The
Theory
of the
American
Novel

The Theory of the American Novel

Edited with
an Introduction by
GEORGE PERKINS
Eastern Michigan University

Holt, Rinehart and Winston
New York / Chicago / San Francisco / Atlanta
Dallas / Montreal / Toronto / London / Sydney

Introduction and Notes Copyright © 1970
by Holt, Rinehart and Winston
All rights reserved, including the right to reproduce
this book or portions thereof in any form.
Library of Congress Catalog Card Number: 71-97847
2813921
SBN: 03-081392-1
Printed in the United States of America
123456789

For my Mother and Father

"Gentlemen, even if one allows that he is an important writer, are we next to invite an elephant to be Professor of Zoology?"

—Reaction of a member of the staff when a "Great University" in England briefly considered the appointment of Vladimir Nabokov to a chair of literature (as quoted in Andrew Field, *Nabokov: His Life in Art,* [Boston and Toronto, 1967], p. 11).

PREFACE

This book was begun under the assumption that novelists writing on the art of the novel are at least as interesting as professional critics who are not themselves novelists: fundamental to an understanding of any art work that moves beyond the work itself is an understanding of the thoughts of the man who made it. The artist's word is neither the first word (he wrote that when he wrote the novel) nor the last word (that, too, is the novel), but if he has chosen to speak on either his art in general or some particular expression of it, he cannot be overlooked. Nevertheless, with a few notable exceptions (one, really), American novelists have received scant attention as critics. Although they have been represented occasionally in this way in American literature textbooks, the more general books containing novel theory by novelists have dealt in the past almost exclusively with the English and continental European novel. This book attempts to redress the balance.

Several principles have determined the shape of the book. I have thought it best to begin with those novelists I believe have the best claims to lasting interest either on the grounds of intrinsic merit or historical importance and seek within their work for the best that they have had to say. If there are major critical statements by minor novelists, I have intentionally passed them by. Within the work of a given writer I have sought public statements rather than private ones, avoiding the casual comment, the interview, and the letter, and attempting to represent the man by what he has most thought about rather than by what has slipped unconsidered from his mouth or pen. Exceptions to this rule have been made with caution, and generally because there was nothing better. Where possible I have preferred to represent the writer speaking about his own work; when he speaks of the work of others, it is generally those whom he knows best and with whom he most deeply sympathizes. Working within these guidelines, I have had no conscious preference for either the familiar or the obscure, but have sought only the best. The arrangement is chronological, author by author and selection by selection within the work of each author, except that where there are letters I have grouped them together at the end of each section. However, in settling on an over-all chronology I have ignored the inherent arbitrariness of assigning places by birth date and have tried to place writers in the order in which their first significant work appeared. Preferring the developed argument to the short excerpt, I have included as many complete pieces as possible. Omissions have been indicated by ellipses. I have avoided the most obvious alternative to a chronological order—an order grouping statements by subject matter—on the grounds that the additional cutting required to get the statements into the most clear thematic relationship to one another involves too much distortion of their meaning in context. Those readers who wish to bring together various judgments of Hawthorne or James or various statements on the nature of romance or on morality in literature will be helped by the index.

My work has been aided considerably by various individuals and institutions. I wish particularly to thank Alfred Appel, Jr., Mr. and Mrs. Vladimir Nabokov, and Robert W. Stallman for courtesies extended regarding the selections from Nabokov and Crane. Some of the letters included have been reprinted with the kind permission of the Henry W. and Albert A. Berg Collection of The New York Public Library, Astor, Lenox and Tilden Foundations; the Houghton Library, by permission of the Harvard College Library; and the Josiah K. Lilly Collection, Indiana University Library. Edna Dixson of Eastern Michigan University helped with the typing. My wife, Barbara Miller Perkins, lent her knowledge and support from beginning to end.

In a special way this book is a result of my teaching in 1966-1967 at Edinburgh University. The students in my honors seminars on the Classic American Novel, Realism and Naturalism in the American Novel, and Fitzgerald, Hemingway, and Faulkner made me look at American literature from a wider perspective than is common in the United States. Discussions with my colleagues—all of them, but especially Professors Kenneth Fielding and John MacQueen—suggested the direction this book might take and helped me define its limits. I began it as a book for Great Britain and ended believing that it is for all readers of English who are interested in the novel as an art form.

—GEORGE PERKINS

Ann Arbor, Michigan
March 14, 1969

INTRODUCTION:
The Novelist as American

For a variety of reasons the novelist in America has always felt a special need to explain the conditions of his art. At first the need was primarily for apology: how was he to justify his concern for art in a country too busy with practical affairs to display much interest in a man who was not in the public's sense productive and too rooted in the Puritan ethic for any reaction except distrust to the moral or esthetic value of his work? How could he produce a literature in a country devoid of the heritage to inspire it and lacking the culture to appreciate it? "In the four quarters of the globe, who reads an American book?" said Sydney Smith, writing in the *Edinburgh Review* in 1820. His comment was to reverberate throughout the literate portions of the United States for the rest of the nineteenth century and remain in the twentieth century as a frequently quoted ornament in literary histories and textbooks of American literature.

In 1820 the comment seemed fair enough, but with the hindsight of history it appears to have come at a singularly inappropriate time. Smith could not have known that even as he wrote his essay Washington Irving was preparing *The Sketch Book* for publication. Nor could he have known that that same year was to see the publication of the first novel of a retired American naval officer, James Fenimore Cooper, who was soon to be the toast of the literary centers of Europe (that first novel, *Precaution,* was not an auspicious beginning, but within three years the appearance of *The Pioneers* had given the world the immortal Leatherstocking). Similarly, within the decade Poe was to publish his first poems and shortly thereafter Emerson, Hawthorne, Longfellow, and Melville had announced their talents to the world. By mid-century Americans had produced enough respectable literature that one of them was willing to compare the best in the United States with the best in England and provide an outrageous answer to Sydney Smith. Herman Melville, reviewing Hawthorne's *Mosses from an Old Manse* in 1850, invoked the magic name of Shakespeare:

> There are minds that have gone as far as Shakspeare into the universe. And hardly a mortal man, who, at some time or other, has not felt as great thoughts in him as any you will find in Hamlet. We must not inferentially malign mankind for the sake of any one man, whoever he may be. This is too cheap a purchase of contentment for conscious mediocrity to make. Besides, this absolute and unconditional adoration of Shakspeare has grown to be a part of our Anglo-Saxon superstitions. The Thirty-Nine Articles are now Forty. Intolerance has come to exist in this matter. You must believe in Shakspeare's unapproachability, or quit the country. But what sort of a belief is this for an American, a man who is bound to carry republican progressiveness into Literature as well as into Life? Believe me, my friends, that men, not very much inferior to Shakspeare, are this day being born on the banks of the Ohio. And the day will come when you shall say, Who reads a book by an Englishman that is a modern?

Even here, though, in the reference to "conscious mediocrity," there is the hint of apology that was so persistent in American novelists in the nineteenth century. At the time that he wrote Melville was finishing *Moby Dick,* one of the masterworks of his century in any language, yet he could not forget that he was writing for a public not yet ready to appreciate him and that he would be judged by standards formed in another country. In the midst of his most jingoistic statement of a literary manifest destiny for the United States, he remembered that his faith was not the faith of his countrymen: "You must believe in Shakspeare's unapproachability or quit the country."

For all the success that came to American writers in the years after 1820, the fact remained that in many ways the United States was not an environment conducive to literature. The average man admired the great literary men who suddenly appeared in New England and elsewhere, and as the century wore on, he devoted a good many of his leisure hours to reading periodicals and books and attending the lectures of the great in the remarkably successful lyceums that sprang up in almost every city and town. But this esteem, important as it was, was not enough to remove the sense of isolation from the writer, and at bottom it was clear that the age was utilitarian and that his was not one of the "useful" arts. A clear sense of what was probably the prevailing attitude toward any pursuit that was not immediately practical emerged from the pen of one of America's early folk heroes when Davy Crockett turned author long enough to write his autobiography:

> But I don't know of anything in my book to be criticised on by honorable men. Is it on my spelling?—that's not my trade. Is it on my grammar?—I hadn't time to learn it, and make no pretensions to it. Is it on the order and arrangement of my book?—I never wrote one before, and never read very many; and, of course, know mighty little about that. Will it be on the authorship of the book?—this I claim, and I'll hang on to it like a wax plaster. The whole book is my own, and every sentiment and sentence in it. I would not be such a fool, or knave either, as to deny that I have had it run hastily over by a friend or so, and that some little alterations have been made in the spelling and grammar; and I am not so sure that it is not the worse of even that, for I despise this way of spelling contrary to nature. And as for grammar, it's pretty much a thing of nothing at last, after all the fuss that's made about it. In some places, I wouldn't suffer either the spelling, or grammar, or anything else to be touched; and therefore it will be found in my own way.

> But if anybody complains that I have had it looked over,

> I can only say to him, her, or them—as the case may be—that
> while critics were learning grammar, and learning to spell,
> I and "Doctor Jackson, LL. D." were fighting in the wars;
> and if our books, and messages, and proclamations, and cab-
> inet writings, and so forth, and so on, should need a little
> looking over, and a little correcting of the spelling and the
> grammar to make them fit for use, its just nobody's business.
> Big men have more important matters to attend to than cross-
> ing their *t*'s—, and dotting their *i*'s—, and such like small
> things.

Crockett's point of view is, in some ways, a compelling one. Certainly his literary contemporaries did little to fight the Indians, settle the West, or legislate the laws for the new nation, and none of them died with him at the Alamo. Never-theless, while big men were doing those things, another, per-haps rarer, kind of big men were trying to create a literature for the new nation and to justify for themselves and others the pursuit of eternal phantoms in a country vibrantly alive with the here and now.

As the years went by American novelists were not always apologetic (though one feels a touch of that in the best of them even today), but they did retain the habit of explanation and justification. Toward the end of the nineteenth century, secure in the knowledge that some good work in the novel had already been done in the United States, they turned the habit from apology to theory and fretted much more than their British counterparts over what is real in literature and what is not real, whether one ought to aim in one direction or the other, and how to arrive there once the goal had been clearly specified. In the twentieth century they have maintained the tradition, sometimes theorizing less, but almost always willing to talk at length about what, how, and why they have written. The result has been a body of criticism touching every aspect of the novelist's art.

One of their chief concerns has been with the idea of an American novel, the possibility that the writer's situation in the United States demanded that he produce a work that was in some nationalistic way unique to his time and experience. This idea arose first out of what many American novelists have seen as two related conditions: the isolation of the writer and the poverty of his material. Ultimately, of course, the isolation cannot matter very much if the writer is to get anything done, and he may even turn it to his advantage as William Faulkner did, but the sense of isolation has generally been there, a force to be overcome. With rare exceptions the American novelist has not been surrounded, at the beginning of his career at least, with intellectually stimulating friends and acquaintances knowledgable about his art and sympathetic to his work. There have been no Bloomsbury groups in American literature. There have been notable literary friendships (Hawthorne and Melville, Howells and Twain, Wolfe and his editor, Maxwell Perkins), but they have generally been formed after the initial good work was done. Even such help as has been given to a young man who has not yet made his name has been provided most often not by numerous friends but by one or two significant chance acquaintances (Phil Stone bringing the bookish sophistication of a Harvard undergraduate to a high school drop-out named William Faulkner in Oxford, Mississippi).

Allied to the condition of isolation has been the belief that the American novelist has been especially hampered by the limitations of his material. Although this view is no longer as popular as it was during the early years of the republic, it has been historically important in the development of the American novel, having much to do with its shift away from the small-scale study of domestic manners so important to the novelistic tradition in England. The argument has been that there must be manners before one can write a novel about them. Failing to find psychological and emotional depths or the solidity of a historical milieu in the lives of his immediate neighbors, the American novelist has depended more than his British counterpart on the shadowlands of his own imagination. As Henry James put it in commenting on the achievement of Hawthorne, "The moral is that the flower of art blooms only where the soil is deep, that it takes a great deal of history to produce a little literature, that it needs a complex social machinery to set a writer in motion." Under circumstances where social machinery is relatively simple the temptation of romance is great, but as Hawthorne himself had lamented, even that solution is not an easy one:

> No author, without a trial, can conceive of the difficulty of writing a romance about a country where there is no shadow, no antiquity, no mystery, no picturesque and gloomy wrong, nor anything but a commonplace prosperity in broad and simple daylight, as is happily the case with my dear native land.

Recognizing the limitations of material, however, writers have often argued (and have demonstrated in their works) that they need not be crippling to the artistic effect. Henry James, for example, differed in this respect in theory and practice. The epitome of the expatriate writer, choosing Europe essentially because of the limitations of home, he at the same time has argued most memorably that a skillful writer can achieve distinction despite the limitations of his personal circumstances. Much can be made of little:

> Experience is never limited, and it is never complete; it is an immense sensibility, a kind of huge spider-web of the finest silken threads suspended in the chamber of consciousness, and catching every air-borne particle in its tissue. It is the very atmosphere of the mind; and when the mind is imaginative—much more when it happens to be that of a man of genius—it takes to itself the faintest hints of life, it converts the very pulses of the air into revelations. The young lady living in a village has only to be a damsel upon whom nothing is lost to make it quite unfair (as it seems to me) to declare to her that she shall have nothing to say about the military. Greater miracles have been seen than that, imagination assisting, she should speak the truth about some of these gentlemen.

Arguing that one should "write from experience and experience only," he adds an injunction of significant illumination when considered with regard to the history of the American novel: "Try to be one of the people on whom nothing is lost!"

Similarly, Charles Brockden Brown, one of the first American novelists, had argued for the supremacy over its material of the recording and translating mind:

> No man can reasonably boast of greater experience than another. He that has traveled over a greater extent of country, associated with a greater number of persons than another, is not to be necessarily deemed more thoroughly acquainted either with man or nature. There is no sphere, however limited, in which human nature may not successfully be studied, and in which sufficient opportunities are not afforded for the exercise of the deepest penetration. . . .

A century later, Stephen Crane, confessing his own lack of any directly personal knowledge of war when he wrote *The Red Badge of Courage,* put it this way:

> I know what the psychologists say, that a fellow can't comprehend a condition that he has never experienced. . . . Of course, I have never been in a battle, but I believe that I got my sense of the rage of conflict on the football field, or else fighting is a hereditary instinct, and I wrote intuitively. . . .

And finally, Faulkner, who might be said to be the man who has made the most of the least:

> I'm inclined to think that my material, the South, is not very important to me. I just happen to know it, and dont have time in one life to learn another one and write at the same time. Though the one I know is probably as good as another, life is a phenomenon but not a novelty, the same frantic steeplechase toward nothing everywhere and man stinks the same stink no matter where in time.

To emphasize the isolation of the artist in America and the poverty of his materials, however, is to regard his situation from a negative standpoint that not all American novelists have shared. Beginning with his sense of difference from his English and European contemporaries, in some moods the American novelist has insisted upon essential advantages to be found in his situation and in others he has found stimulation in the challenge of creating a new literature to match the new environment. Thomas Wolfe, finding that the life of the artist was hard, expressed awe at his sense of the magnitude of the task:

> It seems to me that the task is one whose physical proportions are vaster and more difficult here than in any other nation on the earth. It is not merely that in the cultures of Europe and of the Orient the American artist can find no antecedent scheme, no structural plan, no body of tradition that can give his own work the validity and truth that it must have. It is not merely that he must make somehow a new tradition for himself, derived from his own life and from the enormous space and energy of American life, the structure of his own design; it is not merely that he is confronted by these problems; it is even more than this, that the labor of a complete and whole articulation, the discovery of an entire universe and of a complete language, is the task that lies before him.

Earlier, when neither the nation nor the task was so huge, there was still for some authors the sense of untapped wealth to be found outside of the meagre social life lamented by Hawthorne and James. For Charles Brockden Brown, "The incidents of Indian hostility, and the perils of the Western wilderness, are far more suitable" for engaging reader sympathy than the trappings of the conventional Gothic romance, "and for a native of America to overlook these would admit of no apology." William Gilmore Simms took pride in the fact that his *The Yemassee* was "an *American* romance. It is so styled as much of the material could have been furnished by no other country." As time went on and the wilderness became more tame and more familiar, other men found a distinctive interest in the new societies that had grown up under the stimulus of new conditions. If there was little sense of history behind the towns of the Midwest prairies or the Pacific slopes, there was uniqueness in their very being that augured well for a literature rooted in the local. Howells founded his theories of realism upon a close observation of the immediate surroundings of the writer and particularly welcomed to the pages of the

Atlantic those writers most steeped in the colors of rural America. Garland prophetically expressed his confidence that the local novel would "redeem American literature," especially in the South and with the American Negro, and suggested that "when the real Pacific literature comes . . . It will be such a literature as no other locality could produce, a literature that could not have been written in any other time, or among other surroundings." It was his faith that the writer need not lament his time and place but instead should seek for a way to deal with the riches that have been given to him: "The sun of truth strikes each part of the earth at a little different angle."

In time arguments such as these came to hold such sway with Americans that Fitzgerald was to believe that writers like Howells and Garland had been too persuasive and later novelists too timid in their refusal to carry literature beyond the bounds of the merely and restrictively local. Writing in the mid-1920s he surveyed the immediate past:

> During the past seven years we have had at least half a dozen treatments of the American farmer, ranging from New England to Nebraska; at least a dozen canny books about youth, some of them with surveys of the American universities for background; more than a dozen novels reflecting various aspects of New York, Chicago, Washington, Detroit, Indianapolis, Wilmington, and Richmond; innumerable novels dealing with American politics, business, society, science, racial problems, art, literature, and moving pictures, and with Americans abroad at peace or in war; finally several novels of change and growth, tracing the swift decades for their own sweet lavender or protesting vaguely and ineffectually against the industrialization of our beautiful old American life. We have had an Arnold Bennett for every five towns—surely by this time the foundations have been laid! Are we competent only to toil forever upon a never completed first floor whose specifications change from year to year?

The times had come full circle, and the argument for too little material had become an argument for too much. The task was not to find, but to use the abundance and transcend it, to cull from the wealth only that which was meaningful on a more than local scale and to write truly and without distortion. At the time that he wrote Fitzgerald believed that a young man named Hemingway had begun to do that in his first volume, *In Our Time*. Thomas Wolfe, still unpublished, was just beginning to direct his own Herculean strength to the task, and was to find, as has been said, that it was an enormous one.

Whatever problems developed for Americans because they were writing in a new country and of a new society, these problems have been magnified by the fact that throughout most of their history they have measured themselves against standards made in England and Europe. They found themselves pouring new and sometimes not very suitable materials into old molds, and if the materials cracked the molds, it became sometimes a matter of debate whether the material or the molds themselves had better be changed. From almost the beginning there were cries of the need for an American literature written for Americans and to American standards: this was a major assertion of Emerson, for example, in his "The American Scholar," and he simply voiced more compellingly sentiments that had been expressed often enough before. Later in the century there were those who believed that the need was being fulfilled as Howells and James made themselves anathema in England in the 1880s by their confident assertion of the ascendancy of American novels and techniques. For both of them the novels of Dickens and Thackeray were, to use James's word, *"naïf."* To quote Howells:

> The art of fiction, as Jane Austen knew it, declined from her through Scott, and Bulwer, and Dickens, and Charlotte Brontë, and Thackeray, and even George Eliot, because the mania of romanticism had seized upon all Europe, and these great writers could not escape the taint of their time; but it has shown few signs of recovery in England, because English criticism, in the presence of the Continental masterpieces, has continued provincial and special and personal. . . .

Under the circumstances, when an American did write a novel that could stand with the best that Europe could provide (for both Howells and James the earliest that had been unquestionably of that sort was *The Scarlet Letter*) it was a case for special celebration and there was always an eager scanning of the English journals to see if the critics there were in agreement with the critics at home (unfortunately—or so the novelists sometimes complained—recognition at home had too often to wait for recognition abroad). Only in the twentieth century has this sense of a sometimes unwilling submission to the demands of a foreign standard shown signs of slackening. James went abroad to write largely of Americans who also went abroad. Wolfe went abroad to write of the country and the people he had left behind: "I had found out . . . that the way to discover one's own country was to leave it." The difference epitomized a change that had occurred in American literature. It remained for Faulkner to see the American problem not as the parochial one of a new country asserting its own individuality, nor yet the hardly more cosmopolitan one of asserting its equality with its literary contemporaries among nations, but the transcendent task of raising the novel to the level of eternal art, beyond considerations of national boundaries:

> Art is simpler than people think because there is so little to write about. All the moving things are eternal in man's history and have been written before, and if a man writes hard enough, sincerely enough, humbly enough, and with the unalterable determination never never never to be quite satisfied with it, he will repeat them, because art like poverty takes care of its own, shares its bread.

Concerned as they have been with defense and justification, American novelists have also quite naturally been concerned with definition. In *The American Novel and Its Tradition,* Richard Chase notes and tries "to account for the obvious fact that although most of the great American novels are romances, most of the great English novels are not." This difference has been noted by novelists, too, almost from the inception of the art in America. Yet at the same time there has been a continual pull toward realism, with the realists struggling to define their art in ways that would allow them to lay claim to the best of the romances and the romance writers insisting on their right to some of the aims and methods of realism while refusing to allow realism its traditional claims to superiority. Charles Brockden Brown set the pattern: his *Wieland,* particularly, was greatly admired by certain English romantics, and the stuff of his novels generally—Indians, panthers, caves, death by spontaneous combustion, sleep walking, ventriloquism, seduction, murder—was the stuff of unadulterated romance. Yet despite the material there are some remarkably real passages, and when Brown wrote of his art, he sounded at times like the most uncompromising of realists:

> Indeed, I know no rarer or more valuable qualification than that of describing common objects and relating familiar occurrences in such a manner as to render them pleasing and instructing, but when this talent is acquired, materials on which it may usefully and properly be exercised can never be deficient. I cannot conceive that the character of any man is unworthy to be known, and believe that there is no person, the incidents of whose life, if skillfully related, would not furnish as much entertainment by their variety, and novelty as any fictitious narrative that ever was written.

For all the talk about the rigid line between realism and romance it has been the refusal or inability of the novelists to recognize the line in practice that has resulted in some of the greatest American novels.

Even Hawthorne's celebrated characterization of his own novels as romances was in a sense an evasion, a refusal to be limited by the traditional boundaries of realism while taking direct aim at some of the results that had in England prior to that time belonged chiefly to the realistic novel, the novel of Austen rather than Scott. Thus for all the latitude that Hawthorne asks for his romances in the prefaces to them, he insists also that any romance "sins unpardonably so far as it may swerve aside from the truth of the human heart." It is precisely because Hawthorne was so successful in his delineation of the human heart that the two great spokesmen for American realism, Howells and James, later pronounced Hester and

Zenobia to be among the most living of fictional characters, and it was his more general success in portraying life that made Howells place him among *My Literary Passions* and James reflect so much of his influence in his own fiction. As James expressed it, "he virtually offers the most vivid reflection of New England life that has found its way into literature."

In retrospect the realistic movement in the American novel after the Civil War seems foredoomed to failure, at least insofar as it was aimed at producing a Howellsian fiction of the average man in average circumstances. It had its small successes, but the one novel that comes closest to fulfilling the ideal and at the same time achieving lasting significance, Howells's own *Rise of Silas Lapham,* falls considerably short of greatness. At the same time novel, lecture, and demonstration of the differences between realism and romance, *Silas Lapham* inadvertantly illustrates some of the dangers inherent in too rigid classifications when it makes the enemy of realism not romance but the excesses that Howells liked to call "romanticism." Between the extreme of the average on one hand and the excessive on the other, there lies the middle ground where romance and realism merge that has been so successfully cultivated by the best American novelists. Howells himself recognized that profitable middle ground, but appeared to feel that, because the pendulum had swung too far toward romantic excess in the first half of the nineteenth century, it must in his time make a corrective swing in the other direction. As a result he found himself in the inherently contradictory position of prescribing the most rigidly realistic methods and materials for those writers who looked up to him as the dean of American letters, while he was at the same time sharp enough in his critical perceptions to recognize the heavy admixture of romance in some of those writers he admired most among his contemporaries. He did not, for example, make the common mistake of thinking that his close friend Henry James was as determinedly successful a realist as some other critics would have him. In his words, James's "best efforts seem to me those of romance," and a similar elasticity of critical standards placed him among the first to recognize the greatness of young men like Stephen

Crane who gave the American novel a permanent push away from strict Howellsian standards.

One result of the furor over realism was some interesting definitions of romance. Forced to look closely at their own aims and methods as a result of the general bias toward realism at the end of the nineteenth century and the beginning of the twentieth, novelists began to make refinements on the older definitions that had often too simply equated romance with high adventure set far away in space and time. James took the point of view that for the writer there was really no distinction at all, since in any case his chief concern must be the appearance of reality and if he were fortunate enough to achieve that appearance, it did not matter where he got his material and what method he used to develop it. The distinction must be a critical one, made after the fact of composition: hence it was in theory quite possible that a writer might call his work a romance and achieve a realistic effect as in large degree Hawthorne had done, or he might set out to write realistically and all unwittingly turn out a romance as James felt that he himself had done in *The American*. In the preface to the New York Edition of that novel he wrote at some length on his understanding of just what was involved in the concept of romance and how it was that he was able to aim in one direction and write in another. Briefly, it comes down to a subjective judgment, "our general sense of 'the way things happen,'" and any novel, however faithfully intended as a reflection of life, becomes a romance when it violates that sense. Quite simply, James toward the end of his career was convinced that things do not happen in life the way he had made them happen in *The American*. He believed that it would have been better, not if he had made things happen as they do in life (James never made the mistake common to some realists of assuming an identity between life and art), but if he had contrived somehow to make his situation more convincing to the reader's sense of reality—a trick always, since the writer must be aware of his own deception, but a necessary trick for the serious novelist.

Other writers were more frankly apologists for the validity of the romantic approach, and they, too, felt that new and wider definitions were in order. At the turn of the century one of the best of these, both in theory and practice, was Frank Norris. He, too, had felt the pull of realism and was quick to concede the inferiority of what he called "sentimentalism," but that was for him far different from romance:

> Many people to-day are composing mere sentimentalism, and calling it and causing it to be called romance. . . . The true Romance is a more serious business than this. It is not merely a conjurer's trick-box full of flimsy quackeries, tinsel and claptraps, meant only to amuse, and relying upon deception to do even that. . . . Can we not see in it an instrument, keen, finely tempered, flawless—an instrument with which we may go straight through the clothes and tissues and wrappings of flesh down deep into the red, living heart of things?

Continuing in his defense of romance, Norris distinguished it from realism in a way that may be taken as 1900s final dismissal of the concept of the superiority of realism, a dismissal that pointed the way for the major achievements of the twentieth-century American novel in the hands of such otherwise dissimilar masters as Fitzgerald, Hemingway, and Faulkner:

> Romance, I take it, is the kind of fiction that takes cognizance of variations from the type of normal life. Realism is the kind of fiction that confines itself to the type of normal life. According to this definition, then, Romance may even treat of the sordid, the unlovely—as, for instance, the novels of M. Zola. (Zola has been dubbed a Realist, but he is, on the contrary, the very head of the Romanticists. . . .)
>
> The reason why one claims so much for Romance, and quarrels so pointedly with Realism, is that Realism stultifies itself. It notes only the surface of things. . . . Realism is minute; it is the drama of a broken teacup, the tragedy of a walk down the block, the excitement of an afternoon call, the adventure of an invitation to dinner. It is the visit to my neighbor's house, a formal visit, from which I may draw no conclusions.

For Norris it was important that the novel should cause one
to draw conclusions and not be merely a picture of life. Other
American novelists since his time have felt an equal urgency and the best of them have generally used "variations from
the type of normal life" to cut "down deep into the red, living
heart of things." In only a few more decades Sherwood Anderson could be so far from even a conventional obeisance to
the expectations of realism as to profess amazement rather
than pleasure when his works were called realistic: "I myself
remember with what a shock I heard people say that one of
my own books, *Winesburg, Ohio,* was an exact picture of Ohio
village life." In "A Writer's Conception of Realism" Anderson insisted that he did not know what realism in fiction is:
"art is art. It is not life." The idea was not new, but its general acceptance among American novelists has been one indication of the triumph of romance over realism.

A major reason for the final ascendency of romance in
America has been the Puritan moral imperative that has always
demanded that the serious writer justify his existence in terms
of social utility. In the beginning a born evader such as Hawthorne could escape the demands of a too obvious didacticism
by assuming the relatively harmless cloak of the romantic en-
tertainer, and then, paradoxically, he could make his point
all the more memorable through the freedom afforded by his
genre: witness the gibes at contemporary society in *The Blithedale Romance* and the ingenuous disclaimer in the preface.
Later, when realism sought to answer the charges of immoral-
ity brought against it by unfriendly readers, its best efforts were
undermined by novelists like Norris who sided with the most
Philistine critics in asserting the irrelevancy of realism and
the healthy didacticism of romance. Even the realists themselves have not always made the claims of their art as large
as they might have: James, for example, in praising the excellence of Howells was moved to insert the qualification that
"Mr. Howells's standpoint is an excellent one for seeing a large
part of the truth," leaving the definite impression that another standpoint might see more. Earlier, William Gilmore Simms
had defended the claims of Cooper's romantic novels as against

his first novel of manners not in terms of the considerably greater artistic success of the romances, but in terms of the greater seriousness of the romantic genre. Of the novel of manners he wrote:

> The ordinary events of the household, or of the snug family circle, suggest the only materials; and a large gathering of the set, at ball or dinner, affords incident of which the novelist is required to make the highest use. Writers of much earnestness of mood, originality of thought, or intensity of imagination, seldom engage in this class of writing.

Similarly, although Simms claimed that the Indians in his own novel, *The Yemassee,* were "true to the Indian as our ancestors knew him" and that the work was to that extent realistic, he insisted that it was as a whole a romance. "The Romance is of loftier origin than the Novel," he wrote. It is "the substitute of modern times for the epic or the drama."

The question of the moral superiority of the romantic or the realistic viewpoint is only one facet of a larger question that has continually faced the American novelist: what is the place of his art in society? Relatively few writers have been content to stand fast on the belief, sometimes expressed, that art is its own justification. A few have ignored the question, letting their books speak for themselves, but many have been motivated to seek answers.

Almost all serious novelists have accepted the view that entertainment alone is not enough and have contrasted their own works with what Charles Brockden Brown called "ordinary or frivolous sources of amusement" to be found in the work of other writers. They have taken for granted that literature does have an effect on society and have sought to write themselves, and to encourage others to write, novels that would be morally uplifting rather than sources of corruption to the society at large. Even Hemingway's "what is moral is what you feel good after" is as much an affirmation of a code (and not simply a hedonistic one) that he would like to communicate to the discerning reader as it is a brusque dismissal of readers of little understanding who ask too many questions. Implied

is a message for those who can see and feel (and consequently can also share the perceptions of the writer) that cannot
be made articulate for those more limited souls who cannot
see and feel and for whom no amount of authorial explanation will make clear what ought to be evident in the words and
deeds of the characters.

Insofar as there has been an argument about the place
of morality it has largely resolved itself into questions of the
amount of overt preaching that should go into a novel. Granted that the novel does have an effect on society and that no
serious writer wants that effect to be an immoral one, there
still remains the problem of how best to direct it as a force
for good rather than evil. Whatever tack readers and reviewers have sometimes taken, major novelists have not been so
naïve as to think that a liberal sprinkling of rewards and punish-
ments at the end, coupled with a few words of authorial ap-
proval and condemnation, are enough to redeem a bad book.
The discussion has fortunately held to a higher ground than
that.

Generally it has been the advocates of the romance who
have insisted most on the didactic function of the novel; they
have, in fact, based a good many of their claims for serious
consideration as artists and even the claims for the superiority of their form on the argument that the romance is the form
best suited for use as a teaching medium. In this respect Hawthorne's habit of self-denigration becomes somewhat misleading in the preface to *The House of the Seven Gables* when
he says that he "has considered it hardly worth his while . . . relentlessly to impale the story with its moral as with an iron rod,
—or, rather, as by sticking a pin through a butterfly,—thus at
once depriving it of life, and causing it to stiffen in an ungainly and unnatural attitude." Assuming that one wishes to take
the author at his word it is quite possible to believe that he
did intend first and foremost to bring the story and its characters to life, but reading his own description of the moral that
he says he has provided "not to be deficient in this particular"
and thinking back over the novel it is hard for most readers
to see how he could have done much more "relentlessly to

impale the story with its moral as with an iron rod." Hawthorne, though, is a difficult case, not made any easier by the fact that he wrote at a time when Howells had not yet put the American romancer in an even more defensive position than he had inherited from the attitudes of the eighteenth-century English toward novels and romances. It is often just at the point that he is beginning to appear most clear that the possibilities of irony and ambiguity begin to open up one after another like an endlessly mirrored perspective with truth bouncing crazily into the distance.

The position of Frank Norris is much more clear, perhaps partly because he possessed a lesser talent (and had therefore less to explain) and almost certainly because he had seen some of the issues so clearly spelled out by such realists as Howells and James. For Norris "every novel must do one of three things —it must (1) tell something, (2) show something, or (3) prove something." To the third class belongs "the novel with a purpose," the type that Norris believed to be "the highest form of the novel." Like Hawthorne, Norris believed that a novel cannot be successful without living characters and incidents, and he warned against a situation where "the story may dwindle down and degenerate into mere special pleading, and the novelist become a polemicist, a pamphleteer." He went further than Hawthorne, however, in resolving the dilemma posed by the author who wishes to impale his moral and tell a story at the same time. The secret lies in the mysterious force of creation: the author may be burning to right some wrong or rid the world of some fundamental injustice, but if his novel is to be successful he must be so caught up in the writing of it that "the working out of his *story,* its people, episodes, scenes, and pictures is for the moment the most interesting thing in the world to him, exclusive of everything else." The result is a novel that preaches, because it has been designed from the first to do that, but that in the end has been transmuted from tract to art.

Some of the best American novelists, however, have argued the essential morality of the novel while at the same time insisting that it should not preach. In Stephen Crane's words,

"Preaching is fatal to art in literature. I try to give to readers a slice out of life; and if there is any moral or lesson in it, I do not try to point it out." Implicit here is the Howellsian idea that although one should not "attempt to prove theses by writing stories," still "morality penetrates all things, it is the soul of all things." Even Henry James, almost the epitome in American letters of art for art's sake, could not escape the moral question, though he tried. His "questions of art are questions (in the widest sense) of execution; questions of morality are quite another affair," seems to settle the matter, at least as far as the artist is concerned, but James himself did not quite leave it at that. He, too, could not ignore the ultimate effect of his production on society and argued finally that if the artist was serious, the work could not fail to be:

> There is one point at which the moral sense and the artis-
> tic sense lie very near together; that is in the light of the very
> obvious truth that the deepest quality of a work of art will
> always be the quality of the mind of the producer. In pro-
> portion as that intelligence is fine will the novel, the picture,
> the statue partake of the substance of beauty and truth. To
> be constituted of such elements is, to my vision, to have pur-
> pose enough. No good novel will ever proceed from a sup-
> erficial mind; that seems to me an axiom which, for the art-
> ist in fiction, will cover all needful moral ground. . . .

The difference between those who insist that the novel must preach and those who argue that it cannot preach if it is to live has often been not so much a difference in artistic temperament as a fundamental difference in views of society. The preachers in American literature—Hawthorne, Melville, Norris, and Dreiser, for example—have been the nay-sayers of the American novel, essentially pessimistic about man's capacity to see and choose the right. The non-preachers—Howells, James, Hemingway, Faulkner—have one way or anoth-er displayed an essential faith in the goodness of man and his ultimate triumph. This distinction between those who answer yea and nay to the fundamental human predicament is not an easy one to make for most novelists, particularly since it cuts across traditional divisions between realism and romance and because it suggests a simplicity and a consistency that just do not exist in the works of most major novelists. Still, when American novelists have preached they have usually done so out of a belief that man will not respond unless he is led, that he will not choose the right unless it is forcibly pointed out to him in a world where the temptation to evil is great. When they have not preached, they have displayed their faith in a moral world and the essential goodness of man.

One of the reasons that the romance has possessed such power in the hands of American writers is that they have gone to considerable lengths to give their phantasms the air of reality (as mere romanticists or sentimentalists have not). When Charles Brockden Brown wrote like a romancer and theorized like a realist he suggested a technique that the best American romancers from Hawthorne and Melville to Fitzgerald and Faulkner have followed: the background of the story is carefully built up of the most meticulously arranged details of observed reality. This use of realistic detail is not new, of course—it goes back at least to Defoe in English fiction—but in fiction in England in the nineteenth and twentieth centuries it has more generally been restricted to the traditionally realistic novel than it has in America. It goes without saying that the realists have insisted on the same kind of detail, but it should be noted that even they have not always felt that a merely journalistic reproduction of reality is enough to sustain a novel. As Howells put it, "When realism becomes false to itself, when it heaps up facts merely, and maps life instead of picturing it, realism will perish too." At both the realistic and the romantic end of the spectrum the American novelist has thought of his art as something more than a mirror.

BIBLIOGRAPHY

(Primarily a bibliography of the works from which the contents of this volume have been drawn, this list includes also selected additional sources of novel criticism by the same authors. It is not intended to be comprehensive.)

Anderson, Sherwood
> *Letters of Sherwood Anderson,* H. M. Jones and W. B. Rideout, (eds.) Boston, 1953.
> *A Story Teller's Story,* New York, 1924.
> "A Writer's Conception of Realism," in Paul Rosenfeld (ed.), *The Sherwood Anderson Reader,* Cambridge, Mass., 1947.

Bellow, Saul
> "Distractions of a Fiction Writer," in Granville Hicks (ed.), *The Living Novel,* New York, 1957.
> "Skepticism and the Depth of Life," in James E. Miller, Jr., and Paul D. Herring (eds.), *The Arts and the Public,* Chicago and London, 1967.
> "Where Do We Go from Here: The Future of Fiction," in A. L. Bader (ed.), *To the Young Writer,* Ann Arbor, Mich. 1965.

Brackenridge, Hugh Henry
> "Introduction," *Modern Chivalry,* 6 vols., Philadelphia, Pittsburgh, Carlisle, 1792-1805 (reprinted, enlarged, 4 vols., Wilmington, Del., 1815; *see also* introductions to succeeding volumes).

Brown, Charles Brockden
> "Advertisement," *Wieland,* New York, 1798.

Letters to Henrietta G. and Thomas Jefferson in David Lee Clark, *Charles Brockden Brown: Pioneer Voice of America,* Durham, 1952.

"Preface," *Arthur Mervyn,* New York, 1798.

"To the Public," *Edgar Huntly,* Philadelphia, 1799.

"Walstein's School of History," *Monthly Magazine and American Review,* August - September, 1799 (reprinted in Harry R. Warfel, (ed.), *The Rhapsodist and Other Uncollected Writings,* New York, 1943).

Cather, Willa

"The Novel Démeublé," *Not under Forty,* New York, 1936.

On Writing, New York, 1949 (reprints "The Novel Démeublé").

Clemens, Samuel L.

"The Art of Authorship," *The Art of Authorship,* George Bainton (ed.), New York, 1891.

"Fenimore Cooper's Literary Offenses," *In Defense of Harriet Shelley and Other Essays,* New York, 1918.

"How to Tell a Story," *How to Tell a Story and Other Essays,* New York, 1897.

Letters to William Dean Howells, *Mark Twain-Howells Letters,* Henry Nash Smith and William M. Gibson, (eds.), 2 vols., Cambridge, Mass., 1960.

"Unlearnable Things: From the Contributors' Club," *Atlantic,* (June 1880).

"What Paul Bourget Thinks of Us," *In Defense of Harriet Shelley.*

Cooper, James Fenimore

James F. Beard, Jr. (ed.), *Early Critical Essays (1820 - 1822),* Gainesville, Fla., 1955.

The Letters and Journals of James Fenimore Cooper, James F. Beard, (ed.), 6 vols., Cambridge, Mass., 1960 - 1968.

Notions of the Americans, 2 vols., Philadelphia, 1828.

Prefaces, especially to the individual volumes of *Cooper's Novels,* 32 vols., New York, Townsend, 1859 - 1861.

Crane, Stephen

"Harold Frederic," *Chap-Book,* March 15, 1898 (reprinted in Olov W. Fryckstedt, (ed.), *Stephen Crane: Uncollected Writings,* Uppsala, 1963).

"Ouida's Masterpiece," *Book Buyer,* January, 1897 (reprinted in *Uncollected Writings*).

Stephen Crane: Letters, R. W. Stallman and Lillian Gilkes, (eds.), New York, 1960.

Dos Passos, John
  "The Workman and His Tools," *Occasions and Protests,* Chicago, 1964.
Dreiser, Theodore
  A Book about Myself, New York, 1922 (reprinted, with introduction, as *Newspaper Days,* New York, 1931).
  Letters of Theodore Dreiser, Robert H. Elias, (ed.), 3 vols., Philadelphia, 1959.
Farrell, James T.
  "How *Studs Lonigan* Was Written," *The League of Frightened Philistines,* New York, 1945 (first printed as an introduction to the Modern Library *Studs Lonigan,* New York, 1938).
  Literature and Morality, New York, 1947.
  A Note on Literary Criticism, New York, 1936.
Faulkner, William
  Faulkner at Nagano, Robert A. Jelliffe, (ed.), Tokyo, 1956.
  Faulkner in the University, Frederick L. Gwynn and Joseph L. Blotner, (eds.), Charlottesville, Va., 1959.
  Letters to Malcolm Cowley, *The Faulkner-Cowley File,* Malcolm Cowley, (ed.), New York, 1966.
  William Faulkner: Early Prose and Poetry, Carvel Collins, (ed.), Boston, 1962.
  "William Faulkner," *Writers at Work: The Paris Review Interviews,* Malcolm Cowley, (ed.), New York, 1959.
Fitzgerald, F. Scott
  "How to Waste Material: A Note on My Generation," in Arthur Mizener (ed.), *Afternoon of an Author,* New York, 1958.
  The Letters of F. Scott Fitzgerald, Andrew Turnbull (ed.), New York, 1963.
  "One Hundred False Starts," *Afternoon of an Author.*
Garland, Hamlin
  "The Local Novel," *Crumbling Idols,* Boston, 1894.
  "New Fields," *Crumbling Idols.*
Glasgow, Ellen
  "The Sheltered Life," *A Certain Measure,* New York, 1943.
  Letters of Ellen Glasgow, Blair Rouse, (ed.), New York, 1958.
  The Woman Within, New York, 1954.
Hawthorne, Nathaniel
  The American Notebooks, Randall Stewart (ed.), New Haven, 1932.
  The English Notebooks, Randall Stewart (ed.), New York, 1941.
  Letters to Henry W. Longfellow and James T. Fields, *The Port-*

able Hawthorne, Malcolm Cowley (ed.), New York, 1948 (for other letters see James T. Fields, *Yesterdays with Authors,* Boston, 1871; Julian Hawthorne, *Nathaniel Hawthorne and His Wife,* 2 vols., Boston, 1885; Moncure Conway, *Life of Nathaniel Hawthorne,* New York, 1890; *Love Letters of Nathaniel Hawthorne,* 2 vols., Chicago, 1907; Caroline Ticknor, *Hawthorne and His Publisher,* Boston, 1913).

Prefaces to individual volumes. The standard edition has been *The Complete Works of Nathaniel Hawthorne,* George P. Lathrop, (ed.), 12 vols., Boston, 1883. It is now being superseded by *The Centenary Edition of the Works of Nathaniel Hawthorne,* William Charvat, Roy H. Pearce, and C. M. Simpson, (eds.), Columbus, Ohio, 1962-.

Hemingway, Ernest

Death in the Afternoon, New York, 1932.

The Green Hills of Africa, New York, 1935.

A Moveable Feast, New York, 1964.

Howells, William Dean

Criticism and Fiction, New York, 1891 (reprinted, with other essays, Clara M. Kirk and Rudolph Kirk, (eds.), New York, 1959).

"Henry James, Jr.," *The Century,* November, 1882.

Heroines of Fiction, New York, 1901.

Life in Letters of William Dean Howells, Mildred Howells, (ed.), 2 vols., Garden City, New York, 1928.

Literary Friends and Acquaintance, New York, 1900.

Mark Twain-Howells Letters, Henry Nash Smith and William M. Gibson, (eds.), 2 vols., Cambridge, Mass., 1960.

My Literary Passions, New York, 1895.

My Mark Twain, New York, 1910.

James, Henry

"The Art of Fiction," *Partial Portraits,* London and New York, 1888.

The Art of the Novel, R. P. Blackmur, (ed.), New York, 1934 (the prefaces to the New York Edition, with an introduction by Blackmur).

Hawthorne, London, 1879 (New York, 1880).

The Letters of Henry James, Percy Lubbock, (ed.), 2 vols., New York and London, 1920.

The Notebooks of Henry James, F. O. Matthiessen and Kenneth B. Murdock, (eds.), New York and London, 1947.

Preface to "The American," *The Novels and Tales of Henry James* (the New York Edition), Vol. 2, New York, 1907.

Preface to "The Princess Casamassima," *The Novels and Tales of Henry James.*

"William Dean Howells," *Harper's Weekly,* June 19, 1886.

Lewis, Sinclair

From Main Street to Stockholm: Letters of Sinclair Lewis, 1919-1930, Harrison Smith, (ed.), New York, 1952.

Nobel Prize Address (the best text is most readily available in *The Man from Main Street: A Sinclair Lewis Reader,* Harry E. Maule and Melville H. Cane, (eds.), New York, 1953).

Mailer, Norman

Cannibals and Christians, New York, 1966.

"Last Advertisement for Myself before the Way Out," *Advertisements for Myself,* New York, 1959.

Melville, Herman

The Confidence Man, New York, 1857.

"Hawthorne and His Mosses," *Literary World,* August 17 and 24, 1850.

The Letters of Herman Melville, Merrell R. Davis and William H. Gilman, (eds.), New Haven, 1960.

Pierre, New York, 1852.

Nabokov, Vladimir

Forewords to English translations of *Invitation to a Beheading,* New York, 1959; *The Gift,* New York, 1963; *The Defense,* New York, 1964; *The Eye,* New York, 1965; *Despair,* New York, 1966.

"An Interview with Vladimir Nabokov," conducted by Alfred Appel, Jr., *Nabokov: The Man and His Work,* L. S. Dembo, (ed.), Madison, 1967.

Nikolai Gogol, New York, 1944 (revised, 1961).

"On a Book Entitled *Lolita,*" *Anchor Review,* 2 (1957) (reprinted as an afterword to later editions of *Lolita*).

Speak, Memory, rev. ed., New York, 1966 (earlier version published as *Speak, Memory* and also as *Conclusive Evidence*).

Norris, Frank

The Letters of Frank Norris, Franklin Walker, (ed.), San Francisco, 1956.

The Literary Criticism of Frank Norris, Donald Pizer, (ed.), Austin, Texas, 1964.

"The Novel with a 'Purpose,'" *The Responsibilities of the Novelist,* New York, 1903.

"A Plea for Romantic Fiction," *The Responsibilities of the Novelist.*

Simms, William Gilmore

"Advertisement," *The Yemassee,* New York, 1835.

The Letters of William Gilmore Simms, Mary C. Simms Oliphant, Alfred Taylor Odell, and T. C. Duncan Eaves, (eds.) 5 vols., Columbia, S.C., 1952-1956.

Preface, "To Professor Samuel Henry Dickson, M.D.," *The Yemassee,* New York, 1853.

"The Writings of James Fenimore Cooper," *Views and Reviews in American Literature, History and Fiction,* first series, New York, 1846 (second series, 1847; first and second series bound together, 1847; first series reprinted, C. Hugh Holman, (ed.), Cambridge, Mass., 1962).

Sinclair, Upton

The Autobiography of Upton Sinclair, New York, 1962.

Steinbeck, John

"Critics, Critics, Burning Bright," *Saturday Review,* November 11, 1950 (reprinted in *Steinbeck and His Critics*).

"A Letter on Criticism," *Colorado Quarterly,* Autumn, 1955 (reprinted in *Steinbeck and His Critics*).

"Rationale" in E. W. Tedlock, Jr., and C. V. Wicker (eds.), *Steinbeck and His Critics.* Albuquerque, 1957.

Warren, Robert Penn

"'All the King's Men': The Matrix of Experience," *Yale Review,* (December 1963).

Faulkner: A Collection of Critical Essays, Robert Penn Warren (ed.), Englewood Cliffs, New Jersey, 1966 (contains two essays by Warren).

Selected Essays, New York, 1958.

Wharton, Edith

A Backward Glance, New York, 1934.

The Writing of Fiction, New York, 1925.

Wolfe, Thomas

The Letters of Thomas Wolfe, Elizabeth Nowell, (ed.), New York, 1956.

The Story of a Novel, New York, 1936.

Wright, Richard

Black Boy, New York, 1945.

How "Bigger" Was Born, New York, 1940 [a pamphlet, originally a lecture delivered at the New York Public Library in Harlem, printed in part in *Saturday Review* (June 1, 1940), reprinted in longer version in *Black Voices,* Abraham Chapman (ed.), New York, Toronto, and London, 1968].

CONTENTS

**The
Theory
of the
American
Novel**

Hugh Henry Brackenridge

INTRODUCTION TO *MODERN CHIVALRY*

It has been a question for some time past, what would be the best means to fix the English language. Some have thought of Dictionaries, others of Institutes, for that purpose. Swift, I think it was, who proposed, in his letters to the Earl of Oxford, the forming an academy of learned men, in order by their observations and rules, to settle the true spelling, accentuation, and pronunciation, as well as the proper words, and the purest, most simple, and perfect phraseology of language. It has always appeared to me, that if some great master of stile should arise, and without regarding sentiment, or subject, give an example of good language in his composition, which might serve as a model to future speakers and writers, it would do more to fix the orthography, choice of words, idiom of phrase, and structure of sentence, than all the Dictionaries and Institutes that have been ever made. For certainly, it is much more conducive to this end, to place before the eyes what is good writing, than to suggest it to the ear, which may forget in a short time all that has been said.

It is for this reason, that I have undertaken this work; and that it may attain the end the more perfectly, I shall consider language only, not in the least regarding the matter of the work; but as musicians, when they are about to give the most excel-

1

lent melody, pay no attention to the words that are set to
music; but take the most unmeaning phrases, such as sol, fa,
la; so here, culling out the choicest flowers of diction, I shall
pay no regard to the idea; for it is not in the power of human
ingenuity to attain two things perfectly at once. Thus we see
that they mistake greatly, who think to have a clock that can
at once tell the hour of the day, the age of the moon, and the
day of the week, month, or year; because the complexness
of the machine hinders that perfection which the simplicity of the works and movements can alone give. For it is not
in nature to have all things in one. If you are about to chuse
a wife, and expect beauty, you must give up family and fortune; or if you attain these, you must at least want good temper, health, or some other advantage; so to expect good language and good sense, at the same time, is absurd, and not
in the compass of common nature to produce. Attempting
only one thing, therefore, we may entertain the idea of hitting
the point of perfection. It has been owing to an inattention
to this principle, that so many fail in their attempts at good
writing. A Jack of all Trades, is proverbial of a bungler; and
we scarcely ever find any one who excels in two parts of the
same art; much less in two arts at the same time. The smooth
poet wants strength; and the orator of a good voice, is destitute of logical reason and argument. How many have I
heard speak, who, were they to attempt voice only, might
be respectable; but undertaking, at the same time, to carry
sense along with them, they utterly fail, and become contemptible. One thing at once, is the best maxim that ever came into
the mind of man. This might be illustrated by a thousand examples; but I shall not trouble myself with any; as it is not so
much my object to convince others as to shew the motives
by which I myself am governed. Indeed, I could give authority which is superior to all examples; *viz.* that of the poet
Horace; who, speaking on this very subject of excellence in
writing, says, *Quidvis,* that is, whatever you compose, let it
be, *simplex duntaxit & unum:* that is, simple, and one thing
only.

It will be needless for me to say any thing about the critics;

for as this work is intended as a model or rule of good writing, it cannot be the subject of criticism. It is true, Homer has been criticised by a Zoilus and an Aristotle; but the one contented himself with pointing out defects; the other, beauties. But Zoilus has been censured, Aristotle praised; because in a model there can be no defect; error consisting in a deviation from the truth, and faults, in an aberration from the original of beauty; so that where there are no faults there can be no food for criticism, taken in the unfavourable sense of finding fault with the productions of an author. I have no objections, therefore, to any praise that may be given to this work; but to censure or blame must appear absurd; because it cannot be doubted but that it will perfectly answer the end proposed.

Being a book without thought, or the smallest degree of sense, it will be useful to young minds, not fatiguing their understandings, and easily introducing a love of reading and study. Acquiring language at first by this means, they will afterwards gain knowledge. It will be useful especially to young men of light minds intended for the bar or pulpit. By heaping too much upon them, stile and matter at once, you surfeit the stomach, and turn away the appetite from literary entertainment, to horse-racing and cock-fighting. I shall consider myself, therefore, as having performed an acceptable service, to all weak and visionary people, if I can give them something to read without the trouble of thinking. But these are collateral advantages of my work, the great object of which is, as I have said before, to give a model of perfect stile in writing. If hereafter any author of supereminent abilities, should chuse to give this stile a body, and make it the covering to some work of sense, as you would wrap fine silk round a beautiful form, so that there may be, not only vestment, but life in the object, I have no objections; but shall be rather satisfied with having it put to so good a use.

Charles Brockden Brown
ADVERTISEMENT TO *WIELAND*

The following Work is delivered to the world as the first of a series of performances, which the favorable reception of this will induce the Writer to publish. His purpose is neither selfish nor temporary, but aims at the illustration of some important branches of the moral constitution of man. Whether this tale will be classed with the ordinary or frivolous sources of amusement, or be ranked with the few productions whose usefulness secures to them a lasting reputation, the reader must be permitted to decide.

The incidents related are extraordinary and rare. Some of them, perhaps, approach as nearly to the nature of miracles as can be done by that which is not truly miraculous. It is hoped that intelligent readers will not disapprove of the manner in which appearances are solved, but that the solution will be found to correspond with the known principles of human nature. The power which the principal person is said to possess can scarcely be denied to be real. It must be acknowledged to be extremely rare; but no fact, equally uncommon, is supported by the same strength of historical evidence.

Some readers may think the conduct of the younger Wieland impossible. In support of this possibility the Writer must appeal to Physicians and to men conversant with the latent springs and occasional perversions of the human mind. It will not be objected that the instances of similar delusion are rare, because it is the business of moral painters to exhibit their subject in its most instructive and memorable forms. If history furnishes one parallel fact, it is a sufficient vindication of the Writer; but most readers will probably recollect an authentic case, remarkably similar to that of Wieland.

It will be necessary to add, that this narrative is addressed, in an epistolary form, by the Lady whose story it contains, to a small number of friends, whose curiosity, with regard to it, had been greatly awakened. It may likewise be mentioned that these events took place between the conclusion of the French and the beginning of the revolutionary war. The memoirs of Carwin, alluded to at the conclusion of the work, will be published or suppressed according to the reception which is given to the present attempt.

September 3, 1798   C.B.B.

TO THE PUBLIC: PREFACE TO
EDGAR HUNTLY

The flattering reception that has been given, by the public, to Arthur Mervyn, has prompted the writer to solicit a continuance of the same favour, and to offer to the world a new performance.

America has opened new views to the naturalist and politician, but has seldom furnished themes to the moral painter. That new springs of action and new motives to curiosity should operate, that the field of investigation, opened to us by our own country, should differ essentially from those which exist in Europe, may be readily conceived. The sources of amusement to the fancy and instruction to the heart, that are peculiar to ourselves, are equally numerous and inexhaustible. It is the purpose of this work to profit by some of these sources; to exhibit a series of adventures, growing out of the condition of our country, and connected with one of the most common and most wonderful diseases or affections of the human frame.

One merit the writer may at least claim: that of calling forth the passions and engaging the sympathy of the reader by means hitherto unemployed by preceding authors. Puerile superstition and exploded manners, Gothic castles and chimeras, are the materials usually employed for this end. The incidents of Indian hostility, and the perils of the Western wilderness, are far more suitable; and for a native of America to overlook these would admit of no apology. These, therefore, are, in part, the ingredients of this tale, and these he has been ambitious of depicting in vivid and faithful colours. The success of his efforts must be estimated by the liberal and candid reader.

C.B.B.

LETTERS*
To Henrietta G.

. . . Indeed, I know no rarer or more valuable qualification than that of describing common objects and relating familiar occurrences in such a manner as to render them pleasing and instructing, but when this talent is acquired, materials on which it may usefully and properly be exercised can never be deficient. I cannot conceive that the character of any man is unworthy to be known, and believe that there is no person, the incidents of whose life, if skilfully related, would not furnish as much entertainment by their variety, and novelty as any fictitious narrative that ever was written.[1] Fiction, however polished and elaborate, could never yet surpass reality. The life of most men is a continual comedy, which nature has furnished with characters, events, and scenes which cannot be imagined by the strongest power of invention and which, if faithfully related or described, would render the aid of fancy superfluous.

No man can reasonably boast of greater experience than

*Letters and footnotes, except where noted, are from David Lee Clark, *Charles Brockden Brown: Pioneer Voice of America,* Durham: Duke University, 1952. Clark reprints the letter to Henrietta G. from a journal in which Brown recorded the progress of an otherwise obscure love. Reprinted with permission of Duke University Press.

[1]Brown's statement anticipates Wordsworth's by many years.

another. He that has traveled over a greater extent of country, associated with a greater number of persons than another, is not to be necessarily deemed more thoroughly acquainted either with man or nature. There is no sphere, however limited, in which human nature may not successfully be studied, and in which sufficient opportunities are not afforded for the exercise of the deepest penetration, and as a philosopher is able [to] derive amusement [and] instruction from contemplating a post or a stone, so he whose descriptive powers are vigorous can always make the delineation of them a source of pleasure and improvement. The book of nature, like every other volume, is useful to the reader exactly in proportion to his sagacity and to the attention with which he peruses it, but what advantage can he derive from it, whose rapid and unsteady glances can produce none but general and indeterminate ideas, who dwells not on a single object long enough to know its properties? Nothing is more common than this inattentive and unobserving disposition, and those circumstances which though continually passing in our sight we wanted either power, time, or inclination to remark will, when depicted in words and set before us in a light so [clear] and forcible that they cannot fail of arresting our attention, be viewed with singular satisfaction and advantage.

I have long been powerfully impressed with the justness of these opinions and have sometimes conceived the design of relating every domestic incident, and accounting every dialogue and describing every scene that shall occur within a certain and assignable period with the most excessive and elaborate minuteness, relations in which no circumstances, however frivolous and inconsiderable, should be omitted, and pictures in which should be comprised every appendage. It may be questioned whether the force and accuracy of words can be exceeded by the power of the pencil, though to the perfection of *verbal* portraitures, it is obvious that a greater versatility and copiousness of style or greater command of language is indispensably required than many persons have attained. For my part I shall not scruple to pronounce in favor of the writer, but the circumstances in which the representations of the poet and the painter differ have been so frequently explained and are in themselves so manifest to the most negligent observer that I shall not weary my lovely friend with a trite and tedious disquisition, or with attempting regularly to demonstrate my opinion.

My design, to which I have just alluded, I have carried into execution and find that my knowledge of the manners, characters, and mode of speaking of those with whom I live is far more accurate and extensive than before, or than could possibly have been derived from casual observation. I cannot deny that had I listened with equal attention, or examined with equal vigilance, though without any design of recording what I saw or heard, I should have experienced a new and astonishing increase of knowledge, and therefore am convinced that exact and useful observation is practicable without the intervention or assistance of the pen, but the resolution to describe induced a kind of necessity for procuring the materials of description and was a cogent and irresistible incitement to attention, and the permanence of written record furnishes opportunity for reviewing the scene and attending to the dialogue at leisure.

Such, my Harriet, are the opportunities and advantages of silent, indefatigable observation, and though what I have asserted with regard to the number and variety of scenes and characters with which I have been conversant were not strictly true, yet might I not still claim the merit of experience and sagacity? To visit Europe is it necessary to cross the ocean? Cannot I traverse Connecticut or Carolina while sitting in my closet and admire the dignity and affability of Frederick or Joseph[2] though I never dined or walked in company with either, though I never traversed the ramparts of Berlin or Vienna? And cannot I converse with Gellert,[3] Haller,[4] or Gessner,[5] though I never set my foot within the precincts of Zurich, Göttingen, or Leipsic?

[2]Frederick the Great, King of Prussia (1712-1786); Joseph II, King of Austria (1741-1790).
[3]Christian Fürchtegott Gellert (1715-1769) was a German poet, born in Saxony. He wrote the romance *Das Leben der Schwedischen Gräfin von G.* (1746), but was best known for his songs and fables.
[4]Albrecht von Haller (1708-1777), Swiss scientist and poet.
[5]Salomon Gessner (1730-1788), Swiss artist and poet.

To Thomas Jefferson

December 15, 1798

Sir:

After some hesitation a stranger to the person, though not to the character of Thomas Jefferson, ventures to entreat his acceptance of the volume[1] by which this is accompanied. He is unacquainted with the degree in which your time and attention is engrossed by your public office; he knows not in what way your studious hours are distributed and whether mere works of imagination and invention are not excluded from your notice. He is even doubtful whether this letter will be opened or read, or, if read, whether its contents will not be instantly dismissed from your memory; so much a stranger is he, though a citizen of the United States, to the private occupations and modes of judging of the most illustrious of his fellow citizens.

To request your perusal of a work which at the same time is confessed to be unworthy of perusal will be an uncommon proof of absurdity. In thus transmitting my book to you I tac-

[1]*Wieland* [G.P.].

12

itly acknowledge my belief that it is capable of affording you pleasure and of entitling the writer to some portion of your good opinion. If I had not this belief, I should unavoidably be silent.

I am conscious, however, that this form of composition may be regarded by you with indifference or contempt, that social and intellectual theories, that the history of facts in the processes of nature and the operations of government may appear to you the only laudable pursuits; that fictitious narratives in their own nature or in the manner in which they have been hitherto conducted may be thought not to deserve notice, and that, consequently, whatever may be the merit of my book as a fiction, yet it is to be condemned because it is a fiction.

I need not say that my own opinions are different. I am therefore obliged to hope that an artful display of incidents, the powerful delineation of characters and the train of eloquent and judicious reasoning which may be combined in a fictitious work, will be regarded by Thomas Jefferson with as much respect as they are regarded by me.

No man holds a performance which he has deliberately offered to the world in contempt; but, if he be a man of candor and discernment, his favorable judgment of his own work will always be attended by diffidence and fluctuation. I confess I foster the hope that Mr. Jefferson will be induced to open the book that is here offered him; that when he has begun it he will find himself prompted to continue, and that he will not think the time employed upon it tediously or uselessly consumed.

With more than this I dare not flatter myself. That he will be pleased to any uncommon degree, and that, by his recommendation, he will contribute to diffuse the knowledge of its author, and facilitate a favorable reception to future performances, is a benefit far beyond the expectations, though certainly the object of the fondest wishes of

Charles B. Brown

James Fenimore Cooper

THE LITERATURE OF THE UNITED STATES*

. . . The literature of the United States has, indeed, too powerful obstacles to conquer before (to use a mercantile expression) it can ever enter the markets of its own country on terms
of perfect equality with that of England. Solitary and individual works of genius may, indeed, be occasionally brought
to light, under the impulses of the high feeling which has conceived them; but, I fear, a good, wholesome, profitable and
continued pecuniary support, is the applause that talent most
craves. The fact, that an American publisher can get an English work without money, must, for a few years longer, (unless
legislative protection shall be extended to their own authors,)
have a tendency to repress a national literature. No man will
pay a writer for an epic, a tragedy, a sonnet, a history, or a
romance, when he can get a work of equal merit for nothing.
I have conversed with those who are conversant on the subject, and, I confess, I have been astonished at the information
they imparted.

A capital American publisher has assured me that there
are not a dozen writers in this country, whose works he should

*From *Notions of the Americans,* Philadelphia, 1828, II, 106-109. Title
supplied by the editor.

feel confidence in publishing at all, while he reprints hundreds of English books without the least hesitation. This preference is by no means so much owing to any difference in merit, as to the fact that, when the price of the original author is to be added to the uniform hazard which accompanies all literary speculations, the risk becomes too great. The general taste of the reading world in this country is better than that of England.[1] The fact is both proved and explained by the circumstance that thousands of works that are printed and read in the mother country, are not printed and read here. The publisher on this side of the Atlantic has the advantage of seeing the reviews of every book he wishes to print, and, what is of far more importance, he knows, with the exception of books that he is sure of selling, by means of a name, the decision of the English critics before he makes his choice. Nine times in ten, popularity, which is all he looks for, is a sufficient test of general merit. Thus, while you find every English work of character, or notoriety, on the shelves of an American bookstore, you may ask in vain for most of the trash that is so greedily devoured in the circulating libraries of the mother country, and which would be just as eagerly devoured here, had not a better taste been created by a compelled abstinence. That taste must now be overcome before such works could be sold at all.

When I say that books are not rejected here, from any want of talent in the writers, perhaps I ought to explain. I wish to express something a little different. Talent is sure of too many avenues to wealth and honours, in America, to seek, unnecessarily, an unknown and hazardous path. It is better paid in the ordinary pursuits of life, than it would be likely to be paid by an adventure in which an extraordinary and skilful, because practised, foreign competition is certain. Perhaps high talent does not often make the trial with the American bookseller; but it is precisely for the reason I have named.

[1]The writer does not mean that the best taste of America is better than that of England; perhaps it is not quite so good; but, as a whole, the American reading world requires better books than the whole of the English reading world. [Cooper's note]

The second obstacle against which American literature has to contend, is in the poverty of materials. There is scarcely an ore which contributes to the wealth of the author, that is found, here, in veins as rich as in Europe. There are no annals for the historian; no follies (beyond the most vulgar and commonplace) for the satirist; no manners for the dramatist; no obscure fictions for the writer of romance; no gross and hardy offences against decorum for the moralist; nor any of the rich artificial auxiliaries of poetry. The weakest hand can extract a spark from the flint, but it would baffle the strength of a giant to attempt kindling a flame with a pudding-stone. I very well know there are theorists who assume that the society and institutions of this country are, or ought to be, particularly favourable to novelties and variety. But the experience of one month, in these States, is sufficient to show any observant man the falsity of their position. The effect of a promiscuous assemblage any where, is to create a standard of deportment; and great liberty permits every one to aim at its attainment. I have never seen a nation so much alike in my life, as the people of the United States, and what is more, they are not only like each other, but they are remarkably like that which common sense tells them they ought to resemble. No doubt, traits of character that are a little peculiar, without, however, being either very poetical, or very rich, are to be found in remote districts; but they are rare, and not always happy exceptions. In short, it is not possible to conceive a state of society in which more of the attributes of plain good sense, or fewer of the artificial absurdities of life, are to be found, than here. There is no costume for the peasant, (there is scarcely a peasant at all,) no wig for the judge, no baton for the general, no diadem for the chief magistrate. The darkest ages of their history are illuminated by the light of truth; the utmost efforts of their chivalry are limited by the laws of God; and even the deeds of their sages and heroes are to be sung in a language that would differ but little from a version of the ten commandments. However useful and respectable all this may be in actual life, it indicates but one direction to the man of genius. . . .

PREFACE TO *THE PIONEERS*

As this work professes, in its titlepage, to be a descriptive tale, they who will take the trouble to read it may be glad to know how much of its contents is literal fact, and how much is intended to represent a general picture. The Author is very sensible that, had he confined himself to the latter, always the most effective, as it is the most valuable, mode of conveying knowledge of this nature, he would have made a far better book. But in commencing to describe scenes, and perhaps he may add characters, that were so familiar to his own youth, there was a constant temptation to delineate that which he had known, rather than that which he might have imagined. This rigid adhesion to truth, an indispensable requisite in history and travels, destroys the charm of fiction; for all that is necessary to be conveyed to the mind by the latter had better be done by delineations of principles, and of characters in their classes, than by a too fastidious attention to originals. . . .

PREFACE TO *THE PILOT* (1823)

The privileges of the Historian and of the writer of Romances are very different, and it behooves them equally to respect each other's rights. The latter is permitted to garnish a probable fiction, while he is sternly prohibited from dwelling on improbable truths; but it is the duty of the former to record facts as they have occurred, without a reference to consequences, resting his reputation on a firm foundation of realities, and vindicating his integrity by his authorities. How far and how well the Author has adhered to this distinction between the prerogatives of truth and fiction, his readers must decide; but he cannot forbear desiring the curious inquirers into our annals to persevere, until they shall find good poetical authority for every material incident in this veritable legend.

As to the Critics, he has the advantage of including them all in that extensive class, which is known by the sweeping appellation of "Lubbers." If they have common discretion, they will beware of exposing their ignorance.

If, however, some old seaman should happen to detect any trifling anachronisms in marine usages, or mechanical improvements, the Author begs leave to say to him, with a proper deference for his experience, that it was not so much his intention to describe the customs of a particular age, as to paint those scenes which belong only to the ocean, and to exhibit, in his imperfect manner, a few traits of a people who, from the nature of things, can never be much known.

He will probably be told, that Smollet has done all this, before him, and in a much better manner. It will be seen, however, that though he has navigated the same sea as Smollet, he has steered a different course; or, in other words, that he has considered what Smollet has painted as a picture which is finished, and which is not to be daubed over by every one who may choose to handle a pencil on marine subjects. . . .

PREFACE TO *THE PILOT* (1831)

It is probable a true history of human events would show that a far larger proportion of our acts are the results of sudden impulses and accident, than of that reason of which we so much boast. However true, or false, this opinion may be in more important matters, it is certainly and strictly correct as relates to the conception and execution of this book.

The Pilot was published in 1823. This was not long after the appearance of THE PIRATE, a work which it is hardly necessary to remind the reader, has a direct connection with the sea. In a conversation with a friend, a man of polished taste and extensive reading, the authorship of the Scottish novels came under discussion. The claims of Sir Walter were a little distrusted, on account of the peculiar and minute information that the romances were then very generally thought to display. The Pirate was cited as a very marked instance of this universal knowledge, and it was wondered where a man of Scott's habits and associations could have become so familiar with the sea. The writer had frequently observed that there was much looseness in this universal knowledge, and that the secret of its success was to be traced to the power of creating that *vraisemblance,* which is so remarkably exhibited in those world-renowned fictions, rather than to any very accurate information on the part of their author. It would have been hypercritical to object to the Pirate, that it was not strictly nautical, or true in its details; but, when the reverse was urged as a proof of what, considering the character of other portions of the work, would have been most extraordinary attainments, it was a sort of provocation to dispute the seamanship of the Pirate, a quality to which the book has certainly very little just pretension. The result of this conversation was a sudden determination to produce a work which, if it had no other merit, might present truer pictures of the ocean and ships than any that are to be found in the Pirate. To this unpremeditated decision, purely an impulse, is not only the Pilot due, but a tolerably numerous school of nautical romances that have succeeded it.

The author had many misgivings concerning the success of the undertaking, after he had made some progress in the work; the opinions of his different friends being any thing but encouraging. One would declare that the sea could not be made interesting; that it was tame, monotonous, and without any other movement than unpleasant storms, and that, for his part, the less he got of it the better. The women very generally protested that such a book would have the odor of bilgewater, and that it would give them the *maladie de mer*. Not a single individual among all those who discussed the merits of the project, within the range of the author's knowledge, either spoke, or looked, encouragingly. It is probable that all these persons anticipated a signal failure.

So very discouraging did these ominous opinions get to be, that the writer was, once or twice, tempted to throw his manuscript aside, and turn to something new. A favorable opinion, however, coming from a very unexpected quarter, put a new face on the matter, and raised new hopes. Among the intimate friends of the writer, was an Englishman, who possessed most of the peculiar qualities of the educated of his country. He was learned even, had a taste that was so just as always to command respect, but was prejudiced, and particularly so in all that related to this country and its literature. He could never be persuaded to admire Bryant's Water-Fowl, and this mainly because if it were accepted as good poetry, it must be placed at once amongst the finest fugitive pieces of the language. Of the Thanatopsis he thought better, though inclined to suspect it of being a plagiarism. To the tender mercies of this one-sided critic, who had never affected to compliment the previous works of the author, the sheets of a volume of the Pilot were committed, with scarce an expectation of his liking them. The reverse proved to be the case;—he expressed himself highly gratified, and predicted a success for the book which it probably never attained.

Thus encouraged, one more experiment was made, a seaman being selected for the critic. A kinsman, a namesake, and an old messmate of the author, one now in command on a foreign station, was chosen, and a considerable portion of the first volume was read to him. There is no wish to conceal the satisfaction with which the effect on this listener was observed. He treated the whole matter as fact, and his criticisms were strictly professional, and perfectly just. But the interest he betrayed could not be mistaken. It gave a perfect and most gratifying assurance that the work would be more likely to find favor with nautical men, than with any other class of readers.

The Pilot could scarcely be a favorite with females. The story has little interest for them, nor was it much heeded by the author of the book, in the progress of his labors. His aim was to illustrate vessels and the ocean, rather than to draw any pictures of sentiment and love. In this last respect, the book has small claims on the reader's attention, though it is hoped that the story has sufficient interest to relieve the more strictly nautical features of the work.

It would be affectation to deny that the Pilot met with a most unlooked-for success. The novelty of the design probably contributed a large share of this result. Sea-tales came into vogue, as a consequence; and, as every practical part of knowledge has its uses, something has been gained by letting the landsman into the secrets of the seaman's manner of life. Perhaps, in some small degree, an interest has been awakened in behalf of a very numerous, and what has hitherto been a sort of proscribed class of men, that may directly tend to a melioration of their condition.

PREFACE TO *HOME AS FOUND*

Those who have done us the favor to read HOMEWARD BOUND will at once perceive that the incidents of this book commence at the point where those of the work just mentioned ceased. We are fully aware of the disadvantage of dividing the interest of a tale in this manner; but in the present instance, the separation has been produced by circumstances over which the writer had very little control. As any one who may happen to take up this volume will very soon discover that there is other matter which it is necessary to know, it may be as well to tell all such persons, in commencement, therefore, that their reading will be bootless, unless they have leisure to turn to the pages of Homeward Bound for their cue.

We remember the despair with which that admirable observer of men, Mr. Mathews the comedian, confessed the hopelessness of success, in his endeavors to obtain a sufficiency of prominent and distinctive features to compose an entertainment founded on American character. The whole nation struck him as being destitute of salient points, and as characterized by a respectable mediocrity, that, however useful it might be in its way, was utterly without poetry, humor, or interest to the observer. For one who dealt principally with the more conspicuous absurdities of his fellow-creatures, Mr. Mathews was certainly right; we also believe him to have been right in the main, in the general tenor of his opinion; for this country, in its ordinary aspects, probably presents as barren a field to the writer of fiction, and to the dramatist, as any other on earth; we are not certain that we might not say the most barren. We believe that no attempt to delineate ordinary American life, either on the stage or in the pages of a novel, has been rewarded with success. Even those works in which the desire to illustrate a principle has been the aim, when the picture has been brought within this homely frame, have had to contend with disadvantages that have been commonly found insurmountable. The latter being the intention of this book, the task has been undertaken with a perfect consciousness of all its difficulties, and with scarcely a hope of success. It would be indeed a desperate undertaking, to think of making anything interesting in the way of a *Roman de Société* in this country; still, useful glances may possibly be made even in that direction, and we trust that the fidelity of one or two of our portraits will be recognized by the looker-on, although they will very likely be denied by the sitters themselves.

There seems to be a pervading principle in things, which gives an accumulating energy to any active property that may happen to be in the ascendant at the time being: money produces money; knowledge is the parent of knowledge; and ignorance fortifies ignorance. In a word, like begets like. The governing social evil of America is provincialism; a misfortune that is perhaps inseparable from her situation. Without a social capital, with twenty or more communities divided by distance and political barriers, her people, who are really more homogeneous than any other of the same numbers in the world perhaps, possess no standard for opinion, manners, social maxims, or even language. Every man, as a matter of course, refers to his own particular experience, and praises or condemns agreeably to notions contracted in the circle of his own habits, however narrow, provincial, or erroneous they may happen to be. As a consequence, no useful stage can exist; for the dramatist who should endeavor to delineate the faults of society, would find a formidable party arrayed against him, in a moment, with no party to defend. As another consequence, we see individuals constantly assailed with a wolf-like ferocity, while society is everywhere permitted to pass unscathed.

That the American nation is a great nation, in some particulars the greatest the world ever saw, we hold to be true, and are as ready to maintain as any one can be; but we are also equally ready to concede, that it is very far behind most polished nations in various essentials, and chiefly that it is lamentably in arrears to its own avowed principles. Perhaps this truth will be found to be the predominant thought, throughout the pages of "Home as Found."

PREFACE TO *AFLOAT AND ASHORE*

The writer has published so much truth which the world has insisted was fiction, and so much fiction which has been received as truth, that, in the present instance, he is resolved to say nothing on the subject. Each of his readers is at liberty to believe just as much, or as little, of the matter here laid before him, or her, as may suit his or her notions, prejudices, knowledge of the world, or ignorance. If anybody is disposed to swear he knows precisely where Clawbonny is, that he was well acquainted with old Mr. Hardinge, nay, has often heard him preach—let him make his affidavit, in welcome. Should he get a little wide of the mark, it will not be the first document of that nature which has possessed the same weakness.

It is possible that certain captious persons may be disposed to inquire into the *cui bono?* of such a book. The answer is this. Every thing which can convey to the human mind distinct and accurate impressions of events, social facts, professional peculiarities, or past history, whether of the higher or more familiar character, is of use. All that is necessary is, that the pictures should be true to nature, if not absolutely drawn from living sitters. The knowledge we gain by our looser reading often becomes serviceable in modes and manners little anticipated in the moments when it is acquired.

27

Perhaps the greater portion of all our peculiar opinions have their foundation in prejudices. These prejudices are produced in consequence of its being out of the power of any one man to see, or know, every thing. The most favored mortal must receive far more than half of all that he learns on his faith in others; and it may aid those who can never be placed in positions to judge for themselves of certain phases of men and things, to get pictures of the same, drawn in a way to give them nearer views than they might otherwise obtain. This is the greatest benefit of all light literature in general, it being possible to render that which is purely fictitious even more useful than that which is strictly true, by avoiding extravagances, by portraying with fidelity, and, as our friend Marble might say, by "generalizing" with discretion. . . .

PREFACE TO THE
LEATHER-STOCKING TALES

This series of Stories, which has obtained the name of "The Leather-Stocking Tales," has been written in a very desultory and inartificial manner. The order in which the several books appeared was essentially different from that in which they would have been presented to the world, had the regular course of their incidents been consulted. In "The Pioneers," the first of the series written, the Leather-Stocking is represented as already old, and driven from his early haunts in the forest, by the sound of the axe, and the smoke of the settler. "The Last of the Mohicans," the next book in the order of publication, carried the readers back to a much earlier period in the history of our hero, representing him as middle-aged, and in the fullest vigor of manhood. In "The Prairie," his career terminates, and he is laid in his grave. There, it was originally the intention to leave him, in the expectation that, as in the case of the human mass, he would soon be forgotten. But a latent regard for this character induced the author to resuscitate him in "The Pathfinder," a book that was not long after succeeded by "The Deerslayer," thus completing the series as it now exists.

While the five books that have been written were originally published in the order just mentioned, that of the incidents, insomuch as they are connected with the career of their principal character, is, as has been stated, very different. Taking the life of the Leather-Stocking as a guide, "The Deerslayer" should have been the opening book, for in that work he is seen just emerging into manhood; to be succeeded by "The Last of the Mohicans," "The Pathfinder," "The Pioneers," and "The Prairie." This arrangement embraces the order of events, though far from being that in which the books at first appeared. "The Pioneers" was published in 1822; "The Deerslayer" in 1841; making the interval between them nineteen years. Whether these progressive years have had a tendency to lessen the value of the last-named book by lessening the native fire of its author, or of adding somewhat in the way of improved taste and a more matured judgment, is for others to decide.

If anything from the pen of the writer of these romances is at all to outlive himself, it is, unquestionably, the series of "The Leather-Stocking Tales." To say this, is not to predict a very lasting reputation for the series itself, but simply to express the belief it will outlast any, or all, of the works from the same hand.

It is undeniable that the desultory manner in which "The Leather-Stocking Tales" were written, has, in a measure, impaired their harmony, and otherwise lessened their interest. This is proved by the fate of the two books last published, though probably the two most worthy an enlightened and cultivated reader's notice. If the facts could be ascertained, it is probable the result would show that of all those (in America, in particular) who have read the three first books of the series, not one in ten has a knowledge of the existence even of the two last. Several causes have tended to produce this result. The long interval of time between the appearance of "The Prairie" and that of "The Pathfinder," was itself a reason why the later books of the series should be overlooked. There was no longer novelty to attract attention, and the interest was materially impaired by the manner in which events were necessarily anticipated, in laying the last of the series first before the world. With the generation that is now coming on the stage this fault will be partially removed by the edition contained in the present work, in which the several tales will be arranged solely in reference to their connexion with each other.

The author has often been asked if he had any original in his mind, for the character of Leather-Stocking. In a physical sense, different individuals known to the writer in early life, certainly presented themselves as models, through his recollections; but in a moral sense this man of the forest is purely a creation. The idea of delineating a character that possessed little of civilization but its highest principles as they are exhibited in the uneducated, and all of savage life that is not incompatible with these great rules of conduct, is perhaps natural to the situation in which Natty was placed. He is too proud of his origin to sink into the condition of the wild Indian, and too much a man of the woods not to imbibe as much as was at all desirable, from his friends and companions. In a moral point of view it was the intention to illustrate the effect of seed scattered by the way side. To use his own language, his "gifts" were "white gifts," and he was not disposed to bring on them discredit. On the other hand, removed from nearly all the temptations of civilized life, placed in the best associations of that which is deemed savage, and favorably disposed by nature to improve such advantages, it appeared to the writer that his hero was a fit subject to represent the better qualities of both conditions, without pushing either to extremes.

There was no violent stretch of the imagination, perhaps, in supposing one of civilized associations in childhood, retaining many of his earliest lessons amid the scenes of the forest. Had these early impressions, however, not been sustained by continued, though casual connexion with men of his own color, if not of his own caste, all our information goes to show he would soon have lost every trace of his origin. It is believed that sufficient attention was paid to the particular circumstances in which this individual was placed to justify the picture of his qualities that has been drawn. The Delawares early attracted the attention of missionaries, and were a tribe unusually influenced by their precepts and example. In many instances they became Christians, and cases occurred in which their subsequent lives gave proof of the efficacy of the great moral changes that had taken place within them.

A leading character in a work of fiction has a fair right to the aid which can be obtained from a poetical view of the

subject. It is in this view, rather than in one more strictly circumstantial, that Leather-Stocking has been drawn. The imagination has no great task in portraying to itself a being removed
from the every-day inducements to err, which abound in civilized life, while he retains the best and simplest of his early impressions; who sees God in the forest; hears him in the winds;
bows to him in the firmament that o'ercanopies all; submits to
his sway in a humble belief of his justice and mercy; in a word,
a being who finds the impress of the Deity in all the works of
nature, without any of the blots produced by the expedients,
and passion, and mistakes of man. This is the most that has
been attempted in the character of Leather-Stocking. Had this
been done without any of the drawbacks of humanity, the picture would have been, in all probability, more pleasing than
just. In order to preserve the *vrai-semblable,* therefore, traits
derived from the prejudices, tastes, and even the weaknesses
of his youth, have been mixed up with these higher qualities
and longings, in a way, it is hoped, to represent a reasonable
picture of human nature, without offering to the spectator
a "monster of goodness."

It has been objected to these books that they give a more
favorable picture of the red man than he deserves. The writer
apprehends that much of this objection arises from the habits
of those who have made it. One of his critics, on the appearance of the first work in which Indian character was portrayed,
objected that its "characters were Indians of the school of
Heckewelder,[1] rather than of the school of nature." These
words quite probably contain the substance of the true answer
to the objection. Heckewelder was an ardent, benevolent missionary, bent on the good of the red man, and seeing in him
one who had the soul, reason, and characteristics of a fellow-
being. The critic is understood to have been a very distinguished
agent of the government, one very familiar with Indians, as
they are seen at the councils to treat for the sale of their lands,
where little or none of their domestic qualities come in play,
and where, indeed, their evil passions are known to have the

---

[1] Reverend John Heckewelder, Moravian missionary and writer on the
Indians.

fullest scope. As just would it be to draw conclusions of the
general state of American society from the scenes of the capital,
as to suppose that the negotiating of one of these treaties is
a fair picture of Indian life.

It is the privilege of all writers of fiction, more particularly when their works aspire to the elevation of romances,
to present the *beau-idéal* of their characters to the reader. This
it is which constitutes poetry, and to suppose that the red man
is to be represented only in the squalid misery or in the degrad-
ed moral state that certainly more or less belongs to his condition, is, we apprehend, taking a very narrow view of an author's
privileges. Such criticism would have deprived the world of
even Homer.

William
Gilmore Simms
THE WRITINGS OF
JAMES FENIMORE COOPER

. . . Of Mr. Cooper, little or nothing was known, by the American people at large, until the publication of "the Spy." To a few, perhaps, the novel of "Precaution" had brought him acquainted. That was a very feeble work—coldly correct, elaborately tame—a second or third rate imitation of a very inferior school of writings, known as the social life novel. In works of this class, the imagination can have little play. The exercise of the creative faculty is almost entirely denied. The field of speculation is limited; and the analysis of minute shades of character, is all the privilege which taste and philosophy possess, for lifting the narrative above the province of mere lively dialogue, and sweet and fanciful sentiment. The ordinary events of the household, or of the snug family circle, suggest the only materials; and a large gathering of the set, at ball or dinner, affords incident of which the novelist is required to make the highest use. Writers of much earnestness of mood, originality of thought, or intensity of imagination, seldom engage in this class of writing. Scott attempted it in St. Ronan's Well, and failed;—rising only into the rank of Scott, in such portions of the story as, by a very violent transition, brought him once more into the bolder displays of wild and stirring romance. He consoled himself with the reflection that male writers were not good at these things. His conclusion, that such writings were best handled by the other sex, may be, or not, construed into a sarcasm.

Mr. Cooper failed egregiously in "Precaution." So far as we know, and as we believe, that work fell still-born from the press. But for the success of "the Spy," and the succeeding works, it never would have been heard of. But "the Spy" was an event. It was the boldest and best attempt at the historical romance which had ever been made in America. It is somewhat the practice, at this day, to disparage that story. This is in very bad taste. The book is a good one,—full of faults, perhaps, and blunders; but full also of decided merits, and marked by a boldness of conception, and a courage in progress, which clearly showed the confidence of genius in its own resources. The conception of the Spy, as a character, was a very noble one. A patriot in the humblest condition of life,—almost wholly motiveless unless for his country—enduring the persecutions of friends, the hate of enemies—the doomed by both parties to the gallows—enduring all in secret, without a murmur,—without a word, when a word might have saved him,—all for his country; and all, under the palsying conviction, not only that his country never could reward him, but that, in all probability, the secret of his patriotism must perish with him, and nothing survive but that obloquy under which he was still content to live and labour.

It does not lessen the value of such a novel, nor the ideal truth of such a conception, that such a character is not often to be found. It is sufficiently true if it wins our sympathies and commands our respect. This is always the purpose of the ideal, which, if it can effect such results, becomes at once a model and a reality. The character of the "Spy" was not the only good one of the book. Lawton and Sitgreaves were both good conceptions, though rather exaggerated ones. Lawton was a somewhat too burly Virginian; and his appetite was too strong an ingredient in his chivalry. But, as his origin was British, this may have been due to the truthfulness of portraiture.

The defect of the story was rather in its action than its characters. This is the usual and grand defect in all Mr. Cooper's stories. In truth, there is very little story. He seems to exercise none of his genius in the invention of his fable. There is none of that careful grouping of means to ends, and all, to the one end of the dénouëment, which so remarkably distinguished the genius of Scott, and made all the parts of his story fit as compactly as the work of the joiner,—but he seems to hurry forward in the delineation of scene after scene, as if wholly indifferent to the catastrophe. The consequence is, that his catastrophe is usually forced and unsatisfactory. He is, for this reason, compelled frequently, at the close, to begin the work of invention;—to bring out some latent matter,—to make unlooked for discoveries, and prove his hero, be he hunter or pirate, to have been the son of somebody of unexpected importance;—a discovery which, it is fancied, will secure him a greater degree of the reader's favour, than he could have before commanded. . . .

PREFACE TO THE YEMASSEE
To Professor Samuel Henry Dickson, M.D., of South Carolina

. . . Something, perhaps, should be said of the story as a whole. When I wrote, there was little understood, by readers generally, in respect to the character of the red men; and, of the opinions entertained on the subject, many, according to my own experience, I knew to be incorrect. I had seen the red men of the south in their own homes, on frequent occasions, and had arrived at conclusions in respect to them, and their habits and moral nature, which seemed to me to remove much of that air of mystery which was supposed to disguise most of their ordinary actions. These corrections of the vulgar opinions will be found unobtrusively given in the body of the work, and need not be repeated here. It needs only that I should say that the rude portraits of the red man, as given by those who see him in degrading attitudes only, and in humiliating relation with the whites, must not be taken as a just delineation of the same being in his native woods, unsubdued, a fearless hunter, and without any degrading consciousness of inferiority, and still more degrading habits, to make him wretched and ashamed. My portraits, I contend, are true to the Indian as our ancestors knew him at early periods, and as our people, in certain situations, may know him still. What liberties I have taken with the subject, are wholly with his mythology. That portion of the story, which the reverend critics, with one exception, recognised as sober history, must be admitted to be a pure invention—one, however, based upon such facts and analogies as, I venture to think, will not discredit the proprieties of the invention.

What I shall add to these statements, must be taken from the old preface, which I shall somewhat modify.

You will note that I call "The Yemassee" a romance, and not a novel. You will permit me to insist upon the distinction. I am unwilling that the story shall be examined by any other than those standards which have governed me in its composition; and unless the critic is prepared to adopt with me those leading principles, in accordance with which the book has been written, the sooner we part company the better.

Supported by the authority of common sense and practice, to say nothing of Pope—

"In every work regard the writer's end.
Since none can compass more than they intend—"

I have surely a right to insist upon this particular. It is only when an author departs from his own standard (speaking of his labours as a work of art), that he offends against propriety and merits censure. Reviewing "Atalantis," a fairy tale, full of fanciful machinery, and without a purpose, save the embodiment to the mind's eye of some of those

"Gay creatures of the element,
That, in the colour of the rainbow live,
And play i' the flighted clouds—"

one of my critics—then a very distinguished writer—gravely remarked, in a very popular periodical, "Magic is now beyond the credulity of eight years;" and yet the author *set out* to make a tale of magic, *knowing* it to be thus beyond the range of the probable—knowing that all readers were equally sagacious—and never, for a moment, contemplated the deception of any sober citizen.

The question briefly is—What are the standards of the modern Romance? What is the modern Romance itself? The reply is immediate. The modern Romance is the substitute which the people of the present day offer for the ancient epic. The form is changed; the matter is very much the same; at all events, it differs much more seriously from the English novel than it does from the epic and the drama, because the difference is one of material, even more than of fabrication. The reader who, reading Ivanhoe, keeps Richardson and Fielding beside him, will be at fault in every step of his progress. The domestic novel of those writers, confined to the felicitous narration of common and daily occurring events, and the grouping and delineation of characters in ordinary conditions of society, as altogether a different sort of composition; and if, in a strange doggedness, or simplicity of spirit, such a reader happens to pin his faith to such writers alone, circumscribing the boundless horizon of art to the domestic circle, the Romances of Maturin, Scott, Bulwer, and others of the present day, will be little better than rhapsodical and intolerable nonsense.

When I say that our Romance is the substitute of modern times for the epic or the drama, I do not mean to say that they are exactly the same things, and yet, examined thoroughly, and the differences between them are very slight. These differences depend on the material employed, rather than upon the particular mode in which it is used. The Romance is of loftier origin than the Novel. It approximates the poem. It may be described as an amalgam of the two. It is only with those who are apt to insist upon poetry as verse, and to confound rhyme with poetry, that the resemblance is unapparent. The standards of the Romance—take such a story, for example, as the Ivanhoe of Scott, or the Salathiel of Croly,—are very much those of the epic. It invests individuals with an absorbing interest—it hurries them rapidly through crowding and exacting events, in a narrow space of time—it requires the same unities of plan, of purpose, and harmony of parts, and it seeks for its adventures among the wild and wonderful. It does not confine itself to what is known, or even what is probable. It grasps at the possible; and, placing a human agent in hitherto untried situations, it exercises its ingenuity in extricating him from them, while describing his feelings and his fortunes in his progress. The task has been well or ill done, in proportion to the degree of ingenuity and knowledge which the romancer exhibits in carrying out the details, according to such proprieties as are called for by the circumstances of the story. These proprieties are the standards set up at his starting, and to which he is required religiously to confine himself.

"The Yemassee" is proposed as an *American* romance. It is so styled as much of the material could have been furnished by no other country. Something too much of extravagance—so some may think,—even beyond the usual license of fiction—may enter into certain parts of the narrative. On this subject, it is enough for me to say, that the popular faith yields abundant authority for the wildest of its incidents. The natural romance of our country has been my object, and I have not dared beyond it. For the rest—for the general peculiarities of the Indians, in their undegraded condition—my authorities are numerous in all the writers who have written from their own experience. My chief difficulty, I may add, has risen rather from the discrimination necessary in picking and choosing, than from any deficiency of the material itself. It is needless to add that the historical events are strictly true, and that the outline is to be found in the several chronicles devoted to the region of country in which the scene is laid. A slight anachronism occurs in one of the early chapters, but it has little bearing upon the story, and is altogether unimportant.

But I must not trespass upon your patience, if I do upon your attention. If you read "The Yemassee" *now,* with such changes of mood and judgment as I must acknowledge in my own case, I can hardly hope that it will please you as it did twenty years ago. And yet, my friend, could we both read it as we did then! Ah! how much more grateful our faith than our knowledge! How much do we lose by our gains—how much do our acquisitions cost us!

Yours Faithfully,

W. GILMORE SIMMS.

Charleston, June, 1853.

Nathaniel Hawthorne

PREFACE TO "RAPPACCINI'S DAUGHTER"
From the Writings of Aubépine[1]

We do not remember to have seen any translated specimens of the productions of M. de l'Aubépine—a fact the less to be wondered at, as his very name is unknown to many of his own countrymen as well as to the student of foreign literature. As a writer, he seems to occupy an unfortunate position between the Transcendentalists (who, under one name or another, have their share in all the current literature of the world) and the great body of pen-and-ink men who address the intellect and sympathies of the multitude. If not too refined, at all events too remote, too shadowy, and unsubstantial in his modes of development to suit the taste of the latter class, and yet too popular to satisfy the spiritual or metaphysical requisitions of the former, he must necessarily find himself without an audience except here and there an individual or possibly an isolated clique. His writings, to do them justice, are not altogether destitute of fancy and originality; they might have won him greater reputation but for an inveterate love of allegory, which is apt to invest his plots and characters with the aspect of scenery and people in the clouds, and to steal away the human warmth out of his conceptions. His fictions are sometimes historical, sometimes of the present day, and sometimes, so far as

[1]Hawthorne (French).

can be discovered, have little or no reference either to time or space. In any case, he generally contents himself with a very slight embroidery of outward manners,—the faintest possible counterfeit of real life,—and endeavors to create an interest by some less obvious peculiarity of the subject. Occasionally a breath of Nature, a raindrop of pathos and tenderness, or a gleam of humor, will find its way into the midst of his fantastic imagery, and make us feel as if, after all, we were yet within the limits of our native earth. We will only add to this very cursory notice that M. de l'Aubépine's productions, if the reader chance to take them in precisely the proper point of view, may amuse a leisure hour as well as those of a brighter man; if otherwise, they can hardly fail to look excessively like nonsense.

Our author is voluminous; he continues to write and publish with as much praiseworthy and indefatigable prolixity as if his efforts were crowned with the brilliant success that so justly attends those of Eugene Sue. His first appearance was by a collection of stories in a long series of volumes entitled "Contes deux fois racontées." The titles of some of his more recent works (we quote from memory) are as follows: "Le Voyage Céleste à Chemin de Fer," 3 tom., 1838; "Le nouveau Père Adam et la nouvelle Mère Eve," 2 tom., 1839; "Roderic; ou le Serpent à l'estomac," 2 tom., 1840; "Le Culte du Feu," a folio volume of ponderous research into the religion and ritual of the old Persian Ghebers, published in 1841; "La Soirée du Chateau en Espagne," 1 tom., 8vo, 1842; and "L'Artiste du Beau; ou le Papillon Mécanique," 5 tom., 4to, 1843. Our somewhat wearisome perusal of this startling catalogue of volumes has left behind it a certain personal affection and sympathy, though by no means admiration, for M. de l'Aubépine; and we would fain to do the little in our power towards introducing him favorably to the American public. The ensuing tale is a translation of his "Beatrice; ou la Belle Empoisonneuse," recently published in *La Revue Anti-Aristocratique*. This journal, edited by the Comte de Bearhaven, has for some years past led the defence of liberal principles and popular rights with a faithfulness and ability worthy of all praise.

THE CUSTOM HOUSE:
INTRODUCTORY TO
THE SCARLET LETTER

. . . So little adapted is the atmosphere of a Custom-House to the delicate harvest of fancy and sensibility, that, had I remained there through ten Presidencies yet to come, I doubt whether the tale of "The Scarlet Letter" would ever have been brought before the public eye. My imagination was a tarnished mirror. It would not reflect, or only with miserable dimness, the figures with which I did my best to people it. The characters of the narrative would not be warmed and rendered malleable, by any heat that I could kindle at my intellectual forge. They would take neither the glow of passion nor the tenderness of sentiment, but retained all the rigidity of dead corpses, and stared me in the face with a fixed and ghastly grin of contemptuous defiance. "What have you to do with us?" that expression seemed to say. "The little power you might once have possessed over the tribe of unrealities is gone! You have bartered it for a pittance of the public gold. Go, then, and earn your wages!" In short, the almost torpid creatures of my own fancy twitted me with imbecility, and not without fair occasion.

It was not merely during the three hours and a half which Uncle Sam claimed as his share of my daily life, that this wretched numbness held possession of me. It went with me on my seashore walks and rambles into the country, whenever—which was seldom and reluctantly—I bestirred myself to seek that invigorating charm of Nature, which used to give me such freshness and activity of thought, the moment that I stepped across the threshold of the Old Manse. The same torpor, as regarded the capacity for intellectual effort, accompanied me home, and weighed upon me in the chamber which I most absurdly termed my study. Nor did it quit me, when, late at night, I sat in the deserted parlour, lighted only by the glimmering coal-fire and the moon, striving to picture forth imaginary scenes, which, the next day, might flow out on the brightening page in many-hued description.

If the imaginative faculty refused to act at such an hour, it might well be deemed a hopeless case. Moonlight, in a familiar room, falling so white upon the carpet, and showing all its figures so distinctly,—making every object so minutely visible, yet so unlike a morning or noontide visibility,—is a medium the most suitable for a romance-writer to get acquainted with his illusive guests. There is the little domestic scenery of the well-known apartment; the chairs, with each its separate individuality; the centre-table, sustaining a workbasket, a volume or two, and an extinguished lamp; the sofa; the bookcase; the picture on the wall;—all these details, so completely seen, are so spiritualized by the unusual light, that they seem to lose their actual substance, and become things of intellect. Nothing is too small or too trifling to undergo this change, and acquire dignity thereby. A child's shoe; the doll, seated in her little wicker carriage; the hobby-horse;—whatever, in a word, has been used or played with, during the day, is now invested with a quality of strangeness and remoteness, though still almost as vividly present as by daylight. Thus, therefore, the floor of our familiar room has become a neutral territory, somewhere between the real world and fairy-land, where the Actual and the Imaginary may meet, and each imbue itself with the nature of the other. Ghosts might enter here, without affrighting us. It would be too much in keeping with the scene to excite surprise, were we to look about us and discover a form, beloved, but gone hence, now sitting quietly in a streak of this magic moonshine, with an aspect that would make us doubt whether it had returned from afar, or had never once stirred from our fireside.

The somewhat dim coal-fire has an essential influence in producing the effect which I would describe. It throws its unobtrusive tinge throughout the room, with a faint ruddiness upon the walls and ceiling, and a reflected gleam from the polish of the furniture. This warmer light mingles itself with the cold spirituality of the moonbeams, and communicates, as it were, a heart and sensibilities of human tenderness to the forms which fancy summons up. It converts them from snow-images into men and women. Glancing at the looking-glass, we behold— deep within its haunted verge—the smouldering glow of the half-extinguished anthracite, the white moonbeams on the floor, and a repetition of all the gleam and shadow of the pic- ture, with one remove farther from the actual, and nearer to the imaginative. Then, at such an hour, and with this scene before him, if a man, sitting all alone, cannot dream strange things, and make them look like truth, he need never try to write romances.

But, for myself, during the whole of my Custom-House experience, moonlight and sunshine, and the glow of firelight, were just alike in my regard; and neither of them was of one whit more avail than the twinkle of a tallow-candle. An entire class of susceptibilities, and a gift connected with them,—of no great richness or value, but the best I had,—was gone from me.

It is my belief, however, that, had I attempted a differ- ent order of composition, my faculties would not have been found so pointless and inefficacious. I might, for instance, have contented myself with writing out the narratives of a veteran shipmaster, one of the Inspectors, whom I should be most un- grateful not to mention; since scarcely a day passed that he did not stir me to laughter and admiration by his marvellous gifts as a story-teller. Could I have preserved the picturesque force of his style, and the humorous coloring which nature taught him how to throw over his descriptions, the result, I honestly believe, would have been something new in litera- ture. Or I might readily have found a more serious task. It was a folly, with the materiality of this daily life pressing so intrusively upon me, to attempt to fling myself back into another age; or to insist on creating the semblance of a world out of airy matter, when, at every moment, the impalpable beauty of my soap-bubble was broken by the rude contact of some actual circumstance. The wiser effort would have been, to diffuse thought and imagination through the opaque substance of to-day, and thus to make it a bright transparency; to spiritualize the burden that began to weigh so heavily; to seek, resolutely, the true and indestructible value that lay hidden in the petty and wearisome incidents, and ordinary characters, with which I was now conversant. The fault was mine. The page of life that was spread out before me seemed dull and commonplace, only because I had not fathomed its deeper import. A better book than I shall ever write was there; leaf after leaf presenting itself to me, just as it was written out by the reality of the flitting hour, and vanishing as fast as written, only because my brain wanted the insight and my hand the cunning to transcribe it. At some future day, it may be, I shall remember a few scattered fragments and broken paragraphs, and write them down, and find the letters turn to gold upon the page.

These perceptions have come too late. At the instant, I was only conscious that what would have been a pleasure once was now a hopeless toil. There was no occasion to make much moan about this state of affairs. I had ceased to be a writer of tolerably poor tales and essays, and had become a tolerably good Surveyor of the Customs. . . .

PREFACE TO *TWICE-TOLD TALES*

The Author of "TWICE-TOLD TALES" has a claim to one distinction, which, as none of his literary brethren will care about disputing it with him, he need not be afraid to mention. He was, for a good many years, the obscurest man of letters in America.

These stories were published in magazines and annuals, extending over a period of ten or twelve years, and comprising the whole of the writer's young manhood, without making (so far as he has ever been aware) the slightest impression on the public. One or two among them, the "Rill from the Town Pump," in perhaps a greater degree than any other, had a pretty wide newspaper circulation; as for the rest, he had no grounds for supposing that, on their first appearance, they met with the good or evil fortune to be read by anybody. Throughout the time above specified, he had no incitement to literary effort in a reasonable prospect of reputation or profit, nothing but the pleasure itself of composition—an enjoyment not at all amiss in its way, and perhaps essential to the merit of the work in hand, but which, in the long run, will hardly keep the chill out of a writer's heart, or the numbness out of his fingers. To this total lack of sympathy, at the age when his mind would naturally have been most effervescent, the public owe it (and it is certainly an effect not to be regretted on either part) that the Author can show nothing for the thought and industry of that portion of his life, save the forty sketches, or thereabouts, included in these volumes.

Much more, indeed, he wrote; and some very small part of it might yet be rummaged out (but it would not be worth the trouble) among the dingy pages of fifteen-or-twenty-year-old periodicals, or within the shabby morocco covers of faded souvenirs. The remainder of the works alluded to had a very brief existence, but, on the score of brilliancy, enjoyed a fate vastly superior to that of their brotherhood, which succeeded in getting through the press. In a word, the Author burned them without mercy or remorse, and, moreover, without any subsequent regret, and had more than one occasion to marvel that such very dull stuff, as he knew his condemned manuscripts to be, should yet have possessed inflammability enough to set the chimney on fire!

After a long while the first collected volume of the "Tales" was published. By this time, if the Author had ever been greatly tormented by literary ambition (which he does not remember or believe to have been the case), it must have perished, beyond resuscitation, in the dearth of nutriment. This was fortunate; for the success of the volume was not such as would have gratified a craving desire for notoriety. A moderate edition was "got rid of" (to use the publisher's very significant phrase) within a reasonable time, but apparently without rendering the writer or his productions much more generally known than before. The great bulk of the reading public probably ignored the book altogether. A few persons read it, and liked it better than it deserved. At an interval of three or four years, the second volume was published, and encountered much the same sort of kindly, but calm, and very limited reception. The circulation of the two volumes was chiefly confined to New England; nor was it until long after this period, if it even yet be the case, that the Author could regard himself as addressing the American public, or, indeed, any public at all. He was merely writing to his known or unknown friends.

As he glances over these long-forgotten pages, and considers his way of life while composing them, the Author can very clearly discern why all this was so. After so many sober years, he would have reason to be ashamed if he could not criticise his own work as fairly as another man's; and, though it is little his business, and perhaps still less his interest, he can hardly resist a temptation to achieve something of the sort. If writers were allowed to do so, and would perform the task with perfect sincerity and unreserve, their opinions of their own productions would often be more valuable and instructive than the works themselves.

At all events, there can be no harm in the Author's remarking that he rather wonders how the "TWICE-TOLD TALES" should have gained what vogue they did than that it was so little and so gradual. They have the pale tint of flowers that blossomed in too retired a shade,—the coolness of a meditative habit, which diffuses itself through the feeling and observation of every sketch. Instead of passion there is sentiment; and, even in what purport to be pictures of actual life, we have allegory, not always so warmly dressed in its habiliments of flesh and blood as to be taken into the reader's mind without a shiver. Whether from lack of power, or an unconquerable reserve, the Author's touches have often an effect of tameness; the merriest man can hardly contrive to laugh at his broadest humor; the tenderest woman, one would suppose, will hardly shed warm tears at his deepest pathos. The book, if you would see anything in it, requires to be read in the clear, brown, twilight atmosphere in which it was written; if opened in the sunshine, it is apt to look exceedingly like a volume of blank pages.

With the foregoing characteristics, proper to the production of a person in retirement (which happened to be the Author's category at the time), the book is devoid of others that we should quite as naturally look for. The sketches are not, it is hardly necessary to say, profound; but it is rather more remarkable that they so seldom, if ever, show any design on the writer's part to make them so. They have none of the abstruseness of idea, or obscurity of expression, which mark the written communications of a solitary mind with itself. They never need translation. It is, in fact, the style of a man of society. Every sentence, so far as it embodies thought or sensibility, may be understood and felt by anybody who will give himself the trouble to read it, and will take up the book in a proper mood.

This statement of apparently opposite peculiarities leads us to a perception of what the sketches truly are. They are not the talk of a secluded man with his own mind and heart (had it been so, they could hardly have failed to be more deeply and permanently valuable), but his attempts, and very imperfectly successful ones, to open an intercourse with the world.

The Author would regret to be understood as speaking sourly or querulously of the slight mark made by his earlier literary efforts on the Public at large. It is so far the contrary, that he has been moved to write this Preface chiefly as affording him an opportunity to express how much enjoyment he has owed to these volumes, both before and since their publication. They are the memorials of very tranquil and not unhappy years. They failed, it is true,—nor could it have been otherwise,—in winning an extensive popularity. Occasionally, however, when he deemed them entirely forgotten, a paragraph or an article, from a native or foreign critic, would gratify his instincts of authorship with unexpected praise,—too generous praise, indeed, and too little alloyed with censure, which, therefore, he learned the better to inflict upon himself. And, by the by, it is a very suspicious symptom of a deficiency of the popular element in a book when it calls forth no harsh criticism. This has been particularly the fortune of the "TWICE-TOLD TALES." They made no enemies, and were so little known and talked about that those who read, and chanced to like them, were apt to conceive the sort of kindness for the book which a person naturally feels for a discovery of his own.

This kindly feeling (in some cases, at least) extended to the Author, who, on the internal evidence of his sketches, came to be regarded as a mild, shy, gentle, melancholic, exceedingly sensitive, and not very forcible man, hiding his blushes under an assumed name, the quaintness of which was supposed, somehow or other, to symbolize his personal and literary traits. He is by no means certain that some of his subsequent productions have not been influenced and modified by a natural desire to fill up so amiable an outline, and to act in consonance with the character assigned to him; nor, even now, could he forfeit it without a few tears of tender sensibility. To conclude, however: these volumes have opened the way to most agreeable associations, and to the formation of imperishable friendships; and there are many golden threads interwoven with his present happiness, which he can follow up more or less directly, until he finds their commencement here; so that his pleasant pathway among realities seems to proceed out of the Dreamland of his youth, and to be bordered with just enough of its shadowy foliage to shelter him from the heat of the day. He is therefore satisfied with what the "TWICE-TOLD TALES" have done for him, and feels it to be far better than fame.

PREFACE TO *THE HOUSE OF THE SEVEN GABLES*

When a writer calls his work a Romance, it need hardly be observed that he wishes to claim a certain latitude, both as to its fashion and material, which he would not have felt himself entitled to assume had he professed to be writing a Novel. The latter form of composition is presumed to aim at a very minute fidelity, not merely to the possible, but to the probable and ordinary course of man's experience. The former—while, as a work of art, it must rigidly subject itself to laws, and while it sins unpardonably so far as it may swerve aside from the truth of the human heart—has fairly a right to present that truth under circumstances, to a great extent, of the writer's own choosing or creation. If he think fit, also, he may so manage his atmospherical medium as to bring out or mellow the lights and deepen and enrich the shadows of the picture. He will be wise, no doubt, to make a very moderate use of the privileges here stated, and, especially, to mingle the Marvellous rather as a slight, delicate, and evanescent flavor, than as any portion of the actual substance of the dish offered to the public. He can hardly be said, however, to commit a literary crime even if he disregard this caution.

In the present work, the author has proposed to himself— but with what success, fortunately, it is not for him to judge—

to keep undeviatingly within his immunities. The point of view in which this tale comes under the Romantic definition lies in the attempt to connect a bygone time with the very present that is flitting away from us. It is a legend prolonging itself, from an epoch now gray in the distance, down into our own broad daylight, and bringing along with it some of its legendary mist, which the reader, according to his pleasure, may either disregard, or allow it to float almost imperceptibly about the characters and events for the sake of a picturesque effect. The narrative, it may be, is woven of so humble a texture as to require this advantage, and, at the same time, to render it the more difficult of attainment.

Many writers lay very great stress upon some definite moral purpose, at which they profess to aim their works. Not to be deficient in this particular, the author has provided himself with a moral,—the truth, namely, that the wrong-doing of one generation lives into the successive ones, and, divesting itself of every temporary advantage, becomes a pure and uncontrollable mischief; and he would feel it a singular gratification if this romance might effectually convince mankind,—or, indeed, any one man,—of the folly of tumbling down an avalanche of ill-gotten gold, or real estate, on the heads of an unfortunate posterity, thereby to maim and crush them, until the accumulated mass shall be scattered abroad in its original atoms. In good faith, however, he is not sufficiently imaginative to flatter himself with the slightest hope of this kind. When romances do really teach anything, or produce any effective operation, it is usually through a far more subtle process than the ostensible one. The author has considered it hardly worth his while, therefore, relentlessly to impale the story with its moral as with an iron rod,—or, rather, as by sticking a pin through a butterfly,—thus at once depriving it of life, and causing it to stiffen in an ungainly and unnatural attitude. A high truth, indeed, fairly, finely, and skilfully wrought out, brightening at every step, and crowning the final development of a work of fiction, may add an artistic glory, but it is never any truer, and seldom any more evident, at the last page than at the first.

The reader may perhaps choose to assign an actual locality to the imaginary events of this narrative. If permitted by the historical connection,—which, though slight, was essential to his plan,—the author would very willingly have avoided anything of this nature. Not to speak of other objections, it exposes the romance to an inflexible and exceedingly dangerous species of criticism, by bringing his fancy-pictures almost into positive contact with the realities of the moment. It has been no part of his object, however, to describe local manners, nor in any way to meddle with the characteristics of a community for whom he cherishes a proper respect and natural regard. He trusts not to be considered as unpardonably offending by laying out a street that infringes upon nobody's private rights, and appropriating a lot of land which had no visible owner, and building a house of materials long in use for constructing castles in the air. The personages of the tale—though they give themselves out to be of ancient stability and considerable prominence—are really of the author's own making, or, at all events, of his own mixing; their virtues can shed no lustre, nor their defects redound, in the remotest degree, to the discredit of the venerable town of which they profess to be inhabitants. He would be glad, therefore, if—especially in the quarter to which he alludes—the book may be read strictly as a Romance, having a great deal more to do with the clouds overhead than with any portion of the actual soil of the County of Essex.

PREFACE TO *THE SNOW IMAGE*
To Horatio Bridge, Esq., U.S.N.

MY DEAR BRIDGE,—Some of the more crabbed of my critics, I understand, have pronounced your friend egotistical, indiscreet, and even impertinent, on account of the Prefaces and Introductions with which, on several occasions, he has seen fit to pave the reader's way into the interior edifice of a book. In the justice of this censure I do not exactly concur, for the reasons, on the one hand, that the public generally has negatived the idea of undue freedom on the author's part by evincing, it seems to me, rather more interest in those aforesaid Introductions than in the stories which followed; and that, on the other hand, with whatever appearance of confidential intimacy, I have been especially careful to make no disclosures respecting myself which the most indifferent observer might not have been acquainted with, and which I was not perfectly willing my worst enemy should know. I might further justify myself, on the plea that ever since my youth, I have been addressing a very limited circle of friendly readers, without much danger of being overheard by the public at large; and that the habits thus acquired might pardonably continue, although strangers may have begun to mingle with my audience.

But the charge, I am bold to say, is not a reasonable one, in any view which we can fairly take of it. There is no harm, but, on the contrary, good, in arraying some of the ordinary facts of life in a slightly idealized and artistic guise. I have taken facts which relate to myself, because they chance to be nearest at hand, and likewise are my own property. And, as for egotism, a person, who has been burrowing, to his utmost ability, into the depths of our common nature, for the purposes of psychological romance,—and who pursues his researches in that dusky region, as he needs must, as well by the tact of sympathy as by the light of observation,—will smile at incurring such an imputation in virtue of a little preliminary talk about his external habits, his abode, his casual associates, and other matters entirely upon the surface. These things hide the man, instead of displaying him. You must make quite another kind of inquest, and look through the whole range of his fictitious characters, good and evil, in order to detect any of his essential traits. . . .

Some of these sketches were among the earliest that I wrote, and, after lying for years in manuscript, they at last skulked into the Annuals or Magazines, and have hidden themselves there ever since. Others were the productions of a later period; others, again, were written recently. The comparison of these various trifles—the indices of intellectual conditions at far separate epochs—affects me with a singular complexity of regrets. I am disposed to quarrel with the earlier sketches, both because a mature judgment discerns so many faults, and still more because they come so nearly up to the standard of the best that I can achieve now. The ripened autumnal fruit tastes but little better than the early windfalls. It would, indeed, be mortifying to believe that the summer-time of life has passed away, without any greater progress and improvement than is indicated here. But—at least so I would fain hope—these things are scarcely to be depended upon, as measures of the intellectual and moral man. In youth, men are apt to write more wisely than they really know or feel; and the remainder of life may be not idly spent in realizing and convincing themselves of the wisdom which they uttered long ago. The truth that was only in the fancy then may have since become a substance in the mind and heart. . . .

PREFACE TO
THE BLITHEDALE ROMANCE

In the "BLITHEDALE" of this volume many readers will, probably, suspect a faint and not very faithful shadowing of BROOK FARM, in Roxbury, which (now a little more than ten years ago) was occupied and cultivated by a company of socialists. The author does not wish to deny that he had this community in his mind, and that (having had the good fortune, for a time, to be personally connected with it) he has occasionally availed himself of his actual reminiscences, in the hope of giving a more life-like tint to the fancy-sketch in the following pages. He begs it to be understood, however, that he has considered the institution itself as not less fairly the subject of fictitious handling than the imaginary personages whom he has introduced there. His whole treatment of the affair is altogether incidental to the main purpose of the romance; nor does he put forward the slightest pretensions to illustrate a theory, or elicit a conclusion, favorable or otherwise, in respect to socialism.

In short, his present concern with the socialist community is merely to establish a theatre, a little removed from the highway of ordinary travel, where the creatures of his brain may play their phantasmagorical antics, without exposing them to too close a comparison with the actual events of real lives.

In the old countries, with which fiction has long been conversant, a certain conventional privilege seems to be awarded to the romancer; his work is not put exactly side by side with nature; and he is allowed a license with regard to every-day probability, in view of the improved effects which he is bound to produce thereby. Among ourselves, on the contrary, there is as yet no such Faery Land, so like the real world, that, in a suitable remoteness, one cannot well tell the difference, but with an atmosphere of strange enchantment, beheld through which the inhabitants have a propriety of their own. This atmosphere is what the American romancer needs. In its absence, the beings of imagination are compelled to show themselves in the same category as actually living mortals; a necessity that generally renders the paint and pasteboard of their composition but too painfully discernible. With the idea of partially obviating this difficulty (the sense of which has always pressed very heavily upon him), the author has ventured to make free with his old and affectionately remembered home at BROOK FARM, as being certainly the most romantic episode of his own life,—essentially a day-dream, and yet a fact,—and thus offering an available foothold between fiction and reality. Furthermore, the scene was in good keeping with the personages whom he desired to introduce.

These characters, he feels it right to say, are entirely fictitious. It would, indeed (considering how few amiable qualities he distributes among his imaginary progeny), be a most grievous wrong to his former excellent associates, were the author to allow it to be supposed that he has been sketching any of their likenesses. Had he attempted it, they would at least have recognized the touches of a friendly pencil. But he has done nothing of the kind. The self-concentrated Philanthropist; the high-spirited Woman, bruising herself against the narrow limitations of her sex; the weakly Maiden, whose tremulous nerves endow her with Sibylline attributes; the Minor Poet, beginning life with strenuous aspirations, which die out with his youthful fervor,—all these might have been looked for at BROOK FARM, but, by some accident, never made their appearance there.

The author cannot close his reference to this subject, without expressing a most earnest wish that some one of the many cultivated and philosophic minds, which took an interest in that enterprise, might now give the world its history. Ripley, with whom rests the honorable paternity of the institution, Dana, Dwight, Channing, Burton, Parker, for instance,—with others, whom he dares not name, because they veil themselves from the public eye,—among these is the ability to convey both the outward narrative and the inner truth and spirit of the whole affair, together with the lessons which those years of thought and toil must have elaborated, for the behoof of future experimentalists. Even the brilliant Howadji might find as rich a theme in his youthful reminiscences of BROOK FARM, and a more novel one,—close at hand as it lies,—than those which he has since made so distant a pilgrimage to seek, in Syria and along the current of the Nile.

PREFACE TO *THE MARBLE FAUN*

It is now seven or eight years (so many, at all events, that I cannot precisely remember the epoch) since the author of this romance last appeared before the Public. It had grown to be a custom with him to introduce each of his humble publications with a familiar kind of preface, addressed nominally to the Public at large, but really to a character with whom he felt entitled to use far greater freedom. He meant it for that one congenial friend,—more comprehensive of his purposes, more appreciative of his success, more indulgent of his shortcomings, and, in all respects, closer and kinder than a brother,—that all-sympathizing critic, in short, whom an author never actually meets, but to whom he implicitly makes his appeal whenever he is conscious of having done his best.

The antique fashion of Prefaces recognized this genial personage as the "Kind Reader," the "Gentle Reader," the "Beloved," the "Indulgent," or, at coldest, the "Honored Reader," to whom the prim old author was wont to make his preliminary explanations and apologies, with the certainty that they would be favorably received. I never personally encountered, nor corresponded through the post with this representative essence of all delightful and desirable qualities which a reader can possess. But, fortunately for myself, I never therefore concluded him to be merely a mythic character. I had always a sturdy faith in his actual existence, and wrote for him year after year, during which the great eye of the Public (as well it might) almost utterly overlooked my small productions.

Unquestionably, this gentle, kind, benevolent, indulgent, and most beloved and honored Reader did once exist for me, and (in spite of the infinite chances against a letter's reaching its destination without a definite address) duly received the scrolls which I flung upon whatever wind was blowing, in the faith that they would find him out. But, is he extant now? In these many years, since he last heard from me, may he not have deemed his earthly task accomplished, and have withdrawn to the paradise of gentle readers, wherever it may be, to the enjoyments of which his kindly charity on my behalf must surely have entitled him? I have a sad foreboding that this may be the truth. The "Gentle Reader," in the case of any individual author, is apt to be extremely short-lived; he seldom outlasts a literary fashion, and, except in very rare instances, closes his weary eyes before the writer has half done with him. If I find him at all, it will probably be under some mossy-gravestone, inscribed with a half-obliterated name which I shall never recognize.

Therefore, I have little heart or confidence (especially, writing as I do, in a foreign land, and after a long, long absence from my own) to presume upon the existence of that friend of friends, that unseen brother of the soul, whose apprehensive sympathy has so often encouraged me to be egotistical in my prefaces, careless though unkindly eyes should skim over what was never meant for them. I stand upon ceremony now; and, after stating a few particulars about the work which is here offered to the Public, must make my most reverential bow, and retire behind the curtain.

This Romance was sketched out during a residence of considerable length in Italy, and has been rewritten and prepared for the press in England. The author proposed to himself merely to write a fanciful story, evolving a thoughtful moral, and did not propose attempting a portraiture of Italian manners and character. He has lived too long abroad not to be aware that a foreigner seldom acquires that knowledge of a country at once flexible and profound, which may justify him in endeavoring to idealize its traits.

Italy, as the site of his Romance, was chiefly valuable to him as affording a sort of poetic or fairy precinct, where actualities would not be so terribly insisted upon as they are, and must needs be, in America. No author, without a trial, can conceive of the difficulty of writing a romance about a country where there is no shadow, no antiquity, no mystery, no picturesque and gloomy wrong, nor anything but a commonplace prosperity, in broad and simple daylight, as is happily the case with my dear native land. It will be very long, I trust, before romance-writers may find congenial and easily handled themes, either in the annals of our stalwart republic, or in any characteristic and probable events of our individual lives. Romance and poetry, ivy, lichens, and wall-flowers, need ruin to make them grow. . . .

LETTERS
To Henry Wadsworth Longfellow

Salem, June 4th, 1837

Dear Sir,

Not to burthen you with my correspondence, I have delayed a rejoinder to your very kind and cordial letter, until now. It gratifies me to find that you have occasionally felt an interest in my situation; but your quotation from Jean Paul, about the "lark's nest," makes me smile. You would have been nearer the truth if you had pictured me as dwelling in an owl's nest; for mine is about as dismal; and, like the owl I seldom venture abroad till after dark. By some witchcraft or other— for I really cannot assign any reasonable why and wherefore— I have been carried apart from the main current of life, and find it impossible to get back again. Since we last met—which, I remember, was in Sawtell's room, where you read a farewell poem to the relics of the class—ever since that time, I have secluded myself from society; and yet I never meant any such thing, nor dreamed what sort of life I was going to lead. I have made a captive of myself and put me into a dungeon, and now I cannot find the key to let myself out—and if the door were open, I should be almost afraid to come out. You tell me that you have met with troubles and changes. I know not what they may have been; but I can assure you that trouble is the next best thing to enjoyment, and that there is no fate in this world so horrible as to have no share in either its joys or sorrows. For the last ten years, I have not lived, but only dreamed about living. It may be true that there have been some unsubstantial pleasures here in the shade, which I should have missed in the sunshine, but you cannot conceive how utterly devoid of satisfaction all my retrospects are. I have laid up no treasure of pleasant remembrances, against old age; but there is some comfort in thinking that my future years can hardly fail to be more varied, and therefore more tolerable, than the past.

You give me more credit than I deserve, in supposing that I have led a studious life. I have, indeed, turned over a good many books, but in so desultory a way that it cannot be called study, nor has it left me the fruits of study. As to my literary efforts, I do not think much of them—neither is it worth while to be ashamed of them. They would have been better, I trust, if written under more favorable circumstances. I have had no external excitement—no consciousness that the public would like what I wrote, nor much hope nor a very passionate desire that they should do so. Nevertheless, having nothing else to be ambitious of, I have felt considerably interested in literature; and if my writings had made any decided impression, I should probably have been stimulated to greater exertions; but there has been no warmth of approbation, so that I have always written with benumbed fingers. I have another great difficulty, in the lack of materials; for I have seen so little of the world, that I have nothing but thin air to concoct my stories of, and it is not easy to give a lifelike semblance to such shadowy stuff. Sometimes, through a peep-hole, I have caught a glimpse of the real world; and the two or three articles, in which I have portrayed such glimpses, please me better than the others. I have now, or shall soon have, one sharp spur to exertion, which I lacked at an earlier period; for I see little prospect but that I must scribble for a living. But this troubles me much less than you would suppose. I can turn my pen to all sorts of drudgery, such as children's books, etc., and by and by, I shall get some editorship that will answer my pur-

pose. Frank Pierce, who was with us at college, offered me
his influence to obtain an office in the Exploring Expedition;
but I believe that he was mistaken in supposing that a vacancy
existed. If such a post were attainable, I should certainly accept
it; for, though fixed so long to one spot, I have always had a
desire to run around the world.

The copy of my Tales was sent to Mr. Owen's, the bookseller's in Cambridge. I am glad to find that you had read and liked
some of the stories. To be sure, you could not well help flattering me a little; but I value your praise too highly not to have
faith in its sincerity. When I last heard from the publisher—
which was not very recently—the book was doing pretty well.
Six or seven hundred copies had been sold. I suppose, however,
these awful times have now stopped the sale.

I intend in a week or two to come out of my owl's nest,
and not return to it till late in the summer—employing the interval in making a tour somewhere in New England. You, who
have the dust of distant countries on your "sandal-shoon," cannot imagine how much enjoyment I shall have in this little ex-
cursion. Whenever I get abroad, I feel just as young as I did, ten
years ago. What a letter I am inflicting on you! I trust you will
answer it.

Yours sincerely,

Nath. Hawthorne.

To James T. Fields*

Leamington, Feb. 11th, 1860

Dear Fields,

I received your letter from Florence, and conclude that you are now in Rome, and probably enjoying the carnival—a tame description of which, by the by, I have introduced into my Romance. I thank you most heartily for your kind wishes in favour of the forth-coming work, and sincerely join my own prayers to yours in its behalf, but without much confidence of a good result. My own opinion is, that I am not really a popular writer, and that what popularity I have gained is chiefly accidental, and owing to other causes than my own kind or degree of merit. Possibly I may (or may not) deserve something better than popularity; but looking at all my productions, and especially this latter one, with a cold and critical eye, I can see that they do not make their appeal to the popular mind. It is odd enough, moreover, that my own ·individual taste is for quite another class of works than those which I myself am able to write. If I were to meet with such books as mine, by another writer, I don't believe I should be able to get through them.

*From *The Portable Hawthorne,* ed. by Malcolm Cowley. New York: The Viking Press, Inc., 1948.

Have you ever read the novels of Anthony Trollope? They precisely suit my taste; solid and substantial, written on the strength of beef and through the inspiration of ale, and just as real as if some giant had hewn a great lump out of the earth and put it under a glass case, with all its inhabitants going about their daily business, and not suspecting that they were made a show of. And these books are just as English as a beefsteak. Have they ever been tried in America? It needs an English residence to make them thoroughly comprehensible, but still I should think that the human nature in them would give them a success anywhere.

To return to my own moonshiny Romance; its fate will soon be settled, for Smith & Elder mean to publish on the 28th of this month. Poor Ticknor will have a tight scratch to get his edition out contemporaneously; they having sent him the third volume only a week ago. I think, however, there will be no danger of piracy in America. Perhaps nobody will think it worth stealing.

Give my best regards to William Story, and look well at his Cleopatra, for you will meet her again in one of the chapters which I wrote with most pleasure. If he does not find himself famous henceforth, the fault will be none of mine. I, at least, have done my duty by him, whatever delinquency there may be on the part of other critics.

Smith & Elder (who seem to be pig-headed individuals) persist in calling the book "Transformation," which gives me the idea of Harlequin in a pantomime; but I have strictly enjoined upon Ticknor to call it "The Marble Faun; a Romance of Monte-Beni." . . .

>Most truly yours—
>>Nathl Hawthorne.

Herman Melville

HAWTHORNE AND HIS MOSSES
By a Virginian Spending July in Vermont

A papered chamber in a fine old farm-house, a mile from any other dwelling, and dipped to the eaves in foliage—surrounded by mountains, old woods, and Indian ponds,—this, surely, is the place to write of Hawthorne. Some charm is in this northern air, for love and duty seem both impelling to the task. A man of deep and noble nature has seized me in this seclusion. His wild, witch-voice rings through me; or, in softer cadences, I seem to hear it in the songs of the hill-side birds that sing in the larch trees at my window.

Would that all excellent books were foundlings, without father or mother, that so it might be we could glorify them, without including their ostensible authors! Nor would any true man take exception to this; least of all, he who writes, "When the Artist rises high enough to achieve the Beautiful, the symbol by which he makes it perceptible to mortal senses becomes of little value in his eyes, while his spirit possesses itself in the enjoyment of the reality."[1]

But more than this. I know not what would be the right name to put on the titlepage of an excellent book; but this I feel, that the names of all fine authors are fictitious ones, far more so

---

[1]Hawthorne, "The Artist of the Beautiful."

than that of Junius;[2] simply standing, as they do, for the mystical, ever-eluding spirit of all beauty, which ubiquitously
possesses men of genius. Purely imaginative as this fancy may
appear, it nevertheless seems to receive some warranty from the
fact, that on a personal interview no great author has ever come
up to the idea of his reader. But that dust of which our bodies
are composed, how can it fitly express the nobler intelligences
among us? With reverence be it spoken, that not even in the
case of one deemed more than man, not even in our Saviour,
did his visible frame betoken anything of the augustness of the
nature within. Else, how could those Jewish eye-witnesses fail
to see heaven in his glance! . . .

But it is the least part of genius that attracts admiration.
Where Hawthorne is known, he seems to be deemed a pleasant
writer, with a pleasant style,—a sequestered, harmless man,
from whom any deep and weighty thing would hardly be anticipated—a man who means no meanings. But there is no man,
in whom humor and love, like mountain peaks, soar to such a
rapt height as to receive the irradiations of the upper skies;—
there is no man in whom humor and love are developed in that
high form called genius; no such man can exist without also
possessing, as the indispensable complement of these, a great,
deep intellect, which drops down into the universe like a plummet. Or, love and humor are only the eyes through which such
an intellect views this world. The great beauty in such a mind
is but the product of its strength. What, to all readers, can be
more charming than the piece entitled "Monsieur du Miroir";
and to a reader at all capable of fully fathoming it, what, at the
same time, can possess more mystical depth of meaning?—yes,
there he sits and looks at me,—this "shape of mystery," this
"identical Monsieur du Miroir." "Methinks I should tremble
now, were his wizard power of gliding through all impediments
in search of me, to place him suddenly before my eyes."

How profound, nay appalling, is the moral evolved by
the "Earth's Holocaust"; where—beginning with the hollow
follies and affectations of the world,—all vanities and empty

[2]Sir Philip Francis (?), author of *The Letters of Junius* (1769-1772), a series
of attacks on contemporary British politicians.

theories and forms are, one after another, and by an admirably graduated, growing comprehensiveness, thrown into the allegorical fire, till, at length, nothing is left but the all-engendering heart of man; which remaining still unconsumed, the great conflagration is naught.

Of a piece with this, is the "Intelligence Office," a wondrous symbolizing of the secret workings in men's souls. There are other sketches still more charged with ponderous import.

"The Christmas Banquet," and "The Bosom Serpent," would be fine subjects for a curious and elaborate analysis, touching the conjectural parts of the mind that produced them. For spite of all the Indian-summer sunlight on the hither side of Hawthorne's soul, the other side—like the dark half of the physical sphere—is shrouded in a blackness, ten times black. But this darkness but gives more effect to the ever-moving dawn, that for ever advances through it, and circumnavigates his world. Whether Hawthorne has simply availed himself of this mystical blackness as a means to the wondrous effects he makes it to produce in his lights and shades; or whether there really lurks in him, perhaps unknown to himself, a touch of Puritanic gloom,—this, I cannot altogether tell. Certain it is, however, that this great power of blackness in him derives its force from its appeal to that Calvinistic sense of Innate Depravity and Original Sin, from whose visitations, in some shape or other, no deeply thinking mind is always and wholly free. For, in certain moods, no man can weigh this world without throwing in something, somehow like Original Sin, to strike the uneven balance. At all events, perhaps no writer has ever wielded this terrific thought with greater terror than this same harmless Hawthorne. Still more: this black conceit pervades him through and through. You may be witched by his sunlight,—transported by the bright gildings in the skies he builds over you; but there is the blackness of darkness beyond; and even his bright gildings but fringe and play upon the edges of thunderclouds. In one word, the world is mistaken in this Nathaniel Hawthorne. He himself must often have smiled at its absurd misconception of him. He is immeasurably deeper than the plummet of the mere critic. For it is not the brain that can test such a man; it is only the heart. You cannot come to know greatness by inspecting it; there is no glimpse to be caught of it, except by intuition; you need not ring it, you but touch it, and you find it is gold.

Now, it is that blackness in Hawthorne, of which I have spoken, that so fixes and fascinates me. It may be, nevertheless, that it is too largely developed in him. Perhaps he does not give us a ray of his light for every shade of his dark. But however this may be, this blackness it is that furnishes the infinite obscure of his back-ground,—that back-ground, against which Shakspeare plays his grandest conceits, the things that have made for Shakspeare his loftiest but most circumscribed renown, as the profoundest of thinkers. For by philosophers Shakspeare is not adored as the great man of tragedy and comedy.—"Off with his head; so much for Buckingham!" This sort of rant, interlined by another hand, brings down the house,—those mistaken souls, who dream of Shakspeare as a mere man of Richard-the-Third humps and Macbeth daggers. But it is those deep far-away things in him; those occasional flashings-forth of the intuitive Truth in him; those short, quick probings at the very axis of reality;—these are the things that make Shakspeare, Shakspeare. Through the mouths of the dark characters of Hamlet, Timon, Lear, and Iago, he craftily says, or sometimes insinuates the things which we feel to be so terrifically true, that it were all but madness for any good man, in his own proper character, to utter, or even hint of them. Tormented into desperation, Lear, the frantic king, tears off the mask, and speaks the same madness of vital truth. But, as I before said, it is the least part of genius that attracts admiration. And so, much of the blind, unbridled admiration that has been heaped upon Shakspeare, has been lavished upon the least part of him. And few of his endless commentators and critics seem to have remembered, or even perceived, that the immediate products of a great mind are not so great as that undeveloped and sometimes undevelopable yet dimly-discernible greatness, to which those immediate products are but the infallible indices. In Shakspeare's tomb lies infinitely more than Shakspeare ever wrote. And if I magnify Shakspeare, it is not so much for what he did do as for what he did not do, or refrained from doing. For in this world of lies, Truth is forced to fly like a scared white doe in the woodlands; and only by cunning glimpses will she reveal herself, as in Shakspeare and other masters of the great Art of Telling the Truth,—even though it be covertly and by snatches.

But if this view of the all-popular Shakspeare be seldom taken by his readers, and if very few who extol him have ever read him deeply, or perhaps, only have seen him on the tricky stage (which alone made, and is still making him his mere mob renown)—if few men have time, or patience, or palate, for the spiritual truth as it is in that great genius;—it is then no matter of surprise, that in a contemporaneous age, Nathaniel Hawthorne is a man as yet almost utterly mistaken among men. Here and there, in some quiet arm-chair in the noisy town, or some deep nook among the noiseless mountains, he may be appreciated for something of what he is. But unlike Shakspeare, who was forced to the contrary course by circumstances, Hawthorne (either from simple disinclination, or else from inaptitude) refrains from all the popularizing noise and show of broad farce and blood-besmeared tragedy; content with the still, rich utterance of a great intellect in repose, and which sends few thoughts into circulation, except they be arterialized at his large warm lungs, and expanded in his honest heart.

Nor need you fix upon that blackness in him, if it suit you not. Nor, indeed, will all readers discern it; for it is, mostly, insinuated to those who may best understand it, and account for it; it is not obtruded upon every one alike.

Some may start to read of Shakspeare and Hawthorne on the same page. They may say, that if an illustration were needed, a lesser light might have sufficed to elucidate this Hawthorne, this small man of yesterday. But I am not willingly one of those who, as touching Shakspeare at least, exemplify the maxim of Rochefoucauld, that "we exalt the reputation of some, in order to depress that of others";—who, to teach all noble-souled aspirants that there is no hope for them, pronounce Shakspeare absolutely unapproachable. But Shakspeare has been approached. There are minds that have gone as far as

Shakspeare into the universe. And hardly a mortal man, who, at some time or other, has not felt as great thoughts in him as any you will find in Hamlet. We must not inferentially malign mankind for the sake of any one man, whoever he may be. This is too cheap a purchase of contentment for conscious mediocrity to make. Besides, this absolute and unconditional adoration of Shakspeare has grown to be a part of our Anglo-Saxon superstitions. The Thirty-Nine Articles[3] are now Forty. Intolerance has come to exist in this matter. You must believe in Shakspeare's unapproachability, or quit the country. But what sort of a belief is this for an American, a man who is bound to carry republican progressiveness into Literature as well as into Life? Believe me, my friends, that men, not very much inferior to Shakspeare, are this day being born on the banks of the Ohio. And the day will come when you shall say, Who reads a book by an Englishman that is a modern?[4] The great mistake seems to be, that even with those Americans who look forward to the coming of a great literary genius among us, they somehow fancy he will come in the costume of Queen Elizabeth's day; be a writer of dramas founded upon old English history or the tales of Boccaccio. Whereas, great geniuses are parts of the times, they themselves are the times, and possess a correspondent coloring. It is of a piece with the Jews, who, while their Shiloh[5] was meekly walking in their streets, were still praying for his magnificent coming; looking for him in a chariot, who was already among them on an ass. Nor must we forget that, in his own lifetime, Shakspeare was not Shakspeare, but only Master William Shakspeare of the shrewd, thriving business firm of Condell, Shakspeare & Co., proprietors of the Globe Theatre in London; and by a courtly author, of the name of Chettle[6] was looked at as an "upstart crow," beautified "with other birds' feathers." For, mark it well, imitation is often the first charge brought against real originality. Why this is so,

[3]Of the Church of England.

[4]Cf. Sydney Smith, "In the four quarters of the globe, who reads an American book?," *Edinburgh Review,* 1820.

[5]Messiah.

[6]Rather, Robert Greene.

there is not space to set forth here. You must have plenty of sea-room to tell the Truth in; especially when it seems to have an aspect of newness, as America did in 1492, though it was then just as old, and perhaps older than Asia, only those sagacious philosophers, the common sailors, had never seen it before, swearing it was all water and moonshine there.

Now I do not say that Nathaniel of Salem is greater than William of Avon, or as great. But the difference between the two men is by no means immeasurable. Not a very great deal more, and Nathaniel were verily William.

This, too, I mean, that if Shakspeare has not been equalled, give the world time, and he is sure to be surpassed, in one hemisphere or the other. Nor will it at all do to say, that the world is getting grey and grizzled now, and has lost that fresh charm which she wore of old, and by virtue of which the great poets of past times made themselves what we esteem them to be. Not so. The world is as young to-day as when it was created; and this Vermont morning dew is as wet to my feet, as Eden's dew to Adam's. Nor has nature been all over ransacked by our progenitors, so that no new charms and mysteries remain for this latter generation to find. Far from it. The trillionth part has not yet been said; and all that has been said, but multiplies the avenues to what remains to be said. It is not so much paucity as super-abundance of material that seems to incapacitate modern authors.

Let America, then, prize and cherish her writers; yea, let her glorify them. They are not so many in number as to exhaust her good-will. And while she has good kith and kin of her own, to take to her bosom, let her not lavish her embraces upon the household of an alien. For believe it or not, England, after all, is in many things an alien to us. China has more bonds of real love for us than she. But even were there no strong literary individualities among us, as there are some dozens at least, nevertheless, let America first praise mediocrity even, in her own children, before she praises (for everywhere, merit demands acknowledgment from every one) the best excellence in the children of any other land. Let her own authors, I say, have the priority of appreciation. I was much pleased with a hot-headed Carolina cousin of mine, who once said,—"If there were no other American to stand by, in literature, why, then, I would stand by Pop Emmons and his 'Fredoniad,'[7] and till a better epic came along, swear it was not very far behind the Iliad." Take away the words, and in spirit he was sound.

Not that American genius needs patronage in order to expand. For that explosive sort of stuff will expand though screwed up in a vice, and burst it, though it were triple steel. It is for the nation's sake, and not for her authors' sake, that I would have America be heedful of the increasing greatness among her writers. For how great the shame, if other nations should be before her, in crowning her heroes of the pen! But this is almost the case now. American authors have received more just and discriminating praise (however loftily and ridiculously given, in certain cases) even from some Englishmen, than from their own countrymen. There are hardly five critics in America; and several of them are asleep. As for patronage, it is the American author who now patronizes his country, and not his country him. And if at times some among them appeal to the people for more recognition, it is not always with selfish motives, but patriotic ones.

It is true, that but few of them as yet have evinced that decided originality which merits great praise. But that graceful writer,[8] who perhaps of all Americans has received the most plaudits from his own country for his productions,—that very popular and amiable writer, however good and self-reliant in many things, perhaps owes his chief reputation to the self-acknowledged imitation of a foreign model, and to the studied avoidance of all topics but smooth ones. But it is better to fail in originality than to succeed in imitation. He who has never failed somewhere, that man cannot be great. Failure is the true test of greatness. And if it be said, that continual success is a proof that a man wisely knows his powers,—it is only to be added, that, in that case, he knows them to be small. Let

---

[7]Richard Emmons, *Fredoniad, or Independence Preserved-An Epic Poem of the War of 1812.*

[8]Probably Washington Irving.

us believe it, then, once for all, that there is no hope for us in these smooth, pleasing writers that know their powers. Without malice, but to speak the plain fact, they but furnish an appendix to Goldsmith, and other English authors. And we want no American Goldsmiths: nay, we want no American Miltons. It were the vilest thing you could say of a true American author, that he were an American Tompkins. Call him an American and have done, for you cannot say a nobler thing of him. But it is not meant that all American writers should studiously cleave to nationality in their writings; only this, no American writer should write like an Englishman or a Frenchman; let him write like a man, for then he will be sure to write like an American. Let us away with this leaven of literary flunkeyism towards England. If either must play the flunkey in this thing, let England do it, not us. While we are rapidly preparing for that political supremacy among the nations which prophetically awaits us at the close of the present century, in a literary point of view, we are deplorably unprepared for it; and we seem studious to remain so. Hitherto, reasons might have existed why this should be; but no good reason exists now. And all that is requisite to amendment in this matter, is simply this: that while freely acknowledging all excellence everywhere, we should refrain from unduly lauding foreign writers, and, at the same time, duly recognize meritorious writers that are our own;— those writers who breathe that unshackled, democratic spirit of Christianity in all things, which now takes the practical lead in this world, though at the same time led by ourselves—us Americans. Let us boldly contemn all imitation, though it comes to us graceful and fragrant as the morning; and foster all originality, though at first it be crabbed and ugly as our own pine knots. And if any of our authors fail, or seem to fail, then, in the words of my enthusiastic Carolina cousin, let us clap him on the shoulder, and back him against all Europe for his second round. The truth is, that in one point of view, this matter of a national literature has come to such a pass with us, that in some sense we must turn bullies, else the day is lost, or superiority so far beyond us, that we can hardly say it will ever be ours.

And now, my countrymen, as an excellent author of your

own flesh and blood,—an unimitating, and, perhaps, in his way, an inimitable man—whom better can I commend to you, in the first place, than Nathaniel Hawthorne. He is one of the new, and far better generation of your writers. The smell of your beeches and hemlocks is upon him; your own broad prairies are in his soul; and if you travel away inland into his deep and noble nature, you will hear the far roar of his Niagara. Give not over to future generations the glad duty of acknowledging him for what he is. Take that joy to yourself, in your own generation; and so shall he feel those grateful impulses on him, that may possibly prompt him to the full flower of some still greater achievement in your eyes. And by confessing him you thereby confess others; you brace the whole brotherhood. For genius, all over the world, stands hand in hand, and one shock of recognition runs the whole circle round.

In treating of Hawthorne, or rather of Hawthorne in his writings (for I never saw the man; and in the chances of a quiet plantation life, remote from his haunts, perhaps never shall); in treating of his works, I say, I have thus far omitted all mention of his "Twice-Told Tales," and "Scarlet Letter." Both are excellent, but full of such manifold, strange, and diffusive beauties, that time would all but fail me to point the half of them out. But there are things in those two books, which, had they been written in England a century ago, Nathaniel Hawthorne had utterly displaced many of the bright names we now revere on authority. But I am content to leave Hawthorne to himself, and to the infallible finding of posterity; and however great may be the praise I have bestowed upon him, I feel that in so doing I have more served and honored myself, than him. For at bottom, great excellence is praise enough to itself; but the feeling of a sincere and appreciative love and admiration towards it, this is relieved by utterance; and warm, honest praise, ever leaves a pleasant flavor in the mouth; and it is an honorable thing to confess to what is honorable in others.

But I cannot leave my subject yet. No man can ever read a fine author, and relish him to his very bones while he reads, without subsequently fancying to himself some ideal image of the man and his mind. And if you rightly look for it, you will almost always find that the author himself has somewhere furnished you with his own picture. For poets (whether in prose or verse), being painters of nature, are like their brethren of the pencil, the true portrait-painters, who, in the multitude of likenesses to be sketched, do not invariably omit their own; and in all high instances, they paint them without any vanity, though at times with a lurking something, that would take several pages to properly define.

I submit it, then, to those best acquainted with the man personally, whether the following is not Nathaniel Hawthorne;—and to himself, whether something involved in it does not express the temper of his mind,—that lasting temper of all true, candid men—a seeker, not a finder yet:—

"A man now entered, in neglected attire, with the aspect of a thinker, but somewhat too rough-hewn and brawny for a scholar. His face was full of sturdy vigor, with some finer and keener attribute beneath; though harsh at first, it was tempered with the glow of a large, warm heart, which had force enough to heat his powerful intellect through and through. He advanced to the Intelligencer, and looked at him with a glance of such stern sincerity, that perhaps few secrets were beyond its scope.

"'I seek for Truth,' said he."[9]

Twenty-four hours have elapsed since writing the foregoing. I have just returned from the hay-mow, charged more and more with love and admiration of Hawthorne. For I have just been gleaning through the Mosses, picking up many things here and there that had previously escaped me. And I found that but to glean after this man, is better than to be in at the harvest of others. To be frank (though, perhaps, rather foolish) notwithstanding what I wrote yesterday of these Mosses, I had not then culled them all; but had, nevertheless, been sufficiently sensible of the subtle essence in them, as to write as I did. To what infinite height of loving wonder and admiration I may yet be borne, when by repeatedly banqueting on these Mosses

[9]From "The Intelligence Office," *Mosses from an Old Manse.*

I shall have thoroughly incorporated their whole stuff into my being,—that, I cannot tell. But already I feel that this Hawthorne has dropped germinous seeds into my soul. He expands and deepens down, the more I contemplate him; and further and further, shoots his strong New England roots in the hot soil of my Southern soul. . . .[10]

[10]Here, as throughout, Melville maintains the fiction that he was a "Virginian Spending July in Vermont." He was not a Virginian, of course, and was in actuality spending the summer in Pittsfield, Mass. On July 18, 1850 an aunt had given him a copy of *Mosses from an Old Manse,* which he read with the enthusiasm recorded here and first published in the *Literary World,* August 17 and 24, 1850. He had not met Hawthorne when he wrote the review, though he had by the time it appeared (and Hawthorne then did not know who had written it). By a happy coincidence the Hawthornes spent the summer of 1850 in Lenox, Mass., about six miles from Pittsfield, and the two authors met on a picnic on August 5. During August the Hawthornes were deep in the works of Melville, Nathaniel Hawthorne, like Melville, reading in a hay-mow.

THREE EXCERPTS FROM *THE CONFIDENCE MAN*

CHAPTER 14

Worth the Consideration of Those to Whom it may Prove Worth Considering

As the last chapter was begun with a reminder looking forward, so the present must consist of one glancing backward.

To some, it may raise a degree of surprise that one so full of confidence, as the merchant has throughout shown himself, up to the moment of his late sudden impulsiveness, should, in that instance, have betrayed such a depth of discontent. He may be thought inconsistent, and even so he is. But for this, is the author to be blamed? True, it may be urged that there is nothing a writer of fiction should more carefully see to, as there is nothing a sensible reader will more carefully look for, than that, in the depiction of any character, its consistency should be preserved. But this, though at first blush seeming reasonable enough, may, upon a closer view, prove not so much so. For how does it couple with another requirement—equally insisted upon, perhaps—that, while to all fiction is allowed some play of invention, yet, fiction based on fact should never be contradictory to it; and is it not a fact, that, in real life, a consistent character is a *rara avis?* Which being so, the distaste of readers to the contrary sort in books, can hardly arise from any sense of their untrueness. It may rather be from perplexity as to understanding them. But if the acutest sage be often at his wit's ends to understand living character, shall those who are not sages expect to run and read character in those mere phantoms which flit along a page, like shadows along a wall? That fiction, where every character can, by reason of its consistency, be comprehended at a glance, either exhibits but sections of character, making them appear for wholes, or else is very untrue to reality; while, on the other hand, that author who draws a character, even though to common view incongruous in its parts, as the flying-squirrel, and, at different periods, as much at variance with itself as the butterfly is with the caterpillar into which it changes, may yet, in so doing, be not false but faithful to facts.

If reason be judge, no writer has produced such inconsistent characters as nature herself has. It must call for no small sagacity in a reader unerringly to discriminate in a novel between the inconsistencies of conception and those of life as elsewhere. Experience is the only guide here; but as no one man can be coextensive with *what is,* it may be unwise in every case to rest upon it. When the duck-billed beaver of Australia was first brought stuffed to England, the naturalists, appealing to their classifications, maintained that there was, in reality, no such creature; the bill in the specimen must needs be, in some way, artificially stuck on.

But let nature, to the perplexity of the naturalists, produce her duck-billed beavers as she may, lesser authors, some may hold, have no business to be perplexing readers with duck-billed characters. Always, they should represent human nature not in obscurity, but transparency, which, indeed, is the practice with most novelists, and is, perhaps, in certain cases, some way felt to be a kind of honour rendered by them to their kind. But whether it involve honour or otherwise might be mooted, considering that, if these waters of human nature can be so readily seen through, it may be either that they are very pure or very shallow. Upon the whole, it might rather be thought, that he, who, in view of its inconsistencies, says of human nature the same that, in view of its contrasts, is said of the divine nature, that it is past finding out, thereby evinces a better appreciation of it than he who, by always representing it in a clear light, leaves it to be inferred that he clearly knows all about it.

But though there is a prejudice against inconsistent characters in books, yet the prejudice bears the other way, when what seemed at first their inconsistency, afterward, by the skill of the writer, turns out to be their good keeping. The great masters excel in nothing so much as in this very particular. They challenge astonishment at the tangled web of some character, and then raise admiration still greater at their satisfactory unraveling of it; in this way throwing open, sometimes to the understanding even of school misses, the last complications of that spirit which is affirmed by its Creator to be fearfully and wonderfully made. . . .

CHAPTER 33
Which May Pass for whatever it May Prove to be Worth

But ere be given the rather grave story of Charlemont, a reply must in civility be made to a certain voice which methinks I heard, that, in view of past chapters, and more particularly the last, where certain antics appear, exclaims: How unreal all this is! Who did ever dress or act like your cosmopolitan? And who, it might be returned, did ever dress or act like harlequin?

Strange, that in a work of amusement, this severe fidelity to real life should be exacted by anyone, who, by taking up such a work, sufficiently shows that he is not unwilling to drop real life, and turn, for a time, to something different. Yes, it is, indeed, strange that anyone should clamor for the thing he is weary of; that anyone, who, for any cause, finds real life dull, should yet demand of him who is to divert his attention from it, that he should be true to that dullness.

There is another class, and with this class we side, who sit down to a work of amusement tolerantly as they sit at a play, and with much the same expectations and feelings. They look that fancy shall evoke scenes different from those of the same old crowd round the custom-house counter, and same old dishes on the boarding-house table, with characters unlike those of the same old acquaintances they meet in the same old way every day in the same old street. And as, in real life, the properties will not allow people to act out themselves with that unreserve permitted to the stage; so, in books of fiction, they look not only for more entertainment, but, at bottom, even for more reality, than real life itself can show. Thus, though they want novelty, they want nature, too; but nature unfettered, exhilarated, in effect transformed. In this way of thinking, the people in a fiction, like the people in a play, must dress as nobody exactly dresses, talk as nobody exactly talks, act as nobody exactly acts. It is with fiction as with religion: it should present another world, and yet one to which we feel the tie.

If, then, something is to be pardoned to well-meant endeavor, surely a little is to be allowed to that writer who, in all his scenes, does but seek to minister to what, as he understands it, is the implied wish of the more indulgent lovers of entertainment, before whom harlequin can never appear in a coat too parti-coloured, or cut capers too fantastic.

One word more. Though everyone knows how bootless it is to be in all cases vindicating one's self, never mind how convinced one may be that he is never in the wrong; yet so precious to man is the approbation of his kind, that to rest, though but under an imaginary censure applied to but a work of imagination, is no easy thing. The mention of this weakness will explain why all such readers as may think they perceive something inharmonious between the boisterous hilarity of the cosmopolitan with the bristling cynic, and his restrained good-nature with the boon companion, are now referred to that chapter where some similar apparent inconsistency in another character is, on general principles, modestly endeavored to be apologized for.

CHAPTER 44
In Which the Last Three Words of the Last Chapter are made
the Text of Discourse, which Will be Sure of Receiving More or
Less Attention from Those Readers who do not Skip It

"Quite an original": a phrase, we fancy, rather oftener used
by the young, or the unlearned, or the untravelled, than by
the old, or the well-read, or the man who has made the grand
tour. Certainly, the sense of originality exists at its highest in
an infant, and probably at its lowest in him who has completed
the circle of the sciences.

As for original characters in fiction, a grateful reader will,
on meeting with one, keep the anniversary of that day. True,
we sometimes hear of an author who, at one creation, produces
some two or three score such characters; it may be possible.
But they can hardly be original in the sense that Hamlet is,
or Don Quixote, or Milton's Satan. That is to say, they are not,
in a thorough sense, original at all. They are novel, or singular, or striking, or captivating, or all four at once.

More likely, they are what are called odd characters; but
for that, are no more original, than what is called an odd genius,
in his way, is. But, if original, whence came they? Or where
did the novelist pick them up?

Where does any novelist pick up any character? For the
most part, in town, to be sure. Every great town is a kind of
manshow, where the novelist goes for his stock, just as the
agriculturist goes to the cattle-show for his. But in the one fair,
new species of quadrupeds are hardly more rare, than in the
other are new species of characters—that is, original ones.
Their rarity may still the more appear from this, that, while
characters, merely singular, imply but singular forms, so to
speak, original ones, truly so, imply original instincts.

In short, a due conception of what is to be held for this
sort of personage in fiction would make him almost as much
of a prodigy there, as in real history is a new law-giver, a revo-
lutionizing philosopher, or the founder of a new religion.

In nearly all the original characters, loosely accounted
such in works of invention, there is discernible something pre-

vailingly local, or of the age; which circumstance, of itself, would seem to invalidate the claim, judged by the principles here suggested.

Furthermore, if we consider, what is popularly held to entitle characters in fiction to being deemed original, is but something personal—confined to itself. The character sheds not its characteristic on its surroundings, whereas, the original character, essentially such, is like a revolving Drummond light, raying away from itself all round it—everything is lit by it, everything starts up to it (mark how it is with Hamlet), so that, in certain minds, there follows upon the adequate conception of such a character, an effect, in its way, akin to that which in Genesis attends upon the beginning of things.

For much the same reason that there is but one planet to one orbit, so can there be but one original character to one work of invention. Two would conflict to chaos. In this view, to say that there are more than one to a book, is good presumption there is none at all. But for new, singular, striking, odd, eccentric, and all sorts of entertaining and instructive characters, a good fiction may be full of them. To produce such characters, an author, beside other things, must have seen much, and seen through much: to produce but one original character, he must have had much luck.

There would seem but one point in common between this sort of phenomenon in fiction and all other sorts: it cannot be born in the author's imagination—it being as true in literature as in zoology, that all life is from the egg.

In the endeavour to show, if possible, the impropriety of the phrase, *Quite an Original,* as applied by the barber's friends, we have, at unawares, been led into a dissertation bordering upon the prosy, perhaps upon the smoky. If so, the best use the smoke can be turned to, will be, by retiring under cover of it, in good trim as may be, to the story.

LETTERS
To Nathaniel Hawthorne*

[*Pittsfield 16? April? 1851*]

My Dear Hawthorne,

. . . "The House of the Seven Gables: A Romance. By Nathaniel Hawthorne. One vol. 16mo, pp. 344." The contents of this book do not belie its rich, clustering romantic title. With great enjoyment we spent almost an hour in each separate gable. This book is like a fine old chamber, abundantly, but still judiciously, furnished with precisely that sort of furniture best fitted to furnish it. There are rich hangings, wherein are braided scenes from tragedies! There is old china with rare devices, set out on the carved buffet; there are long and indolent lounges to throw yourself upon; there is an admirabie sideboard, plentifully stored with good viands; there is a smell as of old wine in the pantry; and finally, in one corner, there is a dark little black-letter volume in golden clasps, entitled "Hawthorne: A Problem." It has delighted us; it has piqued a re-perusal; it has robbed us of a day, and made us a present

*Reprinted with permission of Yale University Press from *The Letters of Herman Melville,* ed. Merrell R. Davis and William H. Gilman. New Haven, Conn. 1960.

of a whole year of thoughtfulness; it has bred great exhilaration and exultation with the remembrance that the architect of the Gables resides only six miles off, and not three thousand miles away, in England, say. We think the book, for pleasantness of running interest, surpasses the other works of the author. The curtains are more drawn; the sun comes in more; genialities peep out more. Were we to particularize what most struck us in the deeper passages, we would point out the scene where Clifford, for a moment, would fain throw himself forth from the window to join the procession; or the scene where the judge is left seated in his ancestral chair. Clifford is full of an awful truth throughout. He is conceived in the finest, truest spirit. He is no caricature. He is Clifford. And here we would say that, did circumstances permit, we should like nothing better than to devote an elaborate and careful paper to the full consideration and analysis of the purport and significance of what so strongly characterizes all of this author's writings. There is a certain tragic phase of humanity which, in our opinion, was never more powerfully embodied than by Hawthorne. We mean the tragicalness of human thought in its own unbiassed, native, and profounder workings. We think that into no recorded mind has the intense feeling of the visable truth ever entered more deeply than into this man's. By visable truth, we mean the apprehension of the absolute condition of present things as they strike the eye of the man who fears them not, though they do their worst to him,—the man who, like Russia or the British Empire, declares himself a sovereign nature (in himself) amid the powers of heaven, hell, and earth. He may perish; but so long as he exists he insists upon treating with all Powers upon an equal basis. If any of those other Powers choose to withhold certain secrets, let them; that does not impair my sovereignty in myself; that does not make me tributary. And perhaps, after all, there is *no* secret. We incline to think that the Problem of the Universe is like the Freemason's mighty secret, so terrible to all children. It turns out, at last, to consist in a triangle, a mallet, and an apron,—nothing more! We incline to think that God cannot explain His own secrets, and that He would like a little information upon certain points

Himself. We mortals astonish Him as much as He us. But it is this *Being* of the matter; there lies the knot with which we choke ourselves. As soon as you say *Me*, a *God*, a *Nature*, so soon you jump off from your stool and hang from the beam. Yes, that word is the hangman. Take God out of the dictionary, and you would have Him in the street.

There is the grand truth about Nathaniel Hawthorne. He says NO! in thunder; but the Devil himself cannot make him say *yes*. For all men who say *yes*, lie; and all men who say *no*, — why, they are in the happy condition of judicious, unincumbered travellers in Europe; they cross the frontiers into Eternity with nothing but a carpet-bag, — that is to say, the Ego. Whereas those *yes*-gentry, they travel with heaps of baggage, and, damn them! they will never get through the Custom House. What's the reason, Mr. Hawthorne, that in the last stages of metaphysics a fellow always falls to *swearing* so? I could rip an hour. You see, I began with a little criticism extracted for your benefit from the "Pittsfield Secret Review," and here I have landed in Africa.

Walk down one of these mornings and see me. No nonsense; come. Remember me to Mrs. Hawthorne and the children.

H. Melville.

P.S. The marriage of Phoebe with the daguerreotypist is a fine stroke, because of his turning out to be a *Maule*. If you pass Hepzibah's cent-shop, buy me a Jim Crow (fresh) and send it to me by Ned Higgins.

To Nathaniel Hawthorne*

[Pittsfield 1? June 1851]

My Dear Hawthorne,

. . . In a week or so, I go to New York, to bury myself in a third-story room, and work and slave on my "Whale" while it is driving through the press. *That* is the only way I can finish it now,—I am so pulled hither and thither by circumstances. The calm, the coolness, the silent grass-growing mood in which a man *ought* always to compose,—that, I fear, can seldom be mine. Dollars damn me; and the malicious Devil is forever grinning in upon me, holding the door ajar. My dear Sir, a presentiment is on me,—I shall at last be worn out and perish, like an old nutmeg-grater, grated to pieces by the constant attrition of the wood, that is, the nutmeg. What I feel most moved to write, that is banned,—it will not pay. Yet, altogether, write the *other* way I cannot. So the product is a final hash, and all my books are botches. I'm rather sore, perhaps, in this letter; but see my hand!—four blisters on this palm, made by

*Reprinted with permission of Yale University Press from *The Letters of Herman Melville,* ed. Merrell R. Davis and William H. Gilman. New Haven, Conn., 1960.

hoes and hammers within the last few days. It is a rainy morning; so I am indoors, and all work suspended. I feel cheerfully disposed, and therefore I write a little bluely. Would the Gin were here! If ever, my dear Hawthorne, in the eternal times that are to come, you and I shall sit down in Paradise, in some little shady corner by ourselves; and if we shall by any means be able to smuggle a basket of champagne there (I won't believe in a Temperance Heaven), and if we shall then cross our celestial legs in the celestial grass that is forever tropical, and strike our glasses and our heads together, till both musically ring in concert,—then, O my dear fellow-mortal, how shall we pleasantly discourse of all the things manifold which now so distress us,—when all the earth shall be but a reminiscence, yea, its final dissolution an antiquity. Then shall songs be composed as when wars are over; humorous, comic songs,— "Oh, when I lived in that queer little hole called the world," or, "Oh, when I toiled and sweated below," or, "Oh, when I knocked and was knocked in the fight"—yes, let us look forward to such things. Let us swear that, though now we sweat, yet it is because of the dry heat which is indispensable to the nourishment of the vine which is to bear the grapes that are to give us the champagne hereafter.

But I was talking about the "Whale." As the fishermen say, "he's in his flurry" when I left him some three weeks ago. I'm going to take him by his jaw, however, before long, and finish him up in some fashion or other. What's the use of elaborating what, in its very essence, is so short-lived as a modern book? Though I wrote the Gospels in this century, I should die in the gutter. . . .

H.   Melville

To Nathaniel Hawthorne*

[*Pittsfield 17? Nov. 1851*]

My Dear Hawthorne,

. . . In me divine maganimities are spontaneous and in-
stantaneous—catch them while you can. The world goes round,
and the other side comes up. So now I can't write what I felt.
But I felt pantheistic then—your heart beat in my ribs and mine
in yours, and both in God's. A sense of unspeakable security
is in me this moment, on account of your having understood
the book. I have written a wicked book, and feel spotless as
the lamb. Ineffable socialities are in me. I would sit down and
dine with you and all the gods in old Rome's Pantheon. It is
a strange feeling—no hopefulness is in it, no despair. Content—
that is it; and irresponsibility; but without licentious inclination. I speak now of my profoundest sense of being, not of an
incidental feeling.

Whence come you, Hawthorne? By what right do you
drink from my flagon of life? And when I put it to my lips—lo,

*Reprinted with permission of Yale University Press from *The Letters
of Herman Melville*, ed. Merrell R. Davis and William H. Gilman. New Haven,
Conn., 1960.

they are yours and not mine. I feel that the Godhead is broken up like the bread at the Supper, and that we are the pieces. Hence this infinite fraternity of feeling. Now, sympathizing with the paper, my angel turns over another page. You did not care a penny for the book. But, now and then as you read, you understood the pervading thought that impelled the book—and that you praised. Was it not so? You were archangel enough to despise the imperfect body, and embrace the soul. Once you hugged the ugly Socrates because you saw the flame in the mouth, and heard the rushing of the demon,—the familiar,—and recognized the sound; for you have heard it in your own solitudes.

My dear Hawthorne, the atmospheric skepticisms steal into me now, and make me doubtful of my sanity in writing you thus. But, believe me, I am not mad, most noble Festus![1] But truth is ever incoherent, and when the big hearts strike together, the concussion is a little stunning. Farewell. Don't write a word about the book. That would be robbing me of my miserly delight. I am heartily sorry I ever wrote anything about you—it was paltry.[2] Lord, when shall we be done growing? As long as we have anything more to do, we have done nothing. So, now, let us add Moby Dick to our blessing, and step from that. Leviathan is not the biggest fish;—I have heard of Krakens. . . .

Herman

[1] See Acts 26: 24-25.
[2] "Hawthorne and His Mosses," *Literary World,* August 17, 24, 1850.

To Sophia Hawthorne*

New York Jan. 8th 1852

My Dear Mrs Hawthorne,

. . . It really amazed me that you should find any satisfaction in that book. It is true that some *men* have said they
were pleased with it, but you are the only *woman*—for as a
general thing, women have small taste for the sea. But, then,
since you, with your spiritualizing nature, see more things than
other people, and by the same process, refine all you see, so that
they are not the same things that other people see, but things
which while you think you but humbly discover them, you do in
fact create them for yourself—Therefore, upon the whole, I do
not so much marvel at your expressions concerning Moby Dick.
At any rate, your allusion for example to the "Spirit Spout"[1]
first showed to me that there was a subtile significance in that
thing—but I did not, in that case, *mean* it. I had some vague
idea while writing it, that the whole book was susceptible of

*Reprinted with permission of Yale University Press from *The Letters of
Herman Melville,* ed. Merrell R. Davis and William H. Gilman. New Haven,
Conn., 1960.

[1]*Moby Dick*, chapter 51.

an allegoric construction, & also that *parts* of it were—but the speciality of many of the particular subordinate allegories, were first revealed to me, after reading Mr. Hawthorne's letter, which, without citing any particular examples, yet intimated the part-&-parcel allegoricalness of the whole.—But, My Dear Lady, I shall not again send you a bowl of salt water. The next chalice I shall commend, will be a rural bowl of milk.[2] . . .

Believe Me

Earnestly Thine—

Herman Melville

[2] A reference, perhaps ironic, to *Pierre*.

Samuel L. Clemens

UNLEARNABLE THINGS: FROM THE CONTRIBUTORS' CLUB*

This note comes to me from the home of culture:—

> DEAR MR_____: Your writings interest me very much;
> but I cannot help wishing you would not place adverbs be-
> tween the particle and verb in the Infinitive. For example:
> "to *even* realize," "to *mysteriously* disappear" "to *wholly*
> do away." You should say, *even* to realize; to disappear mys-
> teriously, etc. "rose up" is another mistake—tautology, you
> know. Yours truly
>
> A Boston Girl.

I print the note just as it was written, for one or two reasons: (1.) It flatters a superstition of mine that a person may
learn to excel in only such details of an art as take a particularly strong hold upon his native predilections or instincts.
(2.) It flatters another superstition of mine that whilst all the
details of that art may be of equal importance *he* cannot be
made to feel that it is so. Possibly he may be made to *see* it,
through argument and illustration; but that will be of small
value to him except he *feel* it, also. Culture would be able to

*Atlantic, June, 1880. "The Contributors' Club" was a regular feature,
unsigned.

make him feel it by and by, no doubt, but never very sharply, I think. Now I have certain instincts, and I wholly lack certain others. (Is that "wholly" in the right place?) For instance, I am dead to adverbs; they cannot excite me. To misplace an adverb is a thing which I am able to do with frozen indifference; it can never give me a pang. But when my young lady puts no point after "Mr.;" when she begins "adverb," "verb," and "particle" with the small letter, and aggrandizes "Infinitive" with a capital; and when she puts no comma after "to mysteriously disappear," etc., I am troubled; and when she begins a sentence with a small letter I even *suffer*. Or I suffer, *even*,—I do not know which it is; but she will, because the adverb is in her line, whereas only those minor matters are in mine. Mark these prophetic words: though this young lady's grammar be as the drifted snow for purity, she will never, never, never learn to punctuate while she lives; this is her demon, the adverb is mine. I thank her, honestly and kindly, for her lesson, but I know thoroughly well that I shall never be able to get it into my head. Mind, I do not say I shall not be able to make it *stay* there; I say and mean that I am not capable of *getting it into* my head. There are subtleties which I cannot master at all,—they confuse me, they mean absolutely nothing to me,—and this adverb plague is one of them.

We all have our limitations in the matter of grammar, I suppose. I have never seen a book which had no grammatical defects in it. This leads me to believe that all people have my infirmity, and are afflicted with an inborn inability to feel or mind certain sorts of grammatical particularities. There are people who were not born to spell; these can never be taught to spell correctly. The enviable ones among them are those who do not take the trouble to care whether they spell well or not,—though in truth these latter are absurdly scarce. I have been a correct speller, always; but it is a low accomplishment, and not a thing to be vain of. Why should one take pride in spelling a word rightly when he knows he is spelling it wrongly? *Though* is the right way to spell "though," but it is not *the* right way to spell it. Do I make myself understood?

Some people were not born to punctuate; these cannot

learn the art. They can learn only a rude fashion of it; they cannot attain to its niceties, for these must be *felt;* they cannot be reasoned out. Cast-iron rules will not answer, here, any way; what is one man's comma is another man's colon. One man can't punctuate another man's manuscript any more than one person can make the gestures for another person's speech.

What is known as "dialect" writing looks simple and easy, but it is not. It is exceedingly difficult; it has rarely been done well. A man not born to write dialect cannot learn how to write it correctly. It is a gift. Mr. Harte can write a delightful story; he can *reproduce* Californian scenery so that you see it before you, and hear the sounds and smell the fragrances and feel the influences that go with it and belong to it; he can describe the miner and the gambler perfectly,—as to gait and look and garb; but no human being, living or dead, ever had experience of the dialect which he puts into his people's mouths. Mr. Harte's originality is not questioned; but if it ever shall be, the caviler will have to keep his hands off that dialect, for that *is* original. Mind, I am not objecting to its use; I am not saying its inaccuracy is a fatal blemish. No, it is Mr. Harte's adverb; let him do as he pleases with it; he can no more mend it than I can mine; neither will any but Boston Girls ever be likely to find us out.

Yes, there are things which we cannot learn, and there is no use in fretting about it. I cannot learn adverbs; and what is more I won't. If I try to seat a person at my right hand, I have no trouble, provided I am facing north at the time; but if I am facing south, I get him on my left, sure. As this thing was born in me, and cannot be educated out of me, I do not worry over it or care about it. A gentleman picked me up, last week, and brought me home in his buggy; he drove past the door, and as he approached the circular turn I saw he meant to go around to the left; I was on his left,—that is, I *think* I was, but I have got it all mixed up again in my head; at any rate, I halted him, and asked him to go round the circle the other way. He backed his horse a length or two, put his helm down and "slewed" him to the right, then "came ahead on him," and made the trip. As I got out at the door, he looked puzzled, and asked why

I had particularly wanted to pass to the right around the circle. I said, "Because that would bring me next the door coming back, and I wouldn't have to crowd past your knees." He came near laughing his store teeth out, and said it was all the same whether we drove to the right or to the left in going around the circle; either would bring me back to the house on the side the door was on, since I was on the opposite side when I first approached the circle. I regarded this as false. He was willing to illustrate; so he drove me down to the gate and into the street, turned and drove back past the house, moved leftward around the circle, and brought me back to the door; and as sure as I am sitting here I *was* on the side next the door. I did not believe he could do it again, but he did. He did it eleven times hand running. Was I convinced? No. I was not *capable* of being convinced—*all through.* My sight and intellect (to call it by that name) were convinced, but not my *feeling.* It is simply another case of adverb. It is a piece of dead-corpsy knowledge, which is of no use to me, because I merely *know* it, but do not *understand* it.

The fact is, as the poet has said, we are all fools. The difference is simply in the degree. The mercury in some of the fool-thermometers stands at ten, fifteen, twenty, thirty, and so on; in some it gets up to seventy-five; in some it soars to ninety-nine. I never examine mine,—take no interest in it.

Now as to "rose up." That strikes me as quite a good form; I will use it some more,—that is, when I speak of a person, and wish to signify the full upright position. If I mean less, I will qualify, by saying he rose partly up. It is a form that will answer for the moon sometimes, too. I think it is Bingen on the Rhine who says—

> "The pale moon rose up slowly, and calmly she
>   looked down,
> On the red sands," etc.

But tautology cannot scare me, anyway. Conversation would be intolerably stiff and formal without it; and a mild form of it can limber up even printed matter without doing it serious damage. Some folks are so afraid of a little repetition that they make their meaning vague, when they could just as well make it clear, if only their ogre were out of the way.

Talking of Unlearnable Things, would it be genteel, would it be polite, to ask members of this Club to confess what freightage of this sort they carry? Some of the revelations would be curious and instructive, I think. I am acquainted with one member of it who has never been able to learn nine times eight; he always says, "Nine times seven are sixty-three,"—then counts the rest on his fingers. He is at home in the balance of the multiplication-table. I am acquainted with another member, who, although he has known for many years that when Monday is the first of the month the following Monday will be the eighth, has never been able to *feel* the fact; so he cannot trust it, but always counts on his fingers, to make sure. I have known people who could spell all words correctly but one. They never could get the upper hand of that one; yet as a rule it was some simple, common affair, such as a cat could spell, if a cat could spell at all. I have a friend who has kept his razors in the top drawer and his strop in the bottom drawer for years; when he wants his razors, he always pulls out the bottom drawer— and swears. Change? Could one imagine he never thought of that? He did change; he has changed a dozen times. It didn't do any good; his afflicted mind was able to keep up with the changes and make the proper mistake every time. I knew a man—

THE ART OF AUTHORSHIP*

Your inquiry has set me thinking, but, so far, my thought
fails to materialise. I mean that, upon consideration, I am not
sure that I have methods in composition. I do suppose I have—
I suppose I must have—but they somehow refuse to take shape
in my mind; their details refuse to separate and submit to classification and description; they remain a jumble—visible, like
the fragments of glass when you look in at the wrong end of
a kaleidoscope, but still a jumble. If I could turn the whole
thing around and look in at the other end, why then the figures would flash into form out of the chaos, and I shouldn't
have any more trouble. But my head isn't right for that to-day,
apparently. It might have been, maybe, if I had slept last night.

However, let us try guessing. Let us guess that whenever
we read a sentence and like it, we unconsciously store it away
in our model-chamber; and it goes with the myriad of its fellows to the building, brick by brick, of the eventual edifice
which we call our style. And let us guess that whenever we
run across other forms—bricks—whose colour, or some other
defect, offends us, we unconsciously reject these, and so one
never finds them in our edifice. If I have subjected myself to

*From George Bainton, ed., *The Art of Authorship,* New York; 1891. Twain
had replied to a letter from Bainton.

any training processes, and no doubt I have, it must have been in this unconscious or half-conscious fashion. I think it unlikely that deliberate and consciously methodical training is usual with the craft. I think it likely that the training most in use is of this unconscious sort, and is guided and governed and made by-and-by unconsciously systematic, by an automatically-working taste—a taste which selects and rejects without asking you for any help, and patiently and steadily improves itself without troubling you to approve or applaud. Yes, and likely enough when the structure is at last pretty well up, and attracts attention, *you* feel complimented, whereas you didn't build it, and didn't even consciously superintend. Yes; one notices, for instance, that long, involved sentences confuse him, and that he is obliged to re-read them to get the sense. Unconsciously, then, he rejects that brick. Unconsciously he accustoms himself to writing short sentences as a rule. At times he may indulge himself with a long one, but he will make sure that there are no folds in it, no vaguenesses, no parenthetical interruptions of its view as a whole; when he is done with it, it won't be a sea-serpent, with half of its arches under the water, it will be a torchlight procession.

Well, also he will notice in the course of time, as his reading goes on, that the difference between the *almost right* word and the *right* word is really a large matter—'tis the difference between the lightning-bug and the lightning. After that, of course, that exceedingly important brick, the *exact* word— however, this is running into an essay, and I beg pardon. So I seem to have arrived at this: doubtless I have methods, but they begot themselves, in which case I am only their proprietor, not their father.

HOW TO TELL A STORY

I do not claim that I can tell a story as it ought to be told. I only claim to know how a story ought to be told, for I have been almost daily in the company of the most expert story-tellers for many years.

There are several kinds of stories, but only one difficult kind—the humorous. I will talk mainly about that one. The humorous story is American, the comic story is English, the witty story is French. The humorous story depends for its effect upon the *manner* of the telling; the comic story and the witty story upon the *matter*.

The humorous story may be spun out to great length, and may wander around as much as it pleases, and arrive nowhere in particular; but the comic and witty stories must be brief and end with a point. The humorous story bubbles gently along, the others burst.

The humorous story is strictly a work of art—high and delicate art—and only an artist can tell it; but no art is necessary in telling the comic and the witty story; anybody can do it. The art of telling a humorous story—understand, I mean by word of mouth, not print—was created in America, and has remained at home.

The humorous story is told gravely; the teller does his

best to conceal the fact that he even dimly suspects that there is anything funny about it; but the teller of the comic story tells you beforehand that it is one of the funniest things he has ever heard, then tells it with eager delight, and is the first person to laugh when he gets through. And sometimes, if he has had good success, he is so glad and happy that he will repeat the "nub" of it and glance around from face to face, collecting applause, and then repeat it again. It is a pathetic thing to see.

Very often, of course, the rambling and disjointed humorous story finishes with a nub, point, snapper, or whatever you like to call it. Then the listener must be alert, for in many cases the teller will divert attention from that nub by dropping it in a carefully casual and indifferent way, with the pretense that he does not know it is a nub.

Artemus Ward used that trick a good deal; then when the belated audience presently caught the joke he would look up with innocent surprise, as if wondering what they had found to laugh at. Dan Setchell used it before him, Nye and Riley and others use it to-day.

But the teller of the comic story does not slur the nub; he shouts it at you—every time. And when he prints it, in England, France, Germany, and Italy, he italicizes it, puts some whooping exclamation-points after it, and sometimes explains it in a parenthesis. All of which is very depressing, and makes one want to renounce joking and lead a better life.

Let me set down an instance of the comic method, using an anecdote which has been popular all over the world for twelve or fifteen hundred years. The teller tells it in this way:

THE WOUNDED SOLDIER

In the course of a certain battle a soldier whose leg had been shot off appealed to another soldier who was hurrying by to carry him to the rear, informing him at the same time of the loss which he had sustained; whereupon the generous son of Mars, shouldering the unfortunate, proceeded to carry out his desire. The bullets and cannon-balls were flying in all directions, and presently one of the latter took the wounded man's head off—without, however, his deliverer being aware of it. In no long time he was hailed by an officer, who said:

"Where are you going with that carcass?"

"To the rear, sir—he's lost his leg!"

"His leg, forsooth?" responded the astonished officer, "you mean his head, you booby."

Whereupon the soldier dispossessed himself of his burden, and stood looking down upon it in great perplexity. At length he said:

"It is true, sir, just as you have said." Then after a pause he added, "*But he* TOLD *me* IT WAS HIS LEG!!!!!"

Here the narrator bursts into explosion after explosion of thunderous horse-laughter, repeating that nub from time to time through his gaspings and shriekings and suffocatings.

It takes only a minute and a half to tell that in its comic-story form; and isn't worth the telling, after all. Put into the humorous-story form it takes ten minutes, and is about the funniest thing I have ever listened to—as James Whitcomb Riley tells it.

He tells it in the character of a dull-witted old farmer who has just heard it for the first time, thinks it is unspeakably funny, and is trying to repeat it to a neighbor. But he can't remember it; so he gets all mixed up and wanders helplessly round and round, putting in tedious details that don't belong in the tale and only retard it; taking them out conscientiously and putting in others that are just as useless; making minor mistakes now and then and stopping to correct them and explain how he came to make them; remembering things which he forgot to put in in their proper place and going back to put them in there; stopping his narrative a good while in order to try to recall the name of the soldier that was hurt, and finally remembering that the soldier's name was not mentioned, and remarking placidly that the name is of no real importance, anyway—better, of course, if one knew it, but not essential, after all—and so on, and so on, and so on.

The teller is innocent and happy and pleased with himself, and has to stop every little while to hold himself in and keep from laughing outright; and does hold in, but his body quakes in a jelly-like way with interior chuckles; and at the end of the ten minutes the audience have laughed until they are exhausted, and the tears are running down their faces.

The simplicity and innocence and sincerity and unconsciousness of the old farmer are perfectly simulated, and the result is a performance which is thoroughly charming and delicious. This is art—and fine and beautiful, and only a master can compass it; but a machine could tell the other story.

To string incongruities and absurdities together in a wandering and sometimes purposeless way, and seem innocently unaware that they are absurdities, is the basis of the American art, if my position is correct. Another feature is the slurring of the point. A third is the dropping of a studied remark apparently without knowing it, as if one were thinking aloud. The fourth and last is the pause.

Artemus Ward dealt in numbers three and four a good deal. He would begin to tell with great animation something which he seemed to think was wonderful; then lose confidence, and after an apparently absent-minded pause add an incongruous remark in a soliloquizing way; and that was the remark intended to explode the mine—and it did.

For instance, he would say eagerly, excitedly, "I once knew a man in New Zealand who hadn't a tooth in his head"—here his animation would die out; a silent, reflective pause would follow, then he would say dreamily, and as if to himself, "and yet that man could beat a drum better than any man I ever saw."

The pause is an exceedingly important feature in any kind of story, and a frequently recurring feature, too. It is a dainty thing, and delicate, and also uncertain and treacherous; for it must be exactly the right length—no more and no less—or it fails of its purpose and makes trouble. If the pause is too short the impressive point is passed, and the audience have had time to divine that a surprise is intended—and then you can't surprise them, of course. . . .

WHAT PAUL BOURGET
THINKS OF US

He reports the American joke correctly. In Boston they ask, How much does he know? in New York, How much is he worth? in Philadelphia, Who were his parents? And when an alien observer turns his telescope upon us—advertisedly in our own special interest—a natural apprehension moves us to ask, What is the diameter of his reflector?

I take a great interest in M. Bourget's chapters, for I know by the newspapers that there are several Americans who are expecting to get a whole education out of them; several who foresaw, and also foretold, that our long night was over, and a light almost divine about to break upon the land.

> *His utterances concerning us are bound to be weighty and well timed.*
> *He gives us an object-lesson which should be thoughtfully and profitably studied.*

These well-considered and important verdicts were of a nature to restore public confidence, which had been disquieted by questionings as to whether so young a teacher would be qualified to take so large a class as seventy million, distributed over so extensive a school-house as America, and pull it through without assistance.

I was even disquieted myself, although I am of a cold, calm temperament, and not easily disturbed. I feared for my country. And I was not wholly tranquilized by the verdicts rendered as above. It seemed to me that there was still room for doubt. In fact, in looking the ground over I became more disturbed than I was before. Many worrying questions came up in my mind. Two were prominent. Where had the teacher gotten his equipment? What was his method?

He had gotten his equipment in France.

Then as to his method! I saw by his own intimations that he was an Observer, and had a System—that used by naturalists and other scientists. The naturalist collects many bugs and reptiles and butterflies and studies their ways a long time patiently. By this means he is presently able to group these creatures into families and subdivisions of families by nice shadings of differences observable in their characters. Then he labels all those shaded bugs and things with nicely descriptive group names, and is now happy, for his great work is completed, and as a result he intimately knows every bug and shade of a bug there, inside and out. It may be true, but a person who was not a naturalist would feel safer about it if he had the opinion of the bug. I think it is a pleasant System, but subject to error.

The Observer of Peoples has to be a Classifier, a Grouper, a Deducer, a Generalizer, a Psychologizer; and, first and last, a Thinker. He has to be all these, and when he is at home, observing his own folk, he is often able to prove competency. But history has shown that when he is abroad observing unfamiliar peoples the chances are heavily against him. He is then a naturalist observing a bug, with no more than a naturalist's chance of being able to tell the bug anything new about itself, and no more than a naturalist's chance of being able to teach it any new ways which it will prefer to its own.

To return to that first question. M. Bourget, as teacher, would simply be France teaching America. It seemed to me that the outlook was dark—almost Egyptian, in fact. What would the new teacher, representing France, teach us? Railroading? No. France knows nothing valuable about railroading. Steamshipping? No. France has no superiorities over us in that matter. Steamboating? No. French steamboating is still of Fulton's date—1809. Postal service? No. France is a back number there. Telegraphy? No, we taught her that ourselves. Journalism? No. Magazining? No, that is our own specialty. Government? No; Liberty, Equality, Fraternity, Nobility, Democracy, Adultery—the system is too variegated for our climate. Religion? No, not variegated enough for our climate. Morals? No, we cannot rob the poor to enrich ourselves. Novel-writing? No. M. Bourget and the others know only one plan, and when that is expurgated there is nothing left of the book.

I wish I could think what he is going to teach us. Can it be Deportment? But he experimented in that at Newport and failed to give satisfaction, except to a few. Those few are pleased. They are enjoying their joy as well as they can. They confess their happiness to the interviewer. They feel pretty striped, but they remember with reverent recognition that they had sugar between the cuts. True, sugar with sand in it, but sugar. And true, they had some trouble to tell which was sugar and which was sand, because the sugar itself looked just like the sand, and also had a gravelly taste; still, they knew that the sugar was there, and would have been very good sugar indeed if it had been screened. Yes, they are pleased; not noisily so, but pleased; invaded or streaked, as one may say, with little recurrent shivers of joy—subdued joy, so to speak, not the overdone kind. And they commune together, these, and massage each other with conforting sayings, in a sweet spirit of resignation and thankfulness, mixing these elements in the same proportions as the sugar and the sand, as a memorial, and saying, the one to the other, and to the interviewer: "It was severe—yes it was bitterly severe; but oh, how true it was; and it will do us so much good!"

If it isn't Deportment, what is left? It was at this point that I seemed to get on the right track at last. M. Bourget would teach us to know ourselves; that was it: he would reveal us to ourselves. That would be an education. He would explain us to ourselves. Then we should understand ourselves; and after that be able to go on more intelligently.

It seemed a doubtful scheme. He could explain *us* to *himself*—that would be easy. That would be the same as the naturalist explaining the bug to himself. But to explain the bug to the bug—that is quite a different matter. The bug may not know himself perfectly, but he knows himself better than the naturalist can know him, at any rate.

A foreigner can photograph the exteriors of a nation, but I think that that is as far as he can get. I think that no foreigner can report its interior—its soul, its life, its speech, its thought. I think that a knowledge of these things is acquirable in only one way—not two or four or six—*absorption;* years and years of unconscious absorption; years and years of intercourse with the life concerned; of living it, indeed; sharing personally in its shames and prides, its joys and griefs, its loves and hates, its prosperities and reverses, its shows and shabbinesses, its deep patriotism, its whirlwinds of political passion, its adoration—of flag, and heroic dead, and the glory of the national name. Observation? Of what real value is it? One learns peoples through the heart, not the eyes or the intellect.

There is only one expert who is qualified to examine the souls and the life of a people and make a valuable report—the native novelist. This expert is so rare that the most populous country can never have fifteen conspicuously and confessedly competent ones in stock at one time. This native specialist is not qualified to begin work until he has been absorbing during twenty-five years. How much of his competency is derived from conscious "observation"? The amount is so slight that it counts for next to nothing in the equipment. Almost the whole capital of the novelist is the slow accumulation of *un*conscious observation—absorption. The native expert's intentional observation of manners, speech, character, and ways of life can have value, for the native knows what they mean without having to cipher out the meaning. But I should be astonished to see a foreigner get at the right meanings, catch the elusive shades of these subtle things. Even the native novelist becomes a foreigner, with a foreigner's limitations, when he steps from the state whose life is familiar to him into a state whose life he has not lived. Bret Harte got his California and

his Californians by unconscious absorption, and put both of
them into his tales alive. But when he came from the Pacific
to the Atlantic and tried to do Newport life from study—conscious observation—his failure was absolutely monumental.
Newport is a disastrous place for the unacclimated observer,
evidently.

To return to novel-building. Does the native novelist try
to generalize the nation? No, he lays plainly before you the
ways and speech and life of a few people grouped in a certain
place—his own place—and that is one book. In time he and
his brethren will report to you the life and the people of the
whole nation—the life of a group in a New England village;
in a New York village; in a Texan village; in an Oregon village;
in villages in fifty states and territories; then the farm-life in
fifty states and territories; a hundred patches of life and groups
of people in a dozen widely separated cities. And the Indians
will be attended to; and the cowboys; and the gold and silver
miners; and the negroes; and the Idiots and Congressmen;
and the Irish, the Germans, the Italians, the Swedes, the French,
the Chinamen, the Greasers; and the Catholics, the Metho-
dists, the Presbyterians, the Congregationalists, the Baptists,
the Spiritualists, the Mormons, the Shakers, the Quakers, the
Jews, the Campbellities, the infidels, the Christian Scientists,
the Mind-Curists, the Faith-Curists, the train-robbers, the
White Caps, the Moonshiners. And when a thousand able novels have been written, *there* you have the soul of the people,
the life of the people, the speech of the people; and not anywhere else can these be had. And the shadings of character,
manners, feelings, ambitions, will be infinite.

The nature of a people is always of a similar shade in its
vices and its virtues, in its frivolities and in its labor. *It is this
physiognomy which it is necessary to discover,* and every document is good, from the hall of a casino to the church, from
the foibles of a fashionable woman to the suggestions of a revolutionary leader. I am therefore quite sure that this *American soul,* the principal interest and the great object of my

voyage, appears behind the records of Newport for those who choose to see it.—*M. Paul Bourget.*

[The italics are mine.] It is a large contract which he has undertaken. "Records" is a pretty poor word there, but I think the use of it is due to hasty translation. In the original the word is *fastes*. I think M. Bourget meant to suggest that he expected to find the great "American soul" secreted behind the *ostentations* of Newport; and that he was going to get it out and examine it, and generalize it, and psychologize it, and make it reveal to him its hidden vast mystery: "the nature of the people" of the United States of America. We have been accused of being a nation addicted to inventing wild schemes. I trust that we shall be allowed to retire to second place now.

There isn't a single human characteristic that can be safely labeled "American." There isn't a single human ambition, or religious trend, or drift of thought, or peculiarity of education, or code of principles, or breed of folly, or style of conversation, or preference for a particular subject for discussion, or form of legs or trunk or head or face or expression or complexion, or gait, or dress, or manners, or disposition, or any other human detail, inside or outside, that can rationally be generalized as "American."

Whenever you have found what seems to be an "American" peculiarity, you have only to cross a frontier or two, or go down or up in the social scale, and you perceive that it has disappeared. And you can cross the Atlantic and find it again. . . .

FENIMORE COOPER'S
LITERARY OFFENCES

The Pathfinder and *The Deerslayer* stand at the head
of Cooper's novels as artistic creations. There are others
of his works which contain parts as perfect as are to be found
in these, and scenes even more thrilling. Not one can be compared with either of them as a finished whole.

The defects in both of these tales are comparatively
slight. They were pure works of art.—*Prof. Lounsbury.*

The five tales reveal an extraordinary fulness of invention.

. . . One of the very greatest characters in fiction, Natty
Bumppo . . .

The craft of the woodsman, the tricks of the trapper,
all the delicate art of the forest, were familiar to Cooper from
his youth up.—*Prof. Brander Matthews.*

Cooper is the greatest artist in the domain of romantic
fiction yet produced by America.—*Wilkie Collins.*

It seems to me that it was far from right for the Professor
of English Literature in Yale, the Professor of English Literature in Columbia, and Wilkie Collins to deliver opinions
on Cooper's literature without having read some of it. It would
have been much more decorous to keep silent and let persons
talk who have read Cooper.

Cooper's art has some defects. In one place in *Deerslayer,* and in the restricted space of two-thirds of a page, Cooper has scored 114 offences against literary art out of a possible 115. It breaks the record.

There are nineteen rules governing literary art in the domain of romantic fiction—some say twenty-two. In *Deerslayer* Cooper violated eighteen of them. These eighteen require:

1. That a tale shall accomplish something and arrive somewhere. But the *Deerslayer* tale accomplishes nothing and arrives in the air.

2. They require that the episodes of a tale shall be necessary parts of the tale, and shall help to develop it. But as the *Deerslayer* tale is not a tale, and accomplishes nothing and arrives nowhere, the episodes have no rightful place in the work, since there was nothing for them to develop.

3. They require that the personages in a tale shall be alive, except in the case of corpses, and that always the reader shall be able to tell the corpses from the others. But this detail has often been overlooked in the *Deerslayer* tale.

4. They require that the personages in a tale, both dead and alive, shall exhibit a sufficient excuse for being there. But this detail also has been overlooked in the *Deerslayer* tale.

5. They require that when the personages of a tale deal in conversation, the talk shall sound like human talk, and be talk such as human beings would be likely to talk in the given circumstances, and have a discoverable meaning, also a discoverable purpose, and a show of relevancy, and remain in the neighborhood of the subject in hand, and be interesting to the reader, and help out the tale, and stop when the people cannot think of anything more to say. But this requirement has been ignored from the beginning of the *Deerslayer* tale to the end of it.

6. They require that when the author describes the character of a personage in his tale, the conduct and conversation of that personage shall justify said description. But this law gets little or no attention in the *Deerslayer* tale, as Natty Bumppo's case will amply prove.

7. They require that when a personage talks like an illustrated, gilt-edged, tree-calf, hand-tooled, seven-dollar Friendship's

Offering in the beginning of a paragraph, he shall not talk like a negro minstrel in the end of it. But this rule is flung down and danced upon in the *Deerslayer* tale.

8. They require that crass stupidities shall not be played upon the reader as "the craft of the woodsman, the delicate art of the forest," by either the author or the people in the tale. But this rule is persistently violated in the *Deerslayer* tale.

9. They require that the personages of a tale shall confine themselves to possibilities and let miracles alone; or, if they venture a miracle, the author must so plausibly set it forth as to make it look possible and reasonable. But these rules are not respected in the *Deerslayer* tale.

10. They require that the author shall make the reader feel a deep interest in the personages of his tale and in their fate; and that he shall make the reader love the good people in the tale and hate the bad ones. But the reader of the *Deerslayer* tale dislikes the good people in it, is indifferent to the others, and wishes they would all get drowned together.

11. They require that the characters in a tale shall be so clearly defined that the reader can tell beforehand what each will do in a given emergency. But in the *Deerslayer* tale this rule is vacated.

In addition to these large rules there are some little ones. These require that the author shall

12. Say what he is proposing to say, not merely come near it.

13. Use the right word, not its second cousin.

14. Eschew surplusage.

15. Not omit necessary details.

16. Avoid slovenliness of form.

17. Use good grammar.

18. Employ a simple and straightforward style.

Even these seven are coldly and persistently violated in the *Deerslayer* tale.

Cooper's gift in the way of invention was not a rich endowment; but such as it was he liked to work it, he was pleased with the effects, and indeed he did some quite sweet things with it. In his little box of stage properties he kept six or eight

cunning devices, tricks, artifices for his savages and woods-
men to deceive and circumvent each other with, and he was
never so happy as when he was working these innocent things
and seeing them go. A favorite one was to make a moccasined
person tread in the tracks of the moccasined enemy, and thus
hide his own trail. Cooper wore out barrels and barrels of moccasins in working that trick. Another stage-property that he
pulled out of his box pretty frequently was his broken twig. He
prized his broken twig above all the rest of his effects, and
worked it the hardest. It is a restful chapter in any book of his
when somebody doesn't step on a dry twig and alarm all the reds
and whites for two hundred yards around. Every time a Cooper person is in peril, and absolute silence is worth four dollars
a minute, he is sure to step on a dry twig. There may be a hundred handier things to step on, but that wouldn't satisfy Cooper. Cooper requires him to turn out and find a dry twig; and
if he can't do it, go and borrow one. In fact, the Leather Stock-
ing Series ought to have been called the Broken Twig Series.

   I am sorry there is not room to put in a few dozen instances of the delicate art of the forest, as practised by Natty Bumppo and some of the other Cooperian experts. Perhaps we may
venture two or three samples. Cooper was a sailor—a naval
officer; yet he gravely tells us how a vessel, driving towards a
lee shore in a gale, is steered for a particular spot by her skipper
because he knows of an *undertow* there which will hold her
back against the gale and save her. For just pure woodcraft,
or sailorcraft, or whatever it is, isn't that neat? For several years
Cooper was daily in the society of artillery, and he ought to
have noticed that when a cannon-ball strikes the ground it
either buries itself or skips a hundred feet or so; skips again
a hundred feet or so—and so on, till finally it gets tired and
rolls. Now in one place he loses some "females"—as he always
calls women—in the edge of a wood near a plain at night in
a fog, on purpose to give Bumppo a chance to show off the
delicate art of the forest before the reader. These mislaid people are hunting for a fort. They hear a cannon-blast, and a cannon-ball presently comes rolling into the wood and stops at
their feet. To the females this suggests nothing. The case is

very different with the admirable Bumppo. I wish I may never know peace again if he doesn't strike out promptly and *follow the track* of that cannon-ball across the plain through the dense fog and find the fort. Isn't it a daisy? If Cooper had any real knowledge of Nature's ways of doing things, he had a most delicate art in concealing the fact. For instance: one of his acute Indian experts, Chingachgook (pronounced Chicago, I think), has lost the trail of a person he is tracking through the forest. Apparently that trail is hopelessly lost. Neither you nor I could ever have guessed out the way to find it. It was very different with Chicago. Chicago was not stumped for long. He turned a running stream out of its course, and there, in the slush in its old bed, were that person's moccasin-tracks. The current did not wash them away, as it would have done in all other like cases—no, even the eternal laws of Nature have to vacate when Cooper wants to put up a delicate job of woodcraft on the reader.

We must be a little wary when Brander Matthews tells us that Cooper's books "reveal an extraordinary fulness of invention." As a rule, I am quite willing to accept Brander Matthews's literary judgments and applaud his lucid and graceful phrasing of them; but that particular statement needs to be taken with a few tons of salt. Bless your heart, Cooper hadn't any more invention than a horse; and I don't mean a high-class horse, either; I mean a clothes-horse. It would be very difficult to find a really clever "situation" in Cooper's books, and still more difficult to find one of any kind which he has failed to render absurd by his handling of it. Look at the episodes of "the caves"; and at the celebrated scuffle between Maqua and those others on the table-land a few days later; and at Hurry Harry's queer water-transit from the castle to the ark; and at Deerslayer's half-hour with his first corpse; and at the quarrel between Hurry Harry and Deerslayer later; and at—but choose for yourself; you can't go amiss.

If Cooper had been an observer his inventive faculty would have worked better; not more interestingly, but more rationally, more plausibly. Cooper's proudest creations in the way of "situations" suffer noticeably from the absence of the observer's protecting gift. Cooper's eye was splendidly inaccurate. Cooper seldom saw anything correctly. He saw nearly all things as through a glass eye, darkly. Of course a man who cannot see the commonest little every-day matters accurately is working at a disadvantage when he is constructing a "situation." In the *Deerslayer* tale Cooper has a stream which is fifty feet wide where it flows out of a lake; it presently narrows to twenty as it meanders along for no given reason, and yet when a stream acts like that it ought to be required to explain itself. Fourteen pages later the width of the brook's outlet from the lake has suddenly shrunk thirty feet, and become "the narrowest part of the stream." This shrinkage is not accounted for. The stream has bends in it, a sure indication that it has alluvial banks and cuts them; yet these bends are only thirty and fifty feet long. If Cooper had been a nice and punctilious observer he wou'd have noticed that the bends were oftener nine hundred feet long than short of it.

Cooper made the exit of that stream fifty feet wide, in the first place, for no particular reason; in the second place, he narrowed it to less than twenty to accommodate some Indians. He bends a "sapling" to the form of an arch over this narrow passage, and conceals six Indians in its foliage. They are "laying" for a settler's scow or ark which is coming up the stream on its way to the lake; it is being hauled against the stiff current by a rope whose stationary end is anchored in the lake; its rate of progress cannot be more than a mile an hour. Cooper describes the ark, but pretty obscurely. In the matter of dimensions "it was little more than a modern canal-boat." Let us guess, then, that it was about one hundred and forty feet long. It was of "greater breadth than common." Let us guess, then, that it was about sixteen feet wide. This leviathan had been prowling down bends which were but a third as long as itself, and scraping between banks where it had only two feet of space to spare on each side. We cannot too much admire this miracle. A low-roofed log dwelling occupies "two-thirds of the ark's length"—a dwelling ninety feet long and sixteen feet wide, let us say—a kind of vestibule train. The dwelling has two rooms—each forty-five feet long and sixteen feet wide, let us guess. One of them is the bedroom of the Hutter girls, Judith and Hetty; the other is the parlor in the daytime, at night it is papa's bedchamber. The ark is arriving at the stream's exit now, whose width has been reduced to less than twenty feet to accommodate the Indians—say to eighteen. There is a foot to spare on each side of the boat. Did the Indians notice that there was going to be a tight squeeze there? Did they notice that they could make money by climbing down out of that arched sapling and just stepping aboard when the ark scraped by? No, other Indians would have noticed these things, but Cooper's Indians never notice anything. Cooper thinks they are marvelous creatures for noticing, but he was almost always in error about his Indians. There was seldom a sane one among them.

The ark is one hundred and forty feet long; the dwelling is ninety feet long. The idea of the Indians is to drop softly and secretly from the arched sapling to the dwelling as the ark creeps along under it at the rate of a mile an hour, and butcher the family. It will take the ark a minute and a half to pass under. It will take the ninety foot dwelling a minute to pass under. Now, then, what did the six Indians do? It would take you thirty years to guess, and even then you would have to give it up, I believe. Therefore, I will tell you what the Indians did. Their chief, a person of quite extraordinary intellect for a Cooper Indian, warily watched the canal-boat as it squeezed along under him, and when he had got his calculations fined down to exactly the right shade, as he judged, he let go and dropped. And *missed the house!* That is actually what he did. He missed the house, and landed in the stern of the scow. It was not much of a fall, yet it knocked him silly. He lay there unconscious. If the house had been ninety-seven feet long he would have made the trip. The fault was Cooper's, not his. The error lay in the construction of the house. Cooper was no architect.

There still remained in the roost five Indians. The boat has passed under and is now out of their reach. Let me explain what the five did—you would not be able to reason it out for yourself. No. 1 jumped for the boat, but fell in the water astern of it. Then No. 2 jumped for the boat, but fell in the water still farther astern of it. Then No. 3 jumped for the boat, and fell a good way astern of it. Then No. 4 jumped for the boat, and fell in the water *away* astern. Then even No. 5 made a jump for the boat—for he was a Cooper Indian. In the matter of intellect, the difference between a Cooper Indian and the Indian that stands in front of the cigar-shop is not spacious. The scow episode is really a sublime burst of invention; but it does not thrill, because the inaccuracy of the details throws a sort of air of fictitiousness and general improbability over it. This comes of Cooper's inadequacy as an observer.

The reader will find some examples of Cooper's high talent for inaccurate observation in the account of the shooting match in *The Pathfinder*.

"A common wrought nail was driven lightly into the target, its head having been first touched with paint."

The color of the paint is not stated—an important omission, but Cooper deals freely in important omissions. No, after all, it was not an important omission; for this nail-head is *a hundred yards from* the marksmen, and could not be seen by them at that distance, no matter what its color might be. How far can the best eyes see a common house-fly? A hundred yards? It is quite impossible. Very well; eyes that cannot see a house-fly that is a hundred yards away cannot see an ordinary nail-head at that distance for the size of the two objects is the same. It takes a keen eye to see a fly or a nailhead at fifty yards—one hundred and fifty feet. Can the reader do it?

The nail was lightly driven, its head painted, and game called. Then the Cooper miracles began. The bullet of the first marksman chipped an edge of the nail-head; the next man's bullet drove the nail a little way into the target—and removed all the paint. Haven't the miracles gone far enough now? Not to suit Cooper; for the purpose of this whole scheme is to show off his prodigy, Deerslayer-Hawkeye-Long-Rifle-Leather-Stocking-Pathfinder-Bumppo before the ladies.

" 'Be all ready to clench it, boys!' cried out Pathfinder, stepping into his friend's tracks the instant they were vacant. 'Never mind a new nail; I can see that, though the paint is gone, and what I can see I can hit at a hundred yards, though it were only a mosquito's eye. Be ready to clench!'

"The rifle cracked, the bullet sped its way, and the head of the nail was buried in the wood, covered by the piece of flattened lead."

There, you see, is a man who could hunt flies with a rifle, and command a ducal salary in a Wild West show to-day if we had him back with us.

The recorded feat is certainly surprising just as it stands; but it is not surprising enough for Cooper. Cooper adds a touch. He has made Pathfinder do this miracle with another man's rifle; and not only that, but Pathfinder did not have even the advantage of loading it himself. He had everything against him, and yet he made that impossible shot; and not only made it, but did it with absolute confidence, saying, "Be ready to clench." Now a person like that would have undertaken that same feat with a brickbat, and with Cooper to help he would have achieved it, too.

Pathfinder showed off handsomely that day before the ladies. His very first feat was a thing which no Wild West show can touch. He was standing with the group of marksmen, observing—a hundred yards from the target, mind; one Jasper raised his rifle and drove the centre of the bull's-eye. Then the Quartermaster fired. The target exhibited no result this time. There was a laugh. "It's a dead miss," said Major Lundie. Pathfinder waited an impressive moment or two; then said, in that calm, indifferent, know-it-all way of his, "No, Major, he has covered Jasper's bullet, as will be seen if any one will take the trouble to examine the target."

Wasn't it remarkable! How *could* he see that little pellet fly through the air and enter that distant bullet-hole? Yet that is what he did; for nothing is impossible to a Cooper person. Did any of those people have any deep-seated doubts about this thing? No; for that would imply sanity, and these were all Cooper people.

"The respect for Pathfinder's skill and for his *quickness and accuracy of sight"* (the italics are mine) "was so profound and general, that the instant he made this declaration the spectators began to distrust their own opinions, and a dozen rushed to the target in order to ascertain the fact. There, sure enough, it was found that the Quartermaster's bullet had gone through the hole made by Jasper's, and that, too, so accurately as to require a minute examination to be certain of the circumstance, which, however, was soon clearly established by discovering one bullet over the other in the stump against which the target was placed."

They made a "minute" examination; but never mind, how could they know that there were two bullets in that hole without digging the latest one out? for neither probe nor eyesight could prove the presence of any more than one bullet. Did they dig? No; as we shall see. It is the Pathfinder's turn now; he steps out before the ladies, takes aim, and fires.

But, alas! here is a disappointment; an incredible, an unimaginable disappointment—for the target's aspect is unchanged; there is nothing there but that same old bullet-hole!

"'If one dared to hint at such a thing,' cried Major Duncan, 'I should say that the Pathfinder has also missed the target!'"

As nobody had missed it yet, the "also" was not neccessary; but never mind about that, for the Pathfinder is going to speak.

" 'No, no, Major,' said he, confidently, 'that *would* be a risky declaration. I didn't load the piece, and can't say what was in it; but if it was lead, you will find the bullet driving down those of the Quartermaster and Jasper, else is not my name Pathfinder.'

"A shout from the target announced the truth of this assertion."

Is the miracle sufficient as it stands? Not for Cooper. The Pathfinder speaks again, as he "now slowly advances towards the stage occupied by the females":

" 'That's not all, boys, that's not all; if you find the target touched at all, I'll own to a miss. The Quartermaster cut the wood, but you'll find no wood cut by that last messenger.'"

The miracle is at last complete. He knew—doubtless *saw*—at the distance of a hundred yards—that his bullet had passed into the hole *without fraying the edges*. There were now three bullets in that one hole—three bullets embedded processionally in the body of the stump back of the target. Everybody knew this—somehow or other—and yet nobody had dug any of them out to make sure. Cooper is not a close observer, but he is interesting. He is certainly always that, no matter what happens. And he is more interesting when he is not noticing what he is about than when he is. This is a considerable merit.

The conversations in the Cooper books have a curious sound in our modern ears. To believe that such talk really ever came out of people's mouths would be to believe that there was a time when time was of no value to a person who thought he had something to say; when it was the custom to spread a two-minute remark out to ten; when a man's mouth was a rolling-mill, and busied itself all day long in turning four-foot pigs of thought into thirty-foot bars of conversational railroad iron by attenuation; when subjects were seldom faithfully stuck to, but the talk wandered all around and arrived nowhere; when conversations consisted mainly of irrelevancies, with here and there a relevancy, a relevancy with an embarrassed look, as not being able to explain how it got there.

Cooper was certainly not a master in the construction of dialogue. Inaccurate observation defeated him here as it defeated him in so many other enterprises of his. He even failed to notice that the man who talks corrupt English six days in the week must and will talk it on the seventh, and can't help himself. In the *Deerslayer* story he lets Deerslayer talk the showiest kind of book-talk sometimes, and at other times the basest of base dialects. For instance, when some one asks him if he has a sweetheart, and if so, where she abides, this is his majestic answer:

> " 'She's in the forest—hanging from the boughs of the trees, in a soft rain—in the dew on the open grass—the clouds that float about in the blue heavens—the birds that sing in the woods—the sweet springs where I slake my thirst—and

in all the other glorious gifts that come from God's Providence!' "

And he preceded that, a little before, with this:

" 'It consarns me as all things that touches a fri'nd consarns a fri'nd.' "

And this is another of his remarks:

" 'If I was Injin born, now, I might tell of this, or carry in the scalp and boast of the expl'ite afore the whole tribe; or if my inimy had only been a bear'"—and so on.

We cannot imagine such a thing as a veteran Scotch Commander-in-Chief comporting himself in the field like a windy melodramatic actor, but Cooper could. On one occasion Alice and Cora were being chased by the French through a fog in the neighborhood of their father's fort:

" *'Point de quartier aux coquins!'* cried an eager pursuer, who seemed to direct the operations of the enemy.

" 'Stand firm and be ready, my gallant 60ths!' suddenly exclaimed a voice above them; 'wait to see the enemy; fire low, and sweep the glacis.'

" 'Father! father!' exclaimed a piercing cry from out the mist; 'it is I! Alice! thy own Elsie! spare, O! save your daughters!'

" 'Hold!' shouted the former speaker, in the awful tones of parental agony, the sound reaching even to the woods, and rolling back in solemn echo. ' 'Tis she! God has restored me my children! Throw open the sally-port; to the field, 60ths, to the field! pull not a trigger, lest ye kill my lambs! Drive off these dogs of France with your steel!' "

Cooper's word-sense was singularly dull. When a person has a poor ear for music he will flat and sharp right along without knowing it. He keeps near the tune, but it is *not* the tune. When a person has a poor ear for words, the result is a literary flatting and sharping; you perceive what he is intending to say, but you also perceive that he doesn't *say* it. This is Cooper. He was not a word-musician. His ear was satisfied with the *approximate* word. I will furnish some circumstantial evidence in support of this charge. My instances are gathered from half a dozen pages of the tale called *Deerslayer*. He uses "verbal," for "oral"; "precision," for "facility"; "phenomena," for "marvels"; "necessary," for "predetermined"; "unsophisticated," for "primitive"; "preparation," for "expectancy"; "rebuked," for "subdued"; "dependent on," for "resulting from"; "fact," for "condition"; "fact," for "conjecture"; "precaution," for "caution"; "explain," for "determine"; "mortified," for "disappointed"; "meretricious," for "factitious"; "materially," for "considerably"; "decreasing," for "deepening"; "increasing," for "disappearing"; "embedded," for "enclosed"; "treacherous," for "hostile"; "stood," for "stooped"; "softened," for "replaced"; "rejoined," for "remarked"; "situation," for "condition"; "different," for "differing"; "insensible," for "unsentient"; "brevity," for "celerity"; "distrusted," for "suspicious"; "mental imbecility," for "imbecility"; "eyes," for "sight"; "counteracting," for "opposing"; "funeral obsequies," for "obsequies."

There have been daring people in the world who claimed that Cooper could write English, but they are all dead now—all dead but Lounsbury. I don't remember that Lounsbury makes the claim in so many words, still he makes it, for he says that *Deerslayer* is a "pure work of art." Pure, in that connection, means faultless—faultless in all details—and language is a detail. If Mr. Lounsbury had only compared Cooper's English with the English which he writes himself—but it is plain that he didn't; and so it is likely that he imagines until this day that Cooper's is as clean and compact as his own. Now I feel sure, deep down in my heart, that Cooper wrote about the poorest English that exists in our language, and that the English of *Deerslayer* is the very worst that even Cooper ever wrote.

I may be mistaken, but it does seem to me that *Deerslayer* is not a work of art in any sense; it does seem to me that it is destitute of every detail that goes to the making of a work of art; in truth, it seems to me that *Deerslayer* is just simply a literary *delirium tremens.*

A work of art? It has no invention; it has no order, system, sequence, or result; it has no life-likeness, no thrill, no stir, no seeming of reality; its characters are confusedly drawn, and by their acts and words they prove that they are not the sort of people the author claims that they are; its humor is pathetic; its pathos is funny; its conversations are—oh! indescribable; its love-scenes odious; its English a crime against the language.

Counting these out, what is left is Art. I think we must all admit that.

LETTERS TO
WILLIAM DEAN HOWELLS

Hartford, Jan 18/76

My Dear Howells:*

Thanks, & ever so many, for the good opinion of Tom
Sawyer. Williams[1] has made about 200 rattling pictures for it—
some of them very dainty. Poor devil, what a genius he has,
& how he does murder it with rum. He takes a book of mine,
& without suggestion from anybody builds no end of pictures
just from his reading of it.

There [never] was a man in the world so grateful to another as I was to you day before yesterday, when I sat down
(in still rather wretched health) to set myself to the dreary &
hateful task of making final revision of Tom Sawyer, & discovered, upon opening the package of MS that your pencil
marks were scattered all along. This was splendid, & swept
away all labor. Instead of *reading* the MS, I simply hunted out

---

*Copyright, 1917 by Mark Twain Company; renewed 1945 by Clara
Clemens Samossoud; copyright 1960 by Mark Twain Company. From *Mark
Twain's Letters* ed. by Albert Bigelow Paine. Reprinted by permission of Harper
& Row Publishers.

[1]True W. Williams, who had illustrated other works of Twain as well.

the pencil marks & made the emendations which they suggested. I reduced the boy-battle to a curt paragraph; I finally concluded to cut the Sunday-school speech down to the first two
sentences, (leaving no suggestion of satire, since the book is to
be for boys & girls; I tamed the various obscenities until I
judged that [they] no longer carried offense. So, at a single
sitting I began & finished a revision which I had supposed would
occupy 3 or 4 days & leave me mentally & physically fagged out
at the end. I was careful not to inflict the MS upon you until
I had thoroughly & painstakingly revised it. Therefore, the
only faults left were those that would discover themselves to
others, not me—& these you had pointed out.

There was one expression which perhaps you overlooked.
When Huck is complaining to Tom of the rigorous system in
vogue at the widow's, he says the servants harass him with all
manner of compulsory decencies, & he winds up by saying,
"and they comb me all to hell." (No exclamation point.) Long
ago, when I read that to Mrs. Clemens, she made no comment;
another time I created occasion to read that chapter to her
aunt & her mother (both sensitive & loyal subjects of the kingdom of heaven, so to speak,) & *they* let it pass. I was glad, for
it was the most natural remark in the world for that boy to make
(& he had been allowed few privileges of speech in the book);
when I saw that you, too, had let it go without protest, I was
glad, & afraid, too—afraid you hadn't observed it. Did you?
And did you question the propriety of it? Since the book is
now professedly & confessedly a boy's & girl's book, that dern
word bothers me some nights, but it never did until I had ceased
to regard the volume as being for adults. . . .

Yrs Ever

Mark.

Elmira, July 21/85.

My Dear Howells*—

You are really my only author; I am restricted to you; I wouldn't give a damn for the rest. I bored through Middle-march during the past week, with its labored & tedious analyses of feelings & motives, its paltry & tiresome people, its unexciting & uninteresting story, & its frequent blinding flashes of single-sentence poetry, philosophy, wit, & what-not, & nearly died from the over-work. I wouldn't read another of those books for a farm. I did try to read one other—Daniel Deronda. I dragged through three chapters, losing flesh all the time, & then was honest enough to quit, & confess to myself that I haven't *any* romance-literature appetite, as far as I can see, except for your books.

But what I started to say, was, that I have just read Part II of Indian Summer, & to my mind there isn't a waste-line in it, or one that could be improved. I read it yesterday, ending with that opinion; & read it again to-day, ending with the same opinion emphasized. I haven't read Part I yet, because that number must have reached Hartford after we left; but we are going to send down town for a copy, & when it comes I am to read both parts aloud to the family. It is a beautiful story, & makes a body laugh all the time, & cry inside, & feel so old & so forlorn; & gives him gracious glimpses of his lost youth that fill him with a measureless regret, & build up in him a cloudy sense of his having been a prince, once, in some enchanted far-off land, & of being in exile now, & desolate—& lord, no chance to ever get back there again! That is the thing that hurts. Well, you have done it with marvelous facility—& you make all the motives & feelings perfectly clear without analyzing the guts out of them, the way George Eliot does. I can't stand George Eliot, & Hawthorne & those people; I

see what they are at, a hundred years before they get to it, &
they just tire me to death. And as for the Bostonians,[2] I would
rather be damned to John Bunyan's heaven than read that.

Yrs Ever

Mark.

Hotel Metropole, Vienna, Jan. 22/98.

Dear Howells*—

Look at those ghastly figures. I used to write it "Hartford,
1871." There was no Susy then—there is no Susy now. And
how much lies between—one long lovely stretch of scented
fields, & meadows, & shady woodlands; & suddenly Sahara!
You speak of the glorious days of that old time—& they were.
It is my quarrel—that traps like that are set. Susy & Winnie
given us, in miserable sport, & then taken away.

About the last time I saw you I described to you the culminating disaster in a book I was going to write (& will yet,
when the stroke is further away)—a man's dead daughter
brought to him when he had been through all other possible misfortunes—& I said it couldn't be done as it ought to be done
except by a man who had lived it—it must be written with the
blood out of a man's heart. I could not know, then, how soon I
was to be made competent. I have thought of it many a time
since. If you were here I think we could cry down each other's
necks, as in your dream. For we *are* a pair of old derelicts drift-
ing around, now, with some of our passengers gone & the sunni-
ness of the others in (total) eclipse.

I couldn't get along without work now. I bury myself in
it up to the ears. Long hours—8 & 9 on a stretch, sometimes.
And all the days, Sundays included. It isn't all for print, by

[2]Henry James' novel, then appearing in the *Century Magazine.*

any means, for much of it fails to suit me; 50,000 words of it in the past year. It was because of the deadness which invaded me when Susy died. But I have made a change lately—into dramatic work—& I find it absorbingly entertaining. I don't know that I can write a play that will play; but no matter, I'll write half a dozen that won't, anyway. Dear me, I didn't know there was such fun in it. I'll write twenty that won't play. I get into immense spirits as soon as my day is fairly started. . . .

Mark.

Villa di Quarto [*Florence*], *Jan. 16/04*

Dear 'Owells*—

I've struck it! And I will give it away—to you. You will never know how much enjoyment you have lost until you get to dictating your autobiography; then you will realize, with a pang, that you might have been doing it all your life if you had only had the luck to think of it. And you will be astonished (& charmed) to see how like *talk* it is, & how real it sounds, & how well & compactly & sequentially it constructs itself, & what a dewy & breezy & woodsy freshness it has, & what a darling & worshipful absence of the signs of starch, & flat-iron, & labor & fuss & the other artificialities. Mrs. Clemens is an exacting critic, but I have not talked a sentence yet that she has wanted altered. There are little slips here & there, little inexactnesses, & many desertions of a thought before the end of it has been reached, but these are not blemishes, they are merits, their removal would take away the naturalness of the flow & banish the very thing—the nameless something—which differentiates real narrative from artificial narrative & makes the one so vastly better than the other—the subtle something which makes good talk so much better than the best imitation of it that can be done with a pen.

Try it, & you will see. But with a long-hand scribe, not with a stenographer. At least not at first. Not until you get your hand

*Copyright 1960 by Mark Twain & Company.

in, I should say. There's a good deal of waiting, of course, but that is no matter; soon you do not mind it.

Miss Lyons does the scribing, & is an inspiration, because she takes so much interest in it. I dictate from 10.30 till noon. The result is about 1500 words. Then I am a free man & can read & smoke the rest of the day, for there's not a correction to be made. If I live two years this Auto will cover many volumes, but they will not be published independently, but only as *notes* (copyrightable) to my existing books. Their purpose is, to add 28 years to the life of the existing books. I think the notes will add 50% of matter to each book, & be some shades more readable than the book itself.

I've a good many chapters of Auto—written with a pen from time to time & laid away in envelops—but I expect that when I come to examine them I shall throw them away & do them over again with my mouth, for I feel sure that my quondam satisfaction in them will have vanished & that they will seem poor & artificial & lacking in color. (*Quondam!* long-forgotten old drudge-word!)

One would expect dictated stuff to read like an impromptu speech—brokenly, catchily, repetitiously, & marred by absence of coherence, fluent movement, & the happy things that didn't come till the speech was done—but it isn't so. . . .

Mark.

Stormfield, Redding, Conn.,
Jan. 18, '09.

Dear Howells,*—

I have to write a line, lazy as I am, to say how your Poe article[3] delighted me; and to say that I am in agreement with substantially all you say about his literature. To me his prose

[3]*Harper's Weekly,* Jan. 16, 1909.

is unreadable—like Jane Austin's. No, there is a difference. I could read his prose on salary, but not Jane's. Jane is entirely impossible. It seems a great pity that they allowed her to die a natural death.

Another thing: you grant that God and circumstances sinned against Poe, but you also grant that he sinned against himself—a thing which he couldn't do and didn't do.

It is lively up here now. I wish you could come.

Yrs ever,

Mark.

William Dean Howells

HENRY JAMES, JR.

. . . Mr. James is now so universally recognized that I shall seem to be making an unwarrantable claim when I express my belief that the popularity of his stories was once largely confined to Mr. Fields's assistant.[1] They had characteristics which forbade any editor to refuse them; and there are no anecdotes of thrice-rejected manuscripts finally printed to tell of him; his work was at once successful with all the magazines. But with the readers of "The Atlantic," of "Harper's," of "Lippincott's," of "The Galaxy," of "The Century," it was another affair. The flavor was so strange, that, with rare exceptions, they had to "learn to like" it. Probably few writers have in the same degree compelled the liking of their readers. He was reluctantly accepted, partly through a mistake as to his attitude— through the confusion of his point of view with his private opinion—in the reader's mind. This confusion caused the tears of rage which bedewed our continent in behalf of the "average American girl" supposed to be satirized in Daisy Miller, and prevented the perception of the fact that, so far as the average American girl was studied at all in Daisy Miller, her indestructible innocence, her invulnerable new-worldliness,

---

[1]Howells began his career on the *Atlantic* as assistant to the editor, James T. Fields.

had never been so delicately appreciated. It was so plain that
Mr. James disliked her vulgar conditions, that the very people to whom he revealed her esential sweetness and light were
furious that he should have seemed not to see what existed
through him. In other words, they would have liked him better if he had been a worse artist—if he had been a little more
confidential.

But that artistic impartiality which puzzled so many in
the treatment of Daisy Miller is one of the qualities most valuable in the eyes of those who care how things are done, and
I am not sure that it is not Mr. James's most characteristic quality. As "frost performs the effect of fire," this impartiality comes
at last to the same result as sympathy. We may be quite sure
that Mr. James does not like the peculiar phase of our civilization typified in Henrietta Stackpole; but he treats her with
such exquisite justice that he lets *us* like her. It is an extreme
case, but I confidently allege it in proof.

His impartiality is part of the reserve with which he works
in most respects, and which at first glance makes us say that
he is wanting in humor. But I feel pretty certain that Mr. James
has not been able to disinherit himself to this degree. We A-
mericans are terribly in earnest about making ourselves, indi-
vidually and collectively; but I fancy that our prevailing mood
in the face of all problems is that of an abiding faith which can
afford to be funny. He has himself indicated that we have, as
a nation, as a people, our joke, and every one of us is in the
joke more or less. We may, some of us, dislike it extremely,
disapprove it wholly, and even abhor it, but we are in the joke
all the same, and no one of us is safe from becoming the great
American humorist at any given moment. The danger is not
apparent in Mr. James's case, and I confess that I read him
with a relief in the comparative immunity that he affords from
the national facetiousness. Many of his people are humorously
imagined, or rather humorously *seen,* like Daisy Miller's mother, but these do not give a dominant color; the business in
hand is commonly serious, and the droll people are subordi-
nated. They abound, nevertheless, and many of them are perfectly new finds, like Mr. Tristram in "The American," the

bill-paying father in the "Pension Beaurepas," the anxiously Europeanizing mother in the same story, the amusing little Madame de Belgarde, Henrietta Stackpole, and even Newman himself. But though Mr. James portrays the humorous in character, he is decidedly not on humorous terms with his reader; he ignores rather than recognizes the fact that they are both in the joke.

If we take him at all we must take him on his own ground, for clearly he will not come to ours. We must make concessions to him, not in this respect only, but in several others, chief among which is the motive for reading fiction. By example, at least, he teaches that it is the pursuit and not the end which should give us pleasure; for he often prefers to leave us to our own conjectures in regard to the fate of the people in whom he has interested us. There is no question, of course, but he could tell the story of Isabel in "The Portrait of a Lady" to the end, yet he does not tell it. We must agree, then, to take what seems a fragment instead of a whole, and to find, when we can, a name for this new kind in fiction. Evidently it is the character, not the fate, of his people which occupies him; when he has fully developed their character he leaves them to what destiny the reader pleases.

The analytic tendency seems to have increased with him as his work has gone on. Some of the earlier tales were very dramatic: "A Passionate Pilgrim," which I should rank above all his other short stories, and for certain rich poetical qualities, above everything else that he has done, is eminently dramatic. But I do not find much that I should call dramatic in "The Portrait of a Lady," while I do find in it an amount of analysis which I should call superabundance if it were not all such good literature. The novelist's main business is to possess his reader with a due conception of his characters and the situations in which they find themselves. If he does more or less than this he equally fails. I have sometimes thought that Mr. James's danger was to do more, but when I have been ready to declare this excess an error of his method I have hesitated. Could anything be superfluous that had given me so much pleasure as I read? Certainly from only one point of view,

and this a rather narrow, technical one. It seems to me that
an enlightened criticism will recognize in Mr. James's fiction
a metaphysical genius working to aesthetic results, and will
not be disposed to deny it any method it chooses to employ.
No other novelist, except George Eliot, has dealt so largely
in analysis of motive, has so fully explained and commented
upon the springs of action in the persons of the drama, both
before and after the facts. These novelists are more alike than
any others in their processes, but with George Eliot an ethical purpose is dominant, and with Mr. James an artistic purpose. I do not know just how it should be stated of two such
noble and generous types of character as Dorothea and Isabel Archer, but I think that we sympathize with the former
in grand aims that chiefly concern others, and with the latter
in beautiful dreams that primarily concern herself. Both are
unselfish and devoted women, sublimely true to a mistaken
ideal in their marriages; but, though they come to this common martyrdom, the original difference in them remains. Isabel has her great weaknesses, as Dorothea had, but these seem
to me, on the whole, the most nobly imagined and the most
nobly intentioned women in modern fiction; and I think Isabel is the more subtly divined of the two. If we speak of mere
characterization, we must not fail to acknowledge the perfection of Gilbert Osmond. It was a profound stroke to make him
an American by birth. No European could realize so fully in
his own life the ideal of a European *dilettante* in all the meaning of that cheapened word; as no European could so deeply
and tenderly feel the sweetness and loveliness of the English
past as the sick American, Searle, in "The Passionate Pilgrim."

What is called the international novel is popularly dated
from the publication of "Daisy Miller," though "Roderick Hud-
son" and "The American" had gone before; but it really began
in the beautiful story which I have just named. Mr. James, who
invented this species in fiction, first contrasted in the "Passionate Pilgrim" the New World and Old World moods, ideals,
and prejudices, and he did it there with a richness of poetic
effect which he has since never equalled. I own that I regret
the loss of the poetry, but you cannot ask a man to keep on

being a poet for you; it is hardly for him to choose; yet I compare rather discontentedly in my own mind such impassioned creations as Searle and the painter in "The Madonna of the Future" with "Daisy Miller," of whose slight, thin personality I also feel the indefinable charm, and of the tragedy of whose innocence I recognize the delicate pathos. Looking back to those early stories, where Mr. James stood at the dividing ways of the novel and the romance, I am sometimes sorry that he declared even superficially for the former. His best efforts seem to me those of romance; his best types have an ideal development, like Isabel and Claire Belgarde and Bessy Alden and poor Daisy and even Newman. But, doubtless, he has chosen wisely; perhaps the romance is an outworn form, and would not lend itself to the reproduction of even the ideality of modern life. I myself waver somewhat in my preference—if it is a preference—when I think of such people as Lord Warburton and the Touchetts, whom I take to be all decidedly of this world. The first of these especially interested me as a probable type of the English nobleman, who amiably accepts the existing situation with all its possibilities of political and social change, and insists not at all upon the surviving feudalities, but means to be a manly and simple gentleman in any event. An American is not able to pronounce as to the verity of the type; I only know that it seems probable and that it is charming. It makes one wish that it were in Mr. James's way to paint in some story the present phase of change in England. A titled personage is still mainly an inconceivable being to us; he is like a goblin or a fairy in a story-book. How does he comport himself in the face of all the changes and modifications that have taken place and that still impend? We can hardly imagine a lord taking his nobility seriously; it is some hint of the conditional frame of Lord Warburton's mind that makes him imaginable and delightful to us. . . .

The art of fiction has, in fact, become a finer art in our day than it was with Dickens and Thackeray. We could not suffer the confidential attitude of the latter now, nor the mannerism of the former, any more than we could endure the prolixity of Richardson or the coarseness of Fielding. These great men are of the past—they and their methods and interests; even Trollope and Reade are not of the present. The new school derives from Hawthorne and George Eliot rather than any others; but it studies human nature much more in its wonted aspects, and finds its ethical and dramatic examples in the operation of lighter but not really less vital motives. The moving accident is certainly not its trade; and it prefers to avoid all manner of dire catastrophes. It is largely influenced by French fiction in form; but it is the realism of Daudet rather than the realism of Zola that prevails with it, and it has a soul of its own which is above the business of recording the rather brutish pursuit of a woman by a man, which seems to be the chief end of the French novelist. This school, which is so largely of the future as well as the present, finds its chief exemplar in Mr. James; it is he who is shaping and directing American fiction, at least. It is the ambition of the younger contributors to write like him; he has his following more distinctly recognizable than that of any other English-writing novelist. Whether he will so far control this following as to decide the nature of the novel with us remains to be seen. Will the reader be content to accept a novel which is an analytic study rather than a story, which is apt to leave him arbiter of the destiny of the author's creations? Will he find his account in the unflagging interest of their development? Mr. James's growing popularity seems to suggest that this may be the case; but the work of Mr. James's imitators will have much to do with the final result.

In the meantime it is not surprising that he has his imitators. Whatever exceptions we take to his methods or his results, we cannot deny him a very great literary genius. To me there is a perpetual delight in his way of saying things, and I cannot wonder that younger men try to catch the trick of it. The disappointing thing for them is that it is not a trick, but an inherent virtue. His style is, upon the whole, better than that of any other novelist I know; it is always easy, without being trivial, and it is often stately, without being stiff; it gives a charm to everything he writes; and he has written so much and in such various directions, that we should be judging him very incompletely if we considered him only as a novelist. His

book of European sketches must rank him with the most enlightened and agreeable travelers; and it might be fitly sup-
plemented from his uncollected papers with a volume of American sketches. In his essays on modern French writers he indicates his critical range and grasp; but he scarcely does more,
as his criticisms in "The Atlantic" and "The Nation" and elsewhere could abundantly testify.

There are indeed those who insist that criticism is his true
vocation, and are impatient of his devotion to fiction; but I
suspect that these admirers are mistaken. A novelist he is not,
after the old fashion, or after any fashion but his own; yet since
he has finally made his public in his own way of story-telling—
or call it character-painting if you prefer,—it must be conced-
ed that he has chosen best for himself and his readers in choosing the form of fiction for what he has to say. It is, after all,
what a writer has to say rather than what he has to tell that
we care for nowadays. In one manner or other the stories were
all told long ago; and now we want merely to know what the
novelist thinks about persons and situations. Mr. James gratifies this philosophic desire. If he sometimes forbears to tell
us what he thinks of the last state of his people, it is perhaps
because that does not interest him, and a large-minded criticism might well insist that it was childish to demand that it
must interest him.

I am not sure that my criticism is sufficiently large-minded
for this. I own that I like a finished story; but then also I like
those which Mr. James seems not to finish. This is probably
the position of most of his readers, who cannot very logically account for either preference. We can only make sure that
we have here an annalist, or analyst, as we choose, who fascinates us from his first page to his last, whose narrative or
whose comment may enter into any minuteness of detail without fatiguing us, and can only truly grieve us when it ceases.

CRITICISM AND FICTION

II

. . . "As for those called critics," the author[1] says, "they have generally sought the rule of the arts in the wrong place; they have sought among poems, pictures, engravings, statues, and buildings; but art can never give the rules that make an art. This is, I believe, the reason why artists in general, and poets principally, have been confined in so narrow a circle; they have been rather imitators of one another than of nature. Critics follow them, and therefore can do little as guides. I can judge but poorly of anything while I measure it by no other standard than itself. The true standard of the arts is in every man's power; and an easy observation of the most common, sometimes of the meanest things, in nature will give the truest lights, where the greatest sagacity and industry that slights such observation must leave us in the dark, or, what is worse, amuse and mislead us by false lights."

If this should happen to be true—and it certainly commends itself to acceptance—it might portend an immediate danger to the vested interests of criticism, only that it was written a hundred years ago; and we shall probably have the "sa-

[1]Edmund Burke, *On the Sublime and Beautiful,* 1756.

gacity and industry that slights the observation" of nature long
enough yet to allow most critics the time to learn some more
useful trade than criticism as they pursue it. Nevertheless, I
am in hopes that the communistic era in taste foreshadowed
by Burke is approaching, and that it will occur within the lives
of men now over-awed by the foolish old superstition that literature and art are anything but the expression of life, and
are to be judged by any other test than that of their fidelity
to it. The time is coming, I hope, when each new author, each
new artist, will be considered, not in his proportion to any other
author or artist, but in his relation to the human nature, known
to us all, which it is his privilege, his high duty, to interpret.
"The true standard of the artist is in every man's power" already, as Burke says; Michelangelo's "light of the piazza," the
glance of the common eye, is and always was the best light
on a statue; Goethe's "boys and blackbirds" have in all ages
been the real connoisseurs of berries; but hitherto the mass
of common men have been afraid to apply their own simplicity, naturalness, and honesty to the appreciation of the beautiful. They have always cast about for the instruction of some
one who professed to know better, and who browbeat wholesome common-sense into the self-distrust that ends in sophistication. They have fallen generally to the worst of this bad
species, and have been "amused and misled" (how pretty that
quaint old use of amuse is!) "by the false lights" of critical vanity and self-righteousness. They have been taught to compare
what they see and what they read, not with the things that they
have observed and known, but with the things that some other
artist or writer has done. Especially if they have themselves
the artistic impulse in any direction they are taught to form
themselves, not upon life, but upon the masters who became
masters only by forming themselves upon life. The seeds of
death are planted in them, and they can produce only the still-
born, the academic. They are not told to take their work into
the public square and see if it seems true to the chance passer,
but to test it by the work of the very men who refused and de-
cried any other test of their own work. The young writer who
attempts to report the phrase and carriage of every-day life, who

tries to tell just how he has heard men talk and seen them look, is made to feel guilty of something low and unworthy by the stupid people who would like to have him show how Shakespeare's men talked and looked, or Scott's, or Thackeray's, or Balzac's, or Hawthorne's, or Dickens's; he is instructed to idealize his personages, that is, to take the life-likeness out of them, and put the book-likeness into them. He is approached in the spirit of the wretched pedantry into which learning, much or little, always decays when it withdraws itself and stands apart from experience in an attitude of imagined superiority, and which would say with the same confidence to the scientist: "I see that you are looking at a grasshopper there which you have found in the grass, and I suppose you intend to describe it. Now don't waste your time and sin against culture in that way. I've got a grasshopper here, which has been evolved at considerable pains and expense out of the grasshopper in general; in fact, it's a type. It's made up of wire and card-board, very prettily painted in a conventional tint, and it's perfectly indestructible. It isn't very much like a real grasshopper, but it's a great deal nicer, and it's served to represent the notion of a grasshopper ever since man emerged from barbarism. You may say that it's artificial. Well, it is artificial; but then it's ideal too; and what you want to do is to cultivate the ideal. You'll find the books full of my kind of grasshopper, and scarcely a trace of yours in any of them. The thing that you are proposing to do is commonplace; but if you say that it isn't commonplace, for the very reason that it hasn't been done before, you'll have to admit that it's photographic."

As I said, I hope the time is coming when not only the artist, but the common, average man, who always "has the standard of the arts in his power," will have also the courage to apply it, and will reject the ideal grasshopper wherever he finds it, in science, in literature, in art, because it is not "simple, natural, and honest," because it is not like a real grasshopper. But I will own that I think the time is yet far off, and that the people who have been brought up on the ideal grasshopper, the heroic grasshopper, the impassioned grasshopper, the self-devoted, adventureful, good old romantic cardboard grasshopper, must die out before the simple, honest, and natural grasshopper can have a fair field. I am in no haste to compass the end of these good people, whom I find in the mean time very amusing. It is delightful to meet one of them, either in print or out of it—some sweet elderly lady or excellent gentleman whose youth was pastured on the literature of thirty or forty years ago—and to witness the confidence with which they preach their favorite authors as all the law and the prophets. They have commonly read little or nothing since, or, if they have, they have judged it by a standard taken from these authors, and never dreamed of judging it by nature; they are destitute of the documents in the case of the later writers; they suppose that Balzac was the beginning of realism, and that Zola is its wicked end; they are quite ignorant, but they are ready to talk you down, if you differ from them, with an assumption of knowledge sufficient for any occasion. The horror, the resentment, with which they receive any question of their literary saints is genuine; you descend at once very far in the moral and social scale, and anything short of offensive personality is too good for you; it is expressed to you that you are one to be avoided, and put down even a little lower than you have naturally fallen.

These worthy persons are not to blame; it is part of their intellectual mission to represent the petrifaction of taste, and to preserve an image of a smaller and cruder and emptier world than we now live in, a world which was feeling its way towards the simple, the natural, the honest, but was a good deal "amused and misled" by lights now no longer mistakable for heavenly luminaries. They belong to a time, just passing away, when certain authors were considered authorities in certain kinds, when they must be accepted entire and not questioned in any particular. Now we are beginning to see and to say that no author is an authority except in those moments when he held his ear close to Nature's lips and caught her very accent. These moments are not continuous with any authors in the past, and they are rare with all. Therefore I am not afraid to say now that the greatest classics are sometimes not at all great, and that we can profit by them only when we hold them, like our meanest contemporaries, to a strict accounting, and verify their work by the standard of the arts which we all have in our power, the simple, the natural, and the honest.

Those good people, those curious and interesting if somewhat musty back-numbers, must always have a hero, an idol of some sort, and it is droll to find Balzac, who suffered from their sort such bitter scorn and hate for his realism while he was alive, now become a fetich in his turn, to be shaken in the faces of those who will not blindly worship him. But it is no new thing in the history of literature: whatever is established is sacred with those who do not think. At the beginning of the century, when romance was making the same fight against effete classicism which realism is making to-day against effete romanticism, the Italian poet Monti declared that "the romantic was the cold grave of the Beautiful," just as the realistic is now supposed to be. The romantic of that day and the real of this are in certain degree the same. Romanticism then sought, as realism seeks now, to widen the bounds of sympathy, to level every barrier against aesthetic freedom, to escape from the paralysis of tradition. It exhausted itself in this impulse; and it remained for realism to assert that fidelity to experience and probability of motive are essential conditions of a great imaginative literature. It is not a new theory, but it has never before universally characterized literary endeavor. When realism becomes false to itself, when it heaps up facts merely, and maps life instead of picturing it, realism will perish too. Every true realist instinctively knows this, and it is perhaps the reason why he is careful of every fact, and feels himself bound to express or to indicate its meaning at the risk of over-moralizing. In life he finds nothing insignificant; all tells for destiny and character; nothing that God has made is contemptible. He cannot look upon human life and declare this thing or that thing unworthy of notice, any more than the scientist can declare a fact of the material world beneath the dignity of his inquiry. He feels in every nerve the equality of things and the unity of men; his soul is exalted, not by vain shows and shadows and ideals, but by realities, in which alone the truth lives. In criticism it is his business to break the images

of false gods and misshapen heroes, to take away the poor silly
toys that many grown people would still like to play with. He
cannot keep terms with Jack the Giant-killer or Puss in Boots,
under any name or in any place, even when they reappear as
the convict Vautrec, or the Marquis de Montrivaut, or the
Sworn Thirteen Noblemen. He must say to himself that Balzac, when he imagined these monsters, was not Balzac, he was
Dumas; he was not realistic, he was romantic.

III

Such a critic will not respect Balzac's good work the less
for contemning his bad work. He will easily account for the
bad work historically, and when he has recognized it, will trouble himself no further with it. In his view no living man is a type,
but a character; now noble, now ignoble; now grand, now little; complex, full of vicissitude. He will not expect Balzac to
be always Balzac, and will be perhaps even more attracted
to the study of him when he was trying to be Balzac than when
he had become so. In César Birotteau, for instance, he will be
interested to note how Balzac stood at the beginning of the
great things that have followed since in fiction. There is an
interesting likeness between his work in this and Nicolas Gogol's
in Dead Souls, which serves to illustrate the simultaneity of
the literary movement in men of such widely separated civili-
zations and conditions. Both represent their characters with
the touch of exaggeration which typifies; but in bringing his
story to a close, Balzac employs a beneficence unknown to
the Russian, and almost as universal and as apt as that which
smiles upon the fortunes of the good in the Vicar of Wakefield.
It is not enough to have rehabilitated Birotteau pecuniarily
and socially; he must make him die triumphantly, spectacu-
larly, of an opportune hemorrhage, in the midst of the festivities
which celebrate his restoration to his old home. Before this
happens, human nature has been laid under contribution right
and left for acts of generosity towards the righteous bankrupt;
even the king sends him six thousand francs. It is very pretty;

it is touching, and brings the lump into the reader's throat; but it is too much, and one perceives that Balzac lived too soon to profit by Balzac. The later men, especially the Russians, have known how to forbear the excesses of analysis, to withhold the weakly recurring descriptive and caressing epithets, to let the characters suffice for themselves. All this does not mean that César Birotteau is not a beautiful and pathetic story, full of shrewdly considered knowledge of men, and of a good art struggling to free itself from self-consciousness. But it does mean that Balzac, when he wrote it, was under the burden of the very traditions which he has helped fiction to throw off. He felt obliged to construct a mechanical plot, to surcharge his characters, to moralize openly and baldly; he permitted himself to "sympathize" with certain of his people, and to point out others for the abhorrence of his readers. This is not so bad in him as it would be in a novelist of our day. It is simply primitive and inevitable, and he is not to be judged by it.

IV

In the beginning of any art even the most gifted worker must be crude in his methods, and we ought to keep this fact always in mind when we turn, say from the purblind worshippers of Scott to Scott himself, and recognize that he often wrote a style cumbrous and diffuse; that he was tediously analytical where the modern novelist is dramatic, and evolved his characters by means of long-winded explanation and commentary; that, except in the case of his lower-class personages, he made them talk as seldom man and never woman talked; that he was tiresomely descriptive; that on the simplest occasions he went about half a mile to express a thought that could be uttered in ten paces across lots; and that he trusted his readers' intuitions so little that he was apt to rub in his appeals to them. He was probably right: the generation which he wrote for was duller than this; slower-witted, aesthetically untrained, and in maturity not so apprehensive of an artistic intention as the

children of to-day. All this is not saying Scott was not a great
man; he was a great man, and a very great novelist as compared
with the novelists who went before him. He can still amuse
young people, but they ought to be instructed how false and
how mistaken he often is, with his mediaeval ideals, his blind
Jacobitism, his intense devotion to aristocracy and royalty;
his acquiescence in the division of men into noble and ignoble,
patrician and plebeian, sovereign and subject, as if it were the
law of God; for all which, indeed, he is not to blame as he would
be if he were one of our contemporaries. Something of this
is true of another master, greater than Scott in being less romantic, and inferior in being more German, namely, the great
Goethe himself. He taught us, in novels otherwise now anti-
quated, and always full of German clumsiness, that it was false
to good art—which is never anything but the reflection of life—
to pursue and round the career of the persons introduced, whom
he often allowed to appear and disappear in our knowledge
as people in the actual world do. This is a lesson which the
writers able to profit by it can never be too grateful for; and
it is equally a benefaction to readers; but there is very little
else in the conduct of the Goethean novels which is in advance
of their time; this remains almost their sole contribution to
the science of fiction. They are very primitive in certain characteristics, and unite with their calm, deep insight, an amusing helplessness in dramatization. "Wilhelm retired to his room,
and indulged in the following reflections," is a mode of analysis which would not be practised nowadays; and all that fan-
cifulness of nomenclature in Wilhelm Meister is very drolly
sentimental and feeble. The adventures with robbers seem
as if dreamed out of books of chivalry, and the tendency to
allegorization affects one like an endeavor on the author's
part to escape from the unrealities which he must have felt
harassingly, German as he was. Mixed up with the shadows
and illusions are honest, wholesome, every-day people, who
have the air of wandering homelessly about among them, without definite direction; and the mists are full of a luminosity
which, in spite of them, we know for common-sense and po-

etry. What is useful in any review of Goethe's methods is the recognition of the fact, which it must bring, that the greatest master cannot produce a masterpiece in a new kind. The novel was too recently invented in Goethe's day not to be, even in his hands, full of the faults of apprentice work.

Which brings us again, after this long way about, to the divine Jane and her novels, and that troublesome question about them. She was great and they were beautiful, because she and they were honest, and dealt with nature nearly a hundred years ago as realism deals with it to-day. Realism is nothing more and nothing less than the truthful treatment of material, and Jane Austen was the first and the last of the English novelists to treat material with entire truthfulness. Because she did this, she remains the most artistic of the English novelists, and alone worthy to be matched with the great Scandinavian and Slavic and Latin artists. It is not a question of intellect, or not wholly that. The English have mind enough; but they have not taste enough; or, rather, their taste has been perverted by their false criticism, which is based upon personal preference, and not upon principle; which instructs a man to think that what he likes is good, instead of teaching him first to distinguish what is good before he likes it. The art of fiction, as Jane Austen knew it, declined from her through Scott, and Bulwer, and Dickens, and Charlotte Brontë, and Thackeray, and even George Eliot, because the mania of romanticism had seized upon all Europe, and these great writers could not escape the taint of their time; but it has shown few signs of recovery in England, because English criticism, in the presence of the Continental masterpieces, has continued provincial and special and personal, and has expressed a love and a hate which had to do with the quality of the artist rather than the character of his work. It was inevitable that in their time the English romanticists should treat, as Señor Valdés says, "the barbarous customs of the Middle Ages, softening and disfiguring them, as Walter Scott and his kind did;" that they should "devote themselves to falsifying nature, refining and subtilizing sentiment, and modifying psychology after their own fancy," like Bulwer and Dickens, as well as like Rousseau and Madame de Staël, not to mention Balzac, the worst of all that sort at his worst. This was the natural course of the disease; but it really seems as if it were their criticism that was to blame for the rest: not, indeed, for the performance of this writer or that, for criticism can never affect the actual doing of a thing; but for the esteem in which this writer or that is held through the perpetuation of false ideals. The only observer of English middle-class life since Jane Austen worthy to be named with her was not George Eliot, who was first ethical and then artistic, who transcended her in everything but the form and method most essential to art, and there fell hopelessly below her. It was Anthony Trollope who was most like her in simple honesty and instinctive truth, as unphilosophized as the light of common day; but he was so warped from a wholesome ideal as to wish at times to be like the caricaturist Thackeray, and to stand about in his scene, talking it over with his hands in his pockets, interrupting the action, and spoiling the illusion in which alone the truth of art resides. Mainly, his instinct was too much for his ideal, and with a low view of life in its civic relations and a thoroughly bourgeois soul, he yet produced works whose beauty is surpassed only by the effect of a more poetic writer in the novels of Thomas Hardy. Yet if a vote of English criticism even at this late day, when all continental Europe has the light of aesthetic truth, could be taken, the majority against these artists would be overwhelmingly in favor of a writer who had so little artistic sensibility, that he never hesitated on any occasion, great or small, to make a foray among his characters, and catch them up to show them to the reader and tell him how beautiful or ugly they were; and cry out over their amazing properties.

Doubtless the ideal of those poor islanders will be finally changed. If the truth could become a fad it would be accepted by all their "smart people," but truth is something rather too large for that; and we must await the gradual advance of civilization among them. Then they will see that their criticism has misled them; and that it is to this false guide they owe, not precisely the decline of fiction among them, but its continued debasement as an art.

XXI

It is no doubt such work as Mr. James's that an English essayist (Mr. E. Hughes) has chiefly in mind, in a study of the differences of the English and American novel. He defines the English novel as working from within outwardly, and the American novel as working from without inwardly. The definition is very surprisingly accurate; and the critic's discovery of this fundamental difference is carried into particulars with a distinctness which is as unfailing as the courtesy he has in recognizing the present superiority of American work. He seems to think, however, that the English principle is the better, though why he should think so he does not make so clear. It appears a belated and rather voluntary effect of patriotism, disappointing in a philosopher of his degree; but it does not keep him from very explicit justice to the best characteristics of our fiction. "The American novelist is distinguished for the intellectual grip which he has of his characters. . . . He penetrates below the crust, and he recognizes no necessity of the crust to anticipate what is beneath. . . . He utterly discards heroics; he often even discards anything like a plot. . . . His story proper is often no more than a natural predicament. . . . It is no stage view we have of his characters, but one behind the scenes. . . . We are brought into contact with no strained virtues, illumined by strained lights upon strained heights of situation. . . . Whenever he appeals to the emotions it would seem to be with an appeal to the intellect too. . . . because he weaves his story of the finer, less self-evident though common threads of human nature, seldom calling into play the grosser and more powerful strain. . . . Everywhere in his pages we come across acquaintances undisguised. . . . The characters in an American novel are never unapproachable to the reader. . . . The naturalness, with the every-day atmosphere

which surrounds it, is one great charm of the American novel.
. . . It is throughout examinative, discursory, even more—quiz-
zical. Its characters are undergoing, at the hands of the author,
calm, interested observation. . . . He is never caught identi-
fying himself with them; he must preserve impartiality at all
costs . . . but . . . the touch of nature is always felt, the feeling of kinship always follows. . . . The strength of the American novel is its optimistic faith. . . . If out of this persistent
hopefulness it can evolve for men a new order of trustfulness,
a tenet that between man and man there should be less suspicion, more confidence, since human nature sanctions it,
its mission will have been more than an aesthetic, it will have
been a moral one."

Not all of this will be found true of Mr. James, but all that
relates to artistic methods and characteristics will, and the
rest is true of American novels generally. For the most part
in their range and tendency they are admirable. I will not say
they are all good, or that any of them is wholly good; but I find
in nearly every one of them a disposition to regard our life
without the literary glasses so long thought desirable, and to
see character, not as it is in other fiction, but as it abounds
outside of all fiction. This disposition sometimes goes with
poor enough performance, but in some of our novels it goes
with performance that is excellent; and at any rate it is for the
present more valuable than evenness of performance. It is
what relates American fiction to the only living movement
in imaginative literature, and distinguishes by a superior freshness and authenticity any group of American novels from a
similarly accidental group of English novels, giving them the
same good right to be as the like number of recent Russian
novels, French novels, Spanish novels, Italian novels, Nor-
wegian novels.

It is the difference of the American novelist's ideals from
those of the English novelist that give him his advantage, and
seems to promise him the future. The love of the passionate
and the heroic, as the Englishman has it, is such a crude and
unwholesome thing, so deaf and blind to all the most delicate
and important facts of art and life, so insensible to the subtle

values in either that its presence or absence makes the whole difference, and enables one who is not obsessed by it to thank Heaven that he is not as that other man is.

There can be little question that many refinements of thought and spirit which every American is sensible of in the fiction of this continent, are necessarily lost upon our good kin beyond seas, whose thumb-fingered apprehension requires something gross and palpable for its assurance of reality. This is not their fault, and I am not sure that it is wholly their misfortune: they are made so as not to miss what they do not find, and they are simply content without those subtleties of life and character which it gives us so keen a pleasure to have noted in literature. If they perceive them at all it is as something vague and diaphanous, something that filmily wavers before their sense and teases them, much as the beings of an invisible world might mock one of our material frame by intimations of their presence. It is with reason, therefore, on the part of an Englishman, that Mr. Henley complains of our fiction as a shadow-land, though we find more and more in it the faithful report of our life, its motives and emotions, and all the comparatively etherealized passions and ideals that influence it.

In fact, the American who chooses to enjoy his birthright to the full, lives in a world wholly different from the Englishman's, and speaks (too often through his nose) another language: he breathes a rarefied and nimble air full of shining possibilities and radiant promises which the fog-and-soot-clogged lungs of those less-favored islanders struggle in vain to fill themselves with. But he ought to be modest in his advantage, and patient with the coughing and sputtering of his cousin who complains of finding himself in an exhausted receiver on plunging into one of our novels. To be quite just to the poor fellow, I have had some such experience as that myself in the atmosphere of some of our more attenuated romances.

Yet every now and then I read a book with perfect comfort and much exhilaration, whose scenes the average Englishman would gasp in. Nothing happens; that is, nobody murders or debauches anybody else; there is no arson or pillage of any sort; there is not a ghost, or a ravening beast, or a hairbreadth escape, or a shipwreck, or a monster of self-sacrifice, or a lady five thousand years old in the whole course of the story; "no promenade, no band of music, nossing!" as Mr. Du Maurier's Frenchman said of the meet for a fox-hunt. Yet it is all alive with the keenest interest for those who enjoy the study of individual traits and general conditions as they make themselves known to American experience.

These conditions have been so favorable hitherto (though they are becoming always less so) that they easily account for the optimistic faith of our novel which Mr. Hughes notices. It used to be one of the disadvantages of the practice of romance in America, which Hawthorne more or less whimsically lamented, that there were so few shadows and inequalities in our broad level of prosperity; and it is one of the reflections suggested by Dostoïevsky's novel, The Crime and the Punishment, that whoever struck a note so profoundly tragic in American fiction would do a false and mistaken thing—as false and as mistaken in its way as dealing in American fiction with certain nudities which the Latin peoples seem to find edifying. Whatever their deserts, very few American novelists have been led out to be shot, or finally exiled to the rigors of a winter at Duluth; and in a land where journeymen carpenters and plumbers strike for four dollars a day the sum of hunger and cold is comparatively small, and the wrong from class to class has been almost inappreciable, though all this is changing for the worse. Our novelists, therefore, concern themselves with the more smiling aspects of life, which are the more American, and seek the universal in the individual rather than the social interests. It is worth while, even at the risk of being called commonplace, to be true to our well-to-do actualities; the very passions themselves seem to be softened and modified by conditions which formerly at least could not be said to wrong any one, to cramp endeavor, or to cross lawful desire. Sin and suffering and shame there must always be in the world, I suppose, but I believe that in this new world of ours it is still mainly from one to another one, and oftener still from one to one's self. We have death too in America, and a great deal of disagreeable and painful disease, which the multiplicity of our patent medicines does not seem to cure; but this is tragedy that comes in the very nature of things, and is not peculiarly American, as the large, cheerful average of health and success and happy life is. It will not do to boast, but it is well to be true to the facts, and to see that, apart from these purely mortal troubles, the race here has enjoyed conditions in which most of the ills that have darkened its annals might be averted by honest work and unselfish behavior. . . .

XXIV

One of the great newspapers the other day invited the prominent American authors to speak their minds upon a point in the theory and practice of fiction which had already vexed some of them. It was the question of how much or how little the American novel ought to deal with certain facts of life which are not usually talked of before young people, and especially young ladies. Of course the question was not decided, and I forget just how far the balance inclined in favor of a larger freedom in the matter. But it certainly inclined that way; one or two writers of the sex which is somehow supposed to have purity in its keeping (as if purity were a thing that did not practically concern the other sex, preoccupied with serious affairs) gave it a rather vigorous tilt to that side. In view of this fact it would not be the part of prudence to make an effort to dress the balance; and indeed I do not know that I was going to make any such effort. But there are some things to say, around and about the subject, which I should like to have some one else say, and which I may myself possibly be safe in suggesting.

One of the first of these is the fact, generally lost sight of by those who censure the Anglo-Saxon novel for its prudishness that it is really not such a prude after all; and that if it is sometimes apparently anxious to avoid those experiences of life not spoken of before young people, this may be an appearance only. Sometimes a novel which has this shuffling air, this effect of truckling to propriety, might defend itself, if it could speak for itself, by saying that such experiences happened not to come within its scheme and that, so far from maiming or mutilating itself in ignoring them, it was all the more faithfully representative of the tone of modern life in dealing with love that was chaste, and with passion so honest that it could be openly spoken of before the tenderest society bud at dinner. It might say that the guilty intrigue, the betrayal, the extreme flirtation even, was the exceptional thing in life, and unless the scheme of the story necessarily involved it, that it would be bad art to lug it in, and as bad taste as to introduce such topics in a mixed company. It could say very justly that the novel in our civilization now always addresses a mixed company, and that the vast majority of the company are ladies, and that very many, if not most, of these ladies are young girls. If the novel were written for men and for married women alone, as in continental Europe, it might be altogether different. But the simple fact is that it is not written for them alone among us, and it is a question of writing, under cover of our universal acceptance, things for young girls to read which you would be put out-of-doors for saying to them, or of frankly giving notice of your intention, and so cutting yourself off from the pleasure—and it is a very high and sweet one—of appealing to these vivid, responsive intelligences, which are none the less brilliant and admirable because they are innocent.

One day a novelist who liked, after the manner of other men, to repine at his hard fate, complained to his friend, a critic, that he was tired of the restriction he had put upon himself in this regard; for it is a mistake, as can be readily shown, to suppose that others impose it. "See how free those French fellows are!" he rebelled. "Shall we always be shut up to our tradition of decency?"

"Do you think it's much worse than being shut up to their tradition of indecency?" said his friend.

Then that novelist began to reflect, and he remembered how sick the invariable motive of the French novel made him. He perceived finally that, convention for convention, ours was not only more tolerable, but on the whole was truer to life, not only to its complexion, but also to its texture. No one will pretend that there is not vicious love beneath the surface of our society; if he did, the fetid explosions of the divorce trials would refute him; but if he pretended that it was in any just sense characteristic of our society, he could be still more easily refuted. Yet it exists, and it is unquestionably the material of tragedy, the stuff from which intense effects are wrought. The question, after owning this fact, is whether these intense effects are not rather cheap effects. I incline to think they are, and I will try to say why I think so, if I may do so without offence. The material itself, the mere mention of it, has an instant fascination; it arrests, it detains, till the last word is said, and while there is anything to be hinted. This is what makes a love intrigue of some sort all but essential to the popularity of any fiction. Without such an intrigue the intellectual equipment of the author must be of the highest, and then he will succeed only with the highest class of readers. But any author who will deal with a guilty love intrigue holds all readers in his hand, the highest with the lowest, as long as he hints the slightest hope of the smallest potential naughtiness. He need not at all be a great author; he may be a very shabby wretch, if he has but the courage or the trick of that sort of thing. The critics will call him "virile" and "passionate;" decent people will be ashamed to have been limed by him; but the low average will only ask another chance of flocking into his net. If he happens to be an able writer, his really fine and costly work will be unheeded, and the lure to the appetite will be chiefly remembered. There may be other qualities which make reputations for other men, but in his case they will count for nothing. He pays this penalty for his success in that kind; and every one pays some such penalty who deals with some such material. It attaches in like manner to the triumphs of the writers who now almost form a school among us, and who may be said to have established themselves in an easy popularity simply by the study of erotic shivers and fervors. They may find their account in the popularity, or they may not; there is no question of the popularity.

But I do not mean to imply that their case covers the whole ground. So far as it goes, though, it ought to stop the mouths of those who complain that fiction is enslaved to propriety among us. It appears that of a certain kind of impropriety it is free to give us all it will, and more. But this is not what serious men and women writing fiction mean when they rebel against the limitations of their art in our civilization. They have no desire to deal with nakedness, as painters and sculptors freely do in the worship of beauty; or with certain facts of life, as the stage does, in the service of sensation. But they ask why, when the conventions of the plastic and histrionic arts liberate their followers to the portrayal of almost any phase of the physical or of the emotional nature, an American novelist may not write a story on the lines of Anna Karenina or Madame Bovary. Sappho they put aside, and from Zola's work they avert their eyes. They do not condemn him or Daudet, necessarily, or accuse their motives; they leave them out of the question; they do not want to do that kind of thing. But they do sometimes wish to do another kind, to touch one of the most serious and sorrowful problems of life in the spirit of Tolstoï and Flaubert, and they ask why they may not. At one time, they remind us, the Anglo-Saxon novelist did deal with such problems—De Foe in his spirit, Richardson in his, Goldsmith in his. At what moment did our fiction lose this privilege? In what fatal hour did the Young Girl arise and seal the lips of Fiction, with a touch of her finger, to some of the most vital interests of life?

Whether I wished to oppose them in their aspiration for greater freedom, or whether I wished to encourage them, I should begin to answer them by saying that the Young Girl had never done anything of the kind. The manners of the novel have been improving with those of its readers; that is all. Gentlemen no longer swear or fall drunk under the table, or abduct young ladies and shut them up in lonely country-houses, or so habitually set about the ruin of their neighbors' wives, as they once did. Generally, people now call a spade an agricultural implement; they have not grown decent without having also grown a little squeamish, but they have grown comparatively decent; there is no doubt about that. They require of a novelist whom they respect unquestionable proof of his seriousness, if he proposes to deal with certain phases of life; they require a sort of scientific decorum. He can no longer expect to be received on the ground of entertainment only; he assumes a higher function, something like that of a physician or a priest, and they expect him to be bound by laws as sacred as those of such professions; they hold him solemnly pledged not to betray them or abuse their confidence. If he will accept the conditions, they give him their confidence, and he may then treat to his greater honor, and not at all to his disadvantage, of such experiences, such relations of men and women as George Eliot treats in Adam Bede, in Daniel Deronda, in Romola, in almost all her books; such as Hawthorne treats in the Scarlet Letter; such as Dickens treats in David Copperfield; such as Thackeray treats in Pendennis, and glances at in every one of his fictions; such as most of the masters of English fiction have at some time treated more or less openly. It is quite false or quite mistaken to suppose that our novels have left untouched these most important realities of life. They have only not made them their stock in trade; they have kept a true perspective in regard to them; they have relegated them in their pictures of life to the space and place they occupy in life itself, as we know it in England and America. They have kept a correct proportion, knowing perfectly well that unless the novel is to be a map, with everything scrupulously laid down in it, a faithful record of life in far the greater extent could be made to the exclusion of guilty love and all its circumstances and consequences.

I justify them in this view not only because I hate what is cheap and meretricious, and hold in peculiar loathing the cant of the critics who require "passion" as something in itself admirable and desirable in a novel, but because I prize fidelity in the historian of feeling and character. Most of these critics who demand "passion" would seem to have no conception of any passion but one. Yet there are several other passions: the passion of grief, the passion of avarice, the passion of pity, the passion of ambition, the passion of hate, the passion of envy, the passion of devotion, the passion of friendship; and all these have a greater part in the drama of life than the passion of love, and infinitely greater than the passion of guilty love. Wittingly or unwittingly, English fiction and American fiction have recognized this truth, not fully, not in the measure it merits, but in greater degree than most other fiction.

Henry James
HAWTHORNE

. . . Whatever may have been Hawthorne's private lot, he has the importance of being the most beautiful and most eminent representative of a literature. The importance of the literature may be questioned, but at any rate, in the field of letters, Hawthorne is the most valuable example of the American genius. That genius has not, as a whole, been literary; but Hawthorne was on his limited scale a master of expression. He is the writer to whom his countrymen most confidently point when they wish to make a claim to have enriched the mother-tongue, and, judging from present appearances, he will long occupy this honourable position. If there is something very fortunate for him in the way that he borrows an added relief from the absence of competitors in his own line, and from the general flatness of the literary field that surrounds him, there is also, to a spectator, something almost touching in his situation. He was so modest and delicate a genius that we may fancy him appealing from the lonely honour of a representative attitude—perceiving a painful incongruity between his imponderable literary baggage and the large conditions of American life. Hawthorne, on the one side, is so subtle and slender and unpretending, and the American world, on the other, is so vast

and various and substantial, that it might seem to the author
of *The Scarlet Letter* and the *Mosses from an Old Manse,*
that we render him a poor service in contrasting his proportions with those of a great civilization. But our author must
accept the awkward as well as the graceful side of his fame;
for he has the advantage of pointing a valuable moral. This
moral is that the flower of art blooms only where the soil
is deep, that it takes a great deal of history to produce a little
literature, that it needs a complex social machinery to set a
writer in motion. American civilization has hitherto had other
things to do than to produce flowers, and before giving birth
to writers it has wisely occupied itself with providing something for them to write about. Three or four beautiful plants
of trans-Atlantic growth are the sum of what the world usually
recognises, and in this modest nosegay the genius of Hawthorne
is admitted to have the rarest and sweetest fragrance.

His very simplicity has been in his favour; it has helped
him to appear complete and homogeneous. To talk of his
being national would be to force the note and make a mistake of proportion; but he is, in spite of the absence of the
realistic quality, intensely and vividly local. Out of the soil
of New England he sprang—in a crevice of that immitiga-
ble granite he sprouted and bloomed. Half of the interest
that he possesses for an American reader with any turn for
analysis must reside in his latent New England savour; and
I think it no more than just to say that whatever entertainment he may yield to those who know him at a distance,
it is an almost indispensable condition of properly appre-
ciating him to have received a personal impression of the
manners, the morals, indeed of the very climate, of the great
region of which the remarkable city of Boston is the me-
tropolis. The cold, bright air of New England seems to blow
through his pages, and these, in the opinion of many people, are the medium in which it is most agreeable to make
the acquaintance of that tonic atmosphere. As to whether
it is worth while to seek to know something of New England
in order to extract a more intimate quality from *The House
of Seven Gables* and *The Blithedale Romance*, I need not

pronounce; but it is certain that a considerable observation of the society to which these productions were more directly addressed is a capital preparation for enjoying them. I have alluded to the absence in Hawthorne of that quality of realism which is now so much in fashion, an absence in regard to which there will of course be more to say; and yet I think I am not fanciful in saying that he testifies to the sentiments of the society in which he flourished almost as pertinently (proportions observed) as Balzac and some of his descendants—MM. Flaubert and Zola—testify to the manners and morals of the French people. He was not a man with a literary theory; he was guiltless of a system, and I am not sure that he had ever heard of Realism, this remarkable compound having (although it was invented some time earlier) come into general use only since his death. He had certainly not proposed to himself to give an account of the social idiosyncrasies of his fellow-citizens, for his touch on such points is always light and vague, he has none of the apparatus of an historian, and his shadowy style of portraiture never suggests a rigid standard of accuracy. Nevertheless, he virtually offers the most vivid reflection of New England life that has found its way into literature. His value in this respect is not diminished by the fact that he has not attempted to portray the usual Yankee of comedy, and that he has been almost culpably indifferent to his opportunities for commemorating the variations of colloquial English that may be observed in the New World. His characters do not express themselves in the dialect of the *Biglow Papers*—their language, indeed, is apt to be too elegant, too delicate. They are not portraits of actual types, and in their phraseology there is nothing imitative. But none the less, Hawthorne's work savours thoroughly of the local soil—it is redolent of the social system in which he had his being. . . .

If Hawthorne was in a sombre mood, and if his future was painfully vague, *The Scarlet Letter* contains little enough of gaiety or of hopefulness. It is densely dark, with a single spot of vivid colour in it; and it will probably long remain the most consistently gloomy of English novels of the first order. But I just now called it the author's masterpiece, and I imagine it will continue to be, for other generations than ours, his most substantial title to fame. The subject had probably lain a long time in his mind, as his subjects were apt to do; so that he appears completely to possess it, to know it and feel it. It is simpler and more complete than his other novels; it achieves more perfectly what it attempts, and it has about it that charm, very hard to express, which we find in an artist's work the first time he has touched his highest mark—a sort of straightness and naturalness of execution, an unconsciousness of his public, and freshness of interest in his theme. It was a great success, and he immediately found himself famous. The writer of these lines, who was a child at the time, remembers dimly the sensation the book produced, and the little shudder with which people alluded to it, as if a peculiar horror were mixed with its attractions. He was too young to read it himself; but its title, upon which he fixed his eyes as the book lay upon the table, had a mysterious charm. He had a vague belief, indeed, that the "letter" in question was one of the documents that come by the post, and it was a source of perpetual wonderment to him that it should be of such an unaccustomed hue. Of course it was difficult to explain to a child the significance of poor Hester Prynne's blood-coloured A. But the mystery was at last partly dispelled by his being taken to see a collection of pictures (the annual exhibition of the National Academy), where he encountered a representation of a pale, handsome woman, in a quaint black dress and a white coif, holding between her knees an elfish-looking little girl, fantastically dressed, and crowned with flowers. Embroidered on the woman's breast was a great crimson A, over which the child's fingers, as she glanced strangely out of the picture, were maliciously playing. I was told that this was Hester Prynne and little Pearl, and that when I grew older I might read their interesting history. But the picture remained vividly imprinted on my mind; I had been vaguely frightened and made uneasy by it; and when, years afterwards, I first read the novel, I seemed to myself to have read it before, and to be familiar

with its two strange heroines. I mention this incident simply
as an indication of the degree to which the success of *The
Scarlet Letter* had made the book what is called an actuality.
Hawthorne himself was very modest about it; he wrote to his
publisher, when there was a question of his undertaking another
novel, that what had given the history of Hester Prynne its
"vogue" was simply the introductory chapter. In fact, the
publication of *The Scarlet Letter* was in the United States a
literary event of the first importance. The book was the finest
piece of imaginative writing yet put forth in the country.
There was a consciousness of this in the welcome that was
given it—a satisfaction in the idea of America having produced a novel that belonged to literature, and to the fore-
front of it. Something might at last be sent to Europe as exquisite in quality as anything that had been received, and
the best of it was that the thing was absolutely American;
it belonged to the soil, to the air; it came out of the very
heart of New England.

It is beautiful, admirable, extraordinary; it has in the
highest degree that merit which I have spoken of as the mark
of Hawthorne's best things—an indefinable purity and light-
ness of conception, a quality which in a work of art affects
one in the same way as the absence of grossness does in a
human being. His fancy, as I just now said, had evidently
brooded over the subject for a long time; the situation to
be represented had disclosed itself to him in all its phases.
When I say in all its phases, the sentence demands modi-
fication; for it is to be remembered that if Hawthorne laid
his hand upon the well-worn theme, upon the familiar combination of the wife, the lover, and the husband, it was, after
all, but to one period of the history of these three persons
that he attached himself. The situation is the situation after
the woman's fault has been committed, and the current of
expiation and repentance has set in. In spite of the relation
between Hester Prynne and Arthur Dimmesdale, no story
of love was surely ever less of a "love-story." To Hawthorne's
imagination the fact that these two persons had loved each
other too well was of an interest comparatively vulgar; what

appealed to him was the idea of their moral situation in the long years that were to follow. The story, indeed, is in a secondary degree that of Hester Prynne; she becomes, really, after the first scene, an accessory figure; it is not upon her the *dénoûment* depends. It is upon her guilty lover that the author projects most frequently the cold, thin rays of his fitfully-moving lantern, which makes here and there a little luminous circle, on the edge of which hovers the livid and sinister figure of the injured and retributive husband. The story goes on, for the most part, between the lover and the husband—the tormented young Puritan minister, who carries the secret of his own lapse from pastoral purity locked up beneath an exterior that commends itself to the reverence of his flock, while he sees the softer partner of his guilt standing in the full glare of exposure and humbling herself to the misery of atonement—between this more wretched and pitiable culprit, to whom dishonour would come as a comfort and the pillory as a relief, and the older, keener, wiser man, who, to obtain satisfaction for the wrong he has suffered, devises the infernally ingenious plan of conjoining himself with his wronger, living with him, living upon him; and while he pretends to minister to his hidden ailment and to sympathise with his pain, revels in his unsuspected knowledge of these things, and stimulates them by malignant arts. The attitude of Roger Chillingworth, and the means he takes to compensate himself—these are the highly original elements in the situation that Hawthorne so ingeniously treats. None of his works are so impregnated with that after-sense of the old Puritan consciousness of life to which allusion has so often been made. If, as M. Montégut says, the qualities of his ancestors *filtered* down through generations into his composition, *The Scarlet Letter* was, as it were, the vessel that gathered up the last of the precious drops. And I say this not because the story happens to be of so-called historical cast, to be told of the early days of Massachusetts, and of people in steeple-crowned hats and sad-coloured garments. The historical colouring is rather weak than otherwise; there is little elaboration of detail, of the modern realism of research; and the author has made no great point of causing his figures to speak the English of their period. Nevertheless, the book is full of the moral presence of the race that invented Hester's penance—diluted and complicated with other things, but still perfectly recognisable. Puritanism, in a word, is there, not only objectively, as Hawthorne tried to place it there, but subjectively as well. Not, I mean, in his judgment of his characters in any harshness of prejudice, or in the obtrusion of a moral lesson; but in the very quality of his own vision, in the tone of the picture, in a certain coldness and exclusiveness of treatment.

The faults of the book are, to my sense, a want of reality and an abuse of the fanciful element—of a certain superficial symbolism. The people strike me not as characters, but as representatives, very picturesquely arranged, of a single state of mind; and the interest of the story lies, not in them, but in the situation, which is insistently kept before us, with little progression, though with a great deal, as I have said, of a certain stable variation; and to which they, out of their reality, contribute little that helps it to live and move. I was made to feel this want of reality, this over-ingenuity, of *The Scarlet Letter*, by chancing not long since upon a novel which was read fifty years ago much more than to-day, but which is still worth reading—the story of *Adam Blair*, by John Gibson Lockhart. This interesting and powerful little tale has a great deal of analogy with Hawthorne's novel—quite enough, at least, to suggest a comparison between them; and the comparison is a very interesting one to make, for it speedily leads us to larger considerations than simple resemblances and divergences of plot.

Adam Blair, like Arthur Dimmesdale, is a Calvinistic minister who becomes the lover of a married woman, is overwhelmed with remorse at his misdeed, and makes a public confession of it; then expiates it by resigning his pastoral office and becoming a humble tiller of the soil, as his father had been. The two stories are of about the same length, and each is the masterpiece (putting aside, of course, as far as Lockhart is concerned, the *Life of Scott*) of the author. They deal alike with the manners of a rigidly theological society, and even in certain details they correspond. In each of them, between the guilty pair, there is a charming little girl; though I hasten to say that Sarah Blair (who is not the daughter of the heroine, but the legitimate offspring of the hero, a widower) is far from being as brilliant and graceful an apparition as the admirable little Pearl of *The Scarlet Letter*. The main difference between the two tales is the fact that in the American story the husband plays an all-important part, and in the Scottish plays almost none at all. *Adam Blair* is the history of the passion, and *The Scarlet Letter* the history of its sequel; but nevertheless, if one has read the two books at a short interval, it is impossible to avoid confronting them. I confess that a large portion of the interest of *Adam Blair*, to my mind, when once I had perceived that it would repeat in a great measure the situation of *The Scarlet Letter*, lay in noting its difference of tone. It threw into relief the passionless quality of Hawthorne's novel, its element of cold and ingenious fantasy, its elaborate imaginative delicacy. These things do not precisely constitute a weakness in *The Scarlet Letter*; indeed, in a certain way they constitute a great strength; but the absence of a certain something warm and straightforward, a trifle more grossly human and vulgarly natural, which one finds in *Adam Blair*, will always make Hawthorne's tale less touching to a large number of even very intelligent readers, than a love-story told with the robust, synthetic pathos which served Lockhart so well. His novel is not of the first rank (I should call it an excellent second-rate one), but it borrows a charm from the fact that his vigorous, but not strongly imaginative, mind was impregnated with the reality of his subject. He did not always succeed in rendering this reality; the expression is sometimes awkward and poor. But the reader feels that his vision was clear, and his feeling about the matter very strong and rich. Hawthorne's imagination, on the other hand, plays with his theme so incessantly, leads it such a dance through the moon-lighted air of his intellect, that the thing cools off, as it were, hardens and stiffens, and,

producing effects much more exquisite, leaves the reader
with a sense of having handled a splendid piece of silver-
smith's work. Lockhart, by means much more vulgar, produces at moments a greater illusion, and satisfies our inevitable desire for something, in the people in whom it is sought
to interest us, that shall be of the same pitch and the same
continuity with ourselves. Above all, it is interesting to see
how the same subject appears to two men of a thoroughly different cast of mind and of a different race. Lockhart
was struck with the warmth of the subject that offered itself
to him, and Hawthorne with its coldness; the one with its
glow, its sentimental interest—the other with its shadow,
its moral interest. Lockhart's story is as decent, as severe-
ly draped, as *The Scarlet Letter;* but the author has a more
vivid sense than appears to have imposed itself upon Hawthorne, of some of the incidents of the situation he describes;
his tempted man and tempting woman are more actual and
personal; his heroine in especial, though not in the least a delicate or a subtle conception, has a sort of credible, visible,
palpable property, a vulgar roundness and relief, which are
lacking to the dim and chastened image of Hester Prynne.
But I am going too far; I am comparing simplicity with sub-
tlety, the usual with the refined. Each man wrote as his turn
of mind impelled him, but each expressed something more
than himself. Lockhart was a dense, substantial Briton, with
a taste for the concrete, and Hawthorne was a thin New
Englander, with a miasmatic conscience.

In *The Scarlet Letter* there is a great deal of symbolism; there is, I think, too much. It is overdone at times, and
becomes mechanical; it ceases to be impressive, and grazes
triviality. The idea of the mystic *A* which the young minister finds imprinted upon his breast and eating into his flesh,
in sympathy with the embroidered badge that Hester is condemned to wear, appears to me to be a case in point. This
suggestion should, I think, have been just made and dropped;
to insist upon it and return to it, is to exaggerate the weak
side of the subject. Hawthorne returns to it constantly, plays
with it, and seems charmed by it; until at last the reader

feels tempted to declare that his enjoyment of it is puerile. In the admirable scene, so superbly conceived and beautifully executed, in which Mr. Dimmesdale, in the stillness of the night, in the middle of the sleeping town, feels impelled to go and stand upon the scaffold where his mistress had formerly enacted her dreadful penance, and then, seeing Hester pass along the street, from watching at a sickbed, with little Pearl at her side, calls them both to come and stand there beside him—in this masterly episode the effect is almost spoiled by the introduction of one of these superficial conceits. What leads up to it is very fine—so fine that I cannot do better than quote it as a specimen of one of the striking pages of the book.

> But before Mr. Dimmesdale had done speaking, a light gleamed far and wide over all the muffled sky. It was doubtless caused by one of those meteors which the nightwatcher may so often observe burning out to waste in the vacant regions of the atmosphere. So powerful was its radiance that it thoroughly illuminated the dense medium of cloud betwixt the sky and earth. The great vault brightened, like the dome of an immense lamp. It showed the familiar scene of the street with the distinctness of mid-day, but also with the awfulness that is always imparted to familiar objects by an unaccustomed light. The wooden houses, with their jutting stories and quaint gable-peaks; the doorsteps and thresholds, with the early grass springing up about them; the garden-plots, black with freshly-turned earth; the wheel-track, little worn, and, even in the market-place, margined with green on either side;—all were visible, but with a singularity of aspect that seemed to give another moral interpretation to the things of this world than they had ever borne before. And there stood the minister, with his hand over his heart; and Hester Prynne, with the embroidered letter glimmering on her bosom; and little Pearl, herself a symbol, and the connecting link between these two. They stood in the noon of that strange and solemn splendour, as if it were the light that is to reveal all secrets, and the daybreak that shall unite all that belong to one another.

That is imaginative, impressive, poetic; but when, almost immediately afterwards, the author goes on to say that "the minister looking upward to the zenith, beheld there the appearance of an immense letter—the letter *A*—marked out in lines of dull red light," we feel that he goes too far, and is in danger of crossing the line that separates the sublime from its intimate neighbour. We are tempted to say that this is not moral tragedy, but physical comedy. In the same way, too much is made of the intimation that Hester's badge had a scorching property, and that if one touched it one would immediately withdraw one's hand. Hawthorne is perpetually looking for images which shall place themselves in picturesque correspondence with the spiritual facts with which he is concerned, and of course the search is of the very essence of poetry. But in such a process discretion is everything, and when the image becomes importunate it is in danger of seeming to stand for nothing more serious than itself. When Hester meets the minister by appointment in the forest, and sits talking with him while little Pearl wanders away and plays by the edge of the brook, the child is represented as at last making her way over to the other side of the woodland stream, and disporting herself there in a manner which makes her mother feel herself, "in some indistinct and tantalising manner, estranged from Pearl; as if the child, in her lonely ramble through the forest, had strayed out of the sphere in which she and her mother dwelt together, and was now vainly seeking to return to it." And Hawthorne devotes a chapter to this idea of the child's having, by putting the brook between Hester and herself, established a kind of spiritual gulf, on the verge of which her little fantastic person innocently mocks at her mother's sense of bereavement. This conception belongs, one would say, quite to the lighter order of a story-teller's devices, and the reader hardly goes with Hawthorne in the large development he gives to it. He hardly goes with him either, I think, in his extreme predilection for a small number of vague ideas which are represented by such terms as "sphere" and "sympathies." Hawthorne makes too liberal a use of these two substantives; it is the solitary defect of his style; and it counts as a defect partly because the words in question are a sort of specialty with certain writers immeasurably inferior to himself.

I had not meant, however, to expatiate upon his defects, which are of the slenderest and most venial kind. *The Scarlet Letter* has the beauty and harmony of all original and complete conceptions, and its weaker spots, whatever they are, are not of its essence; they are mere light flaws and inequalities of surface. One can often return to it; it supports familiarity, and has the inexhaustible charm and mystery of great works of art. It is admirably written. Hawthorne afterwards polished his style to a still higher degree; but in his later productions—it is almost always the case in a writer's later productions—there is a touch of mannerism. In *The Scarlet Letter* there is a high degree of polish, and at the same time a charming freshness; his phrase is less conscious of itself. His biographer very justly calls attention to the fact that his style was excellent from the beginning; that he appeared to have passed through no phase of learning how to write, but was in possession of his means, from the first, of his handling a pen. . . .

THE ART OF FICTION

I should not have affixed so comprehensive a title to these few remarks, necessarily wanting in any completeness upon a subject the full consideration of which would carry us far, did I not seem to discover a pretext for my temerity in the interesting pamphlet lately published under this name by Mr. Walter Besant. Mr. Besant's lecture[1] at the Royal Institution—the original form of his pamphlet—appears to indicate that many persons are interested in the art of fiction, and are not indifferent to such remarks, as those who practise it may attempt to make about it. I am therefore anxious not to lose the benefit of this favourable association, and to edge in a few words under cover of the attention which Mr. Besant is sure to have excited. There is something very encouraging in his having put into form certain of his ideas on the mystery of story-telling.

It is a proof of life and curiosity—curiosity on the part of the brotherhood of novelists as well as on the part of their readers. Only a short time ago it might have been supposed that the English novel was not what the French call *discutable*. It had no air of having a theory, a conviction, a consciousness of itself behind it—of being the expression of an artistic faith,

[1]Walter Besant, English novelist and critic, lectured at the Royal Institution April 25, 1884.

the result of choice and comparison. I do not say it was necessarily the worse for that: it would take much more courage
than I possess to intimate that the form of the novel as Dickens
and Thackeray (for instance) saw it had any taint of incomplete-
ness. It was, however, *naïf* (if I may help myself out with another
French word); and evidently if it be destined to suffer in any way
for having lost its *naïveté* it has now an idea of making sure
of the corresponding advantages. During the period I have
alluded to there was a comfortable, good-humoured feeling abroad that a novel is a novel, as a pudding is a pudding,
and that our only business with it could be to swallow it.
But within a year or two, for some reason or other, there
have been signs of returning animation—the era of discussion would appear to have been to a certain extent opened.
Art lives upon discussion, upon experiment, upon curiosity, upon variety of attempt, upon the exchange of views and
the comparison of standpoints; and there is a presumption
that those times when no one has anything particular to
say about it, and has no reason to give for practice or preference, though they may be times of honour, are not times
of development—are times, possibly even, a little of dullness. The successful application of any art is a delightful
spectacle, but the theory too is interesting; and though there
is a great deal of the latter without the former I suspect there
has never been a genuine success that has not had a latent
core of conviction. Discussion, suggestion, formulation,
these things are fertilizing when they are frank and sincere.
Mr. Besant has set an excellent example in saying what he
thinks, for his part, about the way in which fiction should
be written, as well as about the way in which it should be
published; for his view of the "art," carried on into an appendix, covers that too. Other labourers in the same field
will doubtless take up the argument, they will give it the
light of their experience, and the effect will surely be to make
our interest in the novel a little more what it had for some
time threatened to fail to be—a serious, active, inquiring
interest, under protection of which this delightful study may,

in moments of confidence, venture to say a little more what it thinks of itself.

It must take itself seriously for the public to take it so. The old superstition about fiction being "wicked" has doubtless died out in England; but the spirit of it lingers in a certain oblique regard directed toward any story which does not more or less admit that it is only a joke. Even the most jocular novel feels in some degree the weight of the proscription that was formerly directed against literary levity: the jocularity does not always succeed in passing for orthodoxy. It is still expected, though perhaps people are ashamed to say it, that a production which is after all only a "make-believe" (for what else is a "story"?) shall be in some degree apologetic—shall renounce the pretension of attempting really to represent life. This, of course, any sensible, wide-awake story declines to do, for it quickly perceives that the tolerance granted to it on such a condition is only an attempt to stifle it disguised in the form of generosity. The old evangelical hostility to the novel, which was as explicit as it was narrow, and which regarded it as little less favourable to our immortal part than a stage-play, was in reality far less insulting. The only reason for the existence of a novel is that it does attempt to represent life. When it relinquishes this attempt, the same attempt that we see on the canvas of the painter, it will have arrived at a very strange pass. It is not expected of the picture that it will make itself humble in order to be forgiven; and the analogy between the art of the painter and the art of the novelist is, so far as I am able to see, complete. Their inspiration is the same, their process (allowing for the different quality of the vehicle) is the same, their success is the same. They may learn from each other, they may explain and sustain each other. Their cause is the same, and the honour of one is the honour of another. The Mahometans think a picture an unholy thing, but it is a long time since any Christian did, and it is therefore the more odd that in the Christian mind the traces (dissimulated though they may be) of a suspicion of the sister art should linger to this day. The only

effectual way to lay it to rest is to emphasize the analogy
to which I just alluded—to insist on the fact that as the picture is reality, so the novel is history. That is the only general description (which does it justice) that we may give
of the novel. But history also is allowed to represent life;
it is not, any more than painting, expected to apologize.
The subject-matter of fiction is stored up likewise in documents and records, and if it will not give itself away, as they
say in California, it must speak with assurance, with the
tone of the historian. Certain accomplished novelists have
a habit of giving themselves away which must often bring
tears to the eyes of people who take their fiction seriously. I was lately struck, in reading over many pages of Anthony Trollope, with his want of discretion in this particular. In a digression, a parenthesis or an aside, he concedes
to the reader that he and this trusting friend are only "making believe." He admits that the events he narrates have
not really happened, and that he can give his narrative any
turn the reader may like best. Such a betrayal of a sacred
office seems to me, I confess, a terrible crime; it is what
I mean by the attitude of apology, and it shocks me every
whit as much in Trollope as it would have shocked me in
Gibbon or Macaulay. It implies that the novelist is less occupied in looking for the truth (the truth, of course I mean,
that he assumes, the premises that we must grant him, whatever they may be) than the historian, and in doing so it de-
prives him at a stroke of all his standing-room. To represent and illustrate the past, the actions of men, is the task
of either writer, and the only difference that I can see is,
in proportion as he succeeds, to the honour of the novelist, consisting as it does in his having more difficulty in collecting his evidence, which is so far from being purely literary. It seems to me to give him a great character, the fact
that he has at once so much in common with the philosopher and the painter; this double analogy is a magnificent
heritage.

It is of all this evidently that Mr. Besant is full when
he insists upon the fact that fiction is one of the *fine arts,*

deserving in its turn of all the honours and emoluments that have hitherto been reserved for the successful profession of music, poetry, painting, architecture. It is impossible to insist too much on so important a truth, and the place that Mr. Besant demands for the work of the novelist may be represented, a trifle less abstractly, by saying that he demands not only that it shall be reputed artistic, but that it shall be reputed very artistic indeed. It is excellent that he should have struck this note, for his doing so indicates that there was need of it, that his proposition may be to many people a novelty. One rubs one's eyes at the thought; but the rest of Mr. Besant's essay confirms the revelation. I suspect in truth that it would be possible to confirm it still further, and that one would not be far wrong in saying that in addition to the people to whom it has never occurred that a novel ought to be artistic, there are a great many others who, if this principle were urged upon them, would be filled with an indefinable mistrust. They would find it difficult to explain their repugnance, but it would operate strongly to put them on their guard. "Art," in our Protestant communities, where so many things have got so strangely twisted about, is supposed in certain circles to have some vaguely injurious effect upon those who make it an important consideration, who let it weigh in the balance. It is assumed to be opposed in some mysterious manner to morality, to amusement, to instruction. When it is embodied in the work of the painter (the sculptor is another affair!) you know what it is: it stands there before you, in the honesty of pink and green and a gilt frame; you can see the worst of it at a glance, and you can be on your guard. But when it is introduced into literature it becomes more insidious—there is danger of its hurting you before you know it. Literature should be either instructive or amusing, and there is in many minds an impression that these artistic preoccupations, the search for form, contribute to neither end, interfere indeed with both. They are too frivolous to be edifying, and too serious to be diverting; and they are moreover priggish and paradoxical and superfluous. That, I think, represents the manner in which the latent thought of many people who read novels as an exercise in skipping would explain itself if it were to become articulate. They would argue, of course, that a novel ought to be "good," but they would interpret this term in a fashion of their own, which indeed would vary considerably from one critic to another. One would say that being good means representing virtuous and aspiring characters, placed in prominent positions; another would say that it depends on a "happy ending," on a distribution at the last of prizes, pensions, husbands, wives, babies, millions, appended paragraphs, and cheerful remarks. Another still would say that it means being full of incident and movement, so that we shall wish to jump ahead, to see who was the mysterious stranger, and if the stolen will was ever found, and shall not be distracted from this pleasure by any tiresome analysis or "description." But they would all agree that the "artistic" idea would spoil some of their fun. One would hold it accountable for all the description, another would see it revealed in the absence of sympathy. Its hostility to a happy ending would be evident, and it might even in some cases render any ending at all impossible. The "ending" of a novel is, for many persons, like that of a good dinner, a course of dessert and ices, and the artist in fiction is regarded as a sort of meddlesome doctor who forbids agreeable aftertastes. It is therefore true that this conception of Mr. Besant's of the novel as a superior form encounters not only a negative but a positive indifference. It matters little that as a work of art it should really be as little or as much of its essence to supply happy endings, sympathetic characters, and an objective tone, as if it were a work of mechanics: the association of ideas, however incongruous, might easily be too much for it if an eloquent voice were not sometimes raised to call attention to the fact that it is at once as free and as serious a branch of literature as any other.

Certainly this might sometimes be doubted in presence of the enormous number of works of fiction that appeal to the credulity of our generation, for it might easily seem that there could be no great character in a commodity so quickly and easily produced. It must be admitted that good novels are much compromised by bad ones, and that the field at large suffers discredit from overcrowding. I think, however, that this injury is only superficial, and that the superabundance of written fiction proves nothing against the principle itself. It has been vulgarized, like all other kinds of literature, like everything else to-day, and it has proved more than some kinds accessible to vulgarization. But there is as much difference as there ever was between a good novel and a bad one: the bad is swept with all the daubed canvases and spoiled marble into some unvisited limbo, or infinite rubbish-yard beneath the back-windows of the world, and the good subsists and emits its light and stimulates our desire for perfection. As I shall take the liberty of making but a single criticism of Mr. Besant, whose tone is so full of the love of his art, I may as well have done with it at once. He seems to me to mistake in attempting to say so definitely beforehand what sort of an affair the good novel will be. To indicate the danger of such an error as that has been the purpose of these few pages; to suggest that certain traditions on the subject, applied *a priori,* have already had much to answer for, and that the good health of an art which undertakes so immediately to reproduce life must demand that it be perfectly free. It lives upon exercise, and the very meaning of exercise is freedom. The only obligation to which in advance we may hold a novel, without incurring the accusation of being arbitrary, is that it be interesting. That general responsibility rests upon it, but it is the only one I can think of. The ways in which it is at liberty to accomplish this result (of interesting us) strike me as innumerable, and such as can only suffer from being marked out or fenced in by prescription. They are as various as the temperament of man, and they are successful in proportion as they reveal a particular mind, different from others. A novel is in its broadest definition a personal, a direct impression of life: that to begin with, constitutes its value, which is greater or less according to the intensity of the impression. But there will be no intensity at all, and therefore no value, unless there is freedom to feel and say. The tracing of a line to be followed, of a tone to be taken, of a form to be filled out, is a limitation of that freedom and a suppression of the very thing that we are most curious about. The form, it seems to me, is to be appreciated after the fact: then the author's choice has been made, his standard has been indicated; then we can follow lines and directions and compare tones and resemblances. Then in a word we can enjoy one of the most charming of pleasures, we can estimate quality, we can apply the test of execution. The execution belongs to the author alone; it is what is most personal to him, and we measure him by that. The advantage, the luxury, as well as the torment and responsibility of the novelist, is that there is no limit to what he may attempt as an executant—no limit to his possible experiments, efforts, discoveries, successes. Here it is especially that he works, step by step, like his brother of the brush, of whom we may always say that he has painted his picture in a manner best known to himself. His manner is his secret, not necessarily a jealous one. He cannot disclose it as a general thing if he would; he would be at a loss to teach it to others. I say this with a due recollection of having insisted on the community of method of the artist who paints a picture and the artist who writes a novel. The painter *is* able to teach the rudiments of his practice, and it is possible, from the study of good work (granted the aptitude), both to learn how to paint and to learn how to write. Yet it remains true, without injury to the *rapprochement,* that the literary artist would be obliged to say to his pupil much more than the other, "Ah, well, you must do it as you can!" It is a question of degree, a matter of delicacy. If there are exact sciences, there are also exact arts, and the grammar of painting is so much more definite that it makes the difference.

I ought to add, however, that if Mr. Besant says at the beginning of his essay that the "laws of fiction may be laid down and taught with as much precision and exactness as the laws of harmony, perspective, and proportion," he mitigates what might appear to be an extravagance by applying his remark to "general" laws, and by expressing most of these rules in a manner with which it would certainly be unaccommodating to disagree. That the novelist must write from his experience, that his "characters must be real and such as might be met with in actual life"; that "a young lady brought up in a quiet country village should avoid descriptions of garrison life," and "a writer whose friends and personal experiences belong to the lower middle-class should carefully avoid introducing his characters into society"; that one should enter one's notes in a common-place book; that one's figures should be clear in outline; that making them clear by some trick of speech or of carriage is a bad method, and "describing them at length" is a worse one; that English Fiction should have a "conscious moral purpose"; that "it is almost impossible to estimate too highly the value of careful workmanship—that is, of style"; that "the most important point of all is the story," that "the story is everything": these are principles with most of which it is surely impossible not to sympathize. That remark about the lower middle-class writer and his knowing his place is perhaps rather chilling; but for the rest I should find it difficult to dissent from any one of these recommendations. At the same time, I should find it difficult positively to assent to them, with the exception, perhaps, of the injunction as to entering one's notes in a common-place book. They scarcely seem to me to have the quality that Mr. Besant attributes to the rules of the novelist—the "precision and exactness" of "the laws of harmony, perspective, and proportion." They are suggestive, they are even inspiring, but they are not exact, though they are doubtless as much so as the case admits of: which is a proof of that liberty of interpretation for which I just contended. For the value of these different injunctions—so beautiful and so vague—is wholly in the meaning one attaches to them. The characters, the situation, which strike one as real will be those that touch and interest one most, but the measure of reality is very difficult to fix. The reality of Don Quixote or of Mr. Micawber is a very delicate shade; it is a reality so coloured by the author's vision that, vivid as it may be, one would hesitate to propose it as a model: one would expose one's self to some very embarassing questions on the part of a pupil. It goes without saying that you will not write a good novel unless you possess the sense of reality; but it will be difficult to give you a recipe for calling that sense into being. Humanity is immense, and reality has a myriad forms; the most one can affirm is that some of the flowers of fiction have the odour of it, and others have not; as for telling you in advance how your nosegay should be composed, that is another affair. It is equally excellent and inconclusive to say that one must write from experience; to our suppositious aspirant such a declaration might savour of mockery. What kind of experience is intended, and where does it begin and end? Experience is never limited, and it is never complete; it is an immense sensibility, a kind of huge spider-web of the finest silken threads suspended in the chamber of consciousness, and catching every air-borne particle in its tissue. It is the very atmosphere of the mind; and when the mind is imaginative—much more when it happens to be that of a man of genius—it takes to itself the faintest hints of life, it converts the very pulses of the air into revelations. The young lady living in a village has only to be a damsel upon whom nothing is lost to make it quite unfair (as it seems to me) to declare to her that she shall have nothing to say about the military. Greater miracles have been seen than that, imagination assisting, she should speak the truth about some of these gentlemen. I remember an English novelist, a woman of genius, telling me that she was much commended for the impression she had managed to give in one of her tales of the nature and way of life of the French Protestant youth. She had been asked where she learned so much about this recondite being, she had been congratulated on her peculiar opportunities. These opportunities consisted in her having once, in Paris, as she ascended a staircase, passed an open door where, in the household of a *pasteur,* some of the young Protestants were seated at table round a finished meal. The glimpse made a picture; it lasted only a moment, but that moment was experience. She had got her direct personal impression, and she turned out her type. She knew what youth was, and what Protestantism; she also had the advantage of having seen what it was to be French, so that she converted these ideas into a concrete image and produced a reality. Above all, however, she was blessed with the faculty which when you give it an inch takes an ell, and which for the artist is a much greater source of strength than any accident of residence or of place in the social scale. The power to guess the unseen from the seen, to trace the implication of things, to judge the whole piece by the pattern, the condition of feeling life in general so completely that you are well on your way to knowing any particular corner of it— this cluster of gifts may almost be said to constitute experience, and they occur in country and in town, and in the most differing stages of education. If experience consists of impressions, it may be said that impressions *are* experience, just as (have we not seen it?) they are the very air we breathe. Therefore, if I should certainly say to a novice, "Write from experience and experience only," I should feel that this was rather a tantalizing monition if I were not careful immediately to add, "Try to be one of the people on whom nothing is lost!"

I am far from intending by this to minimize the importance of exactness—of truth of detail. One can speak best from one's own taste, and I may therefore venture to say that the air of reality (solidity of specification) seems to me to be the supreme virtue of a novel—the merit on which all its other merits (including that conscious moral purpose of which Mr. Besant speaks) helplessly and submissively depend. If it be not there they are all as nothing, and if these be there, they owe their effect to the success with which the author has produced the illusion of life. The cultivation of this success, the study of this exquisite process, form to my taste, the beginning and the end of the art of the novelist. They are his inspiration, his despair, his reward, his torment, his delight. It is here in very truth that he competes with life; it is here that he competes with his brother the painter in *his* attempt to render the look of things, the look that conveys their meaning, to catch the colour, the relief, the expression, the surface, the substance of the human spectacle. It is in regard to this that Mr. Besant is well inspired when he bids him take notes. He cannot possibly take too many, he cannot possibly take enough. All life solicits him, and to "render" the simplest surface, to produce the most momentary illusion, is a very complicated business. His case would be easier, and the rule would be more exact, if Mr. Besant had been able to tell him what notes to take. But this, I fear, he can never learn in any manual; it is the business of his life. He has to take a great many in order to select a few, he has to work them up as he can, and even the guides and philosophers who might have most to say to him must leave him alone when it comes to the application of precepts, as we leave the painter in communion with his palette. That his characters "must be clear in outline," as Mr. Besant says—he feels that down to his boots; but how he shall make them so is a secret between his good angel and himself. It would be absurdly simple if he could be taught that a great deal of "description" would make them so, or that on the contrary the absence of description and the cultivation of dialogue, or the absence of dialogue and the multiplication of "incident," would rescue him from his difficulties. Nothing, for instance, is more possible than that he be of a turn of mind for which this odd, literal opposition of description and dialogue, incident and description, has little meaning and light. People often talk of these things as if they had a kind of internecine distinctness, instead of melting into each other at every breath, and being intimately associated parts of one general effort of expression. I cannot imagine composition existing in a series of blocks, nor conceive, in any novel worth discussing at all, of a passage of description that is not in its intention narrative, a passage of dialogue that is not in its intention descriptive, a touch of truth of any sort that does not partake of the nature of incident, or an incident that derives its interest from any other source than the general and only source of the success of a work of art—that of being illustrative. A novel is a living thing, all one and continuous, like any other organism, and in proportion as it lives will it be found, I think, that in each of the parts there is something of each of the other parts. The critic who over the close texture of a finished work shall pretend to trace a geography of items will mark some frontiers as artificial, I fear, as any that have been known to history. There is an old-fashioned distinction between the novel of character and the novel of incident which must have cost many a smile to the intending fabulist who was keen about his work. It appears to me as little to the point as the equally celebrated distinction between the novel and the romance—to answer as little to any reality. There are bad novels and good novels, as there are bad pictures and good pictures; but that is the only distinction in which I see any meaning, and I can as little imagine speaking of a novel of character as I can imagine speaking of a picture of character. When one says picture one says of character, when one says novel one says of incident, and the terms may be transposed at will. What is character but the determination of incident? What is incident but the illustration of character? What is either a picture or a novel that is *not* of character? What else do we seek in it and find in it? It is an incident for a woman to stand up with her hand resting on a table and look out at you in a certain way; or if it be not an incident I think it will be hard to say what it is. At the same time it is an expression of character. If you say you don't see it (character in *that*— *allons donc!*), this is exactly what the artist who has reasons of his own for thinking he *does* see it undertakes to show you. When a young man makes up his mind that he has not faith enough after all to enter the church as he intended, that is an incident, though you may not hurry to the end of the chapter to see whether perhaps he doesn't change once more. I do not say that these are extraordinary or startling incidents. I do not pretend to estimate the degree of interest proceeding from them, for this will depend upon the skill of the painter. It sounds almost puerile to say that some incidents are intrinsically much more important than others, and I need not take this precaution after having professed my sympathy for the major ones in remarking that the only classification of the novel that I can understand is into that which has life and that which has it not.

The novel and the romance, the novel of incident and that of character—these clumsy separations appear to me to have been made by critics and readers for their own convenience, and to help them out of some of their occasional queer predicaments, but to have little reality or interest for the producer, from whose point of view it is of course that we are attempting to consider the art of fiction. The case is the same with another shadowy category which Mr. Besant apparently is disposed to set up—that of the "modern English novel"; unless indeed it be that in this matter he has fallen into an accidental confusion of standpoints. It is not quite clear whether he intends the remarks in which he alludes to it to be didactic or historical. It is as difficult to suppose a person intending to write a modern English as to suppose him writing an ancient English novel: that is a label which begs the question. One writes the novel, one paints the picture, of one's language and of one's time, and calling it modern English will not, alas! make the difficult task any easier. No more, unfortunately, will calling this or that work of one's fellow-artist a romance—unless it be, of course, simply for the pleasantness of the thing, as for instance when Hawthorne gave this heading to his story of *Blithedale*. The French, who have brought the theory of fiction to remarkable completeness, have but one name for the novel, and have not attempted smaller things in it, that I can see, for that. I can think of no obligation to which the "romancer" would not be held equally with the novelist; the standard of execution is equally high for each. Of course it is of execution that we are talking—that being the only point of a novel that is open to contention. This is perhaps too often lost sight of, only to produce interminable confusions and cross-purposes. We must grant the artist his subject, his idea, his *donnée:* our criticism is applied only to what he makes of it. Naturally I do not mean that we are bound to like it or find it interesting: in case we do not our course is perfectly simple—to let it alone. We may believe that of a certain idea even the most sincere novelist can make nothing at all, and the event may perfectly justify our belief; but the failure will have been a failure to execute, and it is in the execution that the fatal weakness is recorded. If we pretend to respect the artist at all, we must allow him his freedom of choice, in the face, in particular cases, of innumerable presumptions that the choice will not fructify. Art derives a considerable part of its beneficial exercise from flying in the face of presumptions, and some of the most interesting experiments of which it is capable are hidden in the bosom of common things. Gustave Flaubert has written a story about the devotion of a servant-girl to a parrot, and the production, highly-finished as it is, cannot on the whole be called a success. We are perfectly free to find it flat, but I think it might have been interesting; and I, for my part, am extremely glad he should have written it; it is a contribution to our knowledge of what can be done—or what cannot. Ivan Turgenieff has written a tale about a deaf and dumb serf and a lap-dog, and the thing is touching, loving, a little masterpiece. He struck the note of life where Gustave Flaubert missed it—he flew in the face of a presumption and achieved a victory.

Nothing, of course, will ever take the place of the good old fashion of "liking" a work of art or not liking it: the most improved criticism will not abolish that primitive, that ultimate test. I mention this to guard myself from the accusation of intimating that the idea, the subject, of a novel or a picture, does not matter. It matters, to my sense, in the highest degree, and if I might put up a prayer it would be that artists should select none but the richest. Some, as I have already hastened to admit, are much more remunerative than others, and it would be a world happily arranged in which persons intending to treat them should be exempt from confusions and mistakes. This fortunate condition will arrive only, I fear, on the same day that critics become purged from error. Meanwhile, I repeat, we do not judge the artist with fairness unless we say to him,

"Oh, I grant you your starting-point, because if I did not I should seem to prescribe to you, and heaven forbid I should take that responsibility. If I pretend to tell you what you must not take, you will call upon me to tell you then what you must take; in which case I shall be prettily caught. Moreover, it isn't till I have accepted your data that I can begin to measure you. I have the standard, the pitch; I have no right to tamper with your flute and then criticize your music. Of course I may not care for your idea at all; I may think it silly, or stale, or unclean; in which case I wash my hands of you altogether. I may content myself with believing that you will not have succeeded in being interesting, but I shall, of course, not attempt to demonstrate it, and you will be as indifferent to me as I am to you. I needn't remind you that there are all sorts of tastes: who can know it better? Some people, for excellent reasons, don't like to read about carpenters; others, for reasons even better, don't like to read about courtesans. Many object to Americans. Others (I believe they are mainly editors and publishers) won't look at Italians. Some readers don't like quiet subjects; others don't like bustling ones. Some enjoy a complete illusion, others the consciousness of large concessions. They choose their novels accordingly, and if they don't care about your idea they won't, *a fortiori,* care about your treatment."

So that it comes back very quickly, as I have said, to the liking: in spite of M. Zola, who reasons less powerfully than he represents, and who will not reconcile himself to this absoluteness of taste, thinking that there are certain things that people ought to like, and that they can be made to like. I am quite at a loss to imagine anything (at any rate in this matter of fiction) that people *ought* to like or to dislike. Selection will be sure to take care of itself, for it has a constant motive behind it. That motive is simply experience. As people feel life, so they will feel the art that is most closely related to it. This closeness of relation is what we should never forget in talking of the effort of the novel. Many people speak of it as a factitious, artificial form, a product of ingenuity, the business of which is to alter and arrange the things that surround us, to translate them into conventional, traditional moulds. This, however, is a view of the matter which carries us but a very short way, condemns the art to an eternal repetition of a few familiar *clichés,* cuts short its development, and leads us straight up to a dead wall. Catching the very note and trick, the strange irregular rhythm of life, that is the attempt whose strenuous force keeps Fiction upon her feet. In proportion as in what she offers us we see life *without* rearrangement do we feel that we are touching the truth; in proportion as we see it *with* rearrangement do we feel that we are being put off with a substitute, a compromise and convention. It is not uncommon to hear an extraordinary assurance of remark in regard to this matter of rearranging, which is often spoken of as if it were the last word of art. Mr. Besant seems to me in danger of falling into the great error with his rather unguarded talk about "selection." Art is essentially selection, but it is a selection whose main care is to be typical, to be inclusive. For many people art means rose-coloured window-panes, and selection means picking a bouquet for Mrs. Grundy. They will tell you glibly that artistic considerations have nothing to do with the disagreeable, with the ugly; they will rattle off shallow commonplaces about the province of art and the limits of art till you are moved to some wonder in return as to the province and the limits of ignorance. It appears to me that no one can ever have made a seriously artistic attempt without becoming conscious of an immense increase—a kind of revelation—of freedom. One perceives in that case—by the light of a heavenly ray—that the province of art is all life, all feeling, all observation, all vision. As Mr. Besant so justly intimates, it is all experience. That is a sufficient answer to those who maintain that it must not touch the sad things of life, who stick into its divine unconscious bosom little prohibitory inscriptions on the end of sticks, such as we see in public gardens—"It is forbidden to walk on the grass; it is forbidden to touch the flowers; it is not allowed to introduce dogs or to remain after dark; it is requested to keep to the right." The young aspirant in the line of fiction whom we continue to imagine will do nothing without taste, for in that case his freedom would be of little use to him; but the first advantage of his taste will be to reveal to him the absurdity of the little sticks and tickets. If he have taste, I must add, of course he will have ingenuity, and my disrespectful reference to that quality just now was not meant to imply that it is useless in fiction. But it is only a secondary aid; the first is a capacity for receiving straight impressions.

Mr. Besant has some remarks on the question of "the story" which I shall not attempt to criticize, though they seem to me to contain a singular ambiguity, because I do not think I understand them. I cannot see what is meant by talking as if there were a part of a novel which is the story and part of it which for mystical reasons is not—unless indeed the distinction be made in a sense in which it is difficult to suppose that any one should attempt to convey anything. "The story," if it represents anything, represents the subject, the idea, the *donnée* of the novel; and there is surely no "school"—Mr. Besant speaks of a school—which urges that a novel should be all treatment and no subject. There must assuredly be something to treat; every school is intimately conscious of that. This sense of the story being the idea, the starting-point, of the novel, is the only one that I see in which it can be spoken of as something different from its organic whole; and since in proportion as the work is successful the idea permeates and penetrates it, informs and animates it, so that every word and every punctuation-point contribute directly to the expression, in that proportion do we lose our sense of the story being a blade which may be drawn more or less out of its sheath. The story and the novel, the idea and the form, are the needle and thread, and I never heard of a guild of tailors who recommended the use of the thread without the needle, or the needle without the thread. Mr. Besant is not the only critic who may be observed to have spoken as if there were certain things in life which constitute stories, and certain others which do not. I find the same odd implication in an entertaining article in the *Pall Mall Gazette,* devoted, as it happens, to Mr. Besant's lecture. "The story is the thing!" says this graceful writer, as if with a tone of opposition to some other idea. I should think it was, as every painter who, as the time for "sending in" his picture looms in the distance, finds himself still in quest of a subject—as every belated artist not fixed about his theme will heartily agree. There are some subjects which speak to us and others which do not, but he would be a clever man who should undertake to give a rule—an *index expurgatorius*—by which the story and the no-story should be known apart. It is impossible (to me at least) to imagine any such rule which shall not be altogether arbitrary. The writer in the *Pall Mall* opposes the delightful (as I suppose) novel of *Margot la Balafrée* to certain tales in which "Bostonian nymphs" appear to have "rejected English dukes for psychological reasons." I am not acquainted with the romance just designated, and can scarcely forgive the *Pall Mall* critic for not mentioning the name of the author, but the title appears to refer to a lady who may have received a scar in some heroic adventure. I am inconsolable at not being acquainted with this episode, but am utterly at a loss to see why it is a story when the rejection (or acceptance) of a duke is not, and why a reason, psychological or other, is not a subject when a cicatrix is. They are all particles of the multitudinous life with which the novel deals, and surely no dogma which pretends to make it lawful to touch the one and unlawful to touch the other will stand for a moment on its feet. It is the special picture that must stand or fall, according as it seem to possess truth or to lack it. Mr. Besant does not, to my sense, light up the subject by intimating that a story must, under penalty of not being a story, consist of "adventures." Why of adventures more than of green spectacles? He mentions a category of impossible things, and among them he places "fiction without adventure." Why without adventure, more than without matrimony, or celibacy, or parturition, or cholera, or hydropathy, or Jansenism? This seems to me to bring the novel back to the hapless little *rôle* of being an artificial, ingenious thing—bring it down from its large, free character of an immense and exquisite correspondence with life. And what *is* adventure, when it comes to that, and by what sign is the listening pupil to recognize it? It is an adventure—an immense one—for me to write this little article; and for a Bostonian nymph to reject an English duke is an adventure only less stirring, I should say, than for an English duke to be rejected by a Bostonian nymph. I see dramas within dramas in that, and innummerable points of view. A psychological reason is, to my imagination, an object adorably pictorial; to catch the tint of its complexion—I feel as if that idea might inspire one to Titianesque efforts. There are few things more exciting to me, in short, than a psychological reason, and yet, I protest, the novel seems to me the most magnificent form of art. I have just been reading, at the same time, the delightful story of *Treasure Island,* by Mr. Robert Louis Stevenson and, in a manner less consecutive, the last tale from M. Edmond de Goncourt, which is entitled *Chérie.*

One of these works treats of murders, mysteries, islands of dreadful renown, hair-breadth escapes, miraculous coincidences and buried doubloons. The other treats of a little French girl who lived in a fine house in Paris, and died of wounded sensibility because no one would marry her. I call *Treasure Island* delightful, because it appears to me to have succeeded wonderfully in what it attempts; and I venture to bestow no epithet upon *Chérie,* which strikes me as having failed deplorably in what it attempts—that is in tracing the development of the moral consciousness of a child. But one of these productions strikes me as exactly as much of a novel as the other, and as having a "story" quite as much. The moral consciousness of a child is as much a part of life as the islands of the Spanish Main, and the one sort of geography seems to me to have those "surprises" of which Mr. Besant speaks quite as much as the other. For myself (since it comes back in the last resort, as I say, to the preference of the individual), the picture of the child's experience has the advantage that I can at successive steps (an immense luxury, near to the "sensual pleasure" of which Mr. Besant's critic in the *Pall Mall* speaks) say Yes or No, as it may be, to what the artist puts before me. I have been a child in fact, but I have been on a quest for a buried treasure only in supposition, and it is a simple accident that with M. de Goncourt I should have for the most part to say No. With George Eliot, when she painted that country with a far other intelligence, I always said Yes.

The most interesting part of Mr. Besant's lecture is unfortunately the briefest passage—his very cursory allusion to the "conscious moral purpose" of the novel. Here again it is not very clear whether he be recording a fact or laying down a principle; it is a great pity that in the latter case he should not have developed his idea. This branch of the subject is of immense importance, and Mr. Besant's few words point to considerations of the wildest reach, not to be lightly disposed of. He will have treated the art of fiction but superficially who is not prepared to go every inch of the way that these considerations will carry him. It is for this reason that at the beginning of these remarks I was careful to notify the reader

that my reflections on so large a theme have no pretension
to be exhaustive. Like Mr. Besant, I have left the question of
the morality of the novel till the last, and at the last I find I
have used up my space. It is a question surrounded with difficulties, as witness the very first that meets us, in the form
of a definite question, on the threshold. Vagueness, in such
a discussion, is fatal, and what is the meaning of your morality and your conscious moral purpose? Will you not define your
terms and explain how (a novel being a picture) a picture can
be either moral or immoral? You wish to paint a moral picture or carve a moral statue: will you not tell us how you would
set about it? We are discusing the Art of Fiction; questions
of art are questions (in the widest sense) of execution; questions of morality are quite another affair, and will you not let
us see how it is that you find it so easy to mix them up? These
things are so clear to Mr. Besant that he has deduced from
them a law which he sees embodied in English Fiction, and
which is "a truly admirable thing and a great cause for congratulation." It is a great cause for congratulation indeed when
such thorny problems become as smooth as silk. I may add
that in so far as Mr. Besant perceives that in point of fact English Fiction has addressed itself preponderantly to these delicate questions he will appear to many people to have made
a vain discovery. They will have been positively struck, on
the contrary, with the moral timidity of the usual English novelist; with his (or with her) aversion to face the difficulties with
which on every side the treatment of reality bristles. He is apt
to be extremely shy (whereas the picture that Mr. Besant draws
is a picture of boldness), and the sign of his work, for the most
part, is a cautious silence on certain subjects. In the English
novel (by which of course I mean the American as well), more
than in any other, there is a traditional difference between
that which people know and that which they agree to admit
that they know, that which they see and that which they
speak of, that which they feel to be a part of life and that
which they allow to enter into literature. There is the great
difference, in short, between what they talk of in conversation and what they talk of in print. The essence of moral energy

is to survey the whole field, and I should directly reverse Mr. Besant's remark and say not that the English novel has a purpose, but that it has a diffidence. To what degree a purpose in a work of art is a source of corruption I shall not attempt to inquire; the one that seems to me least dangerous is the purpose of making a perfect work. As for our novel, I may say lastly on this score that as we find it in England to-day it strikes me as addressed in a large degree to "young people," and that this in itself constitutes a presumption that it will be rather shy. There are certain things which it is generally agreed not to discuss, not even to mention, before young people. That is very well, but the absence of discussion is not a sympton of the moral passion. The purpose of the English novel—"a truly admirable thing, and a great cause for congratulation"—strikes me therefore as rather negative.

There is one point at which the moral sense and the artistic sense lie very near together; that is in the light of the very obvious truth that the deepest quality of a work of art will always be the quality of the mind of the producer. In proportion as that intelligence is fine will the novel, the picture, the statue partake of the substance of beauty and truth. To be constituted of such elements is, to my vision, to have purpose enough. No good novel will ever proceed from a superficial mind; that seems to me an axiom which, for the artist in fiction, will cover all needful moral ground: if the youthful aspirant take it to heart it will illuminate for him many of the mysteries of "purpose." There are many other useful things that might be said to him, but I have come to the end of my article, and can only touch them as I pass. The critic in the *Pall Mall Gazette,* whom I have already quoted, draws attention to the danger, in speaking of the art of fiction, of generalizing. The danger that he has in mind is rather, I imagine, that of particularizing, for there are some comprehensive remarks which, in addition to those embodied in Mr. Besant's suggestive lecture, might without fear of misleading him be addressed to the ingenuous student. I should remind him first of the magnificence of the form that is open to him, which offers to sight so few restrictions and such innumerable opportunities. The other arts, in comparison, appear confined and hampered; the various conditions under which they are exercised are so rigid and definite. But the only condition that I can think of attaching to the composition of the novel is, as I have already said, that it be sincere. This freedom is a splendid privilege, and the first lesson of the young novelist is to learn to be worthy of it.

"Enjoy it as it deserves [I should say to him]; take possession of it, explore it to its utmost extent, publish it, rejoice in it. All life belongs to you, and do not listen either to those who would shut you up into corners of it and tell you that it is only here and there that art inhabits, or to those who would persuade you that this heavenly messenger wings her way outside of life altogether, breathing a superfine air, and turning away her head from the truth of things. There is no impression of life, no manner of seeing it and feeling it, to which the plan of the novelist may not offer a place; you have only to remember that talents so dissimilar as those of Alexandre Dumas and Jane Austen, Charles Dickens and Gustave Flaubert have worked in this field with equal glory. Do not think too much about optimism and pessimism; try and catch the colour of life itself. In France to-day we see a prodigious effort (that of Emile Zola, to whose solid and serious work no explorer of the capacity of the novel can allude without respect), we see an extraordinary effort vitiated by a spirit of pessimism on a narrow basis. M. Zola is magnificent, but he strikes an English reader as ignorant; he has an air of working in the dark; if he had as much light as energy, his results would be of the highest value. As for the aberrations of a shallow optimism, the ground (of English fiction especially) is strewn with their brittle particles as with broken glass. If you must indulge in conclusions, let them have the taste of a wide knowledge. Remember that your first duty is to be as complete as possible—to make as perfect a work. Be generous and delicate and pursue the prize."

WILLIAM DEAN HOWELLS

As the existence of a man of letters (so far as the public is concerned with it) may be said to begin with his first appearance in literature, that of Mr. Howells, who was born at Martinsville, Ohio, in 1837, and spent his entire youth in his native State, dates properly from the publication of his delightful volume on *Venetian Life*—than which he has produced nothing since of a literary quality more pure—which he put forth in 1865, after his return from the consular post in the city of St. Mark which he had filled for four years. He had, indeed, before going to live in Venice, and during the autumn of 1860, published, in conjunction with his friend Mr. Piatt, a so-called "campaign" biography of Abraham Lincoln; but as this composition, which I have never seen, emanated probably more from a good Republican than from a suitor of the Muse, I mention it simply for the sake of exactitude, adding, however, that I have never heard of the Muse having taken it ill. When a man is a born artist, everything that happens to him confirms his perverse tendency; and it may be considered that the happiest thing that could have been invented on Mr. Howells's behalf was his residence in Venice at the most sensitive and responsive period of life; for Venice, bewritten and bepainted as she has ever been, does nothing to you unless to persuade you that you also can paint, that you also can write. Her only fault is that she sometimes too flatteringly—for she is shameless in the exercise of such arts—addresses the remark to those who cannot. Mr. Howells could, fortunately, for his writing was painting as well in those days. The papers on Venice prove it, equally with the artistic whimsical chapters of the *Italian Journeys,* made up in 1867 from his notes and memories (the latter as tender as most glances shot eastward in working hours across the Atlantic) of the holidays and excursions which carried him occasionally away from his consulate.

The mingled freshness and irony of these things gave them an originality which has not been superseded, to my knowledge, by any impressions of European life from an American standpoint. At Venice Mr. Howells married a lady of artistic accomplishment and association, passed through the sharp alternations of anxiety and hope to which those who spent the long years of the Civil War in foreign lands were inevitably condemned, and of which the effect was not rendered less wearing by the perusal of the London *Times* and the conversation of the British tourist. The irritation, so far as it proceeded from the latter source, may even yet be perceived in Mr. Howells's pages. He wrote poetry at Venice, as he had done of old in Ohio, and his poems were subsequently collected into two thin volumes, the fruit, evidently, of a rigorous selection. They have left more traces in the mind of many persons who read and enjoyed them than they appear to have done in the author's own. It is not nowadays as a cultivator of rhythmic periods that Mr. Howells most willingly presents himself. Everything in the evolution, as we must all learn to call it today, of a talent of this order is interesting, but one of the things that are most so is the separation that has taken place, in Mr. Howells's case, between its early and its later manner. There is nothing in *Silas Lapham,* or in *Doctor Breen's Practice,* or in *A Modern Instance,* or in *The Undiscovered Country,* to suggest that its author had at one time either wooed the lyric Muse or surrendered himself to those Italian initiations without which we of other countries remain always, after all, more or less barbarians. It is often a good, as it is sometimes an evil, that one cannot disestablish

one's past, and Mr. Howells cannot help having rhymed and
romanced in deluded hours, nor would he, no doubt, if he could.
The repudiation of the weakness which leads to such aberrations is more apparent than real, and the spirit which made him
care a little for the poor factitious Old World and the superstition of "form" is only latent in pages which express a marked
preference for the novelties of civilization and a perceptible
mistrust of the purist. I hasten to add that Mr. Howells has had
moments of reappreciation of Italy in later years, and has even
taken the trouble to write a book (the magnificent volume on
Tuscan Cities) to show it. Moreover, the exquisite tale *A Foregone Conclusion,* and many touches in the recent novel of *Indian
Summer* (both this and the *Cities* the fruit of a second visit to
Italy), sound the note of a charming inconsistency.

On his return from Venice he settled in the vicinity of Boston, and began to edit the *Atlantic Monthly,* accommodating
himself to this grave complication with infinite tact and industry. He conferred further distinction upon the magazine; he
wrote the fine series of "Suburban Sketches," one of the least
known of his productions, but one of the most perfect, and
on Sunday afternoons he took a suburban walk—perfect also,
no doubt, in its way. I know not exactly how long this phase of
his career lasted, but I imagine that if he were asked, he would
reply: "Oh, a hundred years." He was meant for better things
than this—things better, I mean, than superintending the private life of even the most eminent periodical—but I am not
sure that I would speak of this experience as a series of wasted
years. They were years rather of economized talent, of observation and accumulation. They laid the foundation of what
is most remarkable, or most, at least, the peculiar sign, in his
effort as a novelist—his unerring sentiment of the American
character. Mr. Howells knows more about it than anyone, and
it was during this period of what we may suppose to have been
rather perfunctory administration that he must have gathered
many of his impressions of it. An editor is in the nature of the
case much exposed, so exposed as not to be protected even by
the seclusion (the security to a superficial eye so complete) of a
Boston suburb. His manner of contact with the world is almost

violent, and whatever bruises he may confer, those he receives are the most telling, inasmuch as the former are distributed among many, and the latter all to be endured by one. Mr. Howells's accessibilities and sufferings were destined to fructify. Other persons have considered and discoursed upon American life, but no one, surely, has *felt* it so completely as he. I will not say that Mr. Howells feels it all equally, for are we not perpetually conscious how vast and deep it is?—but he is an authority upon many of those parts of it which are most representative.

He was still under the shadow of his editorship when, in the intervals of his letter-writing and reviewing, he made his first cautious attempts in the walk of fiction. I say cautious, for in looking back nothing is more clear than that he had determined to advance only step by step. In his first story, *Their Wedding Journey,* there are only two persons, and in his next, *A Chance Acquaintance,* which contains one of his very happiest studies of a girl's character, the number is not lavishly increased.

In *A Foregone Conclusion,* where the girl again is admirable, as well as the young Italian priest, also a kind of maidenly figure, the actors are but four. Today Mr. Howells doesn't count, and confers life with a generous and unerring hand. If the profusion of forms in which it presents itself to him is remarkable, this is perhaps partly because he had the good fortune of not approaching the novel until he had lived considerably, until his inclination for it had ripened. His attitude was as little as possible that of the gifted young person who, at twenty, puts forth a work of imagination of which the merit is mainly in its establishing the presumption that the next one will be better. It is my impression that long after he was twenty he still cultivated the belief that the faculty of the novelist was not in him, and was even capable of producing certain unfinished chapters (in the candor of his good faith he would sometimes communicate them to a listener) in triumphant support of this contention. He believed, in particular, that he could not make people talk, and such have been the revenges of time that a cynical critic might almost say of him today that he cannot make them keep silent. It was life itself that finally dissipated his doubts, life that reasoned with him and persuaded him. The feeling of life is strong in all his tales, and any one of them has this rare (always rarer) and indispensable sign of a happy origin, that it is an impression at first hand. Mr. Howells is literary, on certain sides exquisitely so, though with a singular and not unamiable perversity he sometimes endeavors not to be; but his vision of the human scene is never a literary reminiscence, a reflection of books and pictures, of tradition and fashion and hearsay. I know of no English novelist of our hour whose work is so exclusively a matter of painting what he sees, and who is so sure of what he sees. People are always wanting a writer of Mr. Howells's temperament to see certain things that he doesn't (that he doesn't sometimes even want to), but I must content myself with congratulating the author of *A Modern Instance* and *Silas Lapham* on the admirable quality of his vision. The American life which he for the most part depicts is certainly neither very rich nor very fair, but it is tremendously positive, and as his manner of presenting it is as little as possible conventional, the reader can have no doubt about it. This is an immense luxury; the ingenuous character of the witness (I can give it no higher praise) deepens the value of the report.

Mr. Howells has gone from one success to another, has taken possession of the field, and has become copious without detriment to his freshness. I need not enumerate his works in their order, for, both in America and in England (where it is a marked feature of the growing curiosity felt about American life that they are constantly referred to for information and verification), they have long been in everybody's hands. Quietly and steadily they have become better and better; one may like some of them more than others, but it is noticeable that from effort to effort the author has constantly enlarged his scope. His work is of a kind of which it is good that there should be much today—work of observation, of patient and definite notation. Neither in theory nor in practice is Mr. Howells a romancer; but the romancers can spare him; there will always be plenty of people to do their work. He has definite and downright convictions on the subject of the work that calls out to be done in opposition to theirs, and this fact is a source of much of the interest that he excites.

It is a singular circumstance that to know what one wishes to do should be, in the field of art, a rare distinction; but it is incontestable that, as one looks about in our English and American fiction, one does not perceive any very striking examples of a vivifying faith. There is no discussion of the great question of how best to write, no exchange of ideas, no vivacity nor variety of experiment. A vivifying faith Mr. Howells may distinctly be said to possess, and he conceals it so little as to afford every facility to those people who are anxious to prove that it is the wrong one. He is animated by a love of the common, the immediate, the familiar and vulgar elements of life, and holds that in proportion as we move into the rare and strange we become vague and arbitrary; that truth of representation, in a word, can be achieved only so long as it is in our power to test and measure it. He thinks scarcely anything too paltry to be interesting, that the small and the vulgar have been terribly neglected, and would rather see an exact account of a sentiment or a character he stumbles against every day than a brilliant evocation of a passion or a type he has never seen and does not even particularly believe in. He adores the real, the natural, the colloquial, the moderate, the optimistic, the domestic, and the democratic; looking askance at exceptions and perversities and superiorities, at surprising and incongruous phenomena in general. One must have seen a great deal before one concludes; the world is very large, and life is a mixture of many things; she by no means eschews the strange, and often risks combinations and effects that make one rub one's eyes. Nevertheless, Mr. Howells's standpoint is an excellent one for seeing a large part of the truth, and even if it were less advantageous, there would be a great deal to admire in the firmness with which he has planted himself. He hates a "story", and (this private feat is not impossible) has probably made up his mind very definitely as to what the pestilent thing consists of. In this respect he is more logical than M. Emile Zola, who partakes of the same aversion,

but has greater lapses as well as greater audacities. Mr. Howells hates an artificial fable and a *denouement* that is pressed
into the service; he likes things to occur as they occur in life,
where the manner of a great many of them is not to occur at
all. (He has observed that heroic emotion and brilliant opportunity are not particularly interwoven with our days, and indeed, in the way of omission, he *has* often practiced in his pages
a very considerable boldness. It has not, however, made what
we find there any less interesting and less human.)

The picture of American life on Mr. Howells's canvas is not
of a dazzling brightness, and many readers have probably wondered why it is that (among a sensitive people) he has so successfully escaped the imputation of a want of patriotism. The
manners he describes—the desolation of the whole social prospect in *A Modern Instance* is perhaps the strongest expression of those influences—are eminently of a nature to discour-
age the intending visitor, and yet the westward pilgrim
continues to arrive, in spite of the Bartley Hubbards and the
Laphams, and the terrible practices at the country hotel in
Doctor Breen, and at the Boston boarding-house in *A Woman's
Reason.* This tolerance of depressing revelations is explained
partly, no doubt, by the fact that Mr. Howells's truthfulness
imposes itself—the representation is so vivid that the reader
accepts it as he accepts, in his own affairs, the mystery of fate—
and partly by a very different consideration, which is simply
that if many of his characters are disagreeable, almost all of
them are extraordinarily good, and with a goodness which is
a ground for national complacency. If American life is on the
whole, as I make no doubt whatever, more innocent than that
of any other country, nowhere is the fact more patent than
in Mr. Howells's novels, which exhibit so constant a study of
the actual and so small a perception of evil. His women,
in particular, are of the best—except, indeed, in the sense of
being the best to live with. Purity of life, fineness of conscience,
benevolence of motive, decency of speech, good nature, kindness, charity, tolerance (though, indeed, there is little but each
other's manners for the people to tolerate), govern all the scene;

the only immoralities are aberrations of thought, like that of
Silas Lapham, or excesses of beer, like that of Bartley Hubbard.
In the gallery of Mr. Howells's portraits there are none more
living than the admirable, humorous images of those two
ineffectual sinners. Lapham, in particular, is magnificent,
understood down to the ground, inside and out—a creation
which does Mr. Howells the highest honor. I do not say that
the figure of his wife is as good as his own, only because I wish
to say that it is as good as that of the minister's wife in the history of *Lemuel Barker,* which is unfolding itself from month
to month at the moment I write. These two ladies are exhaustive renderings of the type of virtue that worries. But everything in *Silas Lapham* is superior—nothing more so than the
whole picture of casual female youth and contemporaneous
"engaging" one's self, in the daughters of the proprietor of the
mineral paint.

This production had struck me as the author's highwater
mark, until I opened the monthly sheets of *Lemuel Barker,* in
which the art of imparting a palpitating interest to common
things and unheroic lives is pursued (or is destined, apparently,
to be pursued) to an even higher point. The four (or is it eight?)
repeated "good-mornings" between the liberated Lemuel and
the shopgirl who has crudely been the cause of his being locked
up by the police all night are a poem, an idyl, a trait of genius,
and a compendium of American good nature. The whole episode is inimitable, and I know fellow novelists of Mr. Howells's
who would have given their eyes to produce that interchange
of salutations, which only an American reader, I think, can
understand. Indeed, the only limitation, in general, to his extreme truthfulness is, I will not say his constant sense of the
comedy of life, for that is irresistible, but the verbal drollery
of many of his people. It is extreme and perpetual, but I fear
the reader will find it a venial sin. Theodore Colville, in *Indian
Summer,* is so irrepressibly and happily facetious as to make
one wonder whether the author is not prompting him a little,
and whether he could be quite so amusing without help from
outside. This criticism, however, is the only one I find it urgent

to make, and Mr. Howells doubtless will not suffer from my saying that, being a humorist himself, he is strong in the representation of humorists. There are other reflections that I might indulge in if I had more space. I should like, for instance, to allude in passing, for purposes of respectful remonstrance, to a phrase that he suffered the other day to fall from his pen (in a periodical, but not in a novel), to the effect that the style of a work of fiction is a thing that matters less and less all the while. Why less and less? It seems to me as great a mistake to say so as it would be to say that it matters more and more. It is difficult to see how it can matter either less or more. The style of a novel is a part of the execution of a work of art; the execution of a work of art is a part of its very essence, and that, it seems to me, must have mattered in all ages in exactly the same degree, and be destined always to do so. I can conceive of no state of civilization in which it shall not be deemed important, though of course there are states in which executants are clumsy. I should also venture to express a certain regret that Mr. Howells (whose style, in practice, after all, as I have intimated, treats itself to felicities which his theory perhaps would condemn) should appear increasingly to hold composition too cheap—by which I mean, should neglect the effect that comes from alternation, distribution, relief. He has an increasing tendency to tell his story altogether in conversations, so that a critical reader sometimes wishes, not that the dialogue might be suppressed (it is too good for that), but that it might be distributed, interspaced with narrative and pictorial matter. The author forgets sometimes to paint, to evoke the conditions and appearances, to build in the subject. He is doubtless afraid of doing these things in excess, having seen in other hands what disastrous effects that error may have; but all the same I cannot help thinking that the divinest thing in a valid novel is the compendious, descriptive, pictorial touch, *à la Daudet*.

It would be absurd to speak of Mr. Howells today in the encouraging tone that one would apply to a young writer who had given fine pledges, and one feels half guilty of that mistake if one makes a cheerful remark about his future. And yet we cannot pretend not to take a still more lively interest in his future than we have done in his past. It is hard to see how it can help being more and more fruitful, for his face is turned in the right direction, and his work is fed from sources which play us no tricks.

PREFACE TO *THE AMERICAN**

. . . If in "The American" I invoked the romantic association
without malice prepense, yet with a production of the romantic
effect that is for myself unmistakable, the occasion is of the
best perhaps for penetrating a little the obscurity of that principle. By what art or mystery, what craft of selection, omission or commission, does a given picture of life appear to us
to surround its theme, its figures and images, with the air of
romance while another picture close beside it may affect us
as steeping the whole matter in the element of reality? It is
a question, no doubt, on the painter's part, very much more
of perceived effect, effect *after* the fact, than of conscious
design—though indeed I have ever failed to see how a coher-
ent picture of anything is producible save by a complex of fine
measurements. The cause of the deflexion, in one pronounced
sense or the other, must lie deep, however; so that for the most
part we recognise the character of our interest only after the
particular magic, as I say, has thoroughly operated—and then

in truth but if we be a bit critically minded, if we find our pleasure, that is, in these intimate appreciations (for which, as I am well aware, ninety-nine readers in a hundred have no use whatever). The determining condition would at any rate seem so latent that one may well doubt if the full artistic consciousness ever reaches it; leaving the matter thus a case, ever, not of an author's plotting and planning and calculating, but just of his feeling and seeing, of his conceiving, in a word, and of his thereby inevitably expressing himself, under the influence of one value or the other. These values represent different sorts and degrees of the communicable thrill, and I doubt if any novelist, for instance, ever proposed to commit himself to one kind or the other with as little mitigation as we are sometimes able to find for him. The interest is greatest—the interest of his genius, I mean, and of his general wealth—when he commits himself in both directions; not quite at the same time or to the same effect, of course, but by some need of performing his whole possible revolution, by the law of some rich passion in him for extremes.

Of the men of largest responding imagination before the human scene, of Scott, of Balzac, even of the coarse, comprehensive, prodigious Zola, we feel, I think that the deflexion toward either quarter has never taken place; that neither the nature of the man's faculty nor the nature of his experience has ever quite determined it. His current remains therefore extraordinarily rich and mixed, washing us successively with the warm wave of the near and familiar and the tonic shock, as may be, of the far and strange. (In making which opposition I suggest not that the strange and the far are at all necessarily romantic: they happen to be simply the unknown, which is quite a different matter. The real represents to my perception the things we cannot possibly *not* know, sooner or later, in one way or another; it being but one of the accidents of our hampered state, and one of the incidents of their quantity and number, that particular instances have not yet come our way. The romantic stands, on the other hand, for the things that, with all the facilities in the world, all the wealth and all the courage and all the wit and all the adventure, we never *can* directly know; the things that can reach us only through the beautiful circuit and subterfuge of our thought and our desire.) There have been, I gather, many definitions of romance, as a matter indispensably of boats, or of caravans, or of tigers, or of "historical characters," or of ghosts, or of forgers, or of detectives, or of beautiful wicked women, or of pistols and knives, but they appear for the most part reducible to the idea of the facing of danger, the acceptance of great risks for the fascination, the very love, of their uncertainty, the joy of success if possible and of battle in any case. This would be a fine formula if it bore examination; but it strikes me as weak and inadequate, as by no means covering the true ground and yet as landing us in strange confusions.

The panting pursuit of danger is the pursuit of life itself, in which danger awaits us possibly at every step and faces us at every turn; so that the dream of an intenser experience easily becomes rather some vision of a sublime security like that enjoyed on the flowery plains of heaven, where we may conceive ourselves proceeding in ecstasy from one prodigious phase and form of it to another. And if it be insisted that the measure of the type is then in the *appreciation* of danger—the sign of our projection of the real being the smallness of its dangers, and that of our projection of the romantic the hugeness, the mark of the distinction being in short, as they say of collars and gloves and shoes, the size and "number" of the danger—this discrimination again surely fails, since it makes our difference not a difference of kind, which is what we want, but a difference only of degree, and subject by that condition to the indignity of a sliding scale and a shifting measure. There are immense and flagrant dangers that are but sordid and squalid ones, as we feel, tainting with their quality the very defiances they provoke; while there are common and covert ones, that "look like nothing" and that can be but inwardly and occultly dealt with, which involve the sharpest hazards to life and honour and the highest instant decisions and intrepidities of action. It is an arbitrary stamp that keeps these latter prosaic and makes the former heroic; and yet I should still less subscribe to a mere "subjective" division—I mean one that would place the difference wholly in the temper of the imperilled agent. It would be impossible to have a more romantic temper than Flaubert's Madame Bovary, and yet nothing less resembles a romance than the record of her adventures. To classify it by that aspect—the definition of the spirit that happens to animate her—is like settling the question (as I have seen it witlessly settled) by the presence or absence of "costume." Where again then does costume begin or end?— save with the "run" of one or another sort of play? We must reserve vague labels for artless mixtures.

The only *general* attribute of projected romance that I can see, the only one that fits all its cases, is the fact of the kind of experience with which it deals—experience liberated, so to speak; experience disengaged, disembroiled, disencumbered, exempt from the conditions that we usually know to attach to it and, if we wish so to put the matter, drag upon it, and operating in a medium which relieves it, in a particular interest, of the inconvenience of a *related,* a measurable state, a state subject to all our vulgar communities. The greatest intensity may so be arrived at evidently—when the sacrifice of community, of the "related" sides of situations, has not been too rash. It must to this end not flagrantly betray itself; we must even be kept if possible, for our illusion, from suspecting any sacrifice at all. The balloon of experience is in fact of course tied to the earth, and under that necessity we swing, thanks to a rope of remarkable length, in the more or less commodious car of the imagination; but it is by the rope we know where we are, and from the moment that cable is cut we are at large and unrelated: we only swing apart from the globe—though remaining as exhilarated, naturally, as we like, especially when all goes well. The art of the romancer is, "for the fun of it," insidiously to cut the cable, to cut it without our detecting him. What I have recognised then in "The American," much to my surprise and after long years, is that the experience here represented is the disconnected and uncontrolled experience— uncontrolled by our general sense of "the way things happen"— which romance alone more or less successfully palms off on us. It is a case of Newman's own intimate experience all, that being my subject, the thread of which, from beginning to end, is not once exchanged, however momentarily, for any other thread; and the experience of others concerning us, and concerning him, only so far as it touches him and as he recognises, feels or divines it. There is our general sense of the way things happen—it abides with us indefeasibly, as readers of fiction, from the moment we demand that our fiction shall be intelligible; and there is our particular sense of the way they don't happen, which is liable to wake up unless reflexion and criticism, in us, have been skilfully and successfully drugged. There are drugs enough, clearly—it is all a question of applying them with tact; in which case the way things don't happen may be artfully made to pass for the way things do.

Amusing and even touching to me, I profess, at this time of day, the ingenuity (worthy, with whatever lapses, of a better cause) with which, on behalf of Newman's adventure, this hocus-pocus is attempted: the value of the instance not being diminished either, surely, by its having been attempted in such evident good faith. Yes, all is romantic to my actual vision here, and not least so, I hasten to add, the fabulous felicity of my candour. The way things happen is frankly not the way in which they are represented as having happened, in Paris, to my hero: the situation I had conceived only saddled me with that for want of my invention of something better. The great house of Bellegarde, in a word, would, I now feel, given the circumstances, given the *whole* of the ground, have comported itself in a manner as different as possible from the manner to which my narrative commits it; of which truth, moreover, I am by no means sure that, in spite of what I have called my serenity, I had not all the while an uneasy suspicion. I had dug in my path, alas, a hole into which I was destined to fall. I was so possessed of my idea that Newman should be ill-used—which was the essence of my subject—that I attached too scant an importance to its fashion of coming about. Almost any fashion would serve, I appear to have assumed, that would give me my main chance for him; a matter depending not so much on the particular trick played him as on the interesting face presented by him to *any* damnable trick. So where I part com-

pany with *terra-firma* is in making that projected, that performed outrage so much more showy, dramatically speaking,
than sound. Had I patched it up to greater apparent soundness
my own trick, artistically speaking, would have been played; I
should have cut the cable without my reader's suspecting it.
I doubtless at the time, I repeat, believed I had taken my pre-
cautions; but truly they should have been greater, to impart
the air of truth to the attitude—that is first to the pomp and
circumstance, and second to the queer falsity—of the Bellegardes.

They would positively have jumped then, the Bellegardes,
at my rich and easy American, and not have "minded" in the
least any drawback—especially as, after all, given the pleasant palette from which I have painted him, there were few
drawbacks to mind. My subject imposed on me a group of close-
ly-allied persons animated by immense pretensions—which
was all very well, which might be full of the promise of interest: only of interest felt most of all in the light of comedy and
of irony. This, better understood, would have dwelt in the idea
not in the least of their not finding Newman good enough for
their alliance and thence being ready to sacrifice him, but in
that of their taking with alacrity everything he could give them,
only asking for more and more, and then adjusting their pretensions and their pride to it with all the comfort in life. Such
accommodation of the theory of a noble indifference to the
practice of a deep avidity is the real note of policy in forlorn
aristocracies—and I meant of course that the Bellegardes
should be virtually forlorn. . . .

PREFACE TO *THE PRINCESS CASAMASSIMA**

. . . This in fact I have ever found rather terribly the point—that
the figures in any picture, the agents in any drama, are interesting only in proportion as they feel their respective situations; since the consciousness, on their part, of the complication exhibited forms for us their link of connexion with it.
But there are degrees of feeling—the muffled, the faint, the
just sufficient, the barely intelligent, as we may say; and the
acute, the intense, the complete, in a word—the power to be
finely aware and richly responsible. It is those moved in this
latter fashion who "get most" out of all that happens to them
and who in so doing enable us, as readers of their record, as
participators by a fond attention, also to get most. Their being
finely aware—as Hamlet and Lear, say, are finely aware—*makes*
absolutely the intensity of their adventure, gives the maximum
of sense to what befalls them. We care, our curiosity and our
sympathy care, comparatively little for what happens to the
stupid, the coarse and the blind; care for it, and for the effects

*Reprinted with the permission of Charles Scribner's Sons from the Pref-
aces to Volumes II and V, *The Novels and Tales of Henry James,* Copyright
1907 Charles Scribner's Sons; renewal copyright 1935 Henry James and copyright 1908 Charles Scribner's Sons; renewal copyright 1936 Henry James (respectively).

of it, at the most as helping to precipitate what happens to the more deeply wondering, to the really sentient. Hamlet and Lear are surrounded, amid their complications, by the stupid and the blind, who minister in all sorts of ways to their recorded fate. Persons of markedly limited sense would, on such a principle as that, play a part in the career of my tormented youth; but he wouldn't be of markedly limited sense himself— he would note as many things and vibrate to as many occasions as I might venture to make him.

There wouldn't moreover simply be the question of his suffering—of which we might soon get enough; there would be the question of what, all beset and all perceptive, he should thus adventurously do, thus dream and hazard and attempt. The interest of the attitude and the act would be the actor's imagination and vision of them, together with the nature and degree of their felt return upon him. So the intelligent creature would be required and so some picture of his intelligence involved. The picture of an intelligence appears for the most part, it is true, a dead weight for the reader of the English novel to carry, this reader having so often the wondrous property of caring for the displayed tangle of human relations without caring for its intelligibility. The teller of a story is primarily, none the less, the listener to it, the reader of it, too; and, having needed thus to make it out, distinctly, on the crabbed page of life, to disengage it from the rude human character and the more or less gothic text in which it has been packed away, the very essence of his affair has been the *imputing* of intelligence. The basis of his attention has been that such and such an imbroglio has got started—on the page of life—because of something that some one has felt and more or less understood.

I recognise at the same time, and in planning "The Princess Casamassima" felt it highly important to recognise, the danger of filling too full any supposed and above all any obviously limited vessel of consciousness. If persons either tragically or comically embroiled with life allow us the comic or tragic value of their embroilment in proportion as their struggle is a measured and directed one, it is strangely true, none the less, that beyond a certain point they are spoiled for us by this carrying of a due light. They may carry too much of it for our credence, for our compassion, for our derision. They may be shown as knowing too much and feeling too much—not certainly for their remaining remarkable, but for their remaining "natural" and typical, for their having the needful communities with our own precious liability to fall into traps and be bewildered. It seems probable that if we were never bewildered there would never be a story to tell about us; we should partake of the superior nature of the all-knowing immortals whose annals are dreadfully dull so long as flurried humans are not, for the positive relief of bored Olympians, mixed up with them. Therefore it is that the wary reader for the most part warns the novelist against making his characters too *interpretative* of the muddle of fate, or in other words too divinely, too priggishly clever. "Give us plenty of bewilderment," this monitor seems to say, "so long as there is plenty of slashing out in the bewilderment too. But don't, we beseech you, give us too much intelligence; for intelligence—well, *endangers;* endangers not perhaps the slasher himself, but the very slashing, the subject-matter of any self-respecting story. It opens up too many considerations, possibilities, issues; it *may* lead the slasher into dreary realms where slashing somehow fails and falls to the ground."

That is well reasoned on the part of the reader, who can in spite of it never have an idea—or his earnest discriminations would come to him less easily—of the extreme difficulty, for the painter of the human mixture, of reproducing that mixture aright. "Give us in the persons represented, the subjects of the bewilderment (that bewilderment without which there would be no question of an issue or of the fact of suspense, prime implications in any story) as much experience as possible, but keep down the terms in which you report that experience, because we only understand the very simplest": such in effect are the words in which the novelist constantly hears himself addressed, such the plea made him by the would-be victims of his spell on behalf of that sovereign principle the economy of interest, a principle as to which their instinct is justly strong. He listens anxiously to the charge—nothing can exceed his own solicitude for an economy of interest; but feels himself all in presence of an abyss of ambiguities, the mutual accommodations in which the reader wholly leaves to him. Experience, as I see it, is our apprehension and our measure of what happens to us as social creatures—any intelligent report of which has to be based on that apprehension. The picture of the exposed and entangled state is what is required, and there are certainly always plenty of grounds for keeping down the complexities of a picture. A picture it still has to be, however, and by that condition has to deal effectually with its subject, so that the simple device of more and more keeping down may well not see us quite to our end or even quite to our middle. One suggested way of keeping down, for instance, is not to attribute feeling, or feelings, to persons who wouldn't in all probability have had any to speak of. The less space, within the frame of the picture, their feelings take up the more space is left for their doings—a fact that may at first seem to make for a refinement of economy.

All of which is charming—yet would be infinitely more so if here at once ambiguity didn't yawn; the unreality of the sharp distinction, where the interest of observation is at stake, between doing and feeling. In the immediate field of life, for action, for application, for getting through a job, nothing may so much matter perhaps as the descent of a suspended weight on this, that or the other spot, with all its subjective concomitants quite secondary and irrelevant. But the affair of the painter is not the immediate, it is the reflected field of life, the realm not of application, but of *appreciation*—a truth that makes our measure of effect altogether different. My report of people's experience—my report as a "story-teller"—is essentially my appreciation of it, and there is no "interest" for me in what my hero, my heroine or any one else does save through that admirable process. As soon as I begin to appreciate simplification is imperilled: the sharply distinguished parts of any adventure, any case of endurance and performance, melt together as an appeal. I then see their "doing," that of the persons just mentioned, as, immensely, their feeling, their feeling as their doing; since I can have none of the conveyed sense and taste of their situation without becoming intimate with them. I can't be intimate without that sense and taste, and I can't appreciate save by intimacy, any more than I can report save by a projected light. Intimacy with a man's specific behaviour, with his given case, is desperately certain to make us see it as a whole—in which event arbitrary limitations of our vision lose whatever beauty they may on occasion have pretended to. What a man thinks and what he feels are the history and the character of what he does; on all of which things the logic of intensity rests. Without intensity where is vividness, and without vividness where is presentability? If I have called the most general state of one's most exposed and assaulted figures the state of bewilderment—the condition for instance on which Thackeray so much insists in the interest of *his* exhibited careers, the condition of a humble heart, a bowed head, a patient wonder, a suspended judgement, before the "awful will" and the mysterious decrees of Providence—so it is rather witless to talk of merely getting rid of that displayed mode of reaction, one of the oft-encountered, one of the highly recommended, categories of feeling.

The whole thing comes to depend thus on the *quality* of bewilderment characteristic of one's creature, the quality involved in the given case or supplied by one's data. There are doubtless many such qualities, ranging from vague and crepuscular to sharpest and most critical; and we have but to imagine one of these latter to see how easily—from the moment it gets its head at all—it may insist on playing a part. There we have then at once a case of feeling, of ever so many possible feelings, stretched across the scene like an attached thread on which the pearls of interest are strung. There are threads shorter and less tense, and I am far from implying that the minor, the coarser and less fruitful forms and degrees of moral reaction, as we may conveniently call it, may not yield lively results. They have their subordinate, comparative, illustrative human value—that appeal of the witless which is often so penetrating. Verily even, I think, no "story" is possible without its fools—as most of the fine painters of life, Shakespeare, Cervantes and Balzac, Fielding, Scott, Thackeray, Dickens,

George Meredith, George Eliot, Jane Austen, have abundantly felt. At the same time I confess I never see the *leading* interest of any human hazard but in a consciousness (on the part
of the moved and moving creature) subject to fine intensifi-
cation and wide enlargement. It is as mirrored in that consciousness that the gross fools, the headlong fools, the fatal fools
play their part for us—they have much less to show us in themselves. The troubled life mostly at the centre of our subject—
whatever our subject, for the artistic hour, happens to be—embraces them and deals with them for its amusement and its
anguish: they are apt largely indeed, on a near view, to be all
the cause of its trouble. This means, exactly, that the person
capable of feeling in the given case more than another of what
is to be felt for it, and so serving in the highest degree to *record*
it dramatically and objectively, is the only sort of person on
whom we can count not to betray, to cheapen or, as we say,
give away, the value and beauty of the thing. By so much as
the affair matters *for* some such individual, by so much do
we get the best there is of it, and by so much as it falls within
the scope of a denser and duller, a more vulgar and more shallow capacity, do we get a picture dim and meagre.

The great chroniclers have clearly always been aware
of this; they have at least always either placed a mind of some
sort—in the sense of a reflecting and colouring medium—in
possession of the general adventure (when the latter has not
been purely epic, as with Scott, say, as with old Dumas and
with Zola); or else paid signally, as to the interest created, for
their failure to do so. We may note moreover in passing that
this failure is in almost no case intentional or part of a plan,
but has sprung from their limited curiosity, their short conception of the particular sensibility projected. Edgar of Ravenswood for instance, visited by the tragic tempest of "The
Bride of Lammermoor," has a black cloak and hat and feathers
more than he has a mind; just as Hamlet, while equally sabled
and draped and plumed, while at least equally romantic, has
yet a mind still more than he has a costume. The situation represented is that Ravenswood loves Lucy Ashton through dire
difficulty and danger, and that she in the same way loves him;

but the relation so created between them is by this neglect of the "feeling" question never shown us as primarily taking place. It is shown only in its secondary, its confused and disfigured aspects—where, however, luckily, it is presented with great romantic good faith. The thing has nevertheless paid for its deviation, as I say, by a sacrifice of intensity; the centre of the subject is empty and the development pushed off, all round, toward the frame—which is, so to speak, beautifully rich and curious. But I mention that relation to each other of the appearances in a particular work only as a striking negative case; there are in the connexion I have glanced at plenty of striking positive ones. It is very true that Fielding's hero in "Tom Jones" is but as "finely," that is but as intimately, bewildered as a young man of great health and spirits may be when he hasn't a grain of imagination: the point to be made is, at all events, that his sense of bewilderment obtains altogether on the comic, never on the tragic plane. He has so much "life" that it amounts, for the effect of comedy and application of satire, almost to his having a mind, that is to his having reactions and a full consciousness; besides which his author— *he* handsomely possessed of a mind—has such an amplitude of reflexion for him and round him that we see him through the mellow air of Fielding's fine old moralism, fine old humour and fine old style, which somehow really enlarge, make every one and every thing important. . . .

Hamlin Garland

NEW FIELDS*

The secret of every lasting success in art or literature lies, I
believe, in a powerful, sincere, emotional concept of life first,
and, second, in the acquired power to convey that concept
to others. This leads necessarily to individuality in authorship,
and to freedom from past models.

This *theory* of the veritist is, after all, a statement of his
passion for truth and for individual expression. The passion
does not spring from theory; the theory rises from the love
of the verities, which seems to increase day by day all over
the Western world.

The veritist, therefore, must not be taken to be dogmatic,
only so far as he is personally concerned. He is occupied in
stating his sincere convictions, believing that only in that way
is the cause of truth advanced. He addresses himself to the
mind prepared to listen. He destroys by displacement, not
by attacking directly.

It is a settled conviction with me that each locality must
produce its own literary record, each special phase of life utter

*Reprinted by permission of the publishers from Jane Johnson, editor;
Hamlin Garland, *Crumbling Idols*. Cambridge, Mass.: The Belknap Press of
Harvard University Press, Copyright, 1960, by the President and Fellows of
Harvard College.

its own voice. There is no other way for a true local expression to embody itself. The sun of truth strikes each part of the earth at a little different angle; it is this angle which gives life and infinite variety to literature. It is the subtle differences which life presents in California and Oregon, for example, which will produce, and justify, a Pacific-Coast literature.

In all that I have written upon local literature, I have told the truth as I saw it. That others did not see it in the same light, was to be expected. And in writing upon Pacific-Coast literature, undoubtedly I shall once more be stating the cause of veritism; for the question of Pacific-Coast literature is really the question of genuine American literature. The same principles apply to all sections of the land.

The mere fact that a writer happens to live in California or Oregon will not make him a part of that literature, any more than Stevenson's life in Samoa will make him a Samoan author. A nation, in the early part of its literary history, is likely to sweep together all that can, by any construction, be called its literature; but as it grows rich in real utterances, it eliminates one after the other all those writings which its clearer judgment perceives to be exotics.

The Pacific Coast is almost like another world. Its distance from New York and Boston, its semi-tropic plants, its strange occupations, place it in a section by itself, just as the rest of the nation falls naturally into New England, the South, the Middle States, and the Northwest; and, in the same way, from the Pacific States will continue to come a distinct local literature. Its vitality depends, in my judgment, upon this difference in quality.

I say "continue to come," because we can never overlook the great work done by Joaquin Miller and Bret Harte. They came to this strange new land, young and impressionable. They became filled with the life and landscape almost with the same power and sincerity as if they had been born here. Miller, especially, at his best, got far below superficial wonder. He attained the love for his subjects which is essential to sincere art. The best of his work could not have been produced anywhere else. It is native as Shasta.

But neither of these men must be taken for model. Veritism, as I understand it, puts aside all models, even living writers. Whatever he may do unconsciously, the artist must consciously stand alone before nature and before life. Nature and life have changed since Miller and Harte wrote. The California of to-day is quite different. The creative writer to-day, if true to himself, finds himself interested in other subjects, and finds himself believing in a different treatment of even the same material.

There is no necessity of treating the same material, however. Vast changes, already in progress, invite the writer. The coming in of horticulture, the immigration of farmers from all the Eastern States; the mingling of races; the feudalistic ownership of lands; the nomadic life of the farmhands, the growth of cities, the passing Spanish civilization,—these are a few of the subjects which occur to me as worthy [of] the best work of novelist and dramatist.

Being "a farmer by birth and a novelist by occupation," I saw most clearly the literary possibilities of the farmer's life in the valleys of California and in the stupendous forests of Oregon.

I saw children moving along to school in the shadow of the most splendid mountains; I saw a youth plowing,—behind him rose a row of palms, against which he stood like a figure of bronze in relief; I saw young men and maidens walking down aisles of green and crimson pepper-trees, and the aisles led to blue silhouetted mountains; I saw men herding cattle where the sun beat with hot radiance, and strange cacti held out wild arms; I saw children playing about cabins, setting at defiance the illimitable width and sunless depths of the Oregon forests,— and I thought, "Perhaps one of these is the novelist or painter of the future."

Perhaps the future poet of these spaces is plowing somewhere like that, because it must be that from the splendor and dramatic contrast of such scenes the poet will rise. He always has, and he always will. His feet will be on the soil like Whittier's, and like Miller's; his song will differ from theirs because he will be an individual soul, and because his time and his environment will not be the same.

Why should the Western artists and poets look away to

Greece and Rome and Persia for themes? I have met Western people who were writing blank-verse tragedies of the Middle Ages and painting pictures of sirens and cherubs, and still
considered themselves Western writers and Western artists!
The reason is not hard to find. They had not risen to the perception of the significant and beautiful in their own environment, or they were looking for effects, without regard to their
sincere conviction. They were poets of books, not of life.

This insincerity is fatal to any great work of art. A man
must be moved by something higher than money, by something higher than hope of praise; he must have a sleepless love
in his heart urging him to re-create in the image the life he has
loved. He must be burdened and without rest until he has given
birth to his conception. He will not be questioned when he
comes; he will be known as a product of some one time and
place, a voice speaking the love of his heart.

There was much of dross and effectism in Miller's earlier work, but it was filled with an abounding love of Sierra
mountains and forests and moving things, which made him
the great figure of the Coast. But the literature which is to come
from the Pacific slope, in my judgment, will be intimate and
human beyond any California precedent. It will not dodge
or equivocate. It will state the truth. It will not be spectacular,
it will not deal with the outside (as a tourist must do). It will
deal with the people and their home dramas, their loves and
their ambitions. It will not seek themes. Themes will crowd
upon them and move them.

The lovers who wander down the aisles of orange or lemon
or pepper trees will not marvel at blooms and shrubs. Their
presence and perfume will be familiar and lovely, not strange.
The stark lines of the fir and the broadsword-thrust of the ba-
nana-leaf will not attract their surprised look. All will be as
friendly and grateful as the maple or the Lombardy poplar
to the Iowa school-boy.

A new literature will come with the generation just coming
to manhood and womanhood on the Coast. If rightly educated,
their eyes will turn naturally to the wheat-fields, the forests,
the lanes of orange-trees, the ranges of unsurpassed mountains.

They will try to express in the novel, the drama, in painting and in song, the love and interest they take in the things close at hand.

This literature will not deal with crime and abnormities, nor with deceased persons. It will deal, I believe, with the wholesome love of honest men for honest women, with the heroism of labor, the comradeship of men,—a drama of average types of character, infinitely varied, but always characteristic.

In this literature will be the shadow of mountain-islands, the sweep of dun plains, and dark-blue mountain-ranges silhouetted against a burning yellow sky. It will deal with mighty forests and with man's brave war against the gloom and silence. It will have in it types of vanishing races, and prophecies of coming citizens. It will have the perfume of the orange and lemon trees, the purple dapple of spicy pepper-tree fruit, the grace of drooping, fern-like acacia leaves.

And in the midst of these sights and sounds, moving to and fro in the shadow of these mountains, and feeling the presence of this sea, will be men and women working out the drama of life in a new way, thinking new thoughts, building a happier, sunnier order of things, perhaps, where the laborer will face the winter always without fear and without despondency.

When the real Pacific literature comes, it will not be subject to misunderstanding. It will be such a literature as no other locality could produce, a literature that could not have been written in any other time, or among other surroundings. That is the test of a national literature.

THE LOCAL NOVEL*

The local novel seems to be the heir-apparent to the kingdom of poesy. It is already the most promising of all literary attempts to-day; certainly it is the most sincere. It seems but beginning its work. It is "hopelessly contemporaneous;" that is its strength. It is (at its best) unaffected, natural, emotional. It is sure to become all-powerful. It will redeem American literature, as it has already redeemed the South from its conventional and highly wrought romanticism.

By reason of growing truth and sincerity the fiction of the South has risen from the dead. It is now in the spring season of shooting wilding plants and timorous blades of sown grains. Its future is assured. Its soil is fertilized with the blood of true men. Its women are the repositories of great, vital, sincere, emotional experiences which will inevitably appear in their children, and at last in art, and especially in fiction. The Southern people are in the midst of a battle more momentous than the Rebellion, because it is the result of the Rebellion; that

*Reprinted by permission of the publishers from Jane Johnson, editor; Hamlin Garland, *Crumbling Idols.* Cambridge, Mass.: The Belknap Press of Harvard University Press, Copyright, 1960, by the President and Fellows of Harvard University.

is, the battle of intrenched privilege against the swiftly-spreading democratic idea of equality before the law and in the face of nature.

They have a terribly, mightily dramatic race-problem on their hands. The South is the meeting-place of winds. It is the seat of swift and almost incalculable change; and this change, this battle, this strife of invisible powers, is about to enter their fiction.

The negro has already entered it. He has brought a musical speech to his masters, and to the new fiction. He has brought a strange and pleading song into music. The finest writers of the New South already find him a never-failing source of interest. He is not, of course, the only subject of Southern fiction, nor even the principal figure; but he is a necessary part, and a most absorbingly interesting part.

The future of fiction in the South will also depict the unreconstructed rebel unreservedly, and the race-problem without hate or contempt or anger; for the highest art will be the most catholic in its sympathy. It will delineate vast contending forces, and it will be a great literature.

The negro will enter the fiction of the South, first, as subject; second, as artist in his own right. His first attempts will be imitative, but he will yet utter himself, as surely as he lives. He will contribute a poetry and a novel as peculiarly his own as the songs he sings. He may appear, also, in a strange half-song, half-chant, and possibly in a drama peculiar to himself; but in some form of fiction he will surely utter the sombre and darkly-florid genius for emotional utterance which characterizes him.

In the North the novel will continue local for some time to come. It will delineate the intimate life and speech of every section of our enormous and widely scattered republic. It will catch and fix in charcoal the changing, assimilating races, delineating the pathos and humor and the infinite drama of their swift adjustment to new conditions. California, New Mexico, Idaho, Utah, Oregon, each wonderful locality in our Nation of Nations will yet find its native utterance. The superficial work of the tourist and outsider will not do. The real novelist of these sections is walking behind the plow or trudging to school in these splendid potential environments.

This local movement will include the cities as well, and St. Louis, Chicago, San Francisco, will be delineated by artists born of each city, whose work will be so true that it could not have been written by any one from the outside. The real utterance of a city or a locality can only come when a writer is born out of its intimate heart. To such an one, nothing will be "strange" or "picturesque;" all will be familiar, and full of significance or beauty. The novel of the slums must be written by one who has played there as a child, and taken part in all its amusements; not out of curiosity, but out of pleasure seeking. It cannot be done from above nor from the outside. It must be done out of a full heart and without seeking for effect.

The artist should not look abroad to see how others are succeeding. Success does not always measure merit. It took nearly a third of a century for Whitman and Monet to be recognized. The great artist never conforms. He does not trail after some other man's success. He works out his individual perception of things.

The contrast of city and country, everywhere growing sharper, will find its reflection in this local novel of the immediate future,—the same tragedies and comedies, with the essential difference called local color, and taking place all over the land, wherever cities arise like fungi, unhealthy, yet absorbing as subjects of fictional art. . . .

Stephen Crane
OUIDA'S MASTERPIECE

Most of us forget Ouida. Childhood and childhood's differ-ent ideal is often required to make us rise properly to her height of sentiment. The poetic corner in the human head becomes too soon like some old dusty niche in a forgotten church. It is only occasionally that an ancient fragrance floats out to us, and then, usually, we do not recognize it. We apply some strange name and grin from the depths of our experience and wisdom. Perhaps it is rather a common habit to mistake a sort of a worldly complacence for knowledge.

For my part I had concluded that I had outgrown Ouida. I thought that I recognized the fact that her tears were care-fully moulded globules of the best Cornish tin and that her splendors were really of the substance of shadows on a gar-den wall. And yet a late reading of "Under Two Flags" affected me like some old and honest liquor. It is certainly a refresh-ment. The characters in this book abandon themselves to vir-tue and heroism as the martyrs abandoned themselves to flames. Sacrifice appears to them as the natural course. Pain, death, dishonor, is counted of no moment so long as the quality of personal integrity is defended and preserved. Certainly we may get good from a book of this kind. It imitates the literary plan of the early peoples. They sang, it seems, of nobility of character. To-day we sing of portières and champagne and gowns. "Under Two Flags" has to me, then, a fine ring in the gospel of life it preaches. I confess, of course, that I often find Beauty's perfections depressing. We men of doleful flaws are thrown into moods of profound gloom by the contemplation of such a bejewelled mind. We grow solemn and sad, and feel revengefully that we might like to touch a match to the hem of Beauty's sacred bath-robe, and see if we couldn't incite him to something profane and human—something like a real oath, or, at least, a fit of perfectly manly ill-temper.

Cigarette is finer. In Ouida's drawing of this secondary character we detect something accidental. With Cigarette the novelist did not take so much pains. She never intended Cigarette to be splendid, and perhaps this is why the girl appears to some of us as really the best character in the book. She is a figure of flesh among all these painted gods. She has imperfections, thank heaven, and it is very nice to come upon a good, sound imperfection when one has grown surfeited with the company of gods.

Nevertheless, with all the cavilling of our modern literary class, it is good to hear at times the song of the brave, and "Under Two Flags" is a song of the brave. To the eye of this time it is, of course, a thing of imperfect creation, but it voices nevertheless the old spirit of dauntless deed and sacrifice which is the soul of literature in every age, and we are not growing too tired to listen, although we try to believe so.

HAROLD FREDERIC

. . . It was in Central New York that Frederic was born, and it is there he passed his childish days and his young manhood. He enjoys greatly to tell how he gained his first opinions of the alphabet from a strenuous and enduring study of the letters on an empty soap-box. At an early age he was induced by his parents to arise at 5:30 A.M., and distribute supplies of milk among the worthy populace.

In his clubs, details of this story are well known. He pitilessly describes the gray shine of the dawn that makes the snow appear the hue of lead, and, moreover, his boyish pain at the task of throwing the stiff harness over the sleepy horse, and then the long and circuitous sledding among the customers of the milk route. There is no pretense in these accounts; many self-made men portray their early hardships in a spirit of purest vanity. "And now look!" But there is none of this in Frederic. He simply feels a most absorbed interest in that part of his career which made him so closely acquainted with the voluminous life of rural America. His boyhood extended through that time when the North was sending its thousands to the war, and the lists of dead and wounded were returning in due course. The great country back of the line of fight—the waiting women, the lightless windows, the tables set for three instead of five—was a land elate or forlorn, triumphant or despairing, always strained, eager, listening, tragic in attitude, trembling and quivering like a vast mass of nerves from the shock of the far away conflicts in the South. Those were supreme years, and yet for the great palpitating regions it seems that the mind of this lad was the only sensitive plate exposed to the sunlight of '61 - '65. The book, *In the Sixties,* which contains *The Copperhead, Marsena, The War Widow, The Eve of the Fourth,* and *My Aunt Susan,* breathes the spirit of a Titanic conflict as felt and endured at the homes. One would think that such a book would have taken the American people by storm, but it is true that an early edition of *The Copperhead* sold less than a thousand copies in America. We have sometimes a way of wildly celebrating the shadow of a mullein-stalk against the wall of a woodshed, and remaining intensely ignorant of the vital things that are ours. I believe that at about the time of the appearance of these stories, the critics were making a great deal of noise in an attempt to stake the novelists down to the soil and make them write the impressive common life of the United States. This virtuous struggle to prevent the novelists from going ballooning off over some land of dreams and candy-palaces was distinguished by the fact that, contemporaneously, there was Frederic doing his locality, doing his Mohawk Valley, with the strong trained hand of a great craftsman, and the critics were making such a din over the attempt to have a certain kind of thing done, that they did not recognize its presence. All this goes to show that there are some painful elements in the art of creating an American literature by what may be called the rattlety-bang method. The important figures, the greater men, rise silently, unspurred, undriven. To be sure, they may come in for magnificent cudgelings later, but their approach is noiseless, invincible, and they are upon us like ghosts before the critics have time to begin their clatter.

But there is something dismally unfortunate in the passing of *Seth's Brother's Wife, In the Valley,* the historical novel, and *The Lawton Girl.* Of course, they all had their success in measure, but here was a chance and a reason for every American to congratulate himself. Another thing had been done. For instance, *In the Valley* is easily the best historical novel that our country has borne. Perhaps it is the only good one. *Seth's Brother's Wife* and *The Lawton Girl* are rimmed with fine portrayals. There are writing men who, in some stories, dash over three miles at a headlong pace, and in an adjacent story move like a boat being sailed over ploughed fields; but in Frederic one feels at once the perfect evenness of craft, the undeviating worth of the workmanship. The excellence is always sustained, and these books form, with *In the Sixties,* a row of big American novels. But if we knew it we made no emphatic sign, and it was not until the appearance of *The Damnation of Theron Ware* that the book audiences really said: "Here is a writer!" If I make my moan too strong over this phase of the matter, I have only the excuse that I believe the *In the Sixties* stories to form a most notable achievement in writing times in America. Abner Beech, the indomitable and ferocious farmer, with his impregnable disloyalty or conscience, or whatever; Aunt Susan always at her loom making rag-carpets which, as the war deepened, took on two eloquent colors—the blue of old army overcoats and the black of woman's mourning; the guileless Marsena and the simple tragedy of his death—these characters represent to me living people, as if the book breathed. . . .

LETTERS
To Hamlin Garland*

[March ? 1893]

[Inscribed across the cover of a copy of *Maggie*][1]

It is inevitable that you will be greatly shocked by this book but continue please with all possible courage to the end. For it tries to show that environment is a tremendous thing in the world and frequently shapes lives regardless. If one proves that theory one makes room in Heaven for all sorts of souls (notably an occasional street girl) who are not confidently expected to be there by many excellent people.

It is probable that the reader of this small thing may consider the Author to be a bad man, but, obviously, this is a matter of small consequence to

The Author

*From *Stephen Crane Letters,* ed. by Stallman and Gilkes. Published by the New York University Press, Peter Owen Limited in the British Commonwealth, and from *Stephen Crane: Omnibus* published by Alfred H. Knopf, 1952 and William Heinemann Limited, 1954.

[1]Crane inscribed almost the same words on other copies of *Maggie* as well.

To John Northern Hilliard*

[*Ravensbrook, 1897?*]

. . . I have only one pride—and may it be forgiven me. This single pride is that the English edition of "The Red Badge" has been received with praise by the English reviewers. Mr. George Wyndham, Under Secretary for War in the British Government, says, in an essay,[1] that the book challenges comparison with the most vivid scenes of Tolstoi's "War and Peace" or of Zola's "Downfall"; and the big reviews here praise it for just what I intended it to be, a psychological portrayal of fear. They all insist that I am a veteran of the civil war, whereas the fact is, as you know, I never smelled even the powder of a sham battle. I know what the psychologists say, that a fellow can't comprehend a condition that he has never experienced, and I argued that many times with the Professor. Of course, I have never been in a battle, but I believe that I got my sense of the rage of conflict on the football field, or else

*From *Stephen Crane Letters,* ed. by Stallman and Gilkes. Published by the New York University Press, Peter Owen Limited in the British Commonwealth, and from *Stephen Crane: Omnibus* published by Alfred H. Knopf, 1952 and William Heinemann Limited, 1954.

[1]In *The New Review,* January, 1896.

fighting is a hereditary instinct, and I wrote intuitively; for
the Cranes were a family of fighters in the old days, and in the
Revolution every member did his duty. But be that as it may,
I endeavored to express myself in the simplest and most con-
cise way. If I failed, the fault is not mine. I have been very careful not to let any theories or pet ideas of my own creep into
my work. Preaching is fatal to art in literature. I try to give
to readers a slice out of life; and if there is any moral or lesson
in it, I do not try to point it out. I let the reader find it for himself. The result is more satisfactory to both the reader and myself. As Emerson said, "There should be a long logic beneath
the story, but it should be kept carefully out of sight." Before
"The Red Badge of Courage" was published, I found it difficult to make both ends meet. The book was written during
this period. It was an effort born of pain, and I believe that
it was beneficial to it as a piece of literature. It seems a pity
that this should be so—that art should be a child of suffering;
and yet such seems to be the case. Of course there are fine
writers who have good incomes and live comfortably and contentedly; but if the conditions of their lives were harder, I believe that their work would be better. Bret Harte is an example.
He has not done any work in recent years to compare with
those early California sketches. Personally, I like my little book
of poems, "The Black Riders," better than I do "The Red Badge
of Courage." The reason is, I suppose, that the former is the
more ambitious effort. In it I aim to give my ideas of life as a
whole, so far as I know it, and the latter is a mere episode, or
rather an amplification. Now that I have reached the goal, I
suppose that I ought to be contented; but I am not. I was happier in the old days when I was always dreaming of the thing I
have now attained. I am disappointed with success, and I am
tired of abuse. Over here, happily, they don't treat you as if you
were a dog, but give every one an honest measure of praise or
blame. There are no disgusting personalities.

Frank Norris

THE NOVEL WITH A "PURPOSE"

After years of indoctrination and expostulation on the part of the artists, the people who read appear at last to have grasped this one precept—"the novel must not preach," but "the purpose of the story must be subordinate to the story itself." It took a very long time for them to understand this, but once it became apparent they fastened upon it with a tenacity comparable only to the tenacity of the American schoolboy to the date "1492." "The novel must not preach," you hear them say.

As though it were possible to write a novel without a purpose, even if it is only the purpose to amuse. One is willing to admit that this savors a little of quibbling, for "purpose" and purpose to amuse are two different purposes. But every novel, even the most frivolous, must have some reason for the writing of it, and in that sense must have a "purpose."

Every novel must do one of three things—it must (1) tell something, (2) show something, or (3) prove something. Some novels do all three of these; some do only two; all must do at least one.

The ordinary novel merely tells something, elaborates a complication, devotes itself primarily to *things*. In this class comes the novel of adventure, such as "The Three Musketeers."

The second and better class of novel shows something,

exposes the workings of a temperament, devotes itself primarily to the minds of human beings. In this class falls the novel of character, such as "Romola."

The third, and what we hold to be the best class, proves something, draws conclusions from a whole congeries of forces, social tendencies, race impulses, devotes itself not to a study of men but of man. In this class falls the novel with the purpose, such as "Les Miserables."

And the reason we decide upon this last as the highest form of the novel is because that, though setting a great purpose before it as its task, it nevertheless includes, and is forced to include, both the other classes. It must tell something, must narrate vigorous incidents and must show something, must penetrate deep into the motives and character of typemen, men who are composite pictures of a multitude of men. It must do this because of the nature of its subject, for it deals with elemental forces, motives that stir whole nations. These can not be handled as abstractions in fiction. Fiction can find expression only in the concrete. The elemental forces, then, contribute to the novel with a purpose to provide it with vigorous action. In the novel, force can be expressed in no other way. The social tendencies must be expressed by means of analysis of the characters of the men and women who compose that society, and the two must be combined and manipulated to evolve the purpose—to find the value of x.

The production of such a novel is probably the most arduous task that the writer of fiction can undertake. Nowhere else is success more difficult; nowhere else is failure so easy. Unskilfully treated, the story may dwindle down and degenerate into mere special pleading, and the novelist become a polemicist, a pamphleteer, forgetting that, although his first consideration is to prove his case, his *means* must be living human beings, not statistics, and that his tools are not figures, but pictures from life as he sees it. The novel with a purpose *is,* one contends, a preaching novel. But it preaches by tellings things and showing things. Only, the author selects from the great storehouse of actual life the things to be told and the things to be shown which shall bear upon his problem, his purpose. The preaching, the moralizing, is the result not of direct appeal by the writer, but is made—should be made—to the reader by the very incidents of the story.

But here is presented a strange anomaly, a distinction as subtle as it is vital. Just now one has said that in the composition of the kind of novel under consideration the *purpose* is for the novelist the all-important thing, and yet it is impossible to deny that the *story,* as a mere story, is to the story-writer the one great object of attention. How reconcile then these two apparent contradictions?

For the novelist, the purpose of his novel, the problem he is to solve, is to his story what the keynote is to the sonata. Though the musician can not exaggerate the importance of the keynote, yet the thing that interests him is the sonata itself. The keynote simply co-ordinates the music, systematizes it, brings all the myriad little rebellious notes under a single harmonious code.

Thus, too, the purpose in the novel. It is important as an end and also as an ever-present guide. For the writer it is important only as a note to which his work must be attuned. The moment, however, that the writer becomes really and vitally interested in his purpose his novel fails.

Here is the strange anomaly. Let us suppose that Hardy, say, should be engaged upon a story which had for purpose to show the injustices under which the miners of Wales were suffering. It is conceivable that he could write a story that would make the blood boil with indignation. But he himself, if he is to remain an artist, if he is to write his novel successfully, will, as a novelist, care very little about the iniquitous labor system of the Welsh coal-mines. It will be to him as impersonal a thing as the key is to the composer of a sonata. As a man Hardy may or may not be vitally concerned in the Welsh coal-miner. That is quite unessential. But as a novelist, as an artist, his sufferings must be for him a matter of the mildest interest. They are important, for they constitute his keynote. They are *not* interesting for the reason that the working out of his *story,* its people, episodes, scenes, and pictures is for the moment the most interesting thing in all the world to him, exclusive of everything else. Do you think that Mrs. Stowe was more interested in the slave question than she was in the writing of "Uncle Tom's Cabin"? Her book, her manuscript, the page-to-page progress of the narrative, were more absorbing to her than all the Negroes that were ever whipped or sold. Had it not been so that great purpose-novel never would have succeeded.

Consider the reverse—"Fecondité," for instance. The purpose for which Zola wrote the book ran away with him. He really did care more for the depopulation of France than he did for his novel. Result—sermons on the fruitfulness of women, special pleading, a farrago of dry, dull incidents overburdened and collapsing under the weight of a theme that should have intruded only indirectly.

This is pre-eminently a selfish view of the question, but it is assuredly the only correct one. It must be remembered that the artist has a double personality: himself as a man, and himself as an artist. But, it will be urged, how account for the artist's sympathy in his fictitious characters, his emotion, the actual tears he sheds in telling of their griefs, their deaths, and the like?

The answer is obvious. As an artist his sensitiveness is quickened because they are characters in his novel. It does not at all follow that the same artist would be moved to tears over the report of parallel catastrophes in real life. As an artist, there is every reason to suppose he would welcome the news with downright pleasure. It would be for him "good material." He would see a story in it, a good scene, a great character. Thus the artist. What he would do, how he would feel as a man is quite a different matter.

To conclude, let us consider one objection urged against the novel with a purpose by the plain people who read. For certain reasons, difficult to explain, the purpose novel always ends unhappily. It is usually a record of suffering, a relation of tragedy. And the plain people say, "Ah, we see so much suffering in the world, why put it into novels? We do not want it in novels."

One confesses to very little patience with this sort. "We see so much suffering in the world already." Do they? Is this really true? The people who buy novels are the well-to-do people. They belong to a class whose whole scheme of life is concerned solely with an aim to avoid the unpleasant. Suffering, the great catastrophes, the social throes, that annihilate whole communities, or that crush even isolated individuals—all these are as far removed from them as earthquakes and tidal-waves. Or, even if it were so, suppose that by some miracle these blind eyes were opened and the sufferings of the poor, the tragedies of the house around the corner, really were laid bare. If there is much pain in life, all the more reason that it should appear in a class of literature which, in its highest form, is a sincere transcription of life.

It is the complaint of the coward, this cry against the novel with a purpose, because it brings the tragedies and griefs of others to notice. Take this element from fiction, take from it the power and opportunity to prove that injustice, crime, and inequality do exist, and what is left? Just the amusing novels, the novels that entertain. The juggler in spangles, with his balancing pole and gilt ball, does this. You may consider the modern novel from this point of view. It may be a flippant paper-covered thing of swords and cloaks, to be carried on a railway journey and to be thrown out the window when read, together with the sucked oranges and peanut shells. Or it may be a great force, that works together with the pulpit and the universities for the good of the people, fearlessly proving that power is abused, that the strong grind the faces of the weak, that an evil tree is still growing in the midst of the garden, that undoing follows hard upon unrighteousness, that the course of Empire is not yet finished, and that the races of men have yet to work out their destiny in those great and terrible movements that crush and grind and rend asunder the pillars of the houses of the nations.

Fiction may keep pace with the Great March, but it will

not be by dint of amusing the people. The Muse is a teacher, not a trickster. Her rightful place is with the leaders, but in the last analysis that place is to be attained and maintained not by cap-and-bells, but because of a serious and sincere interest, such as inspires the great teachers, the great divines, the great philosophers, a well-defined, well-seen, courageously sought-for purpose.

A PLEA FOR ROMANTIC FICTION

Let us at the start make a distinction. Observe that one speaks of romanticism and not sentimentalism. One claims that the latter is as distinct from the former as is that other form of art which is called Realism. Romance has been often put upon and overburdened by being forced to bear the onus of abuse that by right should fall to sentiment; but the two should be kept very distinct, for a very high and illustrious place will be claimed for romance, while sentiment will be handed down the scullery stairs.

Many people to-day are composing mere sentimentalism, and calling it and causing it to be called romance; so with those who are too busy to think much upon these subjects, but who none the less love honest literature, Romance, too, has fallen into disrepute. Consider now the cut-and-thrust stories. They are all labeled Romances, and it is very easy to get the impression that Romance must be an affair of cloaks and daggers, or moonlight and golden hair. But this is not so at all. The true Romance is a more serious business than this. It is not merely a conjurer's trick-box full of flimsy quackeries, tinsel and clap-traps, meant only to amuse, and relying upon deception to do even that. Is it not something better than this? Can we not see in it an instrument, keen, finely tempered, flawless—an instrument with which we may go straight through the clothes and tissues and wrappings of flesh down deep into the red, living heart of things?

Is all this too subtle, too merely speculative and intrinsic, too *precieuse* and nice and "literary"? Devoutly one hopes the contrary. So much is made of so-called Romanticism in present-day fiction that the subject seems worthy of discussion, and a protest against the misuse of a really noble and honest formula of literature appears to be timely—misuse, that is, in the sense of limited use. Let us suppose for the moment that a romance can be made out of a cut-and-thrust business. Good Heavens, are there no other things that are romantic, even in this—falsely, falsely called—humdrum world of today? Why should it be that so soon as the novelist addresses himself—seriously—to the consideration of contemporary life he must abandon Romance and take up the harsh, loveless, colorless, blunt tool called Realism?

Now, let us understand at once what is meant by Romance and what by Realism. Romance, I take it, is the kind of fiction that takes cognizance of variations from the type of normal life. Realism is the kind of fiction that confines itself to the type of normal life. According to this definition, then, Romance may even treat of the sordid, the unlovely—as, for instance, the novels of M. Zola. (Zola has been dubbed a Realist, but he is, on the contrary, the very head of the Romanticists.) Also, Realism, used as it sometimes is as a term of reproach, need not be in the remotest sense or degree offensive, but on the other hand respectable as a church and proper as a deacon—as, for instance, the novels of Mr. Howells.

The reason why one claims so much for Romance, and quarrels so pointedly with Realism is that Realism stultifies itself. It notes only the surface of things. For it, Beauty is not even skin deep, but only a geometrical plane, without dimensions and depth, a mere outside. Realism is very excellent so far as it goes, but it goes no further than the Realist himself can actually see, or actually hear. Realism is minute; it is the drama of a broken teacup, the tragedy of a walk down the block, the excitement of an afternoon call, the adventure of an

invitation to dinner. It is the visit to my neighbor's house, a formal visit, from which I may draw no conclusions. I see my neighbor and his friends—very, oh, such very! probable people—and
that is all. Realism bows upon the doormat and goes away and
says to me, as we link arms on the sidewalk: "That is life." And
I say it is not. It is not, as you would very well see if you took
Romance with you to call upon your neighbor.

Lately you have been taking Romance a weary journey
across the water—ages and the flood of years—and haling
her into the fuzzy, musty, worm-eaten, moth-riddled, rust-cor-
roded "Grandes Salles" of the Middle Ages and the Renaissance, and she has found the drama of a bygone age for you
there. But would you take her across the street to your neighbor's front parlor (with the bisque fisher-boy on the mantel and
the photograph of Niagara Falls on glass hanging in the front
window); would you introduce her there? Not you. Would you
take a walk with her on Fifth Avenue, or Beacon Street, or
Michigan Avenue? No, indeed. Would you choose her for a
companion of a morning spent in Wall Street, or an afternoon
in the Waldorf-Astoria? You just guess you would not.

She would be out of place, you say—inappropriate. She
might be awkward in my neighbor's front parlor, and knock
over the little bisque fisher-boy. Well, she might. If she did,
you might find underneath the base of the statuette, hidden
away, tucked away—what? God knows. But something that
would be a complete revelation of my neighbor's secretest
life.

So you think Romance would stop in the front parlor and
discuss medicated flannels and mineral waters with the ladies!
Not for more than five minutes. She would be off upstairs with
you, prying, peeping, peering into the closets of the bedroom,
into the nursery, into the sitting-room; yes, and into that little
iron box screwed to the lower shelf of the closet in the library;
and into those compartments and pigeon-holes of the *secre-
taire* in the study. She would find a heartache (maybe) between
the pillows of the mistress's bed, and a memory carefully secreted in the master's deed-box. She would come upon a great
hope amid the books and papers of the study-table of the young

man's room, and—perhaps—who knows?—an affair, or, great
Heavens, an intrigue, in the scented ribbons and gloves and
hairpins of the young lady's bureau. And she would pick here
a little and there a little, making up a bag of hopes and fears
and a package of joys and sorrows—great ones, mind you—and
then come down to the front door, and, stepping out into the
street, hand you the bags and package and say to you—"That
is Life!"

Romance does very well in the castles of the Middle Ages
and the Renaissance Chateaux, and she has the *entrée* there
and is very well received. That is all well and good. But let
us protest against limiting her to such places and such times.
You will find her, I grant you, in the chatelaine's chamber and
the dungeon of the man-at-arms; but, if you choose to look
for her, you will find her equally at home in the brownstone
house on the corner and in the office building downtown. And
this very day, in this very hour, she is sitting among the rags
and wretchedness, the dirt and despair of the tenements of
the East Side of New York.

"What?" I hear you say, "look for Romance—the lady
of the silken robes and golden crown, our beautiful, chaste
maiden of soft voice and gentle eyes—look for her among the
vicious ruffians, male and female, of Allen Street and Mulberry
Bend?" I tell you she is there, and to your shame be it said you
will not know her in those surroundings. You, the aristocrats,
who demand the fine linen and the purple in your fiction; you,
the sensitive, the delicate, who will associate with your Romance only so long as she wears a silken gown. You will not
follow her to the slums, for you believe that Romance should
only amuse and entertain you, singing you sweet songs and
touching the harp of silver strings with rosy-tipped fingers.
If haply she should call to you from the squalor of a dive, or
the awful degradation of a disorderly house, crying: "Look!
listen! This, too, is life. These, too, are my children! Look at
them, know them and, knowing, help!" Should she call thus
you would stop your ears; you would avert your eyes and you
would answer, "Come from there, Romance. Your place is
not there!" And you would make of her a harlequin, a tum-

bler, a sword-dancer, when, as a matter of fact, she should be by right divine a teacher sent from God.

She will not often wear the robe of silk, the golden crown, the jeweled shoon; will not always sweep the silver harp. An iron note is hers if so she choose, and coarse garments, and stained hands; and, meeting her thus, it is for you to know her as she passes—know her for the same young queen of the blue mantle and lilies. She can teach you if you will be humble to learn—teach you by showing. God help you if at last you take from Romance her mission of teaching; if you do not believe that she has a purpose—a nobler purpose and a mightier than mere amusement, mere entertainment. Let Realism do the entertainment with its meticulous presentation of teacups, rag carpets, wall-paper and haircloth sofas, stopping with these, going no deeper than it sees, choosing the ordinary, the untroubled, the commonplace.

But to Romance belongs the wide world for range, and the unplumbed depths of the human heart, and the mystery of sex, and the problems of life, and the black, unsearched penetralia of the soul of man. You, the indolent, must not always be amused. What matter the silken clothes, what matter the prince's houses? Romance, too, is a teacher, and if—throwing aside the purple—she wears the camel's-hair and feeds upon the locusts, it is to cry aloud unto the people, "Prepare ye the way of the Lord; make straight his path."

Theodore Dreiser

UNPUBLISHED REALISM*

. . . Be that as it may, this posthumous work,[1] never published, so far as I know, was the opening wedge for me into the realm of realism. Being distinctly imitative of Balzac and Zola, the method was new and to me impressive. It has always struck me as curious that the first novel written by an American that I read in manuscript should have been one which by reason of its subject matter and the puritanic character of the American mind could never be published. These two youths knew this. Hazard handed it to me with the statement: "Of course a thing like this could never be published over here. We'd have to get it done abroad." That struck me as odd at the time—the fact that if one wrote a fine thing nevertheless because of an American standard I had not even thought of before, one might not get it published. How queer, I thought. Yet these two incipient artists had already encountered it. They had been

*Reprinted by permission of The World Publishing Company and the Dreiser Trust from *A Book About Myself,* by Theodore Dreiser. Copyright © 1922 by Boni & Liveright, Inc., 1949 by Mrs. Theodore Dreiser. Title supplied by the editor.

[1]By Robert Hazard, one of Dreiser's colleagues on the St. Louis *Globe-Democrat,* and another writer, who had since died. The novel, *Theo,* was set in Paris, which neither author had ever visited.

overawed to the extent of thinking it necessary to write of French, not American life in terms of fact. Such things as they felt called upon to relate occurred only in France, never here— or at least such things, if done here, were never spoken of. I think it nothing less than tragic that these men, or boys, fresh, forceful, imbued with a burning desire to present life as they saw it, were thus completely overawed by the moral hypocrisy of the American mind and did not even dare to think of sending their novel to an American publisher. Hazard was deeply impressed with the futility of attempting to do anything with a book of that kind. The publishers wouldn't stand for it. You couldn't write about life as it was; you had to write about it as somebody else thought it was, the ministers and farmers and dullards of the home. Yet here he was, as was I, busy in a profession that was hourly revealing the fact that this sweetness and light code, this idea of a perfect world which contained neither sin nor shame for any save vile outcasts, criminals and vagrants, was the trashiest lie that was ever foisted upon an all too human world. Not a day, not an hour, but the pages of the very newspaper we were helping to fill with our scribbled observations were full of the most incisive pictures of the lack of virtue, honesty, kindness, even average human intelligence, not on the part of a few but of nearly everybody. Not a business, apparently, not a home, not a political or social organization or an individual but in the course of time was guilty of an infraction of some kind of this seemingly perfect and unbroken social and moral code. But in spite of all this, judging by the editorial page, the pulpit and the noble mouthings of the average citizen speaking for the benefit of his friends and neighbors, all men were honest—only they weren't; all women were virtuous and without evil intent or design—but they weren't; all mothers were gentle, self-sacrificing slaves, sweet pictures for songs and Sunday Schools—only they weren't; all fathers were kind, affectionate, saving, industrious— only they weren't. But when describing actual facts for the news columns, you were not allowed to indicate these things. Side by side with the most amazing columns of crimes of every kind and description would be other amazing columns of sweet

mush about love, undying and sacrificial, editorials about the
perfection of the American man, woman, child, his or her sweet
deeds, intentions and the like—a wonderful dose. And all this
last in the face of the other, which was supposed to represent
the false state of things, merely passing indecencies, accidental errors that did not count. If a man like Hazard or myself
had ventured to transpose a true picture of facts from the news
columns of the papers, from our own reportorial experiences, into a story or novel, what a howl! Ostracism would have
followed much more swiftly in that day than in this, for today
turgid slush approximating at least some of the facts is toler-
ated. Fifteen years later Hazard told me he still had his book
buried in a trunk somewhere, but by then he had turned to
adventurous fiction, and a year later, as I have said, he blew
his brains out. . . .

Upton Sinclair
ON HACK WRITING*

. . . I was a young shark, ready to devour everything in sight.
So for some months I performed the feat of turning out eight
thousand words every day, Sunday included. I tell this to literary men, and they say it could not be done; but I actually
did it, at least until the end of the Spanish-American War. I
kept two stenographers working all the time, taking dictation
one day and transcribing the next. In the afternoon I would
dictate for about three hours, as fast as I could talk; in the evening I would revise the copy that had been brought in from the
previous day, and then take a long walk and think up the incidents of my next day's stunt. That left me mornings to attend
lectures at Columbia University and to practice the violin.
I figured out that by the time I finished this potboiling I had
published an output equal in volume to the works of Walter
Scott.

What was the effect of all this upon me as a writer? It both
helped and hurt. It taught me to shape a story and to hold in
mind what I had thought up; so it fostered facility. On the other
hand, it taught me to use exaggerated phrases and clichés,

*From *The Autobiography of Upton Sinclair* © 1962 by Upton Sinclair.
Reprinted by permission of Harcourt, Brace & World, Inc. Title supplied by
the editor.

and this is something I have fought against, not always successfully. Strange as it may seem, I actually enjoyed the work while I was doing it. Not merely was I earning a living and putting away a little money; I had a sense of fun, and these adventures were a romp. It is significant that the stories pleased their public only so long as they pleased their author. When, at the age of twenty-one, I became obsessed with the desire to write a serious novel, I came to loathe this hackwork, and from that time on I was never able to do it with success, even though, driven by desperate need, I several times made the effort. It was the end of my youth. . . .

BEGINNING *THE JUNGLE**

. . . So, in October 1904 I set out for Chicago, and for seven weeks lived among the wage slaves of the Beef Trust, as we called it in those days. People used to ask me afterward if I had not spent my life in Chicago, and I answered that if I had done so, I could never have written *The Jungle;* I would have taken for granted things that now hit me a sudden violent blow. I went about, white-faced and thin, partly from undernourishment, partly from horror. It seemed to me I was confronting a veritable fortress of oppression. How to breach those walls, or to scale them, was a military problem.

I sat at night in the homes of the workers, foreign-born and native, and they told me their stories, one after one, and I made notes of everything. In the daytime I would wander about the yards, and my friends would risk their jobs to show me what I wanted to see. I was not much better dressed than the workers, and found that by the simple device of carrying a dinner pail I could go anywhere. So long as I kept moving, no one would heed me. When I wanted to make careful observations, I would pass again and again through the same room.

*From *The Autobiography of Upton Sinclair* © 1962 by Upton Sinclair, Reprinted by permission of Harcourt, Brace & World, Inc. Title supplied by the editor.

I went about the district, talking with lawyers, doctors, dentists, nurses, policemen, politicians, real-estate agents— every sort of person. I got my meals at the University Settlement, where I could check my data with the men and women who were giving their lives to this neighborhood. When the book appeared, they were a little shocked to find how bad it seemed to the outside world; but Mary MacDowell and her group stood by me pretty bravely—considering that the packers had given them the cots on which the strike breakers had slept during their sojourn inside the packing plants in violation of city laws!

I remember being invited to Hull House to dinner and sitting next to the saintly Jane Addams. I got into an argument with her consecrated band, and upheld my contention that the one useful purpose of settlements was the making of settlement workers into socialists. Afterward Jane Addams remarked to a friend that I was a young man who had a great deal to learn. Both she and I went on diligently learning, so that when we met again, we did not have so much to argue over.

One stroke of good fortune for me was the presence in Chicago of Adolphe Smith, correspondent of the *Lancet*, the leading medical paper of Great Britain. Smith was one of the founders of the Social-Democratic Federation in England, and at the same time an authority on abattoirs, having studied the packing plants of the world for the *Lancet*. Whenever I was in doubt about the significance of my facts—when I wondered if possibly my horror might be the oversensitiveness of a young idealist—I would fortify myself by Smith's expert, professional horror. "These are not packing plants at all," he declared; "these are packing boxes crammed with wage slaves."

At the end of a month or more, I had my data and knew the story I meant to tell, but I had no characters. Wandering about "back of the yards" one Sunday afternoon I saw a wedding party going into the rear room of a saloon. There were several carriages full of people. I stopped to watch, and as they seemed hospitable, I slipped into the room and stood against the wall. There the opening chapter of *The Jungle* began to take form. There were my characters—the bride, the groom, the old mother and father, the boisterous cousin, the children, the three musicians, everybody. I watched them one after another, fitted them into my story, and began to write the scene in my mind, going over it and over, as was my custom, fixing it fast. I went away to supper, and came back again, and stayed until late at night, sitting in a chair against the wall, not talking to anyone, just watching, imagining, and engraving the details on my mind. It was two months before I got settled at home and first put pen to paper; but the story stayed, and I wrote down whole paragraphs, whole pages, exactly as I had memorized them. . . .

Edith Wharton

ON INSPIRATION*

. . . Many people assume that the artist receives, at the out-set of his career, the mysterious sealed orders known as "In-spiration," and has only to let that sovereign impulse carry him where it will. Inspiration does indeed come at the outset to every creator, but it comes most often as an infant, help-less, stumbling, inarticulate, to be taught and guided; and the beginner, during this time of training his gift, is as likely to misuse it as a young parent to make mistakes in teaching his first child.

There is no doubt that in this day of general "speeding up," the "inspirational" theory is seductive even to those who care nothing for easy triumphs. No writer—especially at the beginning of his career—can help being influenced by the qual-ity of the audience that awaits him; and the young novelist may ask of what use are experience and meditation, when his readers are so incapable of giving him either. The answer is that he will never do his best till he ceases altogether to think

*Reprinted with the permission of Charles Scribner's Sons from *The Writing of Fiction,* pages 20-23 and 73-75 by Edith Wharton. Copyright © 1925 Charles Scribner's Sons; renewal copyright 1953 Frederic R. King. Title supplied by the editor.

of his readers (and his editor and his publisher) and begins
to write, not for himself, but for that *other self* with whom the
creative artist is always in mysterious correspondence, and
who, happily, has an objective existence somewhere, and will
some day receive the message sent to him, though the sender
may never know it. As to experience, intellectual and moral,
the creative imagination can make a little go a long way, provided it remains long enough in the mind and is sufficiently
brooded upon. One good heart-break will furnish the poet
with many songs, and the novelist with a considerable number of novels. But they must have hearts that can break.

Even to the writer least concerned with popularity it is
difficult, at first, to defend his personality. Study and meditation contain their own perils. Counsellors intervene with
contradictory advice and instances. In such cases these counsellors are most often other people's novels: the great novels
of the past, which haunt the beginner like a passion, and the
works of his contemporaries, which pull him this way and that
with too-persuasive hands. His impulse, at first, will be either
to shun them, to his own impoverishment, or to let his dawn-
ing individuality be lost in theirs; but gradually he will come
to see that he must learn to listen to them, take all they can
give, absorb it into himself, and then turn to his own task with
the fixed resolve to see life only through his own eyes.

Even then another difficulty remains; the mysterious dis-
crepancy which sometimes exists between a novelist's vision
of life and his particular kind of talent. Not infrequently an
innate tendency to see things in large masses is combined with
the technical inability to render them otherwise than separate-
ly, meticulously, on a small scale. Perhaps more failures than
one is aware of are due to this particular lack of proportion
between the powers of vision and expression. At any rate, it
is the cause of some painful struggles and arid dissatisfactions;
and the only remedy is resolutely to abandon the larger for
the smaller field, to narrow one's vision to one's pencil, and
do the small thing closely and deeply rather than the big thing
loosely and superficially. Of twenty subjects that tempt the

imagination (subjects one sees one's self doing, oh so wonderfully, if only one were Merimee or Maupassant, or Conrad
or Mr. Kipling!) probably but one is "fit for the hand" of the
limited person one happens to be; and to learn to renounce
the others is a first step toward doing that particular one
well. . . .

THE USE OF DIALOGUE*

. . . The use of dialogue in fiction seems to be one of the few
things about which a fairly definite rule may be laid down.
It should be reserved for the culminating moments, and regarded as the spray into which the great wave of narrative
breaks in curving toward the watcher on the shore. This lifting
and scattering of the wave, the coruscation of the spray, even
the mere material sight of the page broken into short, uneven
paragraphs, all help to reinforce the contrast between such
climaxes and the smooth effaced gliding of the narrative intervals; and the contrast enhances that sense of the passage
of time for the producing of which the writer has to depend
on his intervening narration. Thus the sparing use of dialogue
not only serves to emphasize the crises of the tale but to give
it as a whole a greater effect of continuous development.

Another argument against the substitution of dialogue
for narrative is the wastefulness and round-aboutness of the
method. The greater effect of animation, of presentness,
produced by its excessive use will not help the reader through

*Reprinted with the permission of Charles Scribner's Sons from *The
Writing of Fiction,* pages 20-23 and 73-75 by Edith Wharton. Copyright 1925
Charles Scribner's Sons; renewal copyright 1953 Frederic R. King. Title supplied
by the editor.

more than half the book, whatever its subject; after that he will perceive that he is to be made to pay before the end for his too facile passage through the earlier chapters. The reason is inherent in the method. When, in real life, two or more people are talking together, all that is understood between them is left out of their talk; but when the novelist uses conversation as a means not only of accentuating but of carrying on his tale, his characters have to tell each other many things that each already knows the other knows. To avoid the resulting shock of improbability, their dialogue must be so diluted with irrelevant touches of realistic commonplace, with what might be described as by-talk, that, as in the least good of Trollope's tales, it rambles on for page after page before the reader, resignedly marking time, arrives, bewildered and weary, at a point to which one paragraph of narrative could have carried him.

THE WRITER'S NEED FOR ENCOURAGEMENT*

. . . I have often wondered, in looking back at the slow stammering beginnings of my literary life, whether or not it is a good thing for the creative artist to grow up in an atmosphere where the arts are simply nonexistent. Violent opposition might be a stimulus—but was it helpful or the reverse to have every aspiration ignored, or looked at askance? I have thought over this many times, as I have over most problems of creative art, in the fascinating but probably idle attempt to discover *how it is all done,* and exactly what happens at that "fine point of the soul" where the creative act, like the mystic's union with the Unknowable, really seems to take place. And as I have grown older my point of view has necessarily changed, since I have seen more and more would-be creators, whether in painting, music or letters, whose way has been made smooth from the cradle, geniuses whose families were prostrate before them before they had written a line or composed a measure, and who, in middle age, still sat in ineffectual ecstasy before the blank page or the empty canvas; while, on the other hand, more and more of the baffled, the derided or the ignored have fought their way to achievement. The conclusion is that I am no believer in pampered vocations, and that Schopenhauer's *Was Einer ist* seems to me the gist of the matter. But as regards a case like my own, where a development no doubt naturally slow was certainly retarded by the indifference of every one about me, it is hard to say whether or no I was really hindered. I am inclined to think the drawbacks were outweighed by the advantages; chief among these being the fact that I escaped all premature flattery, all local celebrity, that I had to fight my way to expression through a thick fog of indifference, if not of tacit disapproval, and that when at last I met one or two kindred minds their criticisms were to me as sharp and searching as if they had been professionals in the exercise of their calling. Fortunately the fact that they were personal friends did not affect their judgment, and my craft was held in such small account in the only world I knew that I was always able to take the severest criticism without undue sensitiveness, and not unusually to profit by it. The criticism I have in mind is that given in the course of private talk, and not imparted by the reviews. I have no quarrel with the professional critics, who have often praised me beyond my merits; but the man who has to review fifty books a week, often on a great variety of subjects, can hardly deal as satisfactorily with any one of them as the friend talking over a book with a friend, and I have always found this kind of comment the most helpful. . . .

PASSION AND PATHOLOGY*

. . . My career began in the days when Thomas Hardy, in order to bring out "Jude the Obscure" in a leading New York periodical, was compelled to turn the children of Jude and Sue into adopted orphans; when the most popular young people's magazine in America excluded all stories containing any reference to "religion, love, politics, alcohol or fairies" (this is textual); the days when a well-known New York editor, offering me a large sum for the serial rights of a projected novel, stipulated only that no reference to "an unlawful attachment" should figure in it; when Theodore Roosevelt gently rebuked me for not having caused the reigning Duke of Pianura (in "The Valley of Decision") to make an honest woman of the humble bookseller's daughter who loved him; and when the translator of Dante, my beloved friend, Professor Charles Eliot Norton, hearing (after the appearance of "The House of Mirth") that I was preparing another "society" novel, wrote in alarm imploring me to remember that "no great work of the imagination has ever been based on illicit passion"!

The poor novelists who were my contemporaries (in English-speaking countries) had to fight hard for the right to turn

*Copyright 1933 Edith Wharton, Copyright © renewed 1961 Wm R. Tyler. Title supplied by the editor.

the wooden dolls about which they were expected to make believe into struggling suffering human beings; but we have been avenged, and more than avenged, not only by life but by the novelists, and I hope the latter will see before long that it is as hard to get dramatic interest out of a mob of irresponsible criminals as out of the Puritan marionettes who formed our stock-in-trade. Authentic human nature lies somewhere between the two, and is always there for a new great novelist to rediscover.

The amusing thing about this turn of the wheel is that we who fought the good fight are now jeered at as the prigs and prudes who barred the way to complete expression—as perhaps we should have tried to do, had we known it was to cause creative art to be abandoned for pathology! . . .

Ellen Glasgow

THE SHELTERED LIFE*

Nothing, except the weather report or a general maxim of conduct, is so unsafe to rely upon as a theory of fiction. Every great novel has broken many conventions. The greatest of all novels defies every formula; and only Mr. Percy Lubbock believed that *War and Peace* would be greater if it were another, and an entirely different, book. By this I do not mean to question Mr. Lubbock's critical insight. *The Craft of Fiction* is the best work in its limited field, and it may be studied to advantage by any novelist. In the first chapters there is a masterly analysis of *War and Peace*. Yet, after reading this with appreciation, I still think that Tolstoy was the best judge of what his book was about and how long it should be.

This brings us, in the beginning, to the most sensitive, and, therefore, the most controversial, point in the criticism of prose fiction. It is the habit of overworked or frugal critics to speak as if economy were a virtue, and not a necessity. Yet there are faithful readers who feel with me that a good novel cannot be too long or a bad novel too short. Our company is small but picked with care, and we would die upon the literary barricade defending the noble proportions of *War*

*From *A Certain Measure,* copyright 1938, 1943, by Ellen Glasgow. Reprinted by permission of Harcourt, Brace & World, Inc.

and Peace, of *The Brothers Karamazov,* of *Clarissa Harlowe* in eight volumes, of *Tom Jones,* of *David Copperfield,* of *The Chronicles of Barsetshire,* of *A la Recherche du Temps Perdu,* of *Le Vicomte de Bragelonne.* Tennyson was with us when he said he had no criticism to make of *Clarissa,* except that it might have been longer.

The true novel (I am not concerned with the run-of-the-mill variety) is, like pure poetry, an act of birth, not a device or an invention. It awaits its own time and has its own way to be born and it cannot, by scientific methods, be pushed into the world from behind. After it is born, a separate individual, an organic structure, it obeys its own vital impulses. The heart quickens; the blood circulates; the pulses beat; the whole body moves in response to some inward rhythm; and in time the expanding vitality attains its full stature. But until the breath of life enters a novel, it is as spiritless as inanimate matter.

Having said this much, I may confess that spinning theories of fiction is my favourite amusement. This is, I think, a good habit to cultivate. The exercise encourages readiness and agility while it keeps both head and hand in practice. Besides, if it did nothing else, it would still protect one from the radio and the moving picture and other sleepness, if less sinister, enemies to the lost mood of contemplation. This alone would justify every precept that was ever evolved. Although a work of fiction may be written without a formula or a method, I doubt if the true novel has ever been created without the long brooding season.

I have read, I believe, with as much interest as if it were a novel itself, every treatise on the art of fiction that appeared to me to be promising. That variable branch of letters shares with philosophy the favourite shelf in my library. I know all that such sources of learning as Sir Leslie Stephen, Sir Walter Raleigh, Mr. Percy Lubbock, Sir Arthur Quiller-Couch, Mr. E. M. Forster, and others less eminent, but often more earnest, were able to teach me, or I was able to acquire. Indeed, I know more than they could teach me, for I know also how very little their knowledge can help one in the actual writing of novels. If I were giving advice to a beginner (but there are

no beginners nowadays, there is only the inspired amateur
or the infant pathologist), I should say, probably, something
like this: "Learn the technique of writing, and having learned
it thoroughly, try to forget it. Study the principles of construction, the value of continuity, the arrangement of masses, the
consistent point of view, the revealing episode, the careful
handling of detail, and the fatal pitfalls of dialogue. Then, having mastered, if possible, every rule of thumb, dismiss it into
the labyrinth of the memory. Leave it there to make its own signals and flash its own warnings. The sensitive feeling, "this
is not right" or "something ought to be different" will prove that
these signals are working. Or, perhaps, this inner voice may
be only the sounder instinct of the born novelist.

The truth is that I began being a novelist, as naturally as
I began talking or walking, so early that I cannot remember
when the impulse first seized me. Far back in my childhood,
before I had learned the letters of the alphabet, a character
named Little Willie wandered into the country of my mind,
just as every other major character in my novels has strolled
across my mental horizon when I was not expecting him, when
I was not even thinking of the novel in which he would finally take his place. From what or where he had sprung, why he
was named Little Willie, or why I should have selected a hero
instead of a heroine—all this is still as much of a mystery to
me as it was in my childhood. But there he was, and there he
remained, alive and active, threading his own adventures, from
the time I was three until I was seven or eight, and discovered
Hans Andersen and *Grimms' Fairy Tales*. Every night, as I
was undressed and put to bed by my coloured Mammy, the
romance of Little Willie would begin again exactly where it
had broken off the evening before. In winter, I was undressed
in the firelight on the hearth-rug; but in summer, we moved over
to an open window, which looked out on the sunset, and presently on the first stars in the long green twilight. For years
Little Willie lasted, never growing older, always pursuing his
own narrative and weaving his situations out of his own personality. I can still see him, small, wiry, with lank brown hair
like a thatch, and eyes that seemed to say, "I know a secret!

I know a secret!" Hans Andersen and the brothers Grimm were his familiar companions. He returned once, though somewhat sadly, after I had read all the Waverley Novels; but when I was twelve years old and entered the world of Dickens, he vanished forever.

In those earliest formative years Little Willie outlined, however vaguely, a general pattern of work. He showed me that a novelist must write, not by taking thought alone, but with every cell of his being, that nothing can occur to him that may not sooner or later find its way into his craft. Whatever happened to me or to Mammy Lizzie happened also, strangely transfigured, to Little Willie. I learned, too, and never forgot, that ideas would not come to me if I went out to hunt for them. They would fly when I pursued; but if I stopped and sank down into a watchful reverie,they would flock back again like friendly pigeons. All I had to do before the novel had formed was to leave the creative faculty (or subconscious mind) free to work its own way without urging and without effort. After Dorinda in *Barren Ground* first appeared to me, I pushed her back into some glimmering obscurity, where she remained, buried but alive, for a decade, when she emerged from the yeasty medium with hard round limbs and the bloom of health in her cheeks. Thus I have never wanted for subjects; but on several occasions when, because of illness or from external compulsion, I have tried to invent, rather than subconsciously create, a theme or a character, invariably the effort has resulted in failure. These are the anaemic offspring of the brain, not children of my complete being; and a brood whom I would wish, were it possible, to disinherit.

It is not easy to tell how much of this dependence upon intuition may be attributed to the lack of harmony between my inner life and my early environment. A thoughtful and imaginative child, haunted by that strange sense of exile which visits the subjective mind when it is unhappily placed (and always, apparently, it is unhappily placed or it would not be subjective), I grew up in a charming society, where ideas were accepted as naturally as the universe or the weather, and cards for the old, dancing for the young, and conversation flavoured

with personalities for the middle-aged, were the only arts practised. Several members of my family, it is true, possessed brilliant minds, and were widely and deeply read; but all despised
what they called "local talent"; and my early work was written
in secret to escape ridicule, alert, pointed, and not the less destructive because it was playful. There is more truth than wit in
the gibe that every Southern novelist must first make his reputation in the North. Perhaps this is why so many Southern novelists write of the South as if it were a fabulous country. When
a bound copy of my first book reached me, I hid it under
my pillow while a cousin, who had run in for breakfast, prat-
tled beside my bed of the young men who had quarrelled over
the privilege of taking her to the Easter German, as the Co-
tillion was called. Had I entered the world by way of Oxford,
or even by way of Bloomsbury, I might now be able to speak
or write of my books without a feeling of outraged reserve.
And yet, in the very act of writing these words, my literary
conscience, a nuisance to any writer, inquires if ideas were
really free at Oxford, or even in Bloomsbury, at the end of the
century, and if all the enfranchised spirits who nowadays bab-
ble of prohibited subjects are either wiser or better than the
happy hypocrites of the 'nineties.

From this dubious prelude it might be inferred that I consider the craft of fiction merely another form of mental iner-
tia. On the contrary, I agree with those writers who have found
actual writing to be the hardest work in the world. What I am
concerned with at the moment, however, is the beginning of
a novel alone, not the endless drudgery that wrung from Stevenson the complaint, "The practice of letters is miserably
harassing to the mind; and after an hour or two's work, all the
more human portion of an author is extinct; he will bully, back-
bite, and speak daggers." For being a true novelist, even if one's
work is not worth the price of a cherry to public or publisher,
takes all that one has to give and still something more. Yet the
matter is not one of choice, but of fatality. As with the enjoyment of music, or a love for El Greco, or a pleasure in garden-
ing, or the taste for pomegranates, or a liking for Santayana's
prose, the bent of nature is either there or it is not there.

For my own part, the only method I have deliberately cultivated has been a system of constant renewal. If novels should be, as Sir Leslie Stephen has said, "transfigured experience," then I have endeavoured, whenever it was possible, to deepen experience and to heighten what I prefer to call illumination, to increase my understanding of that truth of life which has not ever become completely reconciled with the truth of fiction. I do not mean by this that life should necessarily be eventful or filled with variable activities. Profound emotion does not inevitably bear "the pageant of a bleeding heart." Several of the most thrilling lives in all literature were lived amid the unconquerable desolation of the Yorkshire moors. Yet it is doubtful if either the exposed heart of Byron or the brazen trumpet of D. H. Lawrence contained such burning realities as were hidden beneath the quiet fortitude of Emily Brontë.

Because of some natural inability to observe and record instead of create, I have never used an actual scene until the impression it left had sifted down into imagined surroundings. A theme becomes real to me only after it is clothed in living values; but these values must be drawn directly from the imagination and indirectly, if at all, from experience. Invariably the characters appear first, and slowly and gradually build up their own world, and spin the situation and atmosphere out of themselves. Strangely enough, the horizon of this real or visionary world is limited by the impressions or recollections of my early childhood. If I were to walk out into the country and pick a scene for a book, it would remain as flat and lifeless as cardboard; but the places I loved or hated between the ages of three and thirteen compose an inexhaustible landscape of memory. Occasionally, it is true, I have returned to a scene to verify details, though for freshness and force I have trusted implicitly to the vision within. And just as my scene is built up from fragments of the past, whether that past existed in fact or in a dream, so the human figures, though not one of them has been copied from my acquaintances, will startle me by displaying a familiar trait or gesture, and I will recognize with a shock some special blending of characteristics.

Frequently these impressions had been buried so long and so deep that I had entirely forgotten them until they floated upward to the surface of thought. Yet they were not dead but living, and recovered warmth and animation after the creative faculty had revived them. In the same way, half-obliterated images, events, or episodes, observed in moments of intense experience, will flash back into a scene or a figure; and this is equally true of the most trivial detail my memory has registered. For example, in one of the tragic hours of my youth, I looked out of a window and saw two sparrows quarrelling in the rain on a roof. Twenty years or more afterwards, a character in one of my novels looks out of a window, in a moment of heartbreak, and sees two sparrows quarrelling in the rain. And immediately, light streamed back, as if it were cast by the rays of a lantern, into the unlit recesses of memory, and I felt the old grief in my heart, and saw the rain fall on the roof and the two sparrows quarrelling there.

Because everything one has seen or heard or thought or felt leaves a deposit that never filters entirely through the essence of mind, I believe a novelist should be perpetually engaged in this effort to refresh and replenish his source. I am confident, moreover, that nothing I have learned either from life or from literature has been wasted. Whatever I have thought or felt deeply has stayed with me, if only in fragments or in a distillation of memory. But the untiring critic within has winnowed, reassorted, and disposed the material I needed.

Not until the unconscious worker has withdrawn from the task, or taken a brief holiday, and the characters have woven their own background and circumstances, does the actual drudgery of moulding the mass-substance begin. Even now, after the groundwork is completed and the subject assembled, I still give time and thought (brooding is the more accurate term) to the construction. I try to avoid hastening the process, and to leave the invisible agent free to flash directions or warnings. The book must have a form. This is essential. It may be shaped like a mill-stone or an hour-glass or an Indian tomahawk or a lace fan—but a shape it must have. Usually a novel assumes its own figure when it enters the world, and the underlying idea moulds the plastic material to its own structure. More deliberately, the point of view is considered and selected, though this may, and often does, proceed naturally from the unities of time and place, or from one completely dominant figure. In *Barren Ground,* a long novel, I felt from the moment Dorinda entered the book that here could be but one point of view. From the first page to the last, no scene or episode or human figure appears outside her field of vision or imagination.

In *The Sheltered Life,* where I knew intuitively that the angle of vision must create the form, I employed two points of view alone, though they were separated by the whole range of experience. Age and youth look on the same scene, the same persons, the same events and occasions, the same tragedy in the end. Between these conflicting points of view the story flows on, as a stream flows in a narrow valley. Nothing happens that is not seen, on one side, through the steady gaze of the old man, seeing life as it is, and, on the other side, by the troubled eyes of the young girl, seeing life as she would wish it to be. Purposely, I have tried here to interpret reality through the dissimilar mediums of thought and emotion. I have been careful to allow no other aspects to impinge on the contrasting visions which create between them the organic whole of the book. This convention, which appears uncertain, when one thinks of it, becomes natural, and even involuntary, when the work grows, develops, pushes out with its own energy, and finds its own tempo.

Patiently, but without success, I have tried to trace the roots of *The Sheltered Life.* The background is that of my girlhood, and the rudiments of the theme must have lain buried somewhere in my consciousness. But I can recall no definite beginning or voluntary act of creation. One moment there was a mental landscape without figures; the next moment, as if they had been summoned by the stroke of a bell, all the characters trooped in together, with every contour, every feature, every attitude, every gesture and expression, complete. In their origin, I exerted no control over them. They were too real for dismemberment; but I could, and I did, select or eliminate whatever in their appearances or behavior seemed to conflict with the general scheme of the book. It was my part to see that the unities were recognized and obeyed.

It is only logical to infer that when a group of imaginary beings assembles, there must be a motive, or at least an adequate reason, for the particular gathering. I knew, or thought I knew, that no visitor had ever entered my mind without a definite cause. These people were there, I felt, according to a design, for a planned attack upon life, and to push them out of the way would spur them to more vehement activity. It was best to ignore them, and this, as nearly as possible, was the course I pursued. Sooner or later, they would let me know why they had come, and what I was expected to do. For me, they were already alive, though I could not as yet distinguish the intricate ties that bound this isolated group into a detached segment of life. So this state of affairs continued for several years. Another novel, *They Stooped to Folly,* engaged my attention, while some distant range of my imagination was still occupied by the Birdsongs and the Archbalds.

Then, at last, *They Stooped to Folly* was finished, was over. Presently it was published; and in company with all my other books that had gone out into the world, it became a homeless wanderer and a stranger. It had ceased to belong to me. I might almost say that it had ceased even to interest me. The place where it had been, the place it had filled to overflowing for nearly three years, was now empty. Were there no other inhabitants? What had become of those troublesome intruders I had once banished to some vague Siberia of the mind?

It was at this crucial instant that the Birdsongs and the Archbalds, under their own names, and wearing their own outward semblances, escaped from remote exile. While I waited, in that unhappy brooding season, which cannot be forced, which cannot be hurried, the vacant scene was flooded with light and animation, and the emerging figures began to breathe, move, speak, and round out their own destinies. I knew instantly, as soon as they returned, what the integral drama would be and why it had occurred. The theme was implicit in the inevitable title. Beyond this, I saw a shallow and aimless society of happiness-hunters, who lived in a perpetual flight from reality, and grasped at any effort-saving illusion of passion or pleasure. Against this background of futility was projected the contrasting character of General Archbald, a lover of wisdom, a humane and civilized soul, oppressed by the burden of tragic remembrance. The stream of events would pass before him, for he would remain permanently at the centre of vision, while, opposing him on the farther side, he would meet the wide, blank, unreflective gaze of inexperience.

In a sudden wholeness of perception, one of those complex apprehensions which come so seldom, yet possess a miraculous power of conviction, I saw the meaning, not only of these special figures, but of their essential place in this theme of age and youth, of the past and the present. They had been drawn together by some sympathetic attraction, or by some deeper sense of recognition in my own consciousness. My task was the simple one of extracting from the situation every thread of significance, every quiver of vitality, every glimmer of understanding. The contours were moulded. I could see the articulation of the parts, as well as the shape of the structure. I could see, too, the fragile surface of a style that I must strive, however unsuccessfully, to make delicate yet unbreakable. I could feel the peculiar density of light and shadow. I could breathe in that strange symbolic smell which was woven and interwoven through the gradually thickening atmosphere of the scene.

As at least one critic has recognized, the old man, left behind by the years, is the central character of the book; and into his lonely spirit I have put much of my ultimate feeling about life. He represents the tragedy, wherever it appears, of the civilized man in a world that is not civilized. And even the title, which I have called inevitable, implies no special age or place. What it implies, to me, is the effort of one human being to stand between another and life. In a larger sense, as this critic perceives, the same tragedy was being repeated in spheres far wider than Queenborough. The First World War was beginning and men were killing each other from the highest possible ideals. This is the final scope of the book's theme. The old man, his point of view, his thwarted strong body, saw the

age pass by him. Not in the South especially; it was throughout the world that ideas, forms, were changing, the familiar
order going, the beliefs and certainties. The shelter for men's
lives, of religion, convention, social prejudice, was at the crumbling point, just as was the case with the little human figures
in the story. . . .[1]

While I am at work on a book I remain, or try to remain,
in a state of immersion. The first draft of a novel, if it is long,
will take two years, and still another year is required for the
final writing. All this time the imaginary setting becomes the
native country of my mind, and the characters are seldom out
of my thoughts. I live with them day and night; they are more
real to me than acquaintances in the flesh. In our nursery copy
of *Gulliver's Travels* there was a picture which seems, when
I recall it now, to illustrate my predicament in the final draft
of a novel. Gulliver lies bound in threads, while the Lilliputians
swarm over him and hamper his struggles. So words swarm over
me and hamper my efforts to seize the right one among them,
to find the right rhythm, the right tone, the right accent. But,
here again, intuition, or perhaps only a flare of organized memory, will come to my aid. Often, when I have searched for hours
for some special word or phrase, and given up in despair, I
have awakened with a start in the night, because the hunted
word or phrase had darted into my mind while I was asleep.

Nevertheless, it is the act of scrupulous revision (the endless pruning and trimming for the sake of a valid and flexible
prose style) that provides the writer's best solace even while
it makes drudgery. Every literary craftsman who respects his
work has, I dare say, this same feeling, and remains restless
and wandering in mind until, in the beginning, he has entered the right climate and, at the end, has tracked down the
right word. Although my characters may develop traits or actions I had not anticipated, though scenes may shift and alter
in perspective, and new episodes may spring out on the way,
still the end shines always as the solitary fixed star above the
flux of creation. I have never written the first word of the first

---

[1]The punctuation is Glasgow's. Nothing is omitted.

sentence until I knew what the last word of the last sentence would be. Sometimes I may rewrite the beginning many times, as I did in *They Stooped to Folly,* and sometimes (though this has actually occurred but once) a shorter book like *The Romantic Comedians,* completely realized before pen was put to paper, may ripple out, of itself, with its own energy. Yet in the difficult first chapter of *They Stooped to Folly,* I could still look ahead, over a procession of characters that had slipped from my control, to the subdued scene at the end, while the concluding paragraph of *The Romantic Comedians* echoed the keynote of the book, and reflected the ironic mood.

The final words to be said of any activity will always be, I suppose, was it worth what it cost? Well, the writing of fiction is worth, I imagine, exactly what digging a ditch or charting the heavens may be worth to the worker, which is not a penny more or less than the release of mind that it brings. Although I may not speak as an authority, at least I can speak from long perseverance. I became a novelist before I was old enough to resist, and I remained a novelist because no other enterprise in life has afforded me the same interest, or provided me with equal contentment. It is true that I have written only for the biased judgment within; but this inner critic has held up an unattainable standard, and has infused a moderate zest of adventure into what may appear, on the surface, to be merely another humdrum way of earning a livelihood. Still, to a beginner who is young and cherishes an ambition to be celebrated, I should recommend the short cut (or royal road) through the radio and Hollywood; and certainly more than one creative writer, in search of swift economic security, would do well to buy a new broom and to set out for the next crossing. But, incredible as it may appear in this practical decade, there are novelists so wanting in a sense of proper values that they place artistic integrity above the voice on the air, the flash on the screen, and the dividends in the bank. There are others who possess an unreasoning faith in their own work; and there are yet others endowed with a comic spirit so robust, or so lively, that it can find diversion anywhere, even in our national exaltation of the inferior. To this happy company of neglected novelists, the ironic art of fiction will reveal its own special delights, and may even, as the years pass, yield its own sufficient, if imponderable, rewards.

In looking back through a long vista, I can see that what I have called the method of constant renewal may be reduced to three ruling principles. Obedience to this self-imposed discipline has enabled me to write novels for nearly forty years, and yet to feel that the substance from which I draw material and energy is as fresh today as it was in my first youthful failure. As time moves on, I still see life in beginnings, moods in conflict, and change as the only permanent law. But the value of these qualities (which may be self-deluding, and are derived, in fact, more from temperament than from technique) has been mellowed by long saturation with experience — by that essence of reality which one distils from life only after it has been lived.

Among the many strange superstitions of the age of science revels the cheerful belief that immaturity alone is enough. Pompous illiteracy, escaped from some Freudian cage, is in the saddle, and the voice of the amateur is the voice of authority. When we turn to the field of prose fiction, we find that it is filled with literary sky-rockets sputtering out in the fog. But the trouble with sky-rockets has always been that they do not stay up in the air. One has only to glance back over the postwar years to discover that the roads of the jazz age are matted thick with fireworks which went off too soon. To the poet, it is true, especially if he can arrange with destiny to die young, the glow of adolescence may impart an unfading magic. But the novel (which must be conceived with a subdued rapture, or with none at all, or even with the unpoetic virtues of industry and patience) requires more substantial ingredients than a little ignorance of life and a great yearning to tell everything one has never known. When I remember Defoe, the father of us all, I am persuaded that the novelist who has harvested well the years, and laid by a rich store of experience, will find his latter period the ripening time of his career.

Transposed into an impersonal method, the three rules of which I have spoken may be so arranged:

1. Always wait between books for the springs to fill up and flow over.

2. Always preserve, within a wild sanctuary, an inaccessible valley of reveries.

3. Always, and as far as it is possible, endeavour to touch life on every side; but keep the central vision of the mind, the inmost light, untouched and untouchable.

In my modest way, these rules have helped me, not only to pursue the one calling for which I was designed alike by character and inclination, but even to enjoy the prolonged study of a world that, as the sardonic insight of Henry Adams perceived, no "sensitive and timid natures could regard without a shudder."

Willa Cather
THE NOVEL DÉMEUBLÉ*

The novel, for a long while, has been overfurnished. The prop-
erty-man has been so busy on its pages, the importance of
material objects and their vivid presentation have been so
stressed, that we take it for granted whoever can observe, and
can write the English language, can write a novel. Often the latter qualification is considered unnecessary.

In any discussion of the novel, one must make it clear
whether one is talking about the novel as a form of amusement,
or as a form of art; since they serve very different purposes
and in very different ways. One does not wish the egg one eats
for breakfast, or the morning paper, to be made of the stuff
of immortality. The novel manufactured to entertain great
multitudes of people must be considered exactly like a cheap
soap or a cheap perfume, or cheap furniture. Fine quality is
a distinct disadvantage in articles made for great numbers of
people who do not want quality but quantity, who do not want
a thing that "wears," but who want change,—a succession of
new things that are quickly threadbare and can be lightly
thrown away. Does anyone pretend that if the Woolworth store

windows were piled high with Tanagra figurines at ten cents, they could for a moment compete with Kewpie brides in the popular esteem? Amusement is one thing; enjoyment of art is another.

Every writer who is an artist knows that his "power of observation," and his "power of description," form but a low part of his equipment. He must have both, to be sure; but he knows that the most trivial of writers often have a very good observation. Mérimée said in his remarkable essay on Gogol; "L'art de choisir parmi les innombrable traits que nous offre la nature est, après tout, bien plus difficile que celui de les observer avec attention et de les rendre avec exactitude."

There is a popular superstition that "realism" asserts itself in the cataloguing of a great number of material objects, in explaining mechanical processes, the methods of operating manufactories and trades, and in minutely and unsparingly describing physical sensations. But is not realism, more than it is anything else, an attitude of mind on the part of the writer toward his material, a vague indication of the sympathy and candour with which he accepts, rather than chooses, his theme? Is the story of a banker who is unfaithful to his wife and who ruins himself by speculation in trying to gratify the caprices of his mistresses, at all reinforced by a masterly exposition of banking, our whole system of credits, the methods of the Stock Exchange? Of course, if the story is thin, these things do reinforce it in a sense,—any amount of red meat thrown into the scale to make the beam dip. But are the banking system and the Stock Exchange worth being written about at all? Have such things any proper place in imaginative art?

The automatic reply to this question is the name of Balzac. Yes, certainly, Balzac tried out the value of literalness in the novel, tried it out to the uttermost, as Wagner did the value of scenic literalness in the music drama. He tried it, too, with the passion of discovery, with the inflamed zest of an unexampled curiosity. If the heat of that furnace could not give hardness and sharpness to material accessories, no other brain will ever do it. To reproduce on paper the actual city of Paris; the houses, the upholstery, the food, the wines, the game of

pleasure, the game of business, the game of finance: a stupendous ambition—but, after all, unworthy of an artist. In exactly so far as he succeeded in pouring out on his pages that mass
of brick and mortar and furniture and proceedings in bank-
ruptcy, in exactly so far he defeated his end. The things by
which he still lives, the types of greed and avarice and ambition and vanity and lost innocence of heart which he created
—are as vital today as they were then. But their material
surroundings, upon which he expended such labour and pains
. . . the eye glides over them. We have had too much of the
interior decorator and the "romance of business" since his day.
The city he built on paper is already crumbling. Stevenson said
he wanted to blue-pencil a great deal of Balzac's "presentation"—and he loved him beyond all modern novelists. But
where is the man who could cut one sentence from the stories of
Mérimée? And who wants any more detail as to how Carmen-
cita and her fellow factory-girls made cigars? Another sort of
novel? Truly. Isn't it a better sort?

In this discussion another great name naturally occurs.
Tolstoi was almost as great a lover of material things as Balzac, almost as much interested in the way dishes were cooked,
and people were dressed, and houses were furnished. But there
is this determining difference: the clothes, the dishes, the haunting interiors of those old Moscow houses, are always so much
a part of the emotions of the people that they are perfectly
synthesized; they seem to exist, not so much in the author's
mind, as in the emotional penumbra of the characters themselves. When it is fused like this, literalness ceases to be literalness—it is merely part of the experience.

If the novel is a form of imaginative art, it cannot be at
the same time a vivid and brilliant form of journalism. Out
of the teeming, gleaming stream of the present it must select
the eternal material of art. There are hopeful signs that some
of the younger writers are trying to break away from mere
verisimilitude, and, following the development of modern painting, to interpret imaginatively the material and social investiture of their characters; to present their scene by suggestion
rather than by enumeration. The higher processes of art are

all processes of simplification. The novelist must learn to write, and then he must unlearn it; just as the modern painter learns to draw, and then learns when utterly to disregard his accomplishment, when to subordinate it to a higher and truer effect. In this direction only, it seems to me, can the novel develop into anything more varied and perfect than all the many novels that have gone,before.

One of the very earliest American romances might well serve as a suggestion to later writers. In *The Scarlet Letter* how truly in the spirit of art is the mise-en-scene presented. That drudge, the theme-writing high-school student, could scarcely be sent there for information regarding the manners and dress and interiors of Puritan society. The material investiture of the story is presented as if unconsciously; by the reserved, fastidious hand of an artist, not by the gaudy fingers of a showman or the mechanical industry of a department-store window-dresser. As I remember it, in the twilight melancholy of that book, in its consistent mood, one can scarcely ever see the actual surroundings of the people; one feels them, rather, in the dusk.

Whatever is felt upon the page without being specifically named there—that, one might say, is created. It is the inexplicable presence of the thing not named, of the overtone divined by the ear but not heard by it, the verbal mood, the emotional aura of the fact or the thing or the deed, that gives high quality to the novel or the drama, as well as to poetry itself.

Literalness, when applied to the presenting of mental reactions and of physical sensations, seems to be no more effective than when it is applied to material things. A novel crowded with physical sensations is no less a catalogue than one crowded with furniture. A book like *The Rainbow* by D. H. Lawrence sharply reminds one how vast a distance lies between emotion and mere sensory reactions. Characters can be almost dehumanized by a laboratory study of the behaviour of their bodily organs under sensory stimuli—can be reduced, indeed, to mere animal pulp. Can one imagine anything more terrible than the story of *Romeo and Juliet* rewritten in prose by D. H. Lawrence?

How wonderful it would be if we could throw all the furniture out of the window; and along with it, all the meaningless reiterations concerning physical sensations, all the tiresome old patterns, and leave the room as bare as the stage of a Greek theatre, or as that house into which the glory of Pentecost descended; leave the scene bare for the play of emotions, great and little—for the nursery tale, no less than the tragedy, is killed by tasteless amplitude. The elder Dumas enunciated a great principle when he said that to make a drama, a man needed one passion, and four walls.

Sherwood Anderson

A WRITER'S
CONCEPTION OF REALISM*

It must be that I am an incurable small-town man. Either that
is true or there is something very special going on here at Olivet[1]
and, after some ten days here, I have about concluded that
it is not the small town in general that has built up in me a kind
of feeling of wonder but Olivet in particular. It has seemed
to me a little like something out of the past and at the same
time something, too, which one looks forward to in the future, and, I must say, not always very hopefully. Just now and
in most of the places in which I have been—I should say ever
since the World War—I have felt a certain tenseness. It has
been rather hard to work in. Everyone seems to be trying to
think nationally and internationally. The old human interest of
one man in another seems to have got lost somewhere. People
seem more and more to be separating themselves into groups
and classes. A man like myself, never anything but a somewhat
liberal democrat, finds his name put into a book called *The
Red Network,* labeled there as a communist writer; in many

*Reprinted by permission of Harold Ober Associates Incorporated. Copy-
right © 1939 by Sherwood Anderson. Renewed 1967 by Eleanor Copenhaver
Anderson.

[1]The essay was first delivered as an address at Olivet College, Olivet, Michigan in 1939.

places the anti-Jewish feeling apparently growing stronger —often, I have noticed, in places where there are no Jews and among men who know personally no Jews; prejudice against the Negro, often stronger in the North now than in the South; and all of these impulses leading to a new suspicion by man of man and making more prevalent and more marked our human loneliness.

Here in Olivet I have seemed to find these impulses that do so much to destroy human relationships strangely absent. I came here, as a man goes into most new places, nowadays, a little afraid. The fear is gone. I may be a bit nervous about trying to speak to you here tonight, but I am not afraid of you. Since I have been here I do not believe I have heard the word 'capitalist' or 'proletariat' used once. What a relief. Here I have heard talk of music, of painting, of the art of living, and even, strangely enough, of education. It is a little like coming, after a long and stormy sea voyage into some quiet bay, and I feel rather like congratulating the young men and women who are here seeking an education that they can live here, for a time, in this atmosphere, before going out to tackle what they will find they must tackle.

I am here tonight to make a public lecture, the first one I have tried to make for two or three years. I am a professional writer with, I admit, a good many marks of the eternal amateur on me, and so I have written out what I want to say. When a man has sat at a desk for as many hours through as many years as I have, he finds that his thoughts, when he has any, run more naturally down through his arms and fingers than up to his mouth and lips.

Just the same, as you have probably been told that I was going to try to tell you something of a writer's conception of realistic fiction, I think I ought to try to keep the talk as much as possible, on the subject of realism. I do not know what reality is. I do not think any of us quite know how much our point of view, and, in fact, all of our touch with life, is influenced by our imaginations.

In my own experience, for example, and in my work as a writer I have always attempted to use materials that came out of my own experiences of life. I have written a good deal about my father, my mother, a certain grandmother who touched my imagination, and about my brothers and sisters, and it has amused me sometimes, in talking with some of my brothers, to see how poorly my conception of our father and mother fitted into their own conceptions. 'Why, I dare say, the woman you have pictured is all right. She is very interesting, but she is not my mother as I knew her,' they say.

This whole matter of what we think of as realism is probably pretty tricky. I have often told myself that, having met some person for the first time, some other human being, man or woman, and having had my first look, I cannot ever even see him or her again.

If this is true, why is it true? It is true because the moment I meet you and if we begin to talk, my imagination begins to play. Perhaps I begin to make up stories about you. This is a trick all writers, and for that matter, all people, do. The writer may merely be more conscious of it. It is our method of work. Very little of the work of the writer is done at his desk or at the typewriter. It is done as he walks about, as he sits in a room with people, and perhaps most of all as he lies in bed at night.

I myself, for example, have all my life had over and over an experience that some of you may also have had. If I have been working intensely, I find myself unable to relax when I go to bed. Often I fall into a half-dream state, and when I do, the faces of people begin to appear before me. They seem to snap into place before my eyes, stay there, sometimes for a short period, sometimes longer. There are smiling faces, leering ugly faces, tired faces, hopeful faces. Almost always they seem to be faces of people I cannot remember ever having met.

However, I am quite sure they are faces of people I have seen.

They may be people I have met quite casually in the street. I have been walking about. At times the faces of people, met thus, quite casually seem full of a strange significance. To quote Herman Melville, 'Who has ever fathomed the strangeness and wonder of man?' I get sometimes the illusion that every man and woman I meet is crying out to me. Sometimes a single glance at a human face seems to tell a whole life story, and there have been times, when I walked thus, when I had to go along with bowed head, looking at the sidewalk. I could not bear looking at any more faces.

I have a kind of illusion about this matter. It is, I have no doubt, due to a story-teller's point of view. I have the feeling that the faces that appear before me thus at night are those of people who want their stories told and whom I have neglected. Once I remember that I wrote a poem on this matter. I think I had better recite it to you. I called my verses,

The Story Teller[2]

Tales are people who sit on the doorstep of the house of my mind.
It is cold outside and they sit waiting.
I look out at a window.
The tales have cold hands,
Their hands are freezing.
A short thickly-built tale arises and threshes his arms about.
His nose is red and he has two gold teeth.
There is an old female tale that sits hunched up in a cloak.
Many tales come to sit for a moment on the doorstep and then go away.
It is too cold for them outside.
The street before the door of the house of my mind is filled with tales.
They murmur and cry out, they are dying of cold and hunger.
I am a helpless man—my hands tremble.
I should be sitting on a bench like a tailor.
I should be weaving warm cloth out of the threads of thought.
The tales should be clothed.
They are freezing on the doorstep of the house of my mind.
I am a helpless man—my hands tremble.
I feel in the darkness but cannot find the doorknob.
I look out at a window.
Many tales are dying in the street before the house of mind.

[2]From *A New Testament,* by Sherwood Anderson.

Now, when it comes to talking about the experiences of a writer, I think I should say something that perhaps most of you realize. The work of any writer, and for that matter of any artist in any of the seven arts, should contain within it the story of his own life. There are certain beliefs I have. One is that every man who writes, writes as well as he can. We are always hearing stories about men writing with their tongues in their cheeks, but the truth is that if, for example, a man devotes his life to writing detective stories, he probably believes in the detectives he puts in his stories. If he writes cowboy stories, he really believes that cowboys in life are like the cowboys of the stories and the movies. They aren't, of course, but he thinks so.

I have myself, I think, been counted among what we call in America the high-brow writers. I am not in the least a high-brow type of man, so I have to ask myself—or did at first when I first began writing—have to ask myself how it came about that I was called a high-brow. And I concluded finally that it was because I happened to be a man who took writing rather seriously and I took it seriously because I enjoyed it so thoroughly.

I remember reading somewhere a sentence by Joseph Conrad. He said that he only lived fully and richly when he was at work writing.

I have always thought of myself as a man who came into writing, let us say, by the back door. I had a rather adventurous youth. I was a laborer, a farm hand and a factory hand until I was twenty-two or twenty-three years old. I was as a youth always a passionate reader.

And I did not read in order to learn to write. I had no notion of being a writer, although it is probable that I always instinctively wanted to be a story-teller. My father was a rather famous story-teller in the little town in which we lived, and I very much admired that quality in him.

And there were other good story-tellers about. I sought them out. I think I perhaps instinctively watched their technique. I became more or less a wanderer and have been one

all of my life. For a time, for two or three years, I led the life
of a wandering vagabond, a tramp, working just enough to
live. I speak of this because I think it was for me a time of learning, or at least trying to learn.

And here I would like to speak of something. When I was
a lad there was a good deal of something going on that may
be rather on the wane now. There was this talk, heard on all
sides, of America being the great land of opportunity. At that
time, such talk pretty much meant getting on, if possible, growing rich, getting to be something big in the world. A lad heard
it on all sides and it was not unkindly meant. The idea of accumulation of possessions got all mixed up with the idea of
happiness and it was rather confusing. I know it got me confused and I suffered for it. I think I should say to some of the
students here who have heard me talk to smaller groups that,
if I have kept emphasizing this idea, there is a reason. I have
spoken here a good deal, perhaps too much, of my own particular experiences in life. It may be I am rather a nut on the
subject, that I too much resent the years I myself spent trying to be what I did not want to be. Some years ago I was asked
to deliver what is called the William Vaughn Moody series of
lectures in the University of Chicago, and through all the lectures I tried to emphasize the idea of smallness as opposed
to bigness; that is to say, the desirability of being just a man
going along rather than something outstanding and special.

The truth probably is that I wanted to get out of the scram-
ble as much as I could for a particular reason. I had a hunch.
It may be that I gradually realized, as I grew out of childhood
into young manhood, that I was losing something. All of us
who are older can remember with what fervor we read when
we were younger. What a rich place our imagined world was!
As we grew older, it seemed to get less rich. I suppose I wanted
to keep it rich.

We all, I dare say, have to face what are called 'the facts
of life,' but I do think we are often inclined to call facts what
are not necessarily facts.

And I think also that the actual training of the imagination, the learning to use it, has a lot to do with human relations. That has something to do with what I want to try to say here.

There is something you can do. Even if you are not actually practicing writers, you can employ something of the writer's technique. When you are puzzled about your own life, as we all are most of the time, you can throw imagined figures of others against a background very like your own, put these imagined figures through situations in which you have been involved. It is a very comforting thing to do, a great relief at times, this occasionally losing sense of self, living in these imagined figures. This thing we call self, as I said here in a talk the other evening, is often very like a disease. It seems to sap you, take something from you, destroy your relationship with others, while even occasionally losing sense of self seems to give you an understanding that you didn't have before you became absorbed.

May it not be that all the people we know are only what we imagine them to be? If, for example, you are as I was at the time of which I am now speaking, a business man, on the whole spending my time seeking my own advantage, you lose interest, while, as opposed to this, as you lose yourself in others, life immediately becomes more interesting. A new world seems to open out before you. Your imagination becomes constantly more and more alive.

And there is a profound pleasure in all of this. At least I know that when I came to it, I found it the pleasantest experience I had ever had. To be sure, I do not want to discount the difficulty. It is very hard to understand any other human being. It is difficult to tell truly the story of another, but it is, I think, rather a grand challenge. I hope you will pardon me for speaking thus seriously about that which interests me so profoundly. You see, I am interested in writing. I am a man in love with his craft.

But I would like to speak a little more clearly if possible on the subject of what, when we think of writers, we call realists. I have said that I do not know what reality is. I do not think any man knows. I remember that some years ago I wrote a short essay that has often since been reproduced and has even, I believe, been used in college text books. I called it 'A Note on Realism.' I think I will read some extracts from it.

'There is something very confusing to both readers and writers about the notion of realism in fiction. As generally understood it is akin to what is called "representation" in painting. The fact is before you and you put it down, adding a high spot here and there, to be sure. No man can quite make himself a camera. Even the most realistic worker pays some tribute to what is called "art." Where does representation end and art begin? The location of the line is often as confusing to practicing artists as it is to the public.'

Recently a young writer came to talk with me about our mutual craft. He spoke with enthusiastic admiration of a certain book—very popular a year or two ago. 'It is the very life. So closely observed. It is the sort of thing I should like to do. I should like to bring life itself within the pages of a book. If I could do that I would be happy.'

I wondered. The book in question had only seemed to me good in spots and the spots had been far apart. There was too much dependence upon the notebook. The writer had seemed to me to have very little to give out of himself. What had happened, I thought, was that the writer of the book had confused the life of reality with the life of the imagination. Easy enough to get a thrill out of people with reality. A man struck by an automobile, a child falling out at the window of a city office building. Such things stir the emotions. No one, however, confuses them with art.

This confusion of the life of the imagination with the life of reality is a trap into which most of our critics seem to me to fall about a dozen times each year. Do the trick over and over, and in they tumble. 'It is life,' they say. 'Another great artist has been discovered.'

What never seems to come quite clear is the simple fact that art is art. It is not life.

The life of the imagination will always remain separated from the life of reality. It feeds upon the life of reality, but it is not that life—cannot be. Mr. John Marin painting Brooklyn Bridge, Henry Fielding writing Tom Jones, are not trying in the novel and the painting to give us reality. They are striving for a realization in art of something out of their own imaginative experiences, fed, to be sure, upon the life immediately about. A quite different matter from making an actual picture of what they see before them.

And here arises a confusion. For some reason—I myself have never exactly understood very clearly—the imagination must constantly feed upon reality or starve. Separate yourself too much from life and you may at moments be a lyrical poet, but you are not an artist. Something within dries up, starves for the want of food. Upon the fact in nature the imagination must constantly feed in order that the imaginative life remain significant. The workman who lets his imagination drift off into some experience altogether disconnected with reality, the attempt of the American to depict life in Europe, the New Englander writing of cowboy life—all that sort of thing—in ninety-nine cases out of a hundred ends in the work of such a man becoming at once full of holes and bad spots. The intelligent reader, tricked often enough by the technical skill displayed in hiding holes, never in the end accepts it as good work. The imagination of the workman has become confused. He has had to depend altogether upon tricks. The whole job is a fake.

The difficulty, I fancy, is that so few workmen in the arts will accept their own limitations. It is only when the limitation is fully accepted that it ceases to be a limitation. Such men scold at the life immediately about. 'It's too dull and commonplace to make good material,' they declare. Off they sail in fancy to the South Seas, to Africa, to China. What they cannot realize is their own dullness. Life is never dull except to the dull.

The writer who sets himself down to write a tale has undertaken something. He has undertaken to conduct his readers on a trip through the world of his fancy. If he is a novelist, his imaginative world is filled with people and events. If he has any sense of decency as a workman, he can no more tell lies about his imagined people, fake them, than he can sell out real people in real life. The thing is constantly done, but no man I have ever met, having done such a trick, has felt very clean about the matter afterward.

On the other hand, when the writer is rather intensely true to the people of his imaginative world, when he has set them down truly, when he does not fake, another confusion arises. Being square with your people in the imaginative world does not mean lifting them over into life, into reality. There is a very subtle distinction to be made, and upon the writer's ability to make this distinction will in the long run depend his standing as a workman.

Having lifted the reader out of the reality of daily life, it is entirely possible for the writer to do his job so well that the imaginative life becomes to the reader for the time real life. Little real touches are added. The people of the town—that never existed except in the fancy—eat food, live in houses, suffer, have moments of happiness, and die. To the writer, as he works, they are very real. The imaginative world in which he is for the time living has become for him more alive than the world of reality ever can become. His very sincerity confuses. Being unversed in the matter of making the delicate distinction that the writer himself sometimes has such a hard time making, they call him a realist. The notion shocks him. 'The deuce, I am nothing of the kind,' he says. 'But such a thing could not have happened in a Vermont town.' 'Why not? Have you not learned that anything can happen anywhere? If a thing can happen in my imaginative world, it can of course happen in the flesh and blood world. Upon what do you fancy my imagination feeds?'

My own belief is that the writer with a notebook in his hand is always a bad workman, a man who distrusts his own imagination. Such a man describes actual scenes accurately, he puts down actual conversation.

But people do not converse in the book world as they do in life. Scenes of the imaginative world are not real scenes.

The life of reality is confused, disorderly, almost always without apparent purpose, whereas in the artist's imaginative life there is purpose. There is determination to give the tale, the song, the painting, form—to make it true and real to the

theme, not to life. Often the better the job is done, the greater the confusion.

I myself remember with what a shock I heard people say
that one of my own books, *Winesburg, Ohio,* was an exact picture of Ohio village life. The book was written in a crowded
tenement district of Chicago. The hint for almost every character was taken from my fellow lodgers in a large rooming
house, many of whom had never lived in a village. The confusion arises out of the fact that others besides practicing artists have imaginations. But most people are afraid to trust their
imaginations and the artist is not.

Would it not be better to have it understood that realism,
in so far as the word means reality to life, is always bad art—although it may possibly be very good journalism?

Which is but another way of saying that all of the so-called
great realists were not realists at all and never intended being.
Madame Bovary did not exist in fact. She existed in the imaginative life of Flaubert and he managed to make her exist in
the imaginative life of his readers.

•   •   •

I have been writing a story. A man is walking in a street and
suddenly turns out of the street into an alleyway. There he
meets another man and a hurried whispered conversation takes
place. In real life they may be but a pair of rather small bootleggers, but they are not that to me.

When I began writing, the physical aspect of one of the
men, the one who walked in the street, was taken rather literally from life. He looked strikingly like a man I once knew,
so much like him in fact that there was a confusion. A matter easy enough to correct.

A stroke of my pen saves me from realism. The man I
knew in life had red hair; he was tall and thin.

With a few words I have changed him completely. Now
he has black hair and a black mustache. He is short and has
broad shoulders. And now he no longer lives in the world of
reality. He is a denizen of my own imaginative world. He can

now begin a life having nothing at all to do with the life of the red-haired man.

If I am to succeed in making him real in this new world, he, like hundreds of other men and women who live only in my own fanciful world, must live and move within the scope of the story or novel into which I have cast him. If I do tricks with him in the imaginative world, sell him out, I become merely a romancer. If, however, I have the courage to let him really live, he will, perhaps, show me the way to a fine story or novel.

But the story or novel will not be a picture of life. I will never have had any intentions of making it that.

And so you will see in this matter of realism what I am trying to say. There is a reality to your book, your story people. They may, in the beginning, be lifted out of life, but once lifted, once become a part of the book, of the story-life—realism, in the sense in which the word is commonly used, no longer exists.

There are, you see, these two kinds of realism, the realism to actual life that is the challenge to the journalist and the realism to the book or the story-life. That I should say is the job of your real story-teller.

Sinclair Lewis

NOBEL PRIZE ADDRESS*

. . . Before I consider the Academy,[1] however, let me sketch a fantasy which has pleased me the last few days in the unavoidable idleness of a rough trip on the Atlantic. I am sure that you know, by now, that the award to me of the Nobel Prize has by no means been altogether popular in America. Doubtless the experience is not new to you. I fancy that when you gave the award even to Thomas Mann, whose "Zauberberg" seems to me to contain the whole of intellectual Europe, even when you gave it to Kipling, whose social significance is so profound that it has been rather authoritatively said that he created the British Empire, even when you gave it to Bernard Shaw, there were countrymen of those authors who complained because you did not choose another.

And I imagined what would have been said had you chosen some American other than myself. Suppose you had taken Theodore Dreiser.

Now to me, as to many other American writers, Dreiser

*Reprinted with permission of Ernst, Cane, Berner & Gitlin from *The Man From Main Street,* Maule and Cane, eds. 2d edition printed by Harcourt, Brace, May 1931.

[1]The American Academy of Arts and Letters. A member had suggested that the award of a Nobel Prize to Lewis was an affront to the United States.

more than any other man, marching alone, usually unappreci-
ated, often hated, has cleared the trail from Victorian and
Howellsian timidity and gentility in American fiction to honesty
and boldness and passion of life. Without his pioneering, I
doubt if any of us could, unless we liked to be sent to jail, seek
to express life and beauty and terror.

My great colleague Sherwood Anderson has proclaimed
this leadership of Dreiser. I am delighted to join him. Dreiser's
great first novel, "Sister Carrie," which he dared to publish
thirty long years ago and which I read twenty-five years ago,
came to housebound and airless America like a great free Western wind, and to our stuffy domesticity gave us the first fresh
air since Mark Twain and Whitman.

Yet had you given the Prize to Mr. Dreiser, you would have
heard groans from America; you would have heard that his
style—I am not exactly sure what this mystic quality "style"
may be, but I find the word so often in the writings of minor
critics that I suppose it must exist—you would have heard that
his style is cumbersome, that his choice of words is insensitive,
that his books are interminable. And certainly respectable
scholars would complain that in Mr. Dreiser's world, men and
women are often sinful and tragic and despairing, instead of
being forever sunny and full of song and virtue, as befits authentic Americans.

And had you chosen Mr. Eugene O'Neill, who has done
nothing much in American drama save to transform it utterly, in
ten or twelve years, from a false world of neat and competent
trickery to a world of splendor and fear and greatness, you
would have been reminded that he has done something far
worse than scoffing—he has seen life as not to be neatly arranged in the study of a scholar but as a terrifying, magnificent
and often quite horrible thing akin to the tornado, the earth-
quake, the devastating fire.

And had you given Mr. James Branch Cabell the Prize, you
would have been told that he is too fantastically malicious.
So would you have been told that Miss Willa Cather, for all
the homely virtue of her novels concerning the peasants of
Nebraska, has in her novel, "The Lost Lady," been so untrue

to America's patent and perpetual and possibly tedious virtuousness as to picture an abandoned woman who remains, nevertheless, uncannily charming even to the virtuous, in a story without any moral; that Mr. Henry Mencken is the worst of all scoffers; that Mr. Sherwood Anderson viciously errs in considering sex as important a force in life as fishing; that Mr. Upton Sinclair, being a Socialist, sins against the perfectness of American capitalistic mass-production; that Mr. Joseph Hergesheimer is un-American in regarding graciousness of manner and beauty of surface as of some importance in the endurance of daily life; and that Mr. Ernest Hemingway is not only too young but, far worse, uses language which should be unknown to gentlemen; that he acknowledges drunkenness as one of men's eternal ways to happiness, and asserts that a soldier may find love more significant than the hearty slaughter of men in battle.

Yes, they are wicked, these colleagues of mine; you would have done almost as evilly to have chosen them as to have chosen me; and as a Chauvinistic American—only, mind you, as an American of 1930 and not of 1880—I rejoice that they are my countrymen and countrywomen, and that I may speak of them with pride even in the Europe of Thomas Mann, H. G. Wells, Galsworthy, Knut Hamsun, Arnold Bennett, Feuchtwanger, Selma Lagerlöf, Sigrid Undset, Verner von Heidenstam, D'Annunzio, Romain Rolland.

It is my fate in this paper to swing constantly from optimism to pessimism and back, but so is it the fate of any one who writes or speaks of anything in America—the most contradictory, the most depressing, the most stirring, of any land in the world today.

Thus, having with no muted pride called the roll of what seem to me to be great men and women in American literary life today, and having indeed omitted a dozen other names of which I should like to boast were there time, I must turn again and assert that in our contemporary American literature, indeed in all American arts save architecture and the film, we—yes, we who have such pregnant and vigorous standards in commerce and science—have no standards, no healing communication, no heroes to be followed nor villains to be condemned, no certain ways to be pursued and no dangerous paths to be avoided.

The American novelist or poet or dramatist or sculptor or painter must work alone, in confusion, unassisted save by his own integrity.

That, of course, has always been the lot of the artist. The vagabond and criminal François Villon had certainly no smug and comfortable refuge in which elegant ladies would hold his hand and comfort his starveling soul and more starved body. He, veritably a great man, destined to outlive in history all the dukes and puissant cardinals whose robes he was esteemed unworthy to touch, had for his lot the gutter and the hardened crust.

Such poverty is not for the artist in America. They pay us, indeed, only too well; that writer is a failure who cannot have his butler and motor and his villa at Palm Beach, where he is permitted to mingle almost in equality with the barons of banking. But he is oppressed ever by something worse than poverty—by the feeling that what he creates does not matter, that he is expected by his readers to be only a decorator or a clown, or that he is good-naturedly accepted as a scoffer whose bark probably is worse than his bite and who probably is a good fellow at heart, who in any case certainly does not count in a land that produces eighty-story buildings, motors by the million, and wheat by the billions of bushels. And he has no institution, no group, to which he can turn for inspiration, whose criticism he can accept and whose praise will be precious to him.

What institutions have we?

The American Academy of Arts and Letters does contain, along with several excellent painters and architects and statesmen, such a really distinguished university-president as Nicholas Murray Butler, so admirable and courageous a scholar as Wilbur Cross, and several first-rate writers: the poets Edwin Arlington Robinson and Robert Frost, the free-minded publicist James Truslow Adams, and the novelists Edith Wharton, Hamlin Garland, Owen Wister, Brand Whitlock and Booth Tarkington.

But it does not include Theodore Dreiser, Henry Mencken, our most vivid critic, George Jean Nathan who, though still young, is certainly the dean of our dramatic critics, Eugene O'Neill, incomparably our best dramatist, the really original and vital poets, Edna St. Vincent Millay and Carl Sandburg, Robinson Jeffers and Vachel Lindsay and Edgar Lee Masters, whose "Spoon River Anthology" was so utterly different from any other poetry ever published, so fresh, so authoritative, so free from any gropings and timidities that it came like a revelation, and created a new school of native American poetry. It does not include the novelists and short-story writers, Willa Cather, Joseph Hergesheimer, Sherwood Anderson, Ring Lardner, Ernest Hemingway, Louis Bromfield, Wilbur Daniel Steele, Fannie Hurst, Mary Austin, James Branch Cabell, Edna Ferber, nor Upton Sinclair, of whom you must say, whether you admire or detest his aggressive socialism, that he is internationally better known than any other American artist whosoever, be he novelist, poet, painter, sculptor, musician, architect.

I should not expect any Academy to be so fortunate as to contain all these writers, but one which fails to contain any of them, which thus cuts itself off from so much of what is living and vigorous and original in American letters, can have no relationship whatever to our life and aspirations. It does not represent literary America of today—it represents only Henry Wadsworth Longfellow.

It might be answered that, after all, the Academy is limited to fifty members; that, naturally, it cannot include everyone of merit. But the fact is that while most of our few giants are excluded, the Academy does have room to include three extraordinarily bad poets, two very melodramatic and insignificant playwrights, two gentlemen who are known only because they are university presidents, a man who was thirty years ago known as a rather clever humorous draughtsman, and several gentlemen of whom—I sadly confess my ignorance—I have never heard.

Let me again emphasize the fact—for it is a fact—that I am not attacking the American Academy. It is a hospitable and generous and decidedly dignified institution. And it is not altogether the Academy's fault that it does not contain many of the men who have significance in our letters. Sometimes it is the fault of those writers themselves. I cannot imagine that grizzly-bear Theodore Dreiser being comfortable at the serenely Athenian dinners of the Academy, and were they to invite Mencken, he would infuriate them with his boisterous jeering. No, I am not attacking—I am reluctantly considering the Academy because it is so perfect an example of the divorce in America of intellectual life from all authentic standards of importance and reality.

Our universities and colleges, or gymnasia, most of them, exhibit the same unfortunate divorce. I can think of four of them, Rollins College in Florida, Middlebury College in Vermont, the University of Michigan, and the University of Chicago—which has had on its roll so excellent a novelist as Robert Herrick, so courageous a critic as Robert Morss Lovett—which have shown an authentic interest in comtemporary creative literature. Four of them. But universities and colleges and musical emporiums and schools for the teaching of theology and plumbing and sign-painting are as thick in America as the motor traffic. Whenever you see a public building with Gothic fenestration on a sturdy backing of Indiana concrete, you may be certain that it is another university, with anywhere from two hundred to twenty thousand students equally ardent about avoiding the disadvantage of becoming learned and about gaining the social prestige contained in the possession of a B.A. degree.

Oh, socially our universities are close to the mass of our citizens, and so are they in the matter of athletics. A great college football game is passionately witnessed by eighty thousand people, who have paid five dollars apiece and motored anywhere from ten to a thousand miles for the ecstasy of watching twenty-two men chase one another up and down a curiously marked field. During the football season, a capable player ranks very nearly with our greatest and most admired heroes—even with Henry Ford, President Hoover, and Colonel Lindbergh. . . .

With a wealth of creative talent in America, our criticism

has most of it been a chill and insignificant activity pursued by jealous spinsters, ex-baseball-reporters, and acid professors. Our Erasmuses have been village schoolmistresses. How should there be any standards when there has been no one capable of setting them up?

The great Cambridge-Concord circle of the middle of the Nineteenth Century—Emerson, Longfellow, Lowell, Holmes, the Alcotts—were sentimental reflections of Europe, and they left no school, no influence. Whitman and Thoreau and Poe and, in some degree, Hawthorne, were outcasts, men alone and despised, berated by the New Humanists of their generation. It was with the emergence of William Dean Howells that we first began to have something like a standard, and a very bad standard it was.

Mr. Howells was one of the gentlest, sweetest, and most honest of men, but he had the code of a pious old maid whose greatest delight was to have tea at the vicarage. He abhorred not only profanity and obscenity but all of what H. G. Wells has called "the jolly coarsenesses of life." In his fantastic vision of life, which he innocently conceived to be realistic, farmers and seamen and factory-hands might exist, but the farmer must never be covered with muck, the seaman must never roll out bawdy chanteys, the factory-hand must be thankful to his good kind employer, and all of them must long for the opportunity to visit Florence and smile gently at the quaintness of the beggars.

So strongly did Howells feel this genteel, this New Humanistic philosophy that he was able vastly to influence his contemporaries, down even to 1914 and the turmoil of the Great War.

He was actually able to tame Mark Twain, perhaps the greatest of our writers, and to put that fiery old savage into an intellectual frock coat and top hat. His influence is not altogether gone today. He is still worshipped by Hamlin Garland, an author who should in every way have been greater than Howells but who under Howells' influence was changed from a harsh and magnificent realist into a genial and insignificant lecturer. Mr. Garland is, so far as we have one, the dean of American letters today, and as our dean, he is alarmed by all of the younger writers who are so lacking in taste as to suggest that men and women do not always love in accordance with the prayer-book, and that common people sometimes use language which would be inappropriate at a women's literary club on Main Street. Yet this same Hamlin Garland, as a young man, before he had gone to Boston and become cultured and Howellsised, wrote two most valiant and revelatory works of realism, "Main-Travelled Roads" and "Rose of Dutcher's Coolly."

I read them as a boy in a prairie village in Minnesota—just such an environment as was described in Mr. Garland's tales. They were vastly exciting to me. I had realized in reading Balzac and Dickens that it was possible to describe French and English common people as one actually saw them. But it had never occurred to me that one might without indecency write of the people of Sauk Centre, Minnesota, as one felt about them. Our fictional tradition, you see, was that all of us in Midwestern villages were altogether noble and happy; that not one of us would exchange the neighborly bliss of living on Main Street for the heathen gaudiness of New York or Paris or Stockholm. But in Mr. Garland's "Main-Travelled Roads" I discovered that there was one man who believed that Midwestern peasants were sometimes bewildered and hungry and vile—and heroic. And, given this vision, I was released; I could write of life as living life.

I am afraid Mr. Garland would be not pleased but acutely annoyed to know that he made it possible for me to write of America as I see it, and not as Mr. William Dean Howells so sunnily saw it. And it is his tragedy, it is a completely revelatory American tragedy, that in our land of freedom, men like Garland, who first blast the roads to freedom, become themselves the most bound.

But, all this time, while men like Howells were so effusively seeking to guide America into becoming a pale edition of an English cathedral town, there were surly and authentic fellows—Whitman and Melville, then Dreiser and James Huneker and Mencken—who insisted that our land had something more than tea-table gentility.

And so, without standards, we have survived. And for the strong young men, it has perhaps been well that we should have no standards. For, after seeming to be pessimistic about my own and much beloved land, I want to close this dirge with a very lively sound of optimism.

I have, for the future of American literature, every hope and every eager belief. We are coming out, I believe, of the stuffiness of safe, sane, and incredibly dull provincialism. There are young Americans today who are doing such passionate and authentic work that it makes me sick to see that I am a little too old to be one of them.

There is Ernest Hemingway, a bitter youth, educated by the most intense experience, disciplined by his own high standards, an authentic artist whose home is in the whole of life; there is Thomas Wolfe, a child of, I believe, thirty or younger, whose one and only novel, "Look Homeward, Angel," is worthy to be compared with the best in our literary production, a Gargantuan creature with great gusto of life; there is Thornton Wilder, who in an age of realism dreams the old and lovely dreams of the eternal romantics; there is John Dos Passos, with his hatred of the safe and sane standards of Babbitt and his splendor of revolution; there is Stephen Benét who, to American drabness, has restored the epic poem with his glorious memory of old John Brown; there are Michael Gold, who reveals the new frontier of the Jewish East Side, and William Faulkner, who has freed the South from hoop-skirts; and there are a dozen other young poets and fictioneers, most of them living now in Paris, most of them a little insane in the tradition of James Joyce, who, however insane they may be, have refused to be genteel and traditional and dull.

I salute them, with a joy in being not yet too far removed from their determination to give to the America that has mountains and endless prairies, enormous cities and lost farm cabins, billions of money and tons of faith, to an America that is as strange as Russia and as complex as China, a literature worthy of her vastness.

F. Scott Fitzgerald

HOW TO WASTE MATERIAL:
A NOTE ON MY GENERATION*

Ever since Irving's preoccupation with the neccessity for an
American background, for some square miles of cleared territory on which colorful variants might presently arise, the
question of material has hampered the American writer. For
one Dreiser who made a single minded and irreproachable
choice there have been a dozen like Henry James who have
stupid-got with worry over the matter, and yet another dozen
who, blinded by the fading tail of Walt Whitman's comet, have
botched their books by the insincere compulsion to write "sig-
nificantly" about America.

Insincere because it is not a compulsion found in themselves—it is "literary" in the most belittling sense. During the
past seven years we have had at least half a dozen treatments
of the American farmer, ranging from New England to Nebraska; at least a dozen canny books about youth, some of them
with surveys of the American universities for background;
more than a dozen novels reflecting various aspects of New
York, Chicago, Washington, Detroit, Indianapolis, Wilming-

ton, and Richmond; innumerable novels dealing with American politics, business, society, science, racial problems, art, literature, and moving pictures, and with Americans abroad at peace or in war; finally several novels of change and growth, tracing the swift decades for their own sweet lavender or protesting vaguely and ineffectually against the industrialization of our beautiful old American life. We have had an Arnold Bennett for every five towns—surely by this time the foundations have been laid! Are we competent only to toil forever upon a never completed first floor whose specifications change from year to year?

In any case we are running through our material like spendthrifts—just as we have done before. In the Nineties there began a feverish search for any period of American history that hadn't been "used," and once found it was immediately debauched into a pretty and romantic story. These past seven years have seen the same sort of literary gold rush; and for all our boasted sincerity and sophistication, the material is being turned out raw and undigested in much the same way. One author goes to a midland farm for three months to obtain the material for an epic of the American husbandmen! Another sets off on a like errand to the Blue Ridge Mountains, a third departs with a Corona for the West Indies—one is justified in the belief that what they get hold of will weigh no more than the journalistic loot brought back by Richard Harding Davis and John Fox, Jr., twenty years ago.

Worse, the result will be doctored up to give it a literary flavor. The farm story will be sprayed with a faint dilution of ideas and sensory impressions from Thomas Hardy; the novel of the Jewish tenement block will be festooned with wreaths from "Ulysses" and the later Gertrude Stein; the document of dreamy youth will be prevented from fluttering entirely away by means of great and half great names—Marx, Spencer, Wells, Edward Fitzgerald—dropped like paper weights here and there upon the pages. Finally the novel of business will be cudgeled into being satire by the questionable but constantly reiterated implication that the author and his readers don't partake of the American commercial instinct and aren't a little jealous.

And most of it—the literary beginnings of what was to have been a golden age—is as dead as if it had never been written. Scarcely one of those who put so much effort and enthusiasm, even intelligence, into it, got hold of any material at all.

To a limited extent this was the fault of two men—one of whom, H. L. Mencken, has yet done more for American letters than any man alive. What Mencken felt the absence of, what he wanted, and justly, back in 1920, got away from him, got twisted in his hand. Not because the "literary revolution" went beyond him but because his idea had always been ethical rather than aesthetic. In the history of culture no pure aesthetic idea has ever served as an offensive weapon. Mencken's invective, sharp as Swift's, made its point by the use of the most forceful prose style now written in English. Immediately, instead of committing himself to an infinite series of pronouncements upon the American novel, he should have modulated his tone to the more urbane, more critical one of his early essay on Dreiser.

But perhaps it was already too late. Already he had begotten a family of hammer and tongs men—insensitive, suspicious of glamour, preoccupied exclusively with the external, the contemptible, the "national" and the drab, whose style was a debasement of his least effective manner and who, like glib children, played continually with his themes in his maternal shadow. These were the men who manufactured enthusiasm when each new mass of raw data was dumped on the literary platform—mistaking incoherence for vitality, chaos for vitality. It was the "new poetry movement" over again, only that this time its victims were worth the saving. Every week some new novel gave its author membership in "that little band who are producing a worthy American literature." As one of the charter members of that little band I am proud to state that it has now swollen to seventy or eighty members.

And through a curious misconception of his work, Sherwood Anderson must take part of the blame for this enthu-

siastic march up a blind alley in the dark. To this day reviewers solemnly speak of him as an inarticulate, fumbling man,
bursting with ideas—when, on the contrary, he is the posses-
sor of a brilliant and almost inimitable prose style, and of scarcely any ideas at all. Just as the prose of Joyce in the hands of,
say, Waldo Frank becomes insignificant and idiotic, so the Anderson admirers set up Hergesheimer as an anti-Christ and
then proceed to imitate Anderson's lapses from that difficult
simplicity they are unable to understand. And here again critics support them by discovering merits in the very disorgan-
ization that is to bring their books to a timely and unregret-
ted doom.

Now the business is over. "Wolf" has been cried too often.
The public, weary of being fooled, has gone back to its Englishmen, its memoirs and its prophets. Some of the late brilliant boys are on lecture tours (a circular informs me that most
of them are to speak upon "the literary revolution!"), some
are writing pot boilers, a few have definitely abandoned the
literary life—they were never sufficiently aware that material, however closely observed, is as elusive as the moment in
which it has its existence unless it is purified by an incorrupt-
ible style and by the catharsis of a passionate emotion.

Of all the work by the young men who have sprung up
since 1920 one book survives—"The Enormous Room" by E.
E. Cummings. It is scarcely a novel; it doesn't deal with the
American scene; it was swamped in the mediocre downpour,
isolated—forgotten. But it lives on, because those few who
cause books to live have not been able to endure the thought
of its mortality. Two other books, both about the war, complete the possible salvage from the work of the younger generation—"Through the Wheat" and "Three Soldiers," but
the former despite its fine last chapters doesn't stand up as
"Les Croix de Bois" and "The Red Badge of Courage," while
the latter is marred by its pervasive flavor of contemporary
indignation. But as an augury that someone has profited by this
dismal record of high hope and stale failure comes the first
work of Ernest Hemingway.

II

"In Our Time" consists of fourteen stories, short and long, with fifteen vivid miniatures interpolated between them. When I try to think of any contemporary American short stories as good as "Big Two-Hearted River," the last one in the book, only Gertrude Stein's "Melanctha," Anderson's "The Egg," and Lardner's "Golden Honeymoon" come to mind. It is the account of a boy on a fishing trip—he hikes, pitches his tent, cooks dinner, sleeps, and next morning casts for trout. Nothing more—but I read it with the most breathless unwilling interest I have experienced since Conrad first bent my reluctant eyes upon the sea.

The hero, Nick, runs through nearly all the stories, until the book takes on almost an autobiographical tint—in fact "My Old Man," one of the two in which this element seems entirely absent, is the least successful of all. Some of the stories show influences but they are invariably absorbed and transmuted, while in "My Old Man" there is an echo of Anderson's way of thinking in those sentimental "horse stories," which inaugurated his respectability and also his decline four years ago.

But with "The Doctor and the Doctor's Wife," "The End of Something," "The Three Day Blow," "Mr. and Mrs. Elliot," and "Soldier's Home" you are immediately aware of something temperamentally new. In the first of these a man is backed down by a half breed Indian after committing himself to a fight. The quality of humilation in the story is so intense that it immediately calls up every such incident in the reader's past. Without the aid of a comment or a pointing finger one knows exactly the sharp emotion of young Nick who watches the scene.

The next two stories describe an experience at the last edge of adolescence. You are constantly aware of the continual snapping of ties that is going on around Nick. In the half stewed, immature conversation before the fire you watch the awakening of that vast unrest that descends upon the emotional type at about eighteen. Again there is not a single recourse to exposition. As in "Big Two-Hearted River," a picture—sharp, nostalgic, tense—develops before your eyes. When the picture is complete a light seems to snap out, the story is over. There is no tail, no sudden change of pace at the end to throw into relief what has gone before.

Nick leaves home penniless; you have a glimpse of him lying wounded in the street of a battered Italian town, and later of a love affair with a nurse on a hospital roof in Milan. Then in one of the best of the stories he is home again. The last glimpse of him is when his mother asks him, with all the bitter world in his heart, to kneel down beside her in the dining room in Puritan prayer.

Anyone who first looks through the short interpolated sketches will hardly fail to read the stories themselves. "The Garden at Mons" and "The Barricade" are profound essays upon the English officer, written on a postage stamp. "The King of Greece's Tea Party," "The Shooting of the Cabinet Ministers," and "The Cigar-store Robbery" particularly fascinated me, as they did when Edmund Wilson first showed them to me in an earlier pamphlet, over two years ago.

Disregard the rather ill considered blurbs upon the cover. It is sufficient that here is no raw food served up by the railroad restaurants of California and Wisconsin. In the best of these dishes there is not a bit to spare. And many of us who have grown weary of admonitions to "watch this man or that" have felt a sort of renewal of excitement at these stories wherein Ernest Hemingway turns a corner into the street.

ONE HUNDRED FALSE STARTS*

Crack!" goes the pistol and off starts this entry. Sometimes he has caught it just right; more often he has jumped the gun. On these occasions, if he is lucky, he runs only a dozen yards, looks around and jogs sheepishly back to the starting place. But too frequently he makes the entire circuit of the track under the impression that he is leading the field, and reaches the finish to find he has no following. The race must be run all over again.

A little more training, take a long walk, cut out that nightcap, no meat at dinner, and stop worrying about politics—

So runs an interview with one of the champion false starters of the writing profession—myself. Opening a leather-bound wastebasket which I fatuously refer to as my "notebook," I pick out at random a small, triangular piece of wrapping paper with a canceled stamp on one side. On the other side is written:

Boopsie Dee was cute.

*"One Hundred False Starts" (Copyright 1933 The Curtis Publishing Company, Inc; renewal copyright © 1961 Frances Scott Fitzgerald Lanahan) is reprinted with the permission of Charles Scribner's Sons and Laurence Pollinger Limited from *Afternoon of an Author* by F. Scott Fitzgerald.

317

Nothing more. No cue as to what was intended to follow that preposterous statement. Boopsie Dee, indeed, confronting me with this single dogmatic fact about herself. Never will I know what happened to her, where and when she picked up her revolting name, and whether her cuteness got her into much trouble.

I pick out another scrap:

> Article: Unattractive Things Girls Do, to pair with counter article by woman: Unattractive Things Men Do.
>   No. 1. Remove glass eye at dinner table.

That's all there is on that scrap. Evidently, an idea that had dissolved into hilarity before it had fairly got under way. I try to revive it seriously. What unattractive things do girls do—I mean universally nowadays—or what unattractive things do a great majority of them do, or a strong minority? I have a few feeble ideas, but no, the notion is dead, I can only think of an article I read somewhere about a woman who divorced her husband because of the way he stalked a chop, and wondering at the same time why she didn't try him out on a chop before she married him. No, that all belongs to a gilded age when people could afford to have nervous breakdowns because of the squeak in daddy's shoes.

Lines to an Old Favorite

There are hundreds of these hunches. Not all of them have to do with literature. Some are hunches about importing a troupe of Ouled Naïl dancers from Africa, about bringing the Grand-Guignol from Paris to New York, about resuscitating football at Princeton—I have two scoring plays that will make a coach's reputation in one season—and there is a faded note to "explain to D. W. Griffith why costume plays are sure to come back." Also my plan for a film version of H. G. Wells' History of the World.

These little flurries caused me no travail—they were opium eater's illusions, vanishing with the smoke of the pipe, or you know what I mean. The pleasure of thinking about them was the exact equivalent of having accomplished them. It is the six-page, ten-page, thirty-page globs of paper that grieve me professionally, like unsuccessful oil shafts; they represent my false starts.

There is, for example, one false start which I have made at least a dozen times. It is—or rather has tried to take shape as—a short story. At one time or another, I have written as many words on it as would make a presentable novel, yet the present version is only about twenty-five hundred words long and hasn't been touched for two years. Its present name—it has gone under various aliases—is The Barnaby Family.

From childhood I have had a daydream—what a word for one whose entire life is spent noting them down—about starting at scratch on a desert island and building a comparatively high state of civilization out of the materials at hand. I always felt that Robinson Crusoe cheated when he rescued the tools from the wreck, and this applies equally to the Swiss Family Robinson, the Two Little Savages, and the balloon castaways of The Mysterious Island. In my story, not only would no convenient grain of wheat, repeating rifle, 4000 H. P. Diesel engine or technocratic butler be washed ashore but even my characters would be helpless city dwellers with no more wood lore than a cuckoo out of a clock.

The creation of such characters was easy, and it was easy washing them ashore:

For three long hours they were prostrated on the beach. Then Donald sat up.

"Well, here we are," he said with sleepy vagueness.

"Where?" his wife demanded eagerly.

"It couldn't be America and it couldn't be the Philippines," he said, "because we started from one and haven't got to the other."

"I'm thirsty," said the child.

Donald's eyes went quickly to the shore.

"Where's the raft?" He looked rather accusingly at Vivian. "Where's the raft?"

"It was gone when I woke up."

"It would be," he exclaimed bitterly. "Somebody might

have thought of bringing the jug of water ashore. If I don't do it, nothing is done in this house—I mean this family."

All right, go on from there. Anybody—you back there in the tenth row—step up! Don't be afraid. Just go on with the story. If you get stuck, you can look up tropical fauna and flora in the encyclopedia, or call up a neighbor who has been shipwrecked.

Anyhow, that's the exact point where my story—and I still think it's a great plot—begins to creak and groan with unreality. I turn around after a while with a sense of uneasiness—how could anybody believe that rubbish about monkeys throwing coconuts?—trot back to the starting place, and I resume my crouch for days and days.

A Murder That Didn't Jell

During such days I sometimes examine a clot of pages which is headed Ideas for Possible Stories. Among others, I find the following:

> Bath water in Princeton or Florida.
> Plot—suicide, indulgence, hate, liver and circumstance.
> Snubbing or having somebody.
> Dancer who found she could fly.

Oddly enough, all these are intelligible, if not enlightening, suggestions to me. But they are all old—old. I am as apt to be stimulated by them as by my signature or the beat of my feet pacing the floor. There is one that for years has puzzled me, that is as great a mystery as Boopsie Dee.

Story: The Winter Was Cold

Characters

Victoria Cuomo
Mark de Vinci
Jason Tenweather
Ambulance surgeon
Stark, a watchman

What was this about? Who were these people? I have no doubt that one of them was to be murdered or else be a murderer. But all else about the plot I have forgotten long ago.

I turn over a little. Here is something over which I linger longer; a false start that wasn't bad, that might have been run out.

Words

When you consider the more expensive article and finally decide on the cheaper one, the salesman is usually thoughtful enough to make it all right for you. "You'll probably get the most wear out of this," he says consolingly, or even, "That's the one I'd choose myself."

The Trimbles were like that. They were specialists in the neat promotion of the next best into the best.

"It'll do to wear around the house," they used to say: or, "We want to wait until we can get a really nice one."

It was at this point that I decided I couldn't write about the Trimbles. They were very nice and I would have enjoyed somebody else's story of how they made out, but I couldn't get under the surface of their lives—what kept them content to make the best of things instead of changing things. So I gave them up.

There is the question of dog stories. I like dogs and would like to write at least one dog story in the style of Mr. Terhune, but see what happens when I take pen in hand:

Dog

THE STORY OF A LITTLE DOG

Only a newsboy with a wizened face, selling his papers on the corner. A big dog fancier, standing on the curb, laughed contemptuously and twitched up the collar of his Airedale coat. Another rich dog man gave a little bark of scorn from a passing taxicab.

But the newsboy was interested in the animal that had crept close to his feet. He was only a cur; his fuzzy coat was inherited from his mother, who had been a fashionable poodle, while in stature he resembled his father, a Great Dane. And somewhere there was a canary concerned, for a spray of yellow feathers projected from his backbone—

You see, I couldn't go on like that. Think of dog owners writing in to the editors from all over the country, protesting that I was no man for that job.

I am thirty-six years old. For eighteen years, save for a short space during the war, writing has been my chief interest in life, and I am in every sense a professional.

Yet even now when, at the recurrent cry of "Baby needs shoes," I sit down facing my sharpened pencils and block of legal-sized paper, I have a feeling of utter helplessness. I may write my story in three days or, as is more frequently the case, it may be six weeks before I have assembled anything worthy to be sent out. I can open a volume from a criminal-law library and find a thousand plots. I can go into highway and byway, parlor and kitchen, and listen to personal revelations that, at the hands of other writers, might endure forever. But all that is nothing—not even enough for a false start.

Twice-Told Tales

Mostly, we authors must repeat ourselves—that's the truth. We have two or three great and moving experiences in our lives—experiences so great and moving that it doesn't seem at the time that anyone else has been so caught up and pounded and dazzled and astonished and beaten and broken and rescued and illuminated and rewarded and humbled in just that way ever before.

Then we learn our trade, well or less well, and we tell our two or three stories—each time in a new disguise—maybe ten times, maybe a hundred, as long as people will listen.

If this were otherwise, one would have to confess to having no individuality at all. And each time I honestly believe that, because I have found a new background and a novel twist, I have really got away from the two or three fundamental tales I have to tell. But it is rather like Ed Wynn's famous anecdote about the painter of boats who was begged to paint some ancestors for a client. The bargain was arranged, but with the painter's final warning that the ancestors would all turn out to look like boats.

When I face the fact that all my stories are going to have a certain family resemblance, I am taking a step toward avoiding false starts. If a friend says he's got a story for me and launches into a tale of being robbed by Brazilian pirates in a swaying straw hut on the edge of a smoking volcano in the Andes, with his fiancée bound and gagged on the roof, I can well believe there were various human emotions involved; but having successfully avoided pirates, volcanoes and fiancées who get themselves bound and gagged on roofs, I can't feel them. Whether it's something that happened twenty years ago or only yesterday, I must start out with an emotion—one that's close to me and that I can understand.

It's an Ill Wind

Last summer I was hauled to the hospital with high fever and a tentative diagnosis of typhoid. My affairs were in no better shape than yours are, reader. There was a story I should have written to pay my current debts, and I was haunted by the fact that I hadn't made a will. If I had really had typhoid I wouldn't have worried about such things, nor made that scene at the hospital when the nurses tried to plump me into an ice bath. I didn't have either the typhoid or the bath, but I continued to rail against my luck that just at this crucial moment I should have to waste two weeks in bed, answering the baby talk of nurses and getting nothing done at all. But three days after I was discharged I had finished a story about a hospital.

The material was soaking in and I didn't know it. I was profoundly moved by fear, apprehension, worry, impatience;

every sense was acute, and that is the best way of accumulating material for a story. Unfortunately, it does not always
come so easily. I say to myself—looking at the awful blank
block of paper— "Now, here's this man Swankins that I've
known and liked for ten years. I am privy to all his private affairs, and some of them are wows. I've threatened to write about
him, and he says to go ahead and do my worst."

But can I? I've been in as many jams as Swankins, but
I didn't look at them the same way, nor would it ever have occurred to me to extricate myself from the Chinese police or
from the clutches of that woman in the way Swankins chose.
I could write some fine paragraphs about Swankins, but build
a story around him that would have an ounce of feeling in it—
impossible.

Or into my distraught imagination wanders a girl named
Elsie about whom I was almost suicidal for a month, in 1916.

"How about me?" Elsie says. "Surely you swore to a lot
of emotion back there in the past. Have you forgotten?"

"No, Elsie, I haven't forgotten."

"Well, then, write a story about me. You haven't seen
me for twelve years, so you don't know how fat I am now and
how boring I often seem to my husband."

"No, Elsie, I—"

"Oh, come on. Surely I must be worth a story. Why, you
used to hang around saying good-bye with your face so miserable and comic that I thought I'd go crazy myself before
I got rid of you. And now you're afraid even to start a story
about me. Your feeling must have been pretty thin if you can't
revive it for a few hours."

"No, Elsie; you don't understand. I have written about
you a dozen times. That funny little rabbit curl to your lip,
I used it in a story six years ago. The way your face all changed
just when you were going to laugh—I gave that characteristic to one of the first girls I ever wrote about. The way I stayed
around trying to say good night, knowing that you'd rush to
the phone as soon as the front door closed behind me—all
that was in a book that I wrote once upon a time."

"I see. Just because I didn't respond to you, you broke me into bits and used me up piecemeal."

"I'm afraid so, Elsie. You see, you never so much as kissed me, except that once with a kind of a shove at the same time, so there really isn't any story."

Plots without emotions, emotions without plots. So it goes sometimes. Let me suppose, however, that I have got under way; two days' work, two thousand words are finished and being typed for a first revision. And suddenly doubts overtake me.

A Jury of One

What if I'm just horsing around? What's going on in this regatta anyhow? Who could care what happens to the girl, when the sawdust is obviously leaking out of her moment by moment? How did I get the plot all tangled up? I am alone in the privacy of my faded blue room with my sick cat, the bare February branches waving at the window, an ironic paper weight that says Business is Good, a New England conscience—developed in Minnesota—and my greatest problem:

"Shall I run it out? Or shall I turn back?"

Shall I say:

"I know I had something to prove, and it may develop farther along in the story?"

Or:

"This is just bullheadedness. Better throw it away and start over."

The latter is one of the most difficult decisions that an author must make. To make it philosophically, before he has exhausted himself in a hundred-hour effort to resuscitate a corpse or disentangle innumerable wet snarls, is a test of whether or not he is really a professional. There are often occasions when such a decision is doubly difficult. In the last stages of a novel, for instance, where there is no question of junking the whole, but when an entire favorite character has to be hauled out by the heels, screeching, and dragging half a dozen good scenes with him.

It is here that these confessions tie up with a general problem as well as with those peculiar to a writer. The decision as to when to quit, as to when one is merely floundering around and causing other people trouble, has to be made frequently in a lifetime. In youth we are taught the rather simple rule never to quit, because we are presumably following programs made by people wiser than ourselves. My own conclusion is that when one has embarked on a course that grows increasingly doubtful and feels the vital forces beginning to be used up, it is best to ask advice, if decent advice is within range. Columbus didn't and Lindbergh couldn't. So my statement at first seems heretical toward the idea that it is pleasantest to live with—the idea of heroism. But I make a sharp division between one's professional life, when, after the period of apprenticeship, not more than 10 per cent of advice is worth a hoot, and one's private and worldly life when often almost anyone's judgment is better than one's own.

Once, not so long ago, when my work was hampered by so many false starts that I thought the game was up at last, and when my personal life was even more thoroughly obfuscated, I asked an old Alabama Negro:

"Uncle Bob, when things get so bad that there isn't any way out, what do you do then?"

Homely Advice, But Sound

The heat from the kitchen stove stirred his white sideburns as he warmed himself. If I cynically expected a platitudinous answer, a reflection of something remembered from Uncle Remus, I was disappointed.

"Mr. Fitzgerald," he said, "when things get that-away I wuks."

It was good advice. Work is almost everything. But it would be nice to be able to distinguish useful work from mere labor expended. Perhaps that is part of work itself—to find the difference. Perhaps my frequent, solitary sprints around the track are profitable. Shall I tell you about another one? Very well. You see, I had this hunch—But in counting the pages, I find that my time is up and I must put my book of mistakes away. On the fire? No! I put it weakly back in the drawer. These old mistakes are now only toys—and expensive ones at that—give them a toy's cupboard and then hurry back into the serious business of my profession. Joseph Conrad defined it more clearly, more vividly than any man of our time:

"My task is by the power of the written word to make you hear, to make you feel—it is, before all, to make you see."

It's not very difficult to run back and start over again—especially in private. What you aim at is to get in a good race or two when the crowd is in the stand.

LETTERS
To Maxwell Perkins*

[Dec. 20?, 1924]

Dear Max:

... With the aid you've given me I can make *Gatsby* perfect. The Chapter 7 (the hotel scene) will never quite be up to mark—I've worried about it too long and I can't quite place Daisy's reaction. But I can improve it a lot. It isn't imaginative energy that's lacking—it's because I'm automatically prevented from thinking it out over again *because I must get all those characters to New York* in order to have the catastrophe on the road going back, and I must have it pretty much that way. So there's no chance of bringing the freshness to it that a new free conception sometimes gives.

The rest is easy and I see my way so clear that I even see the mental quirks that queered it before. Strange to say, my notion of Gatsby's vagueness was O.K. What you and Louise and Mr. Charles Scribner found wanting was that:

I myself didn't know what Gatsby looked like or was en-

*Reprinted with permission of Charles Scribner's Sons and Laurence Pollinger Limited from *The Letters of F. Scott Fitzgerald,* pages 172-173, edited by Andrew Turnbull. Copyright © 1963 Frances Scott Fitzgerald Lanahan.

gaged in and you felt it. If I'd known and kept it from you you'd have been *too impressed with my knowledge to protest.* This is a complicated idea but I'm sure you'll understand. But I know now—and as a penalty for not having known first, in other words to make sure, I'm going to tell more.

It seems of almost mystical significance to me that you thought he was older—the man I had in mind, half-unconsciously, *was* older (a specific individual) and evidently, without so much as a definite word, I conveyed the fact. Or rather I must qualify this Shaw Desmond trash by saying that I conveyed it without a word that I can at present or for the life of me trace. (I think Shaw Desmond was one of your bad bets—I was the other.)

Anyhow after careful searching of the files (of a man's mind here) for the Fuller Magee case and after having had Zelda draw pictures until her fingers ache I know Gatsby better than I know my own child. My first instinct after your letter was to let him go and have Tom Buchanan dominate the book (I suppose he's the best character I've ever done—I think he and the brother in *Salt* and Hurstwood in *Sister Carrie* are the three best characters in American fiction in the last twenty years, perhaps and perhaps not) but Gatsby sticks in my heart. I had him for awhile, then lost him, and now I know I have him again. I'm sorry Myrtle is better than Daisy. Jordan of course was a great idea (perhaps you know it's Edith Cummings) but she fades out. It's Chapter VII that's the trouble with Daisy and it may hurt the book's popularity that it's *a man's book.*

Anyhow I think (for the first time since *The Vegetable* failed) that I'm a wonderful writer and it's your always wonderful letters that help me to go on believing in myself. . . .

Always yours,

Scott Fitz—

To Maxwell Perkins*

Dear Max:

Reading Tom Wolfe's story in the current *Modern Monthly*[1] makes me wish he was the sort of person you could talk to about his stuff. It has all his faults and virtues. It seems to me that with any sense of humor he could see the Dreiserian absurdities of how the circus people "ate the cod, bass, mackerel, halibut, clams and oysters of the New England coast, the terrapin of Maryland, the fat beeves, porks and cereals of the middle west," etc., etc., down to "the pink meated lobsters that grope their way along the sea-floors of America." And then (after one of his fine paragraphs which sounds a note to be expanded later) he remarks that they leave nothing behind except "the droppings of the camel and the elephant in Illinois." A few pages further on his redundance ruined some paragraphs (see the last complete paragraph on page 103) that

*Reprinted with permission of Charles Scribner's Sons and Laurence Pollinger Limited from *The Letters of F. Scott Fitzgerald,* pages 262-263, edited by Andrew Turnbull. Copyright © 1963 Frances Scott Fitzgerald Lanahan.

[1]"Circus at Dawn."

might have been gorgeous. I sympathize with his use of repetition, of Joyce-like words, endless metaphor, but I wish he could have seen the disgust in Edmund Wilson's face when I once tried to interpolate part of a rhymed sonnet in the middle of a novel, disguised as prose. How he can put side by side such a mess as "With chitterling tricker fast-fluttering skirrs of sound the palmy honied birderies came" and such fine phrases as "tongue-trilling chirrs, plumbellied smoothness, sweet lucidity" I don't know. He who has such infinite power of suggestion and delicacy has absolutely no right to glut people on whole meals of caviar. I hope to Christ he isn't taking all these emasculated paeans to his vitality very seriously. I'd hate to see such an exquisite talent turn into one of those muscle-bound and useless giants seen in a circus. Athletes have got to learn their games; they shouldn't just be content to tense their muscles, and if they do they suddenly find when called upon to bring off a necessary effect they are simply liable to hurl the shot into the crowd and not break any records at all. The metaphor is mixed but I think you will understand what I mean, and that he would too—save for his tendency to almost feminine horror if he thinks anyone is going to lay hands on his precious talent. I think his lack of humility is his most difficult characteristic, a lack oddly enough which I associate only with second or third rate writers. He was badly taught by bad teachers and now he hates learning.

There is another side of him that I find myself doubting, but this is something that no one could ever teach or tell him. His lack of feeling other people's passions, the lyrical value of Eugene Gant's love affair with the universe—is that going to last through a whole saga? God, I wish he could discipline himself and really plan a novel. . . .

Ever yours,

Scott

To Ernest Hemingway*

June 1, 1934

Dear Ernest:

. . . Next to go to the mat with you on a couple of technical
points. The reason I had written you a letter was that Dos
dropped in in passing through and said you had brought up
about my book what we talked about once in a café on the
Avenue de Neuilly about composite characters. Now, I don't
entirely dissent from the theory but I don't believe you can
try to prove your point on such a case as Bunny using his own
father as the sire of John Dos Passos, or in the case of this book
that covers ground that you personally paced off about the
same time I was doing it. In either of those cases how could
you trust your own detachment? If you had never met any of
the originals then your opinion would be more convincing.

   Following this out a little farther, when does the proper
and logical combination of events, cause and effect, etc., end

   *Reprinted with permission of Charles Scribner's Sons and Laurence Pol-
linger Limited from *The Letters of F. Scott Fitzgerald,* pages 308-310, edited
by Andrew Turnbull. Copyright © 1963 Frances Scott Fitzgerald Lanahan.

and the field of imagination begin? Again you may be entirely right because I suppose you were applying the idea particularly to the handling of the creative faculty in one's mind rather than to the effect upon the stranger reading it. Nevertheless, I am not sold on the subject, and especially to account for the big flaws of *Tender* on that ground doesn't convince me. Think of the case of the Renaissance artists, and of the Elizabethan dramatists, the first having to superimpose a medieval conception of science and archeology, etc., upon the Bible story; and, in the second, of Shakespeare's trying to interpret the results of his own observation of the life around him on the basis of Plutarch's *Lives* and Hollinshed's *Chronicles.* There you must admit that the feat of building a monument out of three kinds of marble was brought off. You can accuse me justly of not having the power to bring it off, but a theory that it can't be done is highly questionable. I make this point with such persistence because such a conception, if you stick to it, might limit your own choice of materials. The idea can be reduced simply to: you can't say *accurately* that composite characterization hurt my book, but that it only hurt it for you.

To take a case specifically, that of Gerald and Sara. I don't know how much you think you know about my relations with them over a long time, but from certain remarks that you let drop, such as one "Gerald threw you over," I guess that you didn't even know the beginning of our relations. . . .[1]

I think it is obvious that my respect for your artistic life is absolutely unqualified, that save for a few of the dead or dying old men you are the only man writing fiction in America that I look up to very much. There are pieces and paragraphs of your work that I read over and over—in fact, I stopped myself doing it for a year and a half because I was afraid that your particular rhythms were going to creep in on mine by process of infiltration. Perhaps you will recognize some of your remarks in *Tender,* but I did every damn thing I could to avoid that. (By the way, I didn't read the Wescott story of

---

[1]Fitzgerald's punctuation. Nothing is omitted.

Villefranche sailors till I'd done my own version. Think that was the wisest course, for me anyhow, and got a pleasant letter from him in regard to the matter.)

To go back to my theme song, the second technical point that might be of interest to you concerns direct steals from an idea of yours, an idea of Conrad's and a few lines out of David-into-Fox-Garnett. The theory back of it I got from Conrad's preface to *The Nigger,* that the purpose of a work of fiction is to appeal to the lingering after-effects in the reader's mind as differing from, say, the purpose of oratory or philosophy which respectively leave people in a fighting or thoughtful mood. The second contribution to the burglary was your trying to work out some such theory in your troubles with the very end of *A Farewell to Arms.* I remember that your first draft—or at least the first one I saw—gave a sort of old-fashioned Alger book summary of the future lives of the characters: "The priest became a priest under Fascism," etc., and you may remember my suggestion to take a burst of eloquence from anywhere in the book that you could find it and tag off with that; you were against this idea because you felt that the true line of a work of fiction was to take a reader up to a high emotional pitch but then let him down or ease him off. You gave no aesthetic reason for this—nevertheless, you convinced me. The third piece of burglary contributing to this symposium was my admiration of the dying fall in the aforesaid Garnett's book and I imitated it as accurately as it is humanly decent in my own ending of *Tender,* telling the reader in the last pages that, after all, this is just a casual event, and trying to let *him* come to bat for *me* rather than going out to shake his nerves, whoop him up, then leaving him rather in a condition of a frustrated woman in bed. (Did that ever happen to you in your days with MacCallagan or McKisco, Sweetie?) . . .

Ever your friend,

[Scott]

To Frances Turnbull*[1]

November 9, 1938

Dear Frances:

I've read the story carefully and, Frances, I'm afraid the price for doing professional work is a good deal higher than you are prepared to pay at present. You've got to sell you heart, your strongest reactions, not the little minor things that only touch you lightly, the little experiences that you might tell at dinner. This is especially true when you *begin* to write, when you have not yet developed the tricks of interesting people on paper, when you have none of the technique,which it takes time to learn. When, in short, you have *only* your emotions to sell.

   This is the experience of all writers. It was necessary for Dickens to put into *Oliver Twist* the child's passionate resentment at being abused and starved that had haunted his whole childhood. Ernest Hemingway's first stories, *In Our Time,*

*Reprinted with permission of Charles Scribner's Sons and Laurence Pollinger Limited from *The Letters of F. Scott Fitzgerald,* pages 577-578, edited by Andrew Turnbull. Copyright © 1963 Frances Scott Fitzgerald Lanahan.

[1]Frances Turnbull, a sophomore at Radcliffe, had sent Fitzgerald one of her "Sketches by a Debutante."

went right down to the bottom of all that he had ever felt and known. In *This Side of Paradise* I wrote about a love affair that was still bleeding as fresh as the skin wound on a haemophile.

The amateur, seeing how the professional, having learned all that he'll ever learn about writing, can take a trivial thing such as the most superficial reactions of three uncharacterized girls and make it witty and charming—the amateur thinks he or she can do the same. But the amateur can only realize his ability to transfer his emotions to another person by some such desperate and radical expedient as tearing your first tragic love story out of your heart and putting it on pages for people to see.

That, anyhow, is the price of admission. Whether you are prepared to pay it, or whether it coincides or conflicts with your attitude on what is "nice" is something for you to decide. But literature, even light literature, will accept nothing less from the neophyte. It is one of those professions that want the "works." You wouldn't be interested in a soldier who was only a *little* brave.

In the light of this, it doesn't seem worthwhile to analyze why this story isn't salable but I am too fond of you to kid you along about it, as one tends to do at my age. If you ever decide to tell *your* stories, no one would be more interested than

Your old friend,

F. Scott Fitzgerald

P.S. I might say that the writing is smooth and agreeable and some of the pages very apt and charming. You have talent— which is the equivalent of a soldier having the right physical qualifications for entering West Point.

John Dos Passos

THE WORKMAN AND HIS TOOLS*

An apologia at thirty-six. Thirteen years after writing *Three Soldiers,* I had to read it over to correct misprints for a new edition. It was not exactly a comfortable task. The memory of the novel I wanted to write had not faded enough yet to make it easy to read the novel I did write.

The memory of the spring of 1919 . . .[1] Any spring is a time of overturn. But then Lenin was alive. We thought the Soviets were New England townmeetings on a larger scale. Socialism seemed a radiant dawn. The Seattle general strike seemed the beginning of a flood instead of the beginning of an ebb. Americans in Paris were groggy with new things in theatre and painting and music. Picasso was to rebuild the eye. Stravinski was cramming the Russian steppes into our ears. Imperial America was all shiny with the idea of Ritz. Currents of energy seemed breaking out everywhere as young guys climbed out of their uniforms. In every direction the countries of the world stretched out starving and angry, ready for

*Reprinted with permission of John Dos Passos from *Occasions and Protests* by John Dos Passos, published by the Henry Regnery Company. Copyright 1964 by John Dos Passos.

[1]The punctuation here and below is Dos Passos'. The complete essay is reprinted.

anything turbulent and new. Whenever you went to the movies you saw Charlie Chaplin at his best . . . The memory of the spring of 1919 had not faded enough yet to make the spring of 1932 any easier. It wasn't that *today* was any finer in 1919 than in 1932, it was that in 1919 the tomorrows seemed vaster. Growing up is the process of pinching off the buds of tomorrow.

Most of us who were youngsters in 1919 had already, by the spring of 1932, made our beds and lain in them. You wake up one morning and find out that what was to have been a spring-board into reality is a profession. The organization of your life that was to be an instrument to make you see more and clearer, turns out to be blinders made according to a predestined pattern. The boy who thought he was going to be a tramp turns out a nearsighted middleclass intellectual (or a tramp, it's as bad either way). Professional deformations set in. The freeswimming young oyster fastens to the rock and grows a shell.

Well, you're a novelist. Why? Why not? What excuse have you got for not being ashamed of yourself?

Not that there's any reason, I suppose, for being unduly ashamed of the trade of novelist. A novel is a commodity which fulfills a certain need; people need to buy daydreams the way they need to buy ice cream or aspirin or gin. They even need to buy a pinch of intellectual catnip now and then to liven up their thoughts, a few drops of poetry to liven up their feelings. All you need to do to feel good about your work is to turn out the best commodity you can, play the luxury market and to hell with doubt.

The trouble is that mass production involves a change in the relationship between the workman and his tools. In the Middle Ages the mere setting down of the written word was a marvel; something of that marvel got into the words set down. In the Renaissance the printing press suddenly opened up a continent more tremendous than America. Sixteenth and seventeenth century writers are all on fire with it. Now we have linotype, automatic typesetting machines, phototype and offset processes that plaster the world from end to end with print. Certainly eighty percent of the inhabitants of the United States read a mess of print a day, if it's only the advertising on tooth paste or the Sears Roebuck catalogue.

The perfection of the machinery of publication ought to be a stimulant to good work. But first the writer must decide exactly what he's cramming all these words into print for; the Freudian gush about selfexpression that fills the minds of newspaper critics and publishers' logrollers, emphatically won't do. Making a living by selling daydreams, sensations, packets of mental itching powders, may be all right, but I think most people feel it's not much of a life for a healthy adult. You can make money by it, sure; but for a hundred reasons profit is a wornout motive, tending more and more to strangle on its own power and complexity. No producer, even the producer of the shoddiest of five and ten cent store goods, can do much about money; the man who wants to play with the power of money has to go out after it straight, without any other interest. Writing for money is as silly as writing for selfexpression.

What do you write for then? To convince people of something? That's preaching, and is part of the business of everybody who deals with words; not to admit that is to play with a gun and say you didn't know it was loaded. But outside of preaching I think there is such a thing as writing for writing's sake. A cabinetmaker enjoys whittling a dovetail because he's a cabinetmaker; every type of work has its own delight inherent in it. The mind of a generation is its speech. A writer makes aspects of that speech permanent by putting them in print. He whittles at the words and phrases of today and makes forms for the minds of later generations. That's history. A writer who writes straight is an architect of history.

On being invited to join a Communist writer's union. Anybody who can put the words down on paper is a writer in one sense, but being able to put words down on paper no more makes a man a professional writer than the fact that he can scratch up the ground and plant seeds in it makes him a farmer, or that he can trail a handline overboard makes him a fisherman. That is fairly obvious. The difficulty begins when you try to work out what really distinguishes professional writing from the average man's letters to his family and friends.

In times of rapid change when terms are continually turning inside out and the names of things hardly keep their meaning from day to day, it's not possible to write two honest paragraphs without stopping to take crossbearings on every one of the abstractions that were so well ranged in marble niches in the minds of our fathers. The whole question of what writing is has become particularly tangled in these years during which the industry of the printed word has reached its high point in profusion and wealth, and, to a certain extent, in power.

Three words which still have meaning, that I think we can apply to all professional writing, are discovery, originality, invention. The professional writer discovers some aspect of the world and invents out of the speech of his time some particularly apt and original way of putting it down on paper. If the product is compelling enough, it molds and influences ways of thinking to the point of changing and rebuilding the language, which canalizes the mind of the group. The process is not very different from that of scientific discovery and invention. The importance of a writer, as of a scientist, depends on his ability to influence thought. In his relation to society a professional writer is a technician just as much as an engineer is.

As in industrialized science, we have in writing all the steps between the complete belt conveyor factory system of production and one man handicraft. Newspapers, advertising offices, moving picture studios, political propaganda agencies, news magazines produce the collective type of writing where individual work is indistinguishable in the industrial synthesis. Historical and scientific works are often turned out by the laboratory method where various coworkers collaborate under one man's supervision. Songs and ballads are sometimes the result of the spontaneous efforts of a group working together. At present stories and poems are the commonest output of the isolated technician.

Any writer who has ever worked in any of these collective undertakings knows the difficulty of bucking the routine and the officeworker control that seems to be an inseparable part of large industrial enterprises, whether their aims are to make money or to improve human society or to furnish jobs for officeholders. It is a commonplace that business aims, which are to buy cheap and sell dear, are often opposed to the aims of the technician, which are, insofar as he is a technician and not a timeserver, the development of his material and of the technical possibilities of his work. The main problem in the life of every technician is to secure enough freedom from interference from the managers of the society in which he lives to be able to do his work.

As the era of free competition gives way to that of state monopoly, with the corresponding growth of officeworker control, inner office intrigue and the other maladies of bureaucracy, it becomes increasingly hard for the technician to get that freedom. The need for functional hierarchies on an enormous scale and the difficulty of keeping the hierarchies in check through popular control, makes the position of the technician extremely difficult; because, by his very function, he has to give his time to his work instead of to "organizational problems."

When you add to this disability the knowledge that the men behind the desks in the offices control the police power—indirectly in this country, but directly in the Communist countries—which can at their whim put a man in jail or deprive him of his life or of everything that makes life worth living, you can see that the technician, although the mechanical means in his power are growing every day, is in a position of increasing danger and uncertainty.

The only name you can give a situation in which a technician can do his best work, and be free to give rein to those doubts and unclassified impulses of curiosity which are at the root of invention and discovery and original thinking, is "liberty."

Liberty in the abstract is meaningless outside of philosophical chessgames. The word has taken on various misleading political colorations. In America it once meant liberty for the manufacturer to cut wages and throw his workers out on the street if they didn't like it; in labor union parlance it means liberty for the union leaders to force union members to strike whether they want to or not, and to vote as they are told.

But, underneath, the word still has a meaning that we all know, just as we know that a nickel is a nickel even if the Indian and the buffalo have been rubbed off. The writer as a technician must never, no matter how much he is carried away by even the noblest political partisanship in the fight for social justice, allow himself to forget that his real political aim, for himself and his fellows, is liberty.

A man can't discover anything, originate anything, invent anything unless he's at least morally free, without fear or preoccupation so far as his work goes. Maintaining that position in the face of the conflicting pulls of organized life demands a certain amount of nerve. You can see a miniature of the whole thing whenever a man performs even the smallest technical task, such as cleaning a carburetor, or taking a bead on a target with a rifle. His state of mind is entirely different from that of the owner of the car who wants to get somewhere, or of the man himself a second before he puts his eye to the sight, all of a fluster to win the match or in a cold sweat of fear lest his enemy shoot him first.

This state of mind, in which a man is ready to do good work, is a state of selfless relaxation, with no worries or urges except those of the work at hand. There is a kind of happiness about it. It is much nearer the way an ordinary daylaborer feels than it is the way a preacher, propagandist or swivelchair organizer feels. Anybody who has seen war knows the astonishing difference between the attitude of the men at the front, whose work is killing and dying, and that of the atrocity-haunted citizenry in the rear.

At this particular moment in history, when machines and institutions have so outgrown the ability of the mind to dominate them, we need bold and original thought more than ever. It is the business of writers to supply that thought, and not to make of themselves figureheads in political conflicts. I don't mean that a writer hasn't an obligation, like any other citizen, to take part if he can in the struggle against oppression, but his function as a citizen and his function as a technician are different, although the eventual end aimed at may in both cases be the same.

To fight oppression, and to work as best we can for a sane organization of society, we do not have to abandon the morality of freedom. If we do that we are letting the same thuggery in by the back door that we are fighting off in front of the house. I don't see how it is possible to organize effectively for the humane values of life without protecting and demanding during every minute of the fight the liberties of investigation, speech and discussion which are the greatest part of the ends of the struggle. In any organization a man gives up some of his liberty of action. That is necessary discipline. But if men give up their freedom of thought, what follows is boss rule, gang warfare and administrative stagnation.

The dilemma which faces honest technicians is how to combat the imperial and bureaucratic tendencies of the groups whose aims they believe in, without giving aid and comfort to the enemy. By the nature of his function as a technician, the writer finds himself in the dangerous and uncomfortable front line of this struggle.

In such a position a man is exposed to crossfire. He is as likely to be mowed down by his friends as his enemies. The writer has to face that. His only safety lies in the fact that the work of an able technician cannot be replaced. It is of use and a pleasure to mankind. If it weren't for that fact, reluctantly recognized, but everywhere and always recognized, the whole tribe of doubters, inventors and discoverers would have been so often wiped out that the race would have ceased to produce types with those peculiar traits.

It's an old saying, but a very apt one, that a writer writes not to be saved but to be damned. *Publico ergo damnatus.*

I feel that American writers who want to do the most valuable kind of work will find themselves trying to discover the deep currents under the surface of the opinions, the orthodoxies, the heresies, the gossip and the journalistic trivialities of the day. They will find that they have to keep their attention fixed on the simple needs of men and women. A writer can be a propagandist in the most limited sense of the word, or he can use his abilities for partisan invective or personal vituperation, but the living material out of which his work is built must be what used to be known as the humanities. The humanities—in the original sense of the word—are based on sharply whittled exactitudes about men's instincts and compulsions and hungers and thirsts.

There is no escaping the fact that you are dealing with all mankind, starting with all the readers of your language in your generation; with all the varied traditions out of the past and men's feelings and perceptions in the present. No matter how narrow a set of convictions you start from, you will find yourself, in your effort to probe into men and events, less and less able to work within the prescriptions of doctrine; and you will find more and more that you are on the side of the men, women and children alive right now against all the political organizations, however magnificent their aims may be, that regiment and bedevil them; and that you are on the side, not with phrases or opinions, but really and truly, of liberty, fraternity and humanity.

The words are old and dusty and hung with the faded bunting of a thousand political orations, but underneath they are still sound. What men once meant by these words needs defenders today. And if the kind of men who have, in all kinds of direct and devious ways, stood up for them throughout history do not come out for them now to defend them against the gangsterism of the political bosses and the zeal of the administrators, the world soon will be an even worse place for men, women and children to live in than it is at present.

The writer's liberty is indissolubly linked with the liberty of his fellowcitizens. There may have existed societies in the past where thinkers and painters could win their way into some privileged sanctuary where they would be comparatively free to express themselves as they pleased, but in the close-knit society imposed on us by the structure of mass production industry no such sanctuary exists. The writer is free to write and to publish what he believes to be true only insofar as the farmer is free to work his farm as he pleases, as the factory worker is free to move in search of better opportunities, as the bookkeepers or the merchants are able to make their livings as best they can without the supervision of some government's police.

For the ordinary citizen liberty means the freedom to make his own choices as to how he shall live his life, the freedom to be a complete man, instead of half a man. For the writer it is even more profoundly the essence of his being. It is freedom to search for the truth.

All writing which is in any way first rate is an effort to tell the truth. Good writing is useful to society because each first rate piece of work adds a little something new to truth. The old truths don't need retelling; first rate writing must always add something to man's knowledge of himself, of man's behavior when he runs in packs, of the world around him.

First rate writing—the casting of fresh ideas in new and noble words—is true in the profoundest sense of the word. From Homer and Confucius to our own day the first rate writers have managed to bring to light, in a thousand different styles and languages, varying fragments of that basic knowledge of man's hopes and fears, of his strengths and weaknesses, which we have a right to call truth.

Truth is by its very nature painful.

Men are able to live with old truths because they have become encysted in the commonplace, but fresh truths are painful to come by, and even more painful to hear. Particularly do they cause acute agony to the political bosses of this world who make their living by trying to run the lives of their fellowmen.

In a tolerably free society the man who uncovers some tiny capsule of truth has to face the chance of being derided and ignored. If he insists too much he is likely to be lynched. It was the free Athenians who voted the hemlock for Socrates.

In a state managed by policemen a man doesn't even have the opportunity to assume the objective attitude which is the necessary preliminary to the discovery of truth. The race of policemen, throughout history, has been quick to notice the first flicker of enquiry in a man's eye that marks the beginning of the questioning or inventive mood. A trouble-maker: get him out of the way.

Without liberty the writer cannot even begin to entertain those first untoward inquisitive thoughts about himself or the people around him which are the seeds of invention. Unless he can forget everything else in the painful search for some few fresh fragments of truth his work will be of no use to the world.

First rate writing is hard enough to come by under the most favorable conditions. Without liberty it is impossible.

Ernest Hemingway

DIGRESSIONS ON WRITING*

. . . Once I remember Gertrude Stein talking of bullfights spoke
of her admiration for Joselito and showed me some pictures
of him in the ring and of herself and Alice Toklas sitting in
in the first row of the wooden barreras at the bull ring at Valen-
cia with Joselito and his brother Gallo below, and I had just
come from the Near East, where the Greeks broke the legs
of their baggage and transport animals and drove and shoved
them off the quay into the shallow water when they abandoned the city of Smyrna, and I remember saying that I did not
like the bullfights because of the poor horses. I was trying to
write then and I found the greatest difficulty, aside from knowing truly what you really felt, rather than what you were supposed to feel, and had been taught to feel, was to put down
what really happened in action; what the actual things were
which produced the emotion that you experienced. In writing for a newspaper you told what happened and, with one
trick and another, you communicated the emotion aided by

*Reprinted with permission of Charles Scribner's Sons, the Executors of
the Ernest Hemingway Estate, and Jonathan Cape Ltd, from *Death in The Afternoon,* pages 1-4, 52-54, 173, 191-192 and 278 by Ernest Hemingway. Copyright 1932 Charles Scribner's Sons; renewal copyright © 1960 Ernest Hemingway. Title supplied by the editor.

the element of timeliness which gives a certain emotion to any account of something that has happened on that day; but the real thing, the sequence of motion and fact which made the emotion and which would be as valid in a year or in ten years or, with luck and if you stated it purely enough, always, was beyond me and I was working very hard to try to get it. The only place where you could see life and death, *i.e.,* violent death now that the wars were over, was in the bull ring and I wanted very much to go to Spain where I could study it. I was trying to learn to write, commencing with the simplest things, and one of the simplest things of all and the most fundamental is violent death. It has none of the complications of death by disease, or so-called natural death, or the death of a friend or some one you have loved or have hated, but it is death nevertheless, one of the subjects that a man may write of. I had read many books in which, when the author tried to convey it, he only produced a blur, and I decided that this was because either the author had never seen it clearly or at the moment of it, he had physically or mentally shut his eyes, as one might do if he saw a child that he could not possibly reach or aid, about to be struck by a train. In such a case I suppose he would probably be justified in shutting his eyes as the mere fact of the child being about to be struck by the train was all that he could convey, the actual striking would be an anti-climax, so that the moment before striking might be as far as he could represent. But in the case of an execution by a firing squad, or a hanging, this is not true, and if these very simple things were to be made permanent, as, say, Goya tried to make them in *Los Desastros de la Guerra,* it could not be done with any shutting of the eyes. I had seen certain things, certain simple things of this sort that I remembered, but through taking part in them, or, in other cases, having to write of them immediately after and consequently noticing the things I needed for instant recording, I had never been able to study them as a man might, for instance, study the death of his father or the hanging of some one, say, that he did not know and would not have to write of immediately after for the first edition of an afternoon newspaper.

So I went to Spain to see bullfights and to try to write about them for myself. I thought they would be simple and barbarous and cruel and that I would not like them, but that I would see certain definite action which would give me the feeling of life and death that I was working for. I found the definite action; but the bullfight was so far from simple and I liked it so much that it was much too complicated for my then equipment for writing to deal with and, aside from four very short sketches, I was not able to write anything about it for five years—and I wish I would have waited ten. However, if I had waited long enough I probably never would have written anything at all since there is a tendency when you really begin to learn something about a thing not to want to write about it but rather to keep on learning about it always and at no time, unless you are very egotistical, which, of course, accounts for many books, will you be able to say: now I know all about this and will write about it. Certainly I do not say that now; every year I know there is more to learn, but I know some things which may be interesting now, and I may be away from the bullfights for a long time and I might as well write what I know about them now. Also it might be good to have a book about bullfighting in English and a serious book on such an unmoral subject may have some value. . . .

The longest books on Spain are usually written by Germans who make one intensive visit and then never return. I should say that it is probably a good system, if one has to write books on Spain, to write them as rapidly as possible after a first visit as several visits could only confuse the first impressions and make conclusions much less easy to draw. Also the one-visit books are much surer of everything and are bound to be more popular. Books like Richard Ford's have never had the popularity of the bedside mysticism of such a book as *Virgin Spain*. The author of this book once published a piece in a now dead little magazine called *S4N* explaining how he did his writing. Any historian of letters wanting to explain certain phenomena of our writing can look it up in the files of that magazine. My copy is in Paris or I could quote it in full, but the gist of it was how this writer lay naked in his bed in the night and God sent him things to write, how he "was in touch ecstatically with the plunging and immobile all." How he was, through the courtesy of God, *"everywhere* and *everywhen."* The italics are his or maybe they are God's. It didn't say in the article. After God sent it he wrote it. The result was that unavoidable mysticism of a man who writes a language so badly he cannot make a clear statement, complicated by whatever pseudo-scientific jargon is in style at the moment. God sent him some wonderful stuff about Spain, during his short stay there preparatory to writing of the soul of the country, but it is often nonsense. The whole thing is what, to make a belated entry into the pseudo-scientific field, I call erectile writing. It is well known, or not known, whichever you prefer, that due to a certain congestion or other, trees for example look different to a man in that portentous state and a man who is not. All objects look different. They are slightly larger, more mysterious, and vaguely blurred. Try it yourself. Now there has or had arisen in America a school of writers who (this is old Dr. Hemingstein the great psychiatrist deducing) had, it would seem, by conserving these congestions, sought to make all objects mystic through the slight distortion of vision that unrelieved turgidness presents. The school seems to be passing now, or to have passed, and it was an interesting mechanical experiment while it lasted, and full of pretty phallic images drawn in the manner of sentimental valentines, but it would have amounted to more if only the vision of those writers had been a little more interesting and developed when, say, not so congested.

I wonder what such a book as *Virgin Spain* would have been like if written after a few good pieces of that sovereign specific for making a man see clearly. Perhaps it was. We pseudo-scientific coves may be all wrong. But to those inner-searching Viennese eyes peering out from under the shaggy brows of old Dr. Hemingstein, that masterful deducer, it seems as though, had the brain been cleared sufficiently, by a few good pieces, there might have been no book at all.

This too to remember. If a man writes clearly enough

any one can see if he fakes. If he mystifies to avoid a straight statement, which is very different from breaking so-called rules of syntax or grammar to make an effect which can be obtained in no other way, the writer takes a longer time to be known as a fake and other writers who are afflicted by the same necessity will praise him in their own defense. True mysticism should not be confused with incompetence in writing which seeks to mystify where there is no mystery but is really only the necessity to fake to cover lack of knowledge or the inability to state clearly. Mysticism implies a mystery and there are many mysteries; but incompetence is not one of them; nor is overwritten journalism made literature by the injection of a false epic quality. Remember this too: all bad writers are in love with the epic. . . .

Madame,[1] no decision is irrevocable, but as age comes on I feel I must devote myself more and more to the practice of letters. My operatives tell me that through the fine work of Mr. William Faulkner publishers now will publish anything rather than to try to get you to delete the better portions of your works, and I look forward to writing of those days of my youth which were spent in the finest whorehouses in the land amid the most brilliant society there found. I had been saving this background to write of in my old age when with the aid of distance I could examine it most clearly.

Old lady: Has this Mr. Faulkner written well of these places?

Splendidly, Madame. Mr. Faulkner writes admirably of them. He writes the best of them of any writer I have read for many years.

Old lady: I must buy his works.

Madame, you can't go wrong on Faulkner. He's prolific too. By the time you get them ordered there'll be new ones out.

Old lady: If they are as you say there cannot be too many.

Madame, you voice my own opinion. . . .

[1] The *Old lady* has just asked if Hemingway has "abandoned the bull ring."

When writing a novel a writer should create living people; people not characters. A *character* is a caricature. If a writer can make people live there may be no great characters in his book, but it is possible that his book will remain as a whole; as an entity; as a novel. If the people the writer is making talk of old masters; of music; of modern painting; of letters; or of science then they should talk of those subjects in the novel. If they do not talk of those subjects and the writer makes them talk of them he is a faker, and if he talks about them himself to show how much he knows then he is showing off. No matter how good a phrase or a simile he may have if he puts it in where it is not absolutely necessary and irreplaceable he is spoiling his work for egotism. Prose is architecture, not interior decoration, and the Baroque is over. For a writer to put his own intellectual musing, which he might sell for a low price as essays, into the mouths of artificially constructed characters which are more remunerative when issued as people in a novel is good economics, perhaps, but does not make literature. People in a novel, not skillfully constructed *characters,* must be projected from the writer's assimilated experience, from his knowledge, from his head, from his heart and from all there is of him. If he ever has luck as well as seriousness and gets them out entire they will have more than one dimension and they will last a long time. A good writer should know as near everything as possible. Naturally he will not. A great enough writer seems to be born with knowledge. But he really is not; he has only been born with the ability to learn in a quicker ratio to the passage of time than other men and without conscious application, and with an intelligence to accept or reject what is already presented as knowledge: There are some things which cannot be learned quickly and time, which is all we have, must be paid heavily for their acquiring. They are the very simplest things and because it takes a man's life to know them the little new that each man gets from life is very costly and the only heritage he has to leave. Every novel which is truly written contributes to the total of knowledge which is there at the disposal of the next writer who comes, but the next writer must pay, always, a certain nominal percentage in experience to be able to understand and assimilate what is available as his birthright and what he must, in turn, take his departure from. If a writer of prose knows enough about what he is writing about he may omit things that he knows and the reader, if the writer is writing truly enough, will have a feeling of those things as strongly as though the writer had stated them. The dignity of movement of an ice-berg is due to only one-eighth of it being above water. A writer who omits things because he does not know them only makes hollow places in his writing. A writer who appreciates the seriousness of writing so little that he is anxious to make people see he is formally educated, cultured or well-bred is merely a popinjay. And this too remember; a serious writer is not be confounded with a solemn writer. A serious writer may be a hawk or a buzzard or even a popinjay, but a solemn writer is always a bloody owl. . . .

The great thing is to last and get your work done and see and hear and learn and understand; and write when there is something that you know; and not before; and not too damned much after. Let those who want to save the world if you can get to see it clear and as a whole. Then any part you make will represent the whole if it's made truly. The thing to do is work and learn to make it. No. It is not enough of a book, but still there were a few things to be said. There were a few practical things to be said.

William Faulkner

THE *PARIS REVIEW* INTERVIEW*
This conversation took place in New York City, early in 1956.

Interviewer: Mr. Faulkner, you were saying a while ago that you don't like interviews.

Faulkner: The reason I don't like interviews is that I seem to react violently to personal questions. If the questions are about the work, I try to answer them. When they are about me, I may answer or I may not, but even if I do, if the same question is asked tomorrow, the answer may be different.

Interviewer: How about yourself as a writer?

Faulkner: If I had not existed, someone else would have written me, Hemingway, Dostoevski, all of us. Proof of that is that there are about three candidates for the authorship of Shakespeare's plays. But what is important is *Hamlet* and *Midsummer Night's Dream,* not who wrote them, but that somebody did. The artist is of no importance. Only what he creates is important, since there is nothing new to be said. Shakespeare, Balzac, Homer have all written about the same things, and if they had lived one thousand or two thousand years longer, the publishers wouldn't have needed anyone since.

*From *Writers at Work: The Paris Review Interviews,* edited by Malcolm Cowley. All rights reserved. Reprinted by permission of The Viking Press, Inc., and Martin Secker & Warburg Ltd.

Interviewer: But even if there seems nothing more to be said, isn't perhaps the individuality of the writer important?

Faulkner: Very important to himself. Everybody else should be too busy with the work to care about the individuality.

Interviewer: And your contemporaries?

Faulkner: All of us failed to match our dream of perfection. So I rate us on the basis of our splendid failure to do the impossible. In my opinion, if I could write all my work again, I am convinced that I would do it better, which is the healthiest condition for an artist. That's why he keeps on working, trying again; he believes each time that this time he will do it, bring it off. Of course he won't, which is why this condition is healthy. Once he did it, once he matched the work to the image, the dream, nothing would remain but to cut his throat, jump off the other side of that pinnacle of perfection into suicide. I'm a failed poet. Maybe every novelist wants to write poetry first, finds he can't, and then tries the short story, which is the most demanding form after poetry. And, failing at that, only then does he take up novel writing.

Interviewer: Is there any possible formula to follow in order to be a good novelist?

Faulkner: Ninety-nine per cent talent . . . 99 per cent discipline . . . 99 per cent work. He must never be satisfied with what he does. It never is as good as it can be done. Always dream and shoot higher than you know you can do. Don't bother just to be better than your contemporaries or predecessors. Try to be better than yourself. An artist is a creature driven by demons. He don't know why they choose him and he's usually too busy to wonder why. He is completely amoral in that he will rob, borrow, beg, or steal from anybody and everybody to get the work done.

Interviewer: Do you mean the writer should be completely ruthless?

Faulkner: The writer's only responsibility is to his art. He will be completely ruthless if he is a good one. He has a dream. It anguishes him so much he must get rid of it. He has no peace until then. Everything goes by the board: honor, pride, decency, security, happiness, all, to get the book written. If a writer has to rob his mother, he will not hesitate; the "Ode on a Grecian Urn" is worth any number of old ladies.

Interviewer: Then could the *lack* of security, happiness, honor, be an important factor in the artist's creativity?

Faulkner: No. They are important only to his peace and contentment, and art has no concern with peace and contentment.

Interviewer: Then what would be the best environment for a writer?

Faulkner: Art is not concerned with environment either; it doesn't care where it is. If you mean me, the best job that was ever offered to me was to become a landlord in a brothel. In my opinion it's the perfect milieu for an artist to work in. It gives him perfect economic freedom; he's free of fear and hunger; he has a roof over his head and nothing whatever to do except keep a few simple accounts and to go once every month and pay off the local police. The place is quiet during the morning hours, which is the best time of the day to work. There's enough social life in the evening, if he wishes to participate, to keep him from being bored; it gives him a certain standing in his society; he has nothing to do because the madam keeps the books; all the inmates of the house are females and would defer to him and call him "sir." All the bootleggers in the neighborhood would call him "sir." And he would call the police by their first names.

So the only environment the artist needs is whatever peace, whatever solitude, and whatever pleasure he can get at not too high a cost. All the wrong environment will do is run his blood pressure up; he will spend more time being frustrated or outraged. My own experience has been that the tools I need for my trade are paper, tobacco, food, and a little whisky.

Interviewer: Bourbon, you mean?

Faulkner: No, I ain't that particular. Between scotch and nothing, I'll take scotch.

Interviewer: You mentioned economic freedom. Does the writer need it?

Faulkner: No. The writer doesn't need economic freedom. All he needs is a pencil and some paper. I've never known anything good in writing to come from having accepted any free gift of money. The good writer never applies to a foundation. He's too busy writing something. If he isn't first rate he fools himself by saying he hasn't got time or economic freedom. Good art can come out of thieves, bootleggers, or horse swipes. People really are afraid to find out just how much hardship and poverty they can stand. They are afraid to find out how tough they are. Nothing can destroy the good writer. The only thing that can alter the good writer is death. Good ones don't have time to bother with success or getting rich. Success is feminine and like a woman; if you cringe before her, she will override you. So the way to treat her is to show her the back of your hand. Then maybe she will do the crawling.

Interviewer: Can working for the movies hurt your own writing?

Faulkner: Nothing can injure a man's writing if he's a first-rate writer. If a man is not a first-rate writer, there's not anything can help it much. The problem does not apply if he is not first rate, because he has already sold his soul for a swimming pool.

Interviewer: Does a writer compromise in writing for the movies?

Faulkner: Always, because a moving picture is by its nature a collaboration, and any collaboration is compromise because that is what the word means—to give and to take.

Interviewer: Which actors do you like to work with most?

Faulkner: Humphrey Bogart is the one I've worked with best. He and I worked together in *To Have and Have Not* and *The Big Sleep.*

Interviewer: Would you like to make another movie?

Faulkner: Yes, I would like to make one of George Orwell's *1984.* I have an idea for an ending which would prove the thesis I'm always hammering at: that man is indestructible because of his simple will to freedom.

Interviewer: How do you get the best results in working for the movies?

Faulkner: The moving-picture work of my own which seemed best to me was done by the actors and the writer throwing the script away and inventing the scene in actual rehearsal just before the camera turned. If I didn't take, or feel I was capable of taking, motion-picture work seriously, out of simple honesty to motion pictures and myself too, I would not have tried. But I know now that I will never be a good motion-picture writer; so that work will never have the urgency for me which my own medium has.

Interviewer: Would you comment on that legendary Hollywood experience you were involved in?

Faulkner: I had just completed a contract at MGM and was about to return home. The director I had worked with said, "If you would like another job here, just let me know and I will speak to the studio about a new contract." I thanked him and came home. About six months later I wired my director friend that I would like another job. Shortly after that I received a letter from my Hollywood agent enclosing my first week's paycheck. I was surprised because I had expected first to get an official notice or recall and a contract from the studio. I thought to myself the contract is delayed and will arrive in the next mail. Instead, a week later I got another letter from the agent, enclosing my second week's paycheck. That began in November 1932 and continued until May 1933. Then I received a telegram from the studio. It said: *William Faulkner, Oxford, Miss. Where are you? MGM Studio.*

I wrote out a telegram: *MGM Studio, Culver City, California. William Faulkner.*

The young lady operator said, "Where is the message, Mr. Faulkner?" I said, "That's it." She said, "The rule book says that I can't send it without a message, you have to say something." So we went through her samples and selected I forget which one—one of the canned anniversary greeting messages. I sent that. Next was a long-distance telephone call from the studio directing me to get on the first airplane, go to New Orleans, and report to Director Browning. I could have got on a train in Oxford and been in New Orleans eight hours later. But I obeyed the studio and went to Memphis, where an airplane did occasionally go to New Orleans. Three days later one did.

I arrived at Mr. Browning's hotel about six p.m. and reported to him. A party was going on. He told me to get a good night's sleep and be ready for an early start in the morning. I asked him about the story. He said, "Oh, yes. Go to room so and so. That's the continuity writer. He'll tell you what the story is."

I went to the room as directed. The continuity writer was sitting in there alone. I told him who I was and asked him about the story. He said, "When you have written the dialogue I'll let you see the story." I went back to Browning's room and told him what had happened. "Go back," he said, "and tell that so and so—never mind, you get a good night's sleep so we can get an early start in the morning."

So the next morning in a very smart rented launch all of us except the continuity writer sailed down to Grand Isle, about a hundred miles away, where the picture was to be shot, reaching there just in time to eat lunch and have time to run the hundred miles back to New Orleans before dark.

That went on for three weeks. Now and then I would worry a little about the story, but Browning always said, "Stop worrying. Get a good night's sleep so we can get an early start tomorrow morning."

One evening on our return I had barely entered my room when the telephone rang. It was Browning. He told me to come to his room at once. I did so. He had a telegram. It said: *Faulkner is fired. MGM Studio.* "Don't worry," Browning said. "I'll call that so-and-so up this minute and not only make him put you back on the payroll but send you a written apology." There was a knock on the door. It was a page with another telegram. This one said: *Browning is fired. MGM Studio.* So I came back home. I presume Browning went somewhere too. I imagine that continuity writer is still sitting in a room somewhere with his weekly salary check clutched tightly in his hand. They never did finish the film. But they did build a shrimp village—a long platform on piles in the water with sheds built on it something like a wharf. The studio could have bought dozens of them for forty or fifty dollars apiece. Instead, they built one of their own, a false one. That is, a platform with a single wall on it, so that when you opened the door and stepped through it, you stepped right on off to the ocean itself. As they built it, on the first day, the Cajun fisherman paddled up in his narrow tricky pirogue made out of a hollow log. He would sit in it all day long in the broiling sun watching the strange white folks building this strange imitation platform. The next day he was back in the pirogue with his whole family, his wife nursing the baby, the other children, and the mother-in-law, all to sit all that day in the broiling sun to watch this foolish and incomprehensible activity. I was in New Orleans two or three years later and heard that the Cajun people were still coming in for miles to look at that imitation shrimp platform which a lot of white people had rushed in and built and then abandoned.

Interviewer: You say that the writer must compromise in working for the motion pictures. How about his writing? Is he under any obligation to his reader?

Faulkner: His obligation is to get the work done the best he can do it; whatever obligation he has left over after that he can spend any way he likes. I myself am too busy to care about the public. I have no time to wonder who is reading me. I don't care about John Doe's opinion on my or anyone else's work. Mine is the standard which has to be met, which is when the work makes me feel the way I do when I read *La Tentation de Saint Antoine,* or the Old Testament. They make me feel good. So does watching a bird make me feel good. You know that if I were reincarnated, I'd want to come back a buzzard. Nothing hates him or envies him or wants him or needs him. He is never bothered or in danger, and he can eat anything.

Interviewer: What technique do you use to arrive at your standard?

Faulkner: Let the writer take up surgery or bricklaying if he is interested in technique. There is no mechanical way to get the writing done, no short cut. The young writer would be a fool to follow a theory. Teach yourself by your own mistakes; people learn only by error. The good artist believes that nobody is good enough to give him advice. He has supreme vanity. No matter how much he admires the old writer, he wants to beat him.

Interviewer: Then would you deny the validity of technique?

Faulkner: By no means. Sometimes technique charges in and takes command of the dream before the writer himself can get his hands on it. That is *tour de force* and the finished work is simply a matter of fitting bricks neatly together, since the writer knows probably every single word right to the end before he puts the first one down. This happened with *As I Lay Dying.* It was not easy. No honest work is. It was simple in that all the material was already at hand. It took me just about six weeks in the spare time from a twelve-hour-a-day job at manual labor. I simply imagined a group of people and subjected them to the simple universal natural catastrophes, which are flood and fire, with a simple natural motive to give direction to their progress. But then, when technique does not intervene, in another sense writing is easier too. Because with me there is always a point in the book where the characters themselves rise up and take charge and finish the job—say somewhere about page 275. Of course I don't know what would happen if I finished the book on page 274. The quality an artist must have is objectivity in judging his work, plus the honesty and courage not to kid himself about it. Since none of my work has met my own standards, I must judge it on the basis of that one which caused me the most grief and anguish, as the mother loves the child who became the thief or murderer more than the one who became the priest.

Interviewer: What work is that?

Faulkner: The Sound and the Fury. I wrote it five separate times, trying to tell the story, to rid myself of the dream which would continue to anguish me until I did. It's a tragedy of two lost women: Caddy and her daughter. Dilsey is one of my own favorite characters, because she is brave, courageous, generous, gentle, and honest. She's much more brave and honest and generous than me.

Interviewer: How did *The Sound and the Fury* begin?

Faulkner: It began with a mental picture. I didn't realize at the time it was symbolical. The picture was of the muddy seat of a little girl's drawers in a pear tree, where she could see through a window where her grandmother's funeral was taking place and report what was happening to her brothers on the ground below. By the time I explained who they were and what they were doing and how her pants got muddy, I realized it would be impossible to get all of it into a short story and that it would have to be a book. And then I realized the symbolism of the soiled pants, and that image was replaced by the one of the fatherless and motherless girl climbing down the rainpipe to escape from the only home she had, where she had never been offered love or affection or understanding.

I had already begun to tell the story through the eyes of the idiot child, since I felt that it would be more effective as told by someone capable only of knowing what happened, but not why. I saw that I had not told the story that time. I tried to tell it again, the same story through the eyes of another brother. That was still not it. I told it for the third time through the eyes of the third brother. That was still not it. I tried to gather the pieces together and fill in the gaps by making myself the spokesman. It was still not complete, not until fifteen years after the book was published, when I wrote as an appendix to another book the final effort to get the story told and off my mind, so that I myself could have some peace from it. It's the book I feel tenderest towards. I couldn't leave it alone, and I never could tell it right, though I tried hard and would like to try again, though I'd probably fail again.

Interviewer: What emotion does Benjy arouse in you?

Faulkner: The only emotion I can have for Benjy is grief and pity for all mankind. You can't feel anything for Benjy because he doesn't feel anything. The only thing I can feel about him personally is concern as to whether he is believable as I created him. He was a prologue, like the gravedigger in the Elizabethan dramas. He serves his purpose and is gone. Benjy is incapable of good and evil because he had no knowledge of good and evil.

Interviewer: Could Benjy feel love?

Faulkner: Benjy wasn't rational enough even to be selfish. He was an animal. He recognized tenderness and love though he could not have named them, and it was the threat to tenderness and love that caused him to bellow when he felt the change in Caddy. He no longer had Caddy; being an idiot he was not even aware that Caddy was missing. He knew only that something was wrong, which left a vacuum in which he grieved. He tried to fill that vacuum. The only thing he had was one of Caddy's discarded slippers. The slipper was his tenderness and love which he could not have named, but he knew only that it was missing. He was dirty because he couldn't coordinate and because dirt meant nothing to him. He could no more distinguish between dirt and cleanliness than between good and evil. The slipper gave him comfort even though he no longer remembered the person to whom it had once belonged, any more than he could remember why he grieved. If Caddy had reappeared he probably would not have known her.

Interviewer: Does the narcissus given to Benjy have some significance?

Faulkner: The narcissus was given to Benjy to distract his attention. It was simply a flower which happened to be handy that fifth of April. It was not deliberate.

Interviewer: Are there any artistic advantages in casting the novel in the form of an allegory, as the Christian allegory you used in *A Fable?*

Faulkner: Same advantage the carpenter finds in building square corners in order to build a square house. In *A Fable* the Christian allegory was the right allegory to use in that particular story, like an oblong square corner is the right corner with which to build an oblong rectangular house.

Interviewer: Does that mean an artist can use Christianity simply as just another tool, as a carpenter would borrow a hammer?

Faulkner: The carpenter we are speaking of never lacks that hammer. No one is without Christianity, if we agree on what we mean by the word. It is every individual's individual code of behavior by means of which he makes himself a better human being than his nature wants to be, if he followed his nature only. Whatever its symbol—cross or crescent or whatever—that symbol is man's reminder of his duty inside the human race. Its various allegories are the charts against which he measures himself and learns to know what he is. It cannot teach man to be good as the textbook teaches him mathematics. It shows him how to discover himself, evolve for himself a moral code and standard within his capacities and aspirations, by giving him a matchless example of suffering and sacrifice and the promise of hope. Writers have always drawn, and always will draw, upon the allegories of moral consciousness, for the reason that the allegories are matchless—the three men in *Moby Dick,* who represent the trinity of conscience: knowing nothing, knowing but not caring, knowing and caring. The same trinity is represented in *A Fable* by the young Jewish pilot officer, who said, "This is terrible. I refuse to accept it, even if I must refuse life to do so"; the old French Quartermaster General, who said, "This is terrible, but we can weep and bear it"; and the English battalion runner, who said, "This is terrible, I'm going to do something about it."

Interviewer: Are the two unrelated themes in *The Wild Palms* brought together in one book for any symbolic purpose? Is it as certain critics intimate a kind of esthetic counterpoint, or is it merely haphazard?

Faulkner: No, no. That was one story—the story of Charlotte Rittenmeyer and Harry Wilbourne, who sacrificed everything for love, and then lost that. I did not know it would be two separate stories until after I had started the book. When I reached the end of what is now the first section of *The Wild Palms,* I realized suddenly that something was missing, it needed emphasis, something to lift it like counterpoint in music. So I wrote on the "Old Man" story until "The Wild Palms" story rose back to pitch. Then I stopped the "Old Man" story at what is now its first section, and took up "The Wild Palms" story until it began again to sag. Then I raised it to pitch again with another section of its antithesis, which is the story of a man who got his love and spent the rest of the book fleeing from it, even to the extent of voluntarily going back to jail where he would be safe. They are only two stories by chance, perhaps necessity. The story is that of Charlotte and Wilbourne.

Interviewer: How much of your writing is based on personal experience?

Faulkner: I can't say. I never counted up. Because "how much" is not important. A writer needs three things, experience, observation, and imagination, any two of which, at times any one of which, can supply the lack of the others. With me, a story usually begins with a single idea or memory or mental picture. The writing of the story is simply a matter of working up to that moment, to explain why it happened or what it caused to follow. A writer is trying to create believable people in credible moving situations in the most moving way he can. Obviously he must use as one of his tools the environment which he knows. I would say that music is the easiest means in which to express, since it came first in man's experience and history. But since words are my talent, I must try to express clumsily in words what the pure music would have done better. That is, music would express better and simpler, but I prefer to use words, as I prefer to read rather than listen. I prefer silence to sound, and the image produced by words occurs in silence. That is, the thunder and the music of the prose take place in silence.

Interviewer: Some people say they can't understand your writing, even after they read it two or three times. What approach would you suggest for them?

Faulkner: Read it four times.

Interviewer: You mentioned experience, observation, and imagination as being important for the writer. Would you include inspiration?

Faulkner: I don't know anything about inspiration, because I don't know what inspiration is—I've heard about it, but I never saw it.

Interviewer: As a writer you are said to be obsessed with violence.

Faulkner: That's like saying the carpenter is obsessed with his hammer. Violence is simply one of the carpenter's tools. The writer can no more build with one tool than the carpenter can.

Interviewer: Can you say how you started as a writer?

Faulkner: I was living in New Orleans, doing whatever kind of work was necessary to earn a little money now and then. I met Sherwood Anderson. We would walk about the city in the afternoon and talk to people. In the evenings we would meet again and sit over a bottle or two while he talked and I listened. In the forenoon I would never see him. He was secluded, working. The next day we would repeat. I decided that if that was the life of a writer, then becoming a writer was the thing for me. So I began to write my first book. At once I found that writing was fun. I even forgot that I hadn't seen Mr. Anderson for three weeks until he walked in my door, the first time he ever came to see me, and said, "What's wrong? Are you mad at me?" I told him I was writing a book. He said, "My God," and walked out. When I finished the book—it was *Soldier's Pay*—I met Mrs. Anderson on the street. She asked how the book was going, and I said I'd finished it. She said, "Sherwood says that he will make a trade with you. If he doesn't have to read your manuscript he will tell his publisher to accept it." I said, "Done," and that's how I became a writer.

Interviewer: What were the kinds of work you were doing to earn that "little money now and then"?

Faulkner: Whatever came up. I could do a little of almost anything—run boats, paint houses, fly airplanes. I never needed much money because living was cheap in New Orleans then, and all I wanted was a place to sleep, a little food, tobacco, and whisky. There were many things I could do for two or three days and earn enough money to live on for the rest of the month. By temperament I'm a vagabond and a tramp. I don't want money badly enough to work for it. In my opinion it's a shame that there is so much work in the world. One of the saddest things is that the only thing a man can do for eight hours a day, day after day, is work. You can't eat eight hours a day nor drink for eight hours a day nor make love for eight hours—all you can do for eight hours is work. Which is the reason why man makes himself and everybody else so miserable and unhappy.

Interviewer: You must feel indebted to Sherwood Anderson, but how do you regard him as a writer?

Faulkner: He was the father of my generation of American writers and the tradition of American writing which our successors will carry on. He has never received his proper evaluation. Dreiser is his older brother and Mark Twain the father of them both.

Interviewer: What about the European writers of that period?

Faulkner: The two great men in my time were Mann and Joyce. You should approach Joyce's *Ulysses* as the illiterate Baptist preacher approaches the Old Testament: with faith.

Interviewer: How did you get your background in the Bible?

Faulkner: My Great-Grandfather Murry was a kind and gentle man, to us children anyway. That is, although he was a Scot, he was (to us) neither especially pious nor stern either: he was simply a man of inflexible principles. One of them was, everybody, children on up through all adults present, had to have a verse from the Bible ready and glib at tongue-tip when we gathered at the table for breakfast each morning; if you didn't have your scripture verse ready, you didn't have any breakfast; you would be excused long enough to leave the room and swot one up (there was a maiden aunt, a kind of sergeant-major for this duty, who retired with the culprit and gave him a brisk breezing which carried him over the jump next time).

It had to be an authentic, correct verse. While we were little, it could be the same one, once you had it down good, morning after morning, until you got a little older and bigger, when one morning (by this time you would be pretty glib at it, galloping through without even listening to yourself since you were already five or ten minutes ahead, already among the ham and steak and fried chicken and grits and sweet potatoes and two or three kinds of hot bread) you would suddenly find his eyes on you—very blue, very kind and gentle, and even now not stern so much as inflexible; and next morning you had a new verse. In a way, that was when you discovered that your childhood was over; you had outgrown it and entered the world.

Interviewer: Do you read your contemporaries?

Faulkner: No, the books I read are the ones I knew and loved when I was a young man and to which I return as you do to old friends: the Old Testament, Dickens, Conrad, Cervantes—*Don Quixote.* I read that every year, as some do the Bible. Flaubert, Balzac—he created an intact world of his own, a bloodstream running through twenty books—Dostoevski, Tolstoi, Shakespeare. I read Melville occasionally, and of the poets Marlowe, Campion, Jonson, Herrick, Donne, Keats, and Shelley. I still read Housman. I've read these books so often that I don't always begin at page one and read on to the end. I just read one scene, or about one character, just as you'd meet and talk to a friend for a few minutes.

Interviewer: And Freud?

Faulkner: Everybody talked about Freud when I lived in New Orleans, but I have never read him. Neither did Shakespeare. I doubt if Melville did either, and I'm sure Moby Dick didn't.

Interviewer: Do you ever read mystery stories?

Faulkner: I read Simenon because he reminds me something of Chekhov.

Interviewer: What about your favorite characters?

Faulkner: My favorite characters are Sarah Gamp—a cruel, ruthless woman, a drunkard, opportunist, unreliable, most of her character was bad, but at least it was character; Mrs. Harris, Falstaff, Prince Hal, Don Quixote, and Sancho of course. Lady Macbeth I always admire. And Bottom, Ophelia, and Mercutio—both he and Mrs. Gamp coped with life, didn't ask any favors, never whined. Huck Finn, of course, and Jim. Tom Sawyer I never liked much—an awful prig. And then I like Sut Lovingood, from a book written by George Harris about 1840 or '50 in the Tennessee mountains. He had no illusions about himself, did the best he could; at certain times he was a coward and knew it and wasn't ashamed; he never blamed his misfortunes on anyone and never cursed God for them.

Interviewer: Would you comment on the future of the novel?

Faulkner: I imagine as long as people will continue to read novels, people will continue to write them, or vice versa; unless of course the pictorial magazines and comic strips finally atrophy man's capacity to read, and literature really is on its way back to the picture writing in the Neanderthal cave.

Interviewer: And how about the function of the critics?

Faulkner: The artist doesn't have time to listen to the critics. The ones who want to be writers read the reviews, the ones who want to write don't have the time to read reviews. The critic too is trying to say "Kilroy was here." His function is not directed toward the artist himself. The artist is a cut above the critic, for the artist is writing something which will move the critic. The critic is writing something which will move everybody but the artist.

Interviewer: So you never feel the need to discuss your work with anyone?

Faulkner: No, I am too busy writing it. It has got to please me and if it does I don't need to talk about it. If it doesn't please me, talking about it won't improve it, since the only thing to improve it is to work on it some more. I am not a literary man but only a writer. I don't get any pleasure from talking shop.

Interviewer: Critics claim that blood relationships are central in your novels.

Faulkner: That is an opinion and, as I have said, I don't read critics. I doubt that a man trying to write about people is any more interested in blood relationships than in the shape of their noses, unless they are necessary to help the story move. If the writer concentrates on what he does need to be interested in, which is the truth and the human heart, he won't have much time left for anything else, such as ideas and facts like the shape of noses or blood relationships, since in my opinion ideas and facts have very little connection with truth.

Interviewer: Critics also suggest that your characters never consciously choose between good and evil.

Faulkner: Life is not interested in good and evil. Don Quixote was constantly choosing between good and evil, but then he was choosing in his dream state. He was mad. He entered reality only when he was so busy trying to cope with people that he had no time to distinguish between good and evil. Since people exist only in life, they must devote their time simply to being alive. Life is motion, and motion is concerned with what makes man move—which is ambition, power, pleasure. What time a man can devote to morality, he must take by force from the motion of which he is a part. He is compelled to make choices between good and evil sooner or later, because moral conscience demands that from him in order that he can live with himself tomorrow. His moral conscience is the curse he had to accept from the gods in order to gain from them the right to dream.

Interviewer: Could you explain more what you mean by motion in relation to the artist?

Faulkner: The aim of every artist is to arrest motion, which is life, by artificial means and hold it fixed so that a hundred years later, when a stranger looks at it, it moves again since it is life. Since man is mortal, the only immortality possible for him is to leave something behind him that is immortal since it will always move. This is the artist's way of scribbling "Kilroy was here" on the wall of the final and irrevocable oblivion through which he must someday pass.

Interviewer: It has been said by Malcolm Cowley that your characters carry a sense of submission to their fate.

Faulkner: That is his opinion. I would say that some of them do and some of them don't, like everybody else's characters. I would say that Lena Grove in *Light in August* coped pretty well with hers. It didn't really matter to her in her destiny whether her man was Lucas Birch or not. It was her destiny to have a husband and children and she knew it, and so she went out and attended to it without asking help from anyone. She was the captain of her soul. One of the calmest, sanest speeches I ever heard was when she said to Byron Bunch at the very instant of repulsing his final desperate and despairing attempt at rape, "Ain't you ashamed? You might have woke the baby." She was never for one moment confused, frightened, alarmed. She did not even know that she didn't need pity. Her last speech for example: "Here I ain't been traveling but a month, and I'm already in Tennessee. My, my, a body does get around."

The Bundren family in *As I Lay Dying* pretty well coped with theirs. The father having lost his wife would naturally need another one, so he got one. At one blow he not only replaced the family cook, he acquired a gramophone to give them all pleasure while they were resting. The pregnant daughter failed this time to undo her condition, but she was not discouraged. She intended to try again, and even if they all failed right up to the last, it wasn't anything but just another baby.

Interviewer: And Mr. Cowley says you find it hard to create characters between the ages of twenty and forty who are sympathetic.

Faulkner: People between twenty and forty are not sympathetic. The child has the capacity to do but it can't know. It only knows when it is no longer able to do—after forty. Between twenty and forty the will of the child to do gets stronger, more dangerous, but it has not begun to learn to know yet. Since his capacity to do is forced into channels of evil through environment and pressures, man is strong before he is moral. The world's anguish is caused by people between twenty and forty. The people around my home who have caused all the interracial tension—the Milams and the Bryants (in the Emmet Till murder) and the gangs of Negroes who grab a white woman and rape her in revenge, the Hitlers, Napoleons, Lenins—all these people are symbols of human suffering and anguish, all of them between twenty and forty.

Interviewer: You gave a statement to the papers at the time of the Emmet Till killing. Have you anything to add to it here?

Faulkner: No, only to repeat what I said before: that if we Americans are to survive it will have to be because we choose and elect and defend to be first of all Americans; to present to the world one homogeneous and unbroken front, whether of white Americans or black ones or purple or blue or green.

Maybe the purpose of this sorry and tragic error committed in my native Mississippi by two white adults on an afflicted Negro child is to prove to us whether or not we deserve to survive. Because if we in America have reached that point in our desperate culture when we must murder children, no matter for what reason or what color, we don't deserve to survive, and probably won't.

Interviewer: What happened to you between *Soldier's Pay* and *Sartoris*—that is, what caused you to begin the Yoknapatawpha saga?

Faulkner: With *Soldier's Pay* I found out writing was fun. But I found out afterward that not only each book had to have a design but the whole output or sum of an artist's work had to have a design. With *Soldier's Pay* and *Mosquitoes* I wrote for the sake of writing because it was fun. Beginning with *Sartoris* I discovered that my own little postage stamp of native soil was worth writing about and that I would never live long enough to exhaust it, and that by sublimating the actual into the apocryphal I would have complete liberty to use whatever talent I might have to its absolute top. It opened up a gold mine of other people, so I created a cosmos of my own. I can move these people around like God, not only in space but in time too. The fact that I have moved my characters around in time successfully, at least in my own estimation, proves to me my own theory that time is a fluid condition which has no existence except in the momentary avatars of individual people. There is no such thing as *was*—only *is*. If *was* existed, there would be no grief or sorrow. I like to think of the world I created as being a kind of keystone in the universe; that, small as that keystone is, if it were ever taken away the universe itself would collapse. My last book will be the Doomsday Book, the Golden Book, of Yoknapatawpha County. Then I shall break the pencil and I'll have to stop.

Jean Stein vanden Heuvel

LETTERS TO MALCOLM COWLEY*

Oxford. Saturday.
[*Early November, 1944*]

Dear Maitre:

I saw the piece in the Times Book R[eview].¹ It was all right.
If that is a fair sample, I dont think I need to see the rest of
it before publication because I might want to collaborate
and you're doing all right. But if you want comments from me
before you release it, that's another horse. So I'll leave it to
you whether I see it beforehand or not.

Vide the paragraph you quoted: As regards any specific
book, I'm trying primarily to tell a story, in the most effective
way I can think of, the most moving, the most exhaustive. But
I think even that is incidental to what I am trying to do, taking
my output (the course of it) as a whole. I am telling the same

---

*From *The Faulkner-Cowley File* edited by Malcolm Cowley. Copyright
© 1966 by the Estate of William Faulkner. Reprinted by permission of The
Viking Press, Inc., and Chatto and Windus Ltd.

¹"William Faulkner's Human Comedy," *New York Times Book Review,*
Oct. 29, 1944.

story over and over, which is myself and the world. Tom Wolfe was trying to say everything, the world plus 'I' or filtered through 'I' or the effort of 'I' to embrace the world in which he was born and walked a little while and then lay down again, into one volume. I am trying to go a step further. This I think accounts for what people call the obscurity, the involved formless 'style,' endless sentences. I'm trying to say it all in one sentence, between one Cap and one period. I'm still trying to put it all, if possible, on one pinhead. I don't know how to do it. All I know to do is to keep on trying in a new way. I'm inclined to think that my material, the South, is not very important to me. I just happen to know it, and dont have time in one life to learn another one and write at the same time. Though the one I know is probably as good as another, life is a phenomenon but not a novelty, the same frantic steeplechase toward nothing everywhere and man stinks the same stink no matter where in time.

Your divination (vide paragraph) is correct. I didn't intend it, but afterward I dimly saw myself what you put into words. I think though you went a step further than I (unconsciously, I repeat) intended. I think Quentin, not Faulkner, is the correct yardstick here. I was writing the story, but he not I was brooding over a situation. I mean, I was creating him as a character, as well as Sutpen et al. He [Quentin] grieved and regretted the passing of an order the dispossessor of which he was not tough enough to withstand. But more he grieved the fact (because he hated and feared the portentous symptom) that a man like Sutpen, who to Quentin was trash, originless, could not only have dreamed so high but have had the force and strength to have failed so grandly. Quentin probably contemplated Sutpen as the hypersensitive, already self-crucified cadet of an old long-time Republican Philistine house contemplated the ruin of Sampson's portico . . .[2] He grieved and was moved by it but he was still saying 'I told you so' even while he hated himself for saying it.

You are correct; I was first of all (I still think) telling what I thought was a good story, and I believed Quentin could do

[2]Faulkner's punctuation. Nothing is omitted.

it better than I in this case. But I accept gratefully all your implications, even though I didn't carry them consciously and
simultaneously in the writing of it. In principle I'd like to think
I could have. But I dont believe it would have been necessary
to carry them or even to have known their analogous deriva-
tion, to have had them in the story. Art is simpler than people
think because there is so little to write about. All the moving
things are eternal in man's history and have been written before,
and if a man writes hard enough, sincerely enough, humbly
enough, and with the unalterable determination never never
never to be quite satisfied with it, he will repeat them, because
art like poverty takes care of its own, shares its bread.

I am free of Hollywood for six months, must go back then
for the reason that when I was broke in '42 and the air force
didn't want me again, I had to sign a seven year contract with
Warner to get a job. Re the book offer. I wrote Harold Ober,[3]
who forwarded it to me, that I would not undertake it right
now. I can work at Hollywood 6 months, stay at home 6, am
used to it now and have movie work locked off into another
room. I dont want to undertake a book of the nature suggested[4]
because I'm like the old mare who has been bred and dropped
foals 15 - 16 times, and she has a feeling that she has only 3
or 4 more in her, and cant afford to spend one on something
from outside. I am working on something now. Random House
has about 70 pages of it. I will write them to let you see it, if
you would like to. It's not Yoknapatawpha this time, though
I explained above that I'm still trying to put all mankind's history in one sentence.

Thank you for letter,

William Faulkner

My best to Hal Smith when you see him.

---

[3]Faulkner's agent.

[4]"A nonfiction book, on I don't remember what subject" (Cowley).

[*Hollywood*] *Thursday.* [*August 16, 1945*]*

Dear Cowley:

The idea is very fine. I wish we could meet too, but that seems impossible now. I will do anything I can from here.

By all means let us make a Golden Book of my apocryphal county. I have thought of spending my old age doing something of that nature: an alphabetical, rambling genealogy of the people, father to son to son.

I would hate to have to choose between Red Leaves and A Justice, also another one called Lo! from Story Mag. several years ago. The line dividing the Chickasaw and Choctaw nations passed near my home; I merely moved a tribe slightly at need, since they were slightly different people in behavior.

Yes, there is difference between magazine and Hamlet 'Spotted Horses.' One is a magazine story, shorter and more economical: it is a story made from several chapters of the hamlet, reduced to their essentials. What is lacking in it is the justice of the peace al fresco trial regarding the damage done.

What about taking the whole 3rd section of SOUND AND FURY? That Jason is the new South too. I mean, he is the one Compson and Sartoris who met Snopes on his own ground and in a fashion held his own. Jason would have chopped up a Georgian Manse and sold it off in shotgun bungalows as quick as any man. But then, this is not enough to waste that much space on, is it? The next best would be the last section, for the sake of the negroes, that woman Dilsey who 'does the best I kin.'

AS I LAY DYING is simple tour de force, though I like it. But in this case it says little that spotted horses and Wash and Old Man would not tell.

THE HAMLET was incepted as a novel. When I began it, it produced Spotted Horses, went no further. About two years later suddenly I had The HOUND, then JAMSHYD'S COURTYARD, mainly because SPOTTED HORSES had created a character I fell in love with: the itinerant sewing-machine agent named Suratt. Later a man of that name turned up at home, so I changed my man to Ratliff for the reason that my whole town spent much of its time trying to decide just what living man I was writing about, the one literary criticism of the town being 'How in the hell did he remember all that, and when did that happen anyway?'

Meanwhile my book had created Snopes and his clan, who produced stories in their saga which are to fall in a later volume: MULE IN THE YARD, BRASS, etc. This over about ten years, until one day I decided I had better start on the first volume or I'd never get any of it down. So I wrote an induction toward the spotted horse story, which included BARN BURNING and WASH, which I discovered had no place in that book at all. Spotted horses became a longer story, picked up the HOUND (rewritten and much longer and with the character's name changed from Cotton to Snopes) and went on with JAMSHYD'S COURTYARD.

The Indians actually were Chickasaws, or they may so be from now on. RED LEAVES actually were Chickasaws. A JUSTICE could have been either, the reason for their being Chocktaws was the connection with New Orleans, which was more available to Chocktaws, as the map herewith will explain.[1]

At this time the Tallahatchie, running from the Chickasaw across the Chocktaw nation, was navigable; steamboats came up it.

Wish to hell we could spend three days together with these books. Write me any way I can help.

Faulkner

[1]See Cowley, *The Faulkner-Cowley File,* p. 27.

Oxford, Friday. [February 11, 1949]*

Dear Malcolm:

I saw the LIFE with your Hemingway piece.[1] I didn't read it but I know it's all right or you wouldn't have put your name on it; for which reason I know Hemingway thinks it's all right and I hope it will profit him—if there is any profit or increase or increment that a brave man and an artist can lack or need or want.

But I am more convinced and determined than ever that this is not for me.[2] I will protest to the last: no photographs, no recorded documents. It is my ambition to be, as a private individual, abolished and voided from history, leaving it markless, no refuse save the printed books; I wish I had had enough sense to see ahead thirty years ago and, like some of the Elizabethans, not signed them. It is my aim, and every effort bent, that the sum and history of my life, which in the same sentence is my obit and epitaph too, shall be them both: He made the books and he died.

But I still owe you a drunk. I will hold it on demand at sight draft, not transferable of course since you and Muriel will have to be present. But I will furnish someone to do the actual drinking; not myself this time.

Yours,

Bill

---

[1]January 10, 1949.

[2]Cowley had requested Faulkner's permission to do a profile of him for *Life,* but later dropped the project in deference to Faulkner's objections. Later, after the Nobel Prize award, Robert Coughlan was assigned the article, which was researched without Faulkner's cooperation and appeared in two issues, *Life,* October 5 and 12, 1953 and was reprinted as *The Private World of William Faulkner,* New York, 1954. Faulkner reacted in an essay "On Privacy—The American Dream: What Happened to It," *Harper's,* July, 1955. Part of that essay is printed in an expanded form in Cowley, *The Faulkner-Cowley File,* pp. 132-137.

Thomas Wolfe
THE STORY OF A NOVEL*

An editor,[1] who is also a good friend of mine, told me about
a year ago that he was sorry he had not kept a diary about the
work that both of us were doing, the whole stroke, catch, flow,
stop, and ending, the ten thousand fittings, changings, triumphs,
and surrenders that went into the making of a book. This editor
remarked that some of it was fantastic, much incredible, all
astonishing, and he was also kind enough to say that the whole
experience was the most interesting he had known during the
twenty-five years he had been a member of the publishing business.

I propose to tell about this experience. I cannot tell anyone how to write books; I cannot attempt to give anyone rules
whereby he will be enabled to get his books published by publishers or his stories accepted by highpaying magazines. I am
not a professional writer; I am not even a skilled writer; I am
just a writer who is on the way to learning his profession and
to discovering the line, the structure, and the articulation of

*Reprinted with permission of Charles Scribner's Sons from *The Story of
A Novel,* pages 1-12, 30-34, 37-43, 49-61, 73-83, 87-89, 91-93 by Thomas
Wolfe. Copyright 1936 Charles Scribner's Sons; renewal copyright © 1964 Paul
Gitlin, Administrator C.T.A.

[1]Maxwell Perkins, of Scribner's.

the language which I must discover if I do the work I want
to do. It is for just this reason, because I blunder, because every
energy of my life and talent is still involved in this process of
discovery, that I am speaking as I speak here. I am going to
tell the way in which I wrote a book. It will be intensely personal. It was the most intense part of my life for several years.
There is nothing very literary about it. It is a story of sweat
and pain and despair and partial achievement. I don't know
how to write a story yet. I don't know how to write a novel
yet. But I have learned something about myself and about the
work of writing, and if I can, I am going to try to tell what it
is.

I don't know when it occurred to me first that I would
be a writer. I suppose that like a great many other children
in this country of my generation, I may have thought that it
would be a fine thing because a writer was a man like Lord
Byron or Lord Tennyson or Longfellow or Percy Bysshe Shelley. A writer was a man who was far away like these people
I have mentioned, and since I was myself an American and
an American not of the wealthy or university-going sort of
people, it seemed to me that a writer was a man from a kind
of remote people that I could never approach.

I think this has happened to us all—or almost all of us
here in America. We're still more perturbed by the strangeness of the writing profession than any other people I have
known on the earth. It is for this reason, I think, that one finds
among a great number of our people, I mean the laboring,
farming sort of people from which I came, a kind of great wonder and doubt and romantic feeling about writers so that it is
hard for them to understand that a writer may be one of them
and not a man far away like Lord Byron or Tennyson or Percy
Bysshe Shelley. Then there is another kind of American who
has come from the more educated, university-going kind of
people, and these people also become fascinated with the
glamour and difficulty of writing, but in a different way. They
get more involved or fancy than the most involved and fancy
European people of this sort. They become more "Flauberty"
than Flaubert. They establish little magazines that not only split

a hair with best of them, but they split more hairs than Europeans think of splitting. The Europeans say: "Oh, God, where did these people, these aesthetic Americans, ever come from?" Well, we have known it all. I think all of us who have tried to write in this country may have fallen in between these two groups of well-meaning and misguided people, and if we become writers finally, it is in spite of each of them.

I don't know how I became a writer, but I think it was because of a certain force in me that had to write and that finally burst through and found a channel. My people were of the working class of people. My father, a stonecutter, was a man with a great respect and veneration for literature. He had a tremendous memory, and he loved poetry, and the poetry that he loved best was naturally of the rhetorical kind that such a man would like. Nevertheless it was good poetry, Hamlet's Soliloquy, *Macbeth,* Mark Antony's Funeral Oration, Grey's "Elegy," and all the rest of it. I heard it all as a child; I memorized and learned it all.

He sent me to college to the state university. The desire to write, which had been strong during all my days in high school, grew stronger still. I was editor of the college paper, the college magazine, etc., and in my last year or two I was a member of a course in playwriting which had just been established there. I wrote several little one-act plays, still thinking I would become a lawyer or a newspaperman, never daring to believe I could seriously become a writer. Then I went to Harvard, wrote some more plays there, became obsessed with the idea that I had to be a playwright, left Harvard, had my plays rejected, and finally in the autumn of 1926, how, why, or in what manner I have never exactly been able to determine, but probably because the force in me that had to write at length sought out its channel, I began to write my first book in London. I was living all alone at that time. I had two rooms—a bedroom and a sitting room—in a little square in Chelsea in which all the houses had that familiar, smoked brick and cream-yellow-plaster look of London houses. They looked exactly alike.

As I say, I was living alone at that time and in a foreign country. I did not know why I was there or what the direction of my life should be, and that was the way I began to write my book. I think that is one of the hardest times a writer goes through. There is no standard, no outward judgment, by which he can measure what he has done. By day I would write for hours in big ledgers which I had bought for the purpose; then at night I would lie in bed and fold my hands behind my head and think of what I had done that day and hear the solid, leather footbeat of the London bobby as he came by my window, and remember that I was born in North Carolina and wonder why the hell I was now in London lying in the darkened bed, and thinking about words I had that day put down on paper. I would get a great, hollow, utterly futile feeling inside me, and then I would get up and switch on the light and read the words I had written that day, and then I would wonder: why am I here now? why have I come?

By day there would be the great, dull roar of London, the gold, yellow, foggy light you have there in October. The man-swarmed and old, weblike, smoky London! And I loved the place, and I loathed it and abhorred it. I knew no one there, and I had been a child in North Carolina long ago, and I was living there in two rooms in the huge octopal and illimitable web of that overwhelming city. I did not know why I had come, why I was there.

I worked there every day with such feelings as I have described, and came back to America in the winter and worked here. I would teach all day and write all night, and finally about two and a half years after I had begun the book in London, I finished it in New York.

I should like to tell about this, too. I was very young at the time, and I had the kind of wild, exultant vigor which a man has at that period of his life. The book took hold of me and possessed me. In a way, I think it shaped itself. Like every young man, I was strongly under the influence of writers I admired. One of the chief writers at that time was Mr. James Joyce with his book *Ulysses*. The book that I was writing was much influenced, I believe, by his own book, and yet the powerful energy and fire of my own youth played over and, I think, possessed it all. Like Mr. Joyce, I wrote about things that I had known, the immediate life and experience that had been familiar to me in my childhood. Unlike Mr. Joyce, I had no literary experience. I had never had anything published before. My feeling towards writers, publishers, books, that whole fabulous far-away world, was almost as romantically unreal as when I was a child. And yet my book, the characters with which I had peopled it, the color and the weather of the universe which I had created, had possessed me, and so I wrote and wrote with that bright flame with which a young man writes who never has been published, and who yet is sure all will be good and must go well. This is a curious thing and hard to tell about, yet easy to understand in every writer's mind. I wanted fame, as every youth who ever wrote must want it, and yet fame was a shining, bright, and most uncertain thing.

The book was finished in my twenty-eighth year. I knew no publishers and no writers. A friend of mine took the huge manuscript—it was about 350,000 words long—and sent it to a publisher whom she knew. In a few days, a week or two, I received an answer from this man saying that the book could not be published. The gist of what he said was that his house had published several books like it the year before, that all of them had failed, and that, further, the book in its present form was so amateurish, autobiographical, and unskillful that a publisher could not risk a chance on it. I was, myself, so depressed and weary by this time, the illusion of creation which had sustained me for two and a half years had so far worn off, that I believed what the man said. At that time I was a teacher in one of New York's great universities, and when the year came to a close, I went abroad. It was only after I had been abroad almost six months that news came to me from another publisher in America that he had read my manuscript and would like to talk to me about it as soon as I came home.

I came home on New Year's Day that year. The next day I called up the publisher who had written me. He asked me if I would come to his office and talk to him. I went at once, and before I had left his office that morning, I had signed a contract and had a check for five hundred dollars in my hand.

It was the first time, so far as I can remember, that anyone had concretely suggested to me that anything I had written was worth as much as fifteen cents, and I know that I left the publisher's office that day and entered into the great swarm of men and women who passed constantly along Fifth Avenue at Forty-eighth Street and presently I found myself at 110th Street, and from that day to this I have never known how I got there.

For the next six or eight months I taught at the university and worked upon the manuscript of my book with this editor. The book appeared in the month of October, 1929. The whole experience still had elements of that dreamlike terror and unreality that writing had had for me when I had first begun it seriously and had lain in my room in London with my hands below my head and thought: Why am I here? The awful, utter nakedness of print, that thing which is for all of us so namelessly akin to shame, came closer day by day. That I had wanted this exposure, I could not believe. It seemed to me that I had shamelessly exposed myself and yet that subtle drug of my desire and my creating held me with a serpent's eye, and I could do no other. I turned at last to this editor who had worked with me and found me, and I asked him if he could foretell the end and verdict of my labor. He said that he would rather tell me nothing, that he could not prophesy or know what profit I would have. He said, "All that I know is that they cannot let it go, they cannot ignore it. The book will find its way." . . .

The place to work! Yes, the place to work *was* Paris; it *was* Spain; it *was* Italy and Capri and Majorca, but, great God, it was also Keokuk, and Portland, Maine, and Denver, Colorado, and Yancey County, North Carolina, and wherever we might be, if work was there within us at the time. If this was all that I had learned from these voyages to Europe, if the price of all this wandering had been just this simple lesson, it would have been worth the price, but that was not all. I had found out during these years that the way to discover one's own country was to leave it; that the way to find America was to find it in one's heart, one's memory, and one's spirit, and in a foreign land.

I think I may say that I discovered America during these years abroad out of my very need of her. The huge gain of this discovery seemed to come directly from my sense of loss. I had been to Europe five times now; each time I had come with delight, with maddening eagerness to return, and each time how, where, and in what way I did not know, I had felt the bitter ache of homelessness, a desperate longing for America, an overwhelming desire to return.

During that summer in Paris, I think I felt this great homesickness more than ever before, and I really believe that from this emotion, this constant and almost intolerable effort of memory and desire, the material and the structure of the books I now began to write were derived.

The quality of my memory is characterized, I believe, in a more than ordinary degree by the intensity of its sense impressions, its power to evoke and bring back the odors, sounds, colors, shapes, and feel of things with concrete vividness. Now my memory was at work night and day, in a way that I could at first neither check nor control and that swarmed unbidden in a stream of blazing pageantry across my mind, with the million forms and substances of the life that I had left, which was my own, America. I would be sitting, for example, on the terrace of a café watching the flash and play of life before me on the Avenue de l'Opéra, and suddenly I would remember the iron railing that goes along the boardwalk at Atlantic City. I could see it instantly just the way it was, the heavy iron pipe; its raw, galvanized look; the way the joints were fitted together. It was all so vivid and concrete that I could feel my hand upon it and know the exact dimensions, its size and weight and shape. And suddenly I would realize that I had never seen any railing that looked like this in Europe. And this utterly familiar, common thing would suddenly be revealed to me with all the wonder with which we discover a thing which we have seen all our life and yet have never known before. Or again, it would be a bridge, the look of an old iron bridge across an American river, the sound the train makes as it goes across it; the spoke-and-hollow rumble of the ties below; the look of the muddy banks; the slow, thick, yellow wash of an American

river; an old flat-bottomed boat half-filled with water stogged
in the muddy bank; or it would be, most lonely and haunting
of all the sounds I know, the sound of a milk wagon as it entered an American street just at the first grey of the morning,
the slow and lonely clopping of the hoof upon the street, the
jink of bottles, the sudden rattle of a battered old milk can,
the swift and hurried footsteps of the milkman, and again the
jink of bottles, a low word spoken to his horse, and then the
great, slow, clopping hoof receding into silence, and then quiet-
ness and a bird song rising in the street again. Or it would be a
little wooden shed out in the country two miles from my home
town where people waited for the streetcar, and I could see
and feel again the dull and rusty color of the old green paint
and see and feel all of the initials that had been carved out
with jackknives on the planks and benches within the shed,
and smell the warm and sultry smell so resinous and so thrilling, so filled with a strange and nameless excitement of an unknown joy, a coming prophecy, and hear the streetcar as it
came to a stop, the moment of brooding, drowsing silence;
a hot thrum and drowsy stitch at three o'clock; the smell of
grass and hot sweet clover; and then the sudden sense of absence, loneliness, and departure when the streetcar had gone
and there was nothing but the hot and drowsy stitch at three
o'clock again. . . .

There was nothing at first which could be called a novel.
I wrote about night and darkness in America, and the faces
of the sleepers in ten thousand little towns; and of the tides
of sleep and how the rivers flowed forever in the darkness.
I wrote about the hissing glut of tides upon ten thousand miles
of coast; of how the moonlight blazed down on the wilderness
and filled the cat's cold eye with blazing yellow. I wrote about
death and sleep, and of that enfabled rock of life we call the
city. I wrote about October, of great trains that thundered
through the night, of ships and stations in the morning; of men
in harbors and the traffic of the ships.

I spent the winter of that year in England from October
until March, and here perhaps because of the homely familiarity of the English life, the sense of order and repose which

such a life can give one, my work moved forward still another step from this flood-tide chaos of creation. For the first time the work began to take on the lineaments of design. These lineaments were still confused and broken, sometimes utterly lost, but now I really did get the sense at last that I was working on a great block of marble, shaping a figure which no one but its maker could as yet define, but which was emerging more and more into the sinewy lines of composition.

From the beginning—and this was one fact that in all my times of hopelessness returned to fortify my faith in my conviction—the idea, the central legend that I wished my book to express had not changed. And this central idea was this: The deepest search in life, it seemed to me, the thing that in one way or another was central to all living was man's search to find a father, not merely the father of his flesh, not merely the lost father of his youth, but the image of a strength and wisdom external to his need and superior to his hunger, to which the belief and power of his own life could be united.

Yet I was terribly far away from the actual accomplishment of a book—how far away I could not at that time foresee. But four more years would have to pass before the first of a series of books on which I was now embarked would be ready for the press, and if I could have known that in those next four years there would be packed a hundred lives of birth and death, despair, defeat and triumph, and the sheer exhaustion of a brute fatigue, I do not know whether or not I could have found the power within myself to continue. But I was still sustained by the exuberant optimism of youth. My temperament, which is pessimistic about many things, has always been a curiously sanguine one concerning time, and although more than a year had now gone by and I had done no more than write great chants on death and sleep, prepare countless notes and trace here and there the first dim outlines of a formal pattern, I was confident that by the spring or the fall of the next year my book would somehow miraculously be ready.

So far as I can describe with any accuracy, the progress of that winter's work in England was not along the lines of planned design, but along this line that I have mentioned—writing some of the sections which I knew would have to be in the book. Meanwhile what was really going on in my whole creative consciousness, during all this time, although I did not realize it at the moment, was this: What I was really doing, what I had been doing all the time since my discovery of my America in Paris the summer before, was to explore day by day and month by month, with a fanatical intensity, the whole material domain of my resources as a man and as a writer. This exploration went on for a period which I can estimate conservatively as two years and a half. It is still going on, although not with the same all-absorbing concentration, because the work it led to, the work that after infinite waste and labor it helped me wonderfully to define, that work has reached such a state of final definition that the immediate task of finishing it is the one that now occupies the energy and interest of my life.

In a way, during that period of my life, I think I was like the Ancient Mariner who told the Wedding Guest that his frame was wrenched by the woeful agony which forced him to begin his tale before it left him free. In my own experience, my wedding guests were the great ledgers in which I wrote, and the tale which I told to them would have seemed, I am afraid, completely incoherent, as meaningless as Chinese characters, had any reader seen them. I could by no means hope to give a comprehensive idea of the whole extent of this labor because three years of work and perhaps a million and a half words went into these books. It included everything from gigantic and staggering lists of the towns, cities, counties, states, and countries I had been in, to minutely thorough, desperately evocative descriptions of the undercarriage, the springs, wheels, flanges, axle rods, color, weight, and quality of the day coach of an American railway train. There were lists of the rooms and houses in which I had lived or in which I had slept for at least a night, together with the most accurate and evocative descriptions of those rooms that I could write—their size, their shape, the color and design of the wallpaper, the way a towel hung down, the way a chair creaked, a streak of water rust upon the ceiling. There were countless charts, catalogues, descriptions that I can only classify here under the general heading of Amount and Number. What were the total combined populations of all the countries in Europe and America? In how many of those countries had I had some personal and vital experience? In the course of my twenty-nine or thirty years of living, how many people had I seen? How many had I passed by on the streets? How many had I seen on trains and subways, in theaters, at baseball or football games? With how many had I actually had some vital and illuminating experience, whether of joy, pain, anger, pity, love, or simple casual companionship, however brief? . . .

When I returned to America in the spring of 1931, although I had three or four hundred thousand words of material, I had nothing that could be published as a novel. Almost a year and a half had elapsed since the publication of my first book and already people had begun to ask that question which is so well meant, but which as year followed year was to become more intolerable to my ears than the most deliberate mockery: "Have you finished your next book yet?" "When is it going to be published?"

At this time I was sure that a few months of steady work would bring the book to completion. I found a place, a little basement flat in the Assyrian quarter in South Brooklyn, and there I went about my task.

The spring passed into the summer; the summer, into autumn. I was working hard, day after day, and still nothing that had the unity and design of a single work appeared. October came and with it a second full year since the publication of my first book. And now, for the first time, I was irrevocably committed so far as the publication of my book was concerned. I began to feel the sensation of pressure, and of naked desperation, which was to become almost maddeningly intolerable in the next three years. For the first time I began to realize that my project was much larger than I thought it would be. I had still believed at the time of my return from Europe that I was writing a single book, which would be comprised within the limits of about 200,000 words. Now as scene followed scene, as character after character came into being, as my understanding of my material became more comprehensive, I discovered that it would be impossible to write the book I had planned within the limits I had thought would be sufficient.

All of this time I was being baffled by a certain time element in the book, by a time relation which could not be escaped, and for which I was now desperately seeking some structural channel. There were three time elements inherent in the material. The first and most obvious was an element of actual present time, an element which carried the narrative forward, which represented characters and events as living in the present and moving forward into an immediate future. The second time element was of past time, one which represented these same characters as acting and as being acted upon by all the accumulated impact of man's experience so that each moment of their lives was conditioned not only by what they experienced in that moment, but by all that they had experienced up to that moment. In addition to these two time elements, there was a third which I conceived as being time immutable, the time of rivers, mountains, oceans, and the earth; a kind of eternal and unchanging universe of time against which would be projected the transience of man's life, the bitter briefness of his day. It was the tremendous problem of these three time elements that almost defeated me and that cost me countless hours of anguish in the years that were to follow.

As I began to realize the true nature of the task I had set for myself, the image of the river began to haunt my mind. I actually felt that I had a great river thrusting for release inside of me and that I had to find a channel into which its floodlike power could pour. I knew I had to find it or I would be destroyed in the flood of my own creation, and I am sure that every artist who ever lived has had the same experience.

Meanwhile, I was being baffled by a fixed and impossible idea whose error at the time I did not fully apprehend. I was convinced at that time that this whole gigantic plan had to be realized within the limits of a single book which would be called "The October Fair." It was not until more than a year had passed, when I realized finally that what I had to deal with was material which covered almost 150 years in history, demanded the action of more than 2000 characters, and would in its final design include almost every racial type and social class of American life, that I realized that even the pages of a book of 200,000 words were wholly inadequate for the purpose.

How did I finally arrive at this conclusion? I think it is not too much to say that I simply wrote myself into it. During all that year, I was writing furiously, feeling now the full pressure of inexorable time, the need to finish something. I wrote like mad; I finished scene after scene, chapter after chapter. The characters began to come to life, to grow and multiply until they were numbered by the hundreds, but so huge was the extent of my design, as I now desperately realized, that I can liken these chapters only to a row of lights which one sometimes sees at night from the windows of a speeding train, strung out across the dark and lonely countryside.

I would work furiously day after day until my creative energies were utterly exhausted, and although at the end of such a period I would have written perhaps as much as 200,000 words, enough in itself to make a very long book, I would realize with a feeling of horrible despair that what I had completed was only one small section of a single book.

During this time I reached that state of naked need and utter isolation which every artist has got to meet and conquer if he is to survive at all. Before this I had been sustained by that delightful illusion of success which we all have when we dream about the books we are going to write instead of actually doing them. Now I was face to face with it, and suddenly I realized that I had committed my life and my integrity so irrevocably to this struggle that I must conquer now or be destroyed. I was alone with my own work, and now I knew that I had to be alone with it, that no one could help me with it now no matter how anyone might wish to help. For the first time I realized another naked fact which every artist must know, and that is that in a man's work there are contained not only the seeds of life, but the seeds of death, and that that power of creation which sustains us will also destroy us like a leprosy if we let it rot stillborn in our vitals. I had to get it out of me somehow. I saw that now. And now for the first time a terrible doubt began to creep into my mind that I might not live long enough to get it out of me, that I had created a labor so large and so impossible that the energy of a dozen lifetimes would not suffice for its accomplishment.

During this time, however, I was sustained by one piece of inestimable good fortune. I had for a friend a man of immense and patient wisdom and a gentle but unyielding fortitude. I think that if I was not destroyed at this time by the sense of hopelessness which these gigantic labors had awakened in me, it was largely because of the courage and patience of this man. I did not give in because he would not let me give in, and I think it is also true that at this particular time he had the advantage of being in the position of a skilled observer at a battle, I was myself engaged in that battle, covered by its dust and sweat and exhausted by its struggle, and I understood far less clearly than my friend the nature and the progress of the struggle in which I was engaged. At this time there was little that this man could do except observe, and in one way or another keep me at my task, and in many quiet and marvelous ways he succeeded in doing this.

I was now at the place where I must produce, and even the greatest editor can do little for a writer until he has brought from the secret darkness of his own spirit into the common light of day the completed concrete accomplishment of his imagining. My friend, the editor, has likened his own function at this painful time to that of a man who is trying to hang onto the fin of a plunging whale, but hang on he did, and it is to his tenacity that I owe my final release.

Meanwhile, my creative power was functioning at the highest intensity it had ever known. I wrote at times without belief that I would ever finish, with nothing in me but black despair, and yet I wrote and wrote and could not give up writing. And it seemed that despair itself was the very goad that urged me on, that made me write even when I had no belief that I would ever finish. It seemed to me that my life in Brooklyn, although I had been there only two and a half years, went back through centuries of time, through ocean depths of black and bottomless experience which no ordinary scale of hours would ever measure. People have sometimes asked me what happened to my life during these years. They have asked me how I ever found time to know anything that was going on in the world about me when my life was so completely absorbed by this world of writing. Well, it may seem to be an extraordinary fact, but the truth is that never in my whole life have I lived so fully, have I shared so richly in the common life of man as I did during these three years when I was struggling with the giant problem of my own work.

For one thing, my whole sensory and creative equipment, my powers of feeling and reflection—even the sense of hearing, and above all my powers of memory, had reached the greatest degree of sharpness that they had ever known. At the end of the day of savage labor, my mind was still blazing with its effort, could by no opiate of reading, poetry, music, alcohol, or any other pleasure, be put at rest. I was unable to sleep, unable to subdue the tumult of these creative energies, and as a result of this condition, for three years I prowled the streets, explored the swarming web of the million-footed city and came to know it as I had never done before. It was a black time in the history of the nation, a black time in my own life and, I suppose, it is but natural that my own memory of it now should be a pretty grim and painful one.

Everywhere around me, during these years, I saw the evidence of an incalculable ruin and suffering. My own people, the members of my own family, had been ruined, had lost all the material wealth and accumulation of a lifetime in what was called the "depression." And that universal calamity had somehow struck the life of almost every one I knew. Moreover, in this endless quest and prowling of the night through the great web and jungle of the city, I saw, lived, felt, and experienced the full weight of that horrible human calamity.

I saw a man whose life had subsided into a mass of shapeless and filthy rags, devoured by vermin; wretches huddled together for a little warmth in freezing cold squatting in doorless closets upon the foul seat of a public latrine within the very shadow, the cold shelter of palatial and stupendous monuments of wealth. I saw acts of sickening violence and cruel-

ty, the menace of brute privilege, a cruel and corrupt authority trampling ruthlessly below its feet the lives of the poor,
the weak, the wretched, and defenseless of the earth.

And the staggering impact of this black picture of man's
inhumanity to his fellow man, the unending repercussions of
these scenes of suffering, violence, oppression, hunger, cold,
and filth and poverty going on unheeded in a world in which
the rich were still rotten with their wealth left a scar upon my
life, a conviction in my soul which I shall never lose.

And from it all, there has come as the final deposit, a burning memory, a certain evidence of the fortitude of man, his
ability to suffer and somehow to survive. And it is for this reason now that I think I shall always remember this black period
with a kind of joy that I could not at that time have believed
possible, for it was during this time that I lived my life through
to a first completion and through the suffering and labor of
my own life came to share those qualities in the lives of people
all around me. And that is another thing which the making
of a book has done for me. It has given my life that kind of
growth which I think the fulfillment of each work does give
the artist's life, and insofar as I have known these things, I think
that they have added to my stature. . . .

Such was the state my life had come to in the early winter of 1933, and even at that moment, although I could not
see it, the end of my huge labor was in sight. In the middle of
December of that year the editor, of whom I have spoken,
and who, during all this tormented period, had kept a quiet
watch upon me, called me to his home and calmly informed
me that my book was finished. I could only look at him with
stunned surprise, and finally I only could tell him out of the
depth of my own hopelessness, that he was mistaken, that the
book was not finished, that it could never be completed, that
I could write no more. He answered with the same quiet fi-
nality that the book was finished whether I knew it or not, and
then he told me to go to my room and spend the next week
in collecting in its proper order the manuscript which had accumulated during the last two years.

I followed his instructions, still without hope and without

belief. I worked for six days sitting in the middle of the floor surrounded by mountainous stacks of typed manuscript on every side. At the end of a week I had the first part of it together, and just two days before Christmas, 1933, I delivered to him the manuscript of "The October Fair," and a few days later, the manuscript of "The Hills Beyond Pentland." The manuscript of "The Fair" was, at that time, something over 1,000,000 words in length. He had seen most of it in its dismembered fragments during the three preceding years, but now, for the first time, he was seeing it in its sequential order, and once again his intuition was right; he had told me the truth when he said that I had finished the book.

It was not finished in any way that was publishable or readable. It was really not a book so much as it was the skeleton of a book, but for the first time in four years the skeleton was all there. An enormous labor of revision, weaving together, shaping, and, above all, cutting remained, but I had the book now so that nothing, not even the despair of my own spirit, could take it from me. He told me so, and suddenly I saw that he was right.

I was like a man who is drowning and who suddenly, at the last gasp of his dying effort, feels earth beneath his feet again. My spirit was borne upward by the greatest triumph it had ever known, and although my mind was tired, my body exhausted, from that moment on I felt equal to anything on earth.

It was evident that many problems were before us, but now we had the thing, and we welcomed the labor before us with happy confidence. In the first place there was the problem of the book's gigantic length. Even in this skeletonized form the manuscript of "The October Fair" was about twelve times the length of the average novel or twice the length of *War and Peace*. It was manifest, therefore, that it would not only be utterly impossible to publish such a manuscript in a single volume, but that even if it were published in several volumes, the tremendous length of such a manuscript would practically annihilate its chances of ever finding a public which would read it.

This problem now faced us, and the editor grappled with it immediately. As his examination of the manuscript of "The October Fair" proceeded, he found that the book did describe two complete and separate cycles. The first of these was a movement which described the period of wandering and hunger in a man's youth. The second cycle described the period of greater certitude, and was dominated by the unity of a single passion. It was obvious, therefore, that what we had in the two cyclic movements of this book was really the material of two completely different chronicles, and although the second of the two was by far the more finished, the first cycle, of course, was the one which logically we ought to complete and publish first, and we decided on this course.

We took the first part first. I immediately prepared a minutely thorough synopsis which described not only the course of the book from first to last, but which also included an analysis of those chapters which had been completed in their entirety, of those which were completed only in part, and of those which had not been written at all, and with this synopsis before us, we set to work immediately to prepare the book for press. This work occupied me throughout the whole of the year 1934. The book was completed at the beginning of 1935, and was published in March of that year under the title of *Of Time and the River.*

In the first place, the manuscript, even in its unfinished form, called for the most radical cutting, and because of the way in which the book had been written, as well as the fatigue which I now felt, I was not well prepared to do by myself the task that lay ahead of us.

Cutting had always been the most difficult and distasteful part of writing to me; my tendency had always been to write rather than to cut. Moreover, whatever critical faculty I may have had concerning my own work had been seriously impaired, for the time being at least, by the frenzied labor of the past four years. When a man's work has poured from him for almost five years like burning lava from a volcano; when all of it, however superfluous, has been given fire and passion by the white heat of his own creative energy, it is very difficult suddenly to become coldly surgical, ruthlessly detached.

To give a few concrete illustrations of the difficulties that now confronted us: The opening section of the book describes the journey of a train across the State of Virginia at night. Its function in the book is simply to introduce some of the chief characters, to indicate a central situation, to give something of the background from which the book proceeds, and perhaps through the movement of the train across the stillness of the earth to establish a certain beat, evoke a certain emotion which is inherent to the nature of the book. Such a section, therefore, undoubtedly serves an important function, but in proportion to the whole purport of the book, its function is a secondary one and must be related to the whole book in a proportionate way.

Now in the original version, the manuscript which described the journey of the train across Virginia at night was considerably longer than the average novel. What was needed was just an introductory chapter or two, and what I had written was over 100,000 words in length, and this same difficulty, this lack of proportion, was also evident in other parts of the manuscript.

What I had written about the great train was really good. But what I had to face, the very bitter lesson that everyone who wants to write has got to learn, was that a thing may in itself be the finest piece of writing one has ever done, and yet have absolutely no place in the manuscript one hopes to publish. This is a hard thing, but it must be faced, and so we faced it.

My spirit quivered at the bloody execution. My soul recoiled before the carnage of so many lovely things cut out upon which my heart was set. But it had to be done, and we did it.

The first chapter in the original manuscript, a chapter which the editor, himself, admitted was as good a single piece of writing as I had ever done, was relentlessly kicked out, and the reason it was kicked out was that it was really not a true beginning for the book but merely something which led up to the true beginning; therefore it had to go. And so it went all up and down the line. Chapters 50,000 words long were reduced to ten or fifteen thousand words, and having faced this inevitable necessity, I finally acquired a kind of ruthlessness of my own, and once or twice, myself, did more cutting than my editor was willing to allow.

Another fault that has always troubled me in writing is that I have often attempted to reproduce in its entirety the full flood and fabric of a scene in life itself. Thus, in another section of the book, four people were represented as talking to each other for four hours without a break or intermission. All were good talkers; often all talked, or tried to talk, at the same time. The talk was wonderful and living talk because I knew the life and character and the vocabulary of all these people from its living source, and I had forgotten nothing. Yet all the time, all that was actually happening in this scene was that a young woman had got out of her husband's motor car and gone into her mother's house and kept calling to the impatient man outside every time he honked his horn, "All right. All right. I'll be with you in five minutes." These five minutes really lengthened into four hours, while the unfortunate man outside honked upon his horn, and while the two women and two young men of the same family inside carried on a torrential discourse and discussed exhaustively the lives and histories of almost everyone in town, their memories of the past, adventures of the present, and speculations of the future. I put it all down in the original manuscript just as I had seen and known and lived it a thousand times, and even if I do say so myself, the nature of the talk, the living vitality and character of the language, the utter naturalness, the flood-tide river of it all was wonderful, but I had made four people talk 80,000 words—200 printed pages of close type in a minor scene of an enormous book, and of course, good as it was, it was all wrong and had to go. . . .

In January, 1935, I finished the last of my revisions on the proof; the first printed copies came from the press in February. The book was released for final publication early in March. I was not here when it came out. I had taken a ship for Europe the week before, and as the ship got farther and farther from the American shores, my spirits sank lower and lower, reaching, I think, the lowest state of hopeless depression they had ever known. This, I believe, was largely a physical reaction, the inevitable effect of relaxation upon a human organism which had for five years been strained to its utmost limit. My life seemed to me to be like a great spring which had been taut for years and which was now slowly uncoiling from its tension. I had the most extraordinary sense of desolation I had ever known when I thought about my book. I had never realized until now how close I had been to it, how much a part of me it had become, and now that it had been taken away from me, my life felt utterly futile, hollow as a shell. And now that the book was gone, now that there was nothing more that I could do about it, I felt the most abysmal sensation of failure. I have always been somewhat afraid of print, although print is a thing I have tried so hard to achieve. Yet it is literally true that with everything I have ever written, I have felt when the hour of naked print drew nigh a kind of desperation and have even entreated my publisher not only to defer the publication of my book until another season, but have asked the editors of magazines to put off the publication of a story for another month or two until I had a chance to work on it some more, do something to it, I was not always sure what. . . .

The life of the artist at any epoch of man's history has not been an easy one. And here in America, it has often seemed to me, it may well be the hardest life that man has ever known. I am not speaking of some frustration in our native life, some barrenness of spirit, some arid Philistinism which contends against the artist's life and which prevents his growth. I do not speak of these things because I do not put the same belief in them that I once did. I am speaking as I have tried to speak from first to last in the concrete terms of the artist's actual experience, of the nature of the physical task before him. It seems to me that the task is one whose physical proportions are vaster and more difficult here than in any other nation on the earth. It is not merely that in the cultures of Europe and of the Orient the American artist can find no antecedent scheme, no structural plan, no body of tradition that can give his own work the validity and truth that it must have. It is not merely that he must make somehow a new tradition for himself, derived from his own life and from the enormous space and energy of American life, the structure of his own design; it is not merely that he is confronted by these problems; it is even more than this, that the labor of a complete and whole articulation, the discovery of an entire universe and of a complete language, is the task that lies before him.

Such is the nature of the struggle to which henceforth our lives must be devoted. Out of the billion forms of America, out of the savage violence and the dense complexity of all its swarming life; from the unique and single substance of this land and life of ours, must we draw the power and energy of our own life, the articulation of our speech, the substance of our art.

For here it seems to me in hard and honest ways like these we may find the tongue, the language, and the conscience that as men and artists we have got to have. Here, too, perhaps, must we who have no more than what we have, who know no more than what we know, who are no more than what we are, find our America. Here, at this present hour and moment of my life, I seek for mine.

James T. Farrell

HOW *STUDS LONIGAN* WAS WRITTEN*

I

I began writing what has developed into this trilogy in June, 1929. *Judgment Day* was finally completed at the end of January, 1935. In June, 1929, I was a young man who had burned other bridges behind him with the determination to write, whether my efforts brought me success or failure. I was then finishing what happened to be the last quarter in which I was a student at the University of Chicago. Three times before, I had dropped out of classes because I was restless and dissatisfied, resolved to devote my time to writing and to educating myself in my own haphazard manner. For a fourth and last time I had matriculated and I managed to finish out the quarter. Although I read continuously and rather broadly, I could not, after my sophomore year, maintain a steady interest in any of my courses except in composition, where I could write as much as I pleased. I would cut other classes, day after day, finally dropping out, heedless of the loss of credit and the waste of money I had spent in tuition.

*Reprinted by permission of the publisher, The Vanguard Press, from *The League of Frightened Philistines* by James T. Farrell. Copyright, 1938, 1945, by The Vanguard Press, Inc.

My mood and state of mind in those days were, I believe, of the kind which most young writers will recognize. To be a young man with literary aspirations is not to be particularly happy. At first, the desire to write is more strong than is a clear perception of what one wants to write and how one will write it. There are surprising oscillations of mood. One moment the young writer is energetic and hopeful. The next· he is catapulted into a fit of despair, his faith in himself infirm, his self-confidence shattered and broken, his view of the future one in which he sees futile self-sacrifices ending only in dismal failure. There are times when he cannot look his friends in the eye. There are moments when he feels himself to be set against the opposition of the entire world. There are occasions when he turns a caustic wit, a brutal sarcasm and a savage arrogance on others only because he is defending himself from himself. Suddenly he will be devastated by an image of himself in which he sees a nobody who has had the temerity and egotism to want to call himself a writer. He measures himself with his few unpublished manuscripts against the accomplishments of great writers, and his ambition suddenly seems like insanity. Even though he is not particularly conscious of clothes, there are periods when he gazes upon his own shabbiness—his unshined shoes, his worn and unpressed shiny suit, his frayed overcoat, his uncut hair—and he sees these as a badge of his own miserable mediocrity. A sense of failure dogs his steps. Living with himself becomes almost unendurable.

Writing is one of the cruelest of professions. The sense of possible failure in a literary career can torment one pitilessly. And failure in a literary career cannot be measured in dollars and cents. Poverty and the struggle for bread are not the only features of a literary career which can make it so cruel. There is the self-imposed loneliness. There is the endless struggle to perceive freshly and clearly, to realize and re-create a sense of life on paper. There is more than economic competition involved. The writer feels frequently that he is competing with time and with life itself. His hopes will sometimes ride high. His ambitions will soar until they have become so grandiose that they cannot be realized within the space of a single life-

time. The world opens up before the young writer as a grand
and glorious adventure in feeling and in understanding. Nothing
human is unimportant to him. Everything that he sees is ger-
mane to his purpose. Every word that he hears uttered is of
potential use to him. Every mood, every passing fancy, every
trivial thought can have its meaning and its place in the store
of experience which he accumulates. The opportunities for
assimilation are enormous, endless. And there is only one
single short life of struggle in which to assimilate. A melancholy
sense of time becomes a torment. One's whole spirit rebels
against a truism which all men must realize because it applies
to all men. One seethes in rebellion against the realization that
the human being must accept limitations, that he can develop
in one line of effort only at the cost of making many sacrifices
in other lines. Time becomes for the writer the most precious
good in all the world. And how often will he not feel that he
is squandering this precious good? His life then seems like a
sieve through which his days are filtering, leaving behind only
a few, a very few, miserable grains of experience. If he is wast-
ing time today, what assurance can he give himself that he will
not be doing likewise tomorrow? He is struggling with himself
to attain self-discipline. He weighs every failure in his struggle.
He begins to find a sense of death—death before he has fulfilled any of his potentialities—like a dark shadow cast constantly close to his awareness.

Such were some of the components of my own state of
mind when *Studs Lonigan* was begun.

II

In the spring of 1929, I took a course in advanced composition conducted by Professor James Weber Linn. Professor
Linn—with whom I was constantly at loggerheads concerning literary questions—was encouraging. His encouragement,
as well as my arguments with him and with the majority of the
class, assisted me in maintaining my own self-confidence. For
his course I wrote thousands of words. I wrote stories, sketch-

es, book reviews, essays, impressions, anecdotes. Most of these manuscripts related to death, disintegration, human indignity, poverty, drunkenness, ignorance, human cruelty. They attempted to describe dusty and deserted streets, street corners, miserable homes, pool rooms, brothels, dance halls, taxi dances, bohemian sections, express offices, gasoline filling stations, scenes laid in slum districts. The characters were boys, boys' gangs, drunkards, Negroes, expressmen, homosexuals, immigrants and immigrant landlords, filling-station attendants, straw bosses, hitchhikers, bums, bewildered parents. Most of the manuscripts were written with the ideal of objectivity in mind. I realized then that the writer should submit himself to an objective discipline. These early manuscripts of mine were written, in the main, out of such an intention.

One of the stories which I wrote for Professor Linn's course was titled *Studs*. It was originally published in *This Quarter*. *Studs* is the story of a wake, written in the first person. The corpse is a lad from the Fifty-eighth Street neighborhood who had died suddenly at the age of twenty-six. The story describes his background and friends. They have come to the wake and they sit in the rear of the apartment, discussing the mysteries of death in banalities, nostalgically remembering the good old days, contentedly describing the dull details of their current life. The author of the story sits there, half-heartedly trying to join in the conversation, recollecting the past vividly, remembering how these fellows, who are now corpulent and sunk in the trivialities of day-to-day living, were once adventurous boys.

Professor Linn read this story in class and praised it most enthusiastically. I had no genuine opinion concerning it. I had tried to write it as honestly, as clearly and as well as I could. I did not know what I thought of it. The praise which this story received in class greatly encouraged me. I asked Professor Robert Morss Lovett to read it. He kindly consented, and after doing so, he called me to his office and suggested that this story should be developed at greater length, and the *milieu* described in it should be put down in greater detail. I had already begun to think of doing this, and Mr. Lovett's advice clinched the matter for me. In a sense, Professor Linn and Professor Lovett are the spiritual godfathers of *Studs Lonigan.*

When I began working on this material, I envisaged one long novel, ending in a scene similar to that described in the story *Studs.* I saw in the character of Studs Lonigan a number of tendencies at work in a section of American life which I happened to know because it had been part of my own education in living. I began to see Studs, not only as a character for imaginative fiction, but also as a social manifestation. In the early stages of writing this work, I analyzed my character as I considered him in his relations to his own world, his own background. I set as my aim that of unfolding the destiny of Studs Lonigan in his own words, his own actions, his own patterns of thought and feeling. I decided that my task was not to state formally what life meant to me, but to try and re-create a sense of what life meant to Studs Lonigan. I worked on with this project, setting up as an ideal the strictest possible objectivity. As I wrote, the book enlarged and expanded. It grew into two novels, and finally into three. There were numberless changes and expansions of the original conception, alterations in emphasis, reconstructions of the structure of events from the time that the work was first conceived until the last line was written. However, to go into this phase of the work would be dull and would sound too much like a pretentious effort to bring one's laboratory out into public. All works of imaginative fiction go through such a process of change and expansion.

III

Studs Lonigan was conceived as a normal American boy of Irish-Catholic extraction. The social *milieu* in which he lived and was educated was one of spiritual poverty. It was not, contrary to some misconceptions, a slum neighborhood. Had I written *Studs Lonigan* as a story of the slums, it would then have been easy for the reader falsely to place the motivation and causation of the story directly in immediate economic roots. Such a placing of motivation would have obscured one of the most important meanings which I wanted to inculcate into my story: my desire to reveal the concrete effects of spiritual poverty. It is readily known that poverty and slums cause spiritual poverty in many lives. One of the important meanings which I perceived in this story was that here was a neighborhood several steps removed from the slums and dire economic want, and here was manifested a pervasive spiritual poverty.

The fathers, grandfathers, great grandfathers of boys like Studs Lonigan came to America as to a new world. They came from the shores of that island whose history is one of the most bitter of all nations. Most of them were poor immigrants. Some of them could not read or write. They belonged at the bottom of the American social and economic ladder. Many of them did menial work, and the lives which they led were hard. They struggled upward in American society just as have other immigrant groups and races before and after them. Their lives constituted a process in which they were assimilated into the American petty bourgeoisie and the American labor aristocracy. Their lives were dedicated to work, to advancing themselves, to saving and thrift, to raising their families. They rose socially and economically. Ultimately many of them owned buildings and conducted their own small business enterprises. They became politicians, straw bosses, salesmen, boss craftsmen and the like. And they became tired. Their spiritual resources were meager. They believed in the American myth of success and advancement. They believed in the teachings and dogma of their faith. They believed that with homilies, platitudes about faith and work, and little fables about good example, they could educate their children. They believed that thus their children would start off in the race of life with greater advantages than they had had, and that their children would advance so much the farther, so many more rungs on the economic and social ladder.

The story of Studs Lonigan opens on the day that Woodrow Wilson is renominated to run for a second term as President of the United States. It closes in the depths of the Hoover era.

It was during the period of the Wilson Administration that this nation reached upward toward the zenith of its power and became, perhaps, the richest and the most powerful nation in all history. The story of Studs Lonigan was conceived as the story of the education of a normal American boy in this period. The important institutions in the education of Studs Lonigan were the home and the family, the church, the school, and the playground. These institutions broke down and did not serve their desired function. The streets become a potent educative factor in the boy's life. In time, the pool room becomes an important institution in his life. When Studs reaches his young manhood, this nation is moving headlong into one of the most insane eras of our history—the Prohibition era. A word here is necessary concerning the drinking of Studs and his companions. This drinking has a definite social character. When Studs and his companions drink, they do so as a gesture of defiance which is in the spirit of the times. Drinking in those days became a social ritual. Furthermore, when Studs and his companions began drinking, the worst liquor of the Prohibition era was being sold. Those were the days when the newspapers published daily death lists of the number of persons who had died from bootleg liquor and wood alcohol. That was the time when men and boys would take one or two drinks, pass out into unconsciousness and come to their senses only to learn that they would never again have their eyesight. All generations drink more or less in the period of young manhood. But all generations do not drink the kind of bootleg liquor which Studs Lonigan and his companions drank. The health of Studs and many of his friends is impaired and permanently ruined in this story. That very loss of health has, it can be seen now, a social character.

Studs Lonigan is neither a tough nor a gangster. He is not really a hard guy. He is a normal young American of his time and his class. His values become the values of his world. He has as many good impulses as normal human beings have.

In time, because of defeat, of frustration, of a total situation which is characterized by spiritual poverty, these good impulses go more and more into the stream of his reverie. Here we find the source of Studs' constant dream of himself. Studs' dream of himself changes in character as the story progresses. In the beginning, it is a vision of what he is going to be. He is a boy waiting at the threshold of life. His dream of himself is a romantic projection of his future, conceived in the terms and the values of his world. In time, this dream of himself turns backward. It is no longer a romantic projection of things to come. More and more it becomes a nostalgic image turned toward the past. Does this not happen in greater or lesser degree to all of us?

Shortly after I began working on *Studs Lonigan,* I happened to be reading John Dewey's *Human Nature and Conduct,* and I came upon the following sentence which I used as a quotation in *Young Lonigan:* "The poignancy of situations which evoke reflection lies in the fact that we do not know the meaning of the tendencies that are pressing for action." This observation crystallized for me what I was seeking to do. This work grew out of a situation which evoked reflection. The situation revealed to me the final meaning of tendencies which had been pressing for action. And that final situation became death, turning poignancy into tragedy. *Studs Lonigan* was conceived as the story of an American destiny in our time. It deals with the making and the education of an ordinary American boy. My attitude toward it and toward my character here is essentially a simple one. "There but for the grace of God go I." . . . "There but for the grace of God go"—many others.

James T. Farrell

May 5, 1938
New York City

John Steinbeck

CRITICS, CRITICS, BURNING BRIGHT*

. . . My experience in writing has followed an almost invariable pattern. Since by the process of writing a book I have out-grown that book, and since I like to write, I have not written two books alike. Where would be the interest in that? The result has been (and I can prove it with old reviews) that every book has been attacked by a large section of the critical family. I can also prove by old notices that the preceding book is compared favorably over the current one and the one before over the preceding one. To a sensitive reader this would indi-cate that starting nowhere I have consistently gone down. Or perhaps, having made up their minds what the next book would be like, the critics experienced anger when it was different. But there is one advantage in the book over the play to the writer. A book can wait around and perhaps gradually pick up its adherents and defenders while a play cannot. A play goes or dies very quickly. If my books, almost without exception, could have been killed by initial criticism, as a play is, they would have been killed and my work would be very largely unknown.

*"Critics, Critics, Burning Bright" by John Steinbeck. Copyright © 1950 by Elaine Steinbeck and Harry Buchman as Executors of the Estate of John Steinbeck, and the Saturday Review Associates, Inc. Appeared originally in the *Saturday Review of Literature.*, Nov. 11, 1950.

Again I am not criticizing critics. They must translate to their audiences, and to do this they must think as their audiences do. But a book can wait until any frightening innovations have ceased to be objects of fear or derision. If my work had been exclusively for the theatre I believe that it would be unknown—and perhaps rightly so—for the theatre cannot wait.

If a writer likes to write, he will find satisfaction in endless experiment with his medium. He will improvise techniques, arrangements of scenes, rhythms of words, and rhythms of thought. He will constantly investigate and try combinations new to him, sometimes utilizing an old method for a new idea and vice versa. Some of his experiments will inevitably be unsuccessful but he must try them anyway if his interest be alive. This experimentation is not criminal. Perhaps it is not even important, but it is necessary if the writer be not moribund.

And sometimes the experiment, which at first seems outrageous to the critic and the reader who have not been through the process of its development, may become interesting and valid when it is inspected a second and third time. The structure of literature is not endangered thereby in any case and the growth of literature springs from no other source.

I have had fun with my work and I shall insist on continuing to have fun with it. And it has been my great good fortune in the past, as I hope it will be in the future, to find enough people to go along with me to the extent of buying books, so that I may eat and continue to have fun. I do not believe that I can much endanger or embellish the great structure of English literature.

I had a wise uncle who, coming upon me in my teens, with my chin down and shoulders bulging as I fought viciously for a highly problematical literary immortality, said as follows: "You know, if you succeed perfectly in doing what you are trying to do, the most you can hope to gain is the undying hatred of a few generations of undergraduates." Even at that age I was so impressed with his logic that I never put on the gloves with Maupassant or Proust again.

I just like to have fun with whatever equipment I have.

A LETTER ON CRITICISM*

Feb. 5, 1955

Dear Editors:

Thank you for your very kind letter and your offer to make space available for my comment on the two recent articles on the *Grapes of Wrath* which have appeared in the *Quarterly*.[1] I wish I could so comment but I have no opinions nor ideas on the subject. Indeed, both pieces seem to me to be nearer to taxonomy than to criticism. Much of the new criticism with its special terms and parochial approach is interesting to me, although I confess I don't understand it very well, but I cannot see that it has very much to do with the writing of novels good or bad. And since the new critics fight each other even more fiercely than they do the strapped down and laid open subjects of their study, it would seem to me that they do not have a table of constants. In less criticismal terms, I think it is a bunch of crap. As such I am not against it so long as it is un-

*"A letter on Criticism" by John Steinbeck, from *The Colorado Quarterly,* Copyright 1955. By permission of *The Colorado Quarterly* and McIntosh and Otis, Inc.

[1]The editor of *The Colorado Quarterly* had invited Steinbeck to comment on articles by Bernard Bowron and Warren G. French (Summer, 1954 and Winter, 1955).

derstood that the process is a kind of ill tempered parlour game in which nobody gets kissed. What such an approach would do to a student beyond confusing him and perhaps making him shy away from reading, I have no idea. I do not read much criticism of my work any more. In the first place it is valueless as advice or castigation since the criticised piece is finished and I am not likely to repeat it. And in the second place, the intrafrontal disagreements only succeed in puzzling me. Recently a critic proved by parallel passages that I had taken my whole philosophy from a 17th century Frenchman of whom I had never heard. I usually know what I want to say and hope I have the technique to say it clearly and effectively. As Tennessee Williams once said, "I put it down that a way and that's the only way I know to put it down."

I don't think the *Grapes of Wrath* is obscure in what it tries to say. As to its classification and pickling, I have neither opinion nor interest. It's just a book, interesting I hope, instructive in the same way the writing instructed me. Its structure is very carefully worked out and it is no more intended to be inspected than is the skeletal structure of a pretty girl. Just read it, don't count it!

Please believe me when I say I have nothing against the scholarly or critical approach. It does seem to me to have very little to do with the writing or reading of books.

The writing of books is a lonely and difficult job, and it takes all the time I have. Remember the negro boy in Texas who when asked by a priest whether he was a catholic, replied, "Hell no, father, I'm having enough trouble just being a nigger." Well I'm having enough—just being a writer.

I am working now on a long novel, trying to get it straight and clear—trying to fit method to subject and tone to surround the whole—trying to fit the thousand details and people into the pattern. Imagine, if you will, the confusion if criticism should come now. No book would ever get written if the critic could get at the mind of a writer rather than his work. Afterwards, critics are hardly more destructive than silver fish.

Yours,
John Steinbeck

RATIONALE*

Recently I was asked by a University for a Rationale of the corpus of my work. I didn't know the word.

The Oxford Dictionary defines a "Rationale" as: 1. A reasoned exposition of principles, an explanation or statement of reasons, a set of reasoned rules or directions; and 2. The fundamental reason, the logical or rational basis for anything. Or in simpler words—what did you write and why did you write it?

There may be writers who before the fact of writing may have been able to do this. In my own case, I fear that a *rationale* might well be a rationalization, undertaken after the fact— a critic's rather than a writer's approach. It is like asking a prisoner, "Why did you commit murder?" His reply might be "Let me think. I guess I didn't like the guy, and—well I was mad." He can work out why he did it but he can't really remember the emotional pressure which drifted his hand toward the knife.

So in my work I can say, "It must have been this way or this"—but I am not at all sure that I remember. I can say of one book, "I suppose I saw things which made me angry." Of another, "It was just an idea which amused me and I wrote

*"Rationale" by John Steinbeck, from *Steinbeck and His Critics* by Tedlock and Wicker, copyright 1957 the University of New Mexico Press. By permission of the University of New Mexico Press and McIntosh and Otis, Inc.

it." Of another, "It is possible that I was trying to explain some-thing—something that was not clear to me. I may have felt that writing it would make me understand it better."

My basic rationale might be that I like to write. I feel good when I am doing it—better than when I am not. I find joy in the texture and tone and rhythms of words and sentences, and when these happily combine in a "thing" that has texture and tone and emotion and design and architecture, there comes a fine feeling—a satisfaction like that which follows good and shared love. If there have been difficulties and failures over-come, these may even add to the satisfaction.

As for my "reasoned exposition of principles," I suspect that they are no different from those of any man living out his life. Like everyone, I want to be good and strong and virtuous and wise and loved. I think that writing may be simply a method or technique for communication with other individuals; and its stimulus, the loneliness we are born to. In writing, perhaps we hope to achieve companionship. What some people find in religion, a writer may find in his craft or whatever it is,—absorption of the small and frightened and lonely into the whole and complete, a kind of breaking through to glory.

A lady of my acquaintance was asked by her young daugh-ters where babies came from, and after making certain that they really wanted to know, she told them. They listened sol-emnly and at the end, the mother asked, "Now are you sure you understand?"

The oldest girl said, "Yes, we understand what you do—but *why* do you do it?"

The mother thought for a moment and then replied, "Be-cause it's *fun!*"

And that could well be my rationale. My work is and has been fun. Within myself, I find no hunger to inquire further.

Robert Penn Warren

"ALL THE KING'S MEN":
THE MATRIX OF EXPERIENCE*

When I am asked how much *All the King's Men* owes to the actual politics of Louisiana in the '30's, I can only be sure that if I had never gone to live in Louisiana and if Huey Long had not existed, the novel would never have been written. But this is far from saying that my "state" in *All the King's Men* is Louisiana (or any of the other forty-nine stars in our flag), or that my Willie Stark is the late Senator. What Louisiana and Senator Long gave me was a line of thinking and feeling that did eventuate in the novel.

In the summer of 1934 I was offered a job—a much-needed job—as Assistant Professor at the Louisiana State University, in Baton Rouge. It was "Huey Long's University," and definitely on the make—with a sensational football team and with money to spend even for assistant professors at a time when assistant professors were being fired, not hired—as I knew all too well. It was Huey's University, but he, I was assured, would never mess with my classroom. That was to prove true; he was far too adept in the arts of power to care what an assistant professor might have to say. The only time that his presence

*From *All The King's Men:* "The Matrix of Experience" by Robert Penn Warren. Published by the *Yale Review.* Copyright © 1963 by Robert Penn Warren. Reprinted with permission by William Morris Agency.

was ever felt in my classroom was when, in my Shakespeare course, I gave my little annual lecture on the political background of *Julius Caesar;* and then, for the two weeks we spent on the play, backs grew straighter, eyes grew brighter, notes were taken, and the girls stopped knitting in class, or repairing their faces.

In September 1934 I left Tennessee, where I had been living on a farm near Nashville, drove down across Mississippi, crossed the river by ferry (where I can't be sure—was it at Greenville?) and was in North Louisiana. Along the way I picked up a hitchhiker—a country man, the kind you call a red-neck or a wool-hat, aging, aimless, nondescript, beat up by life and hard times and bad luck, clearly tooth-broke and probably gut-shot, standing beside the road in an attitude that spoke of infinite patience and considerable fortitude, holding a parcel in his hand, wrapped in old newspaper and tied with binder twine, waiting for some car to come along. He was, though at the moment I did not sense it, a mythological figure.

He was the god on the battlement, dimly perceived above the darkling tumult and the steaming carnage of the political struggle. He was a voice, a portent, and a natural force like the Mississippi River getting set to bust a levee. Long before the Fascist March on Rome, Norman Douglas, meditating on Naples, had predicted that the fetid slums of Europe would make possible the "inspired idiot." His predictive diagnosis of the origins of fascism—and of communism—may be incomplete, but it is certain that the rutted back roads and slab-side shacks that had spawned my nameless old hitchhiker, with the twine-tied paper parcel in his hand, had, by that fall of 1934, made possible the rise of "Huey." My nameless hitchhiker was, mythologically speaking, Long's *sine qua non.*

So it was appropriate that he should tell me the first episode of the many I had to hear of the myth that was "Huey." The roads, he said, was shore better now. A man could git to market, he said. A man could jist git up and git, if'n a notion come on him. Did'n have to pay no toll at no toll bridge neither. Fer Huey was a free-bridge man. So he went on and told me how, standing on the river bank by a toll bridge (by what river and what bridge was never clear), Huey had made the president of the company that owned the bridge a good, fair cash offer, and the man laughed at him. But, the old hitchhiker said, Huey did'n do nothing but lean over and pick him up a chunk of rock and throwed it off a-ways, and asked did the president-feller see whar the rock hit. The feller said yeah, he seen. Wal, Huey said, the next thing you see is gonna be a big new free bridge right whar that rock hit, and you, you son-of-a-bitch, are goen bankrupt a-ready and doan even know it.

There were a thousand tales, over the years, and some of them were, no doubt, literally and factually true. But they were all true in the world of "Huey"—that world of myth, folklore, poetry, deprivation, rancor, and dimly envisaged hopes. That world had a strange, shifting, often ironical and sometimes irrelevant relation to the factual world of Senator Huey P. Long and his cold manipulation of the calculus of power. The two worlds, we may hazard, merged only at the moment when in September 1935, in the corridor of the Capitol, the little .32 slug bit meanly into the senatorial vitals.

There was another world—this a factual world—made possible by the factual Long, though not inhabited by him. It was a world that I, as an assistant professor, was to catch fleeting glimpses of, and ponder. It was the world of the parasites of power, a world that Long was, apparently, contemptuous of, but knew how to use, as he knew how to use other things of which he was, perhaps, contemptuous. This was a world of a sick yearning for elegance and the sight of one's name on the society page of a New Orleans paper; it was the world of the electric moon devised, it was alleged, to cast a romantic glow over the garden when the president of the University and his wife entertained their politicos and pseudo-socialites; it was a world of pretentiousness, of bloodcurdling struggles for academic preferment, of drool-jawed grab and arrogant criminality. It was a world all too suggestive, in its small-bore, provincial way, of the airs and aspirations that the newspapers attributed to that ex-champagne salesman Von Ribbentrop and to the inner circle of Edda Ciano's friends.

For in Louisiana, in the 1930's, you felt somehow that you were living in the great world, or at least in a microcosm with all the forces and fatalities faithfully, if sometimes comically, drawn to scale. And the little Baton Rouge world of campus and Governor's Mansion and Capitol and the gold bathroom fixtures reported to be in the house of the University contractor was, once the weight of Long's contempt and political savvy had been removed by the bullet of the young Brutus in the Capitol, to plunge idiotically rampant to an end almost as dramatic as the scenes in the last bunkers of Berlin or at the filling station on the outskirts of Milan. The headlines advertised the suicides, and the population of penitentiaries, both Federal and state, received some distinguished additions.

But this is getting ahead of the story. Meanwhile, there was, besides the lurid worlds, the world of ordinary life to look at. There were the people who ran stores or sold insurance or had a farm and tried to survive and pay their debts. There were—visible even from the new concrete speedway that Huey had slashed through the cypress swamps toward New Orleans— the palmetto-leaf and sheet-iron hovels of the moss pickers, rising like some fungoid growth from a hummock under the great cypress knees, surrounded by scum-green water that never felt sunlight, back in that Freudianly contorted cypress gloom of cotton-mouth moccasins big as the biceps of a prizefighter, and owl calls, and the murderous metallic grind of insect life, and the smudge fire at the hovel door, that door being nothing but a hole in a hovel wall, with a piece of croker sack hung over it. There were, a few miles off at the University, your colleagues, some as torpid as a gorged alligator in the cold mud of January and some avid to lick the spit of an indifferent or corrupt administration, but many able and gifted and fired by a will to create, out of the seething stew and heaving magma, a distinguished university.

And there were, of course, the students, like students anywhere in the country in the big state universities, except for the extraordinary number of pretty girls and the preternatural blankness of the gladiators who were housed beneath the stadium to have their reflexes honed, their diet supervised, and—through the efforts of tutors—their heads crammed with just enough of whatever mash was required (I never found out) to get them past their minimal examinations. Among the students there sometimes appeared, too, that awkward boy from the depth of the 'Cajun country or from some scrabble-farm in North Louisiana, with burning ambition and frightening energy and a thirst for learning; and his presence there, you reminded yourself, with whatever complication of irony seemed necessary at the moment, was due to Huey, and to Huey alone. For the "better element" had done next to nothing in fifty years to get that boy out of the grim despair of his ignorance.

Yes, there was the world of the "good families," most of whom hated Huey Long—except, of course, for that percentage who, for one reason or another, had reached an accommodation. They hated him sometimes for good reasons and sometimes for bad, and sometimes for no reason at all, as a mere revulsion of taste; but they never seemed to reflect on what I took to be the obvious fact that if the government of the state had not previously been marked by various combinations of sloth, complacency, incompetence, corruption, and a profound lack of political imagination, there would never have been a Senator Huey P. Long, and my old hitchhiker by the roadside would, in September 1934, have had no tale to tell me.

Conversation in Louisiana always came back to the tales, to the myth, to politics; and to talk politics is talk about power. So conversation turned, by implication at least, on the question of power and ethics, of power and justification, of means and ends, of "historical costs." The big words were not often used, certainly not by the tellers of tales, but the concepts lurked even behind the most ungrammatical folktale. The tales were shot through with philosophy.

The tales were shot through, too, with folk humor, and the ethical ambiguity of folk humor. And the tales, like the political conversations, were shot through, too, with violence—or rather, with hints of the possibility of violence. There was a hint of revolutionary desperation—often synthetically induced. In Louisiana, in '34 and '35, it took nothing to start a rumor of violence. There had been, you might hear, a "battle" at the airport of Baton Rouge. A young filling station operator would proudly display his sawed-off automatic shotgun—I forget which "side" he was on, but I remember his fingers caressing the polished walnut of the stock. Or you might hear that there was going to be a "march" on the Capitol—but not hear by whom or for what.

Melodrama was the breath of life. There had been melodrama in the life I had known in Tennessee, but with a difference: in Tennessee the melodrama seemed to be different from the stuff of life, something superimposed upon life, but in Louisiana people lived melodrama, seemed to live, in fact, for it, for this strange combination of philosophy, humor, and violence. Life was a tale that you happened to be living—and that "Huey" happened to be living before your eyes. And all the while I was reading Elizabethan tragedy, Machiavelli, William James, and American history—and all that I was reading seemed to come alive, in shadowy distortions and sudden clarities, in what I saw around me.

How directly did I try to transpose into fiction Huey P. Long and the tone of that world? The question answers itself in a single fact. The first version of my story was a verse drama; and the actual writing began, in 1938, in the shade of an olive tree by a wheat field near Perugia. In other words, if you are sitting under an olive tree in Umbria and are writing a verse drama, the chances are that you are concerned more with the myth than with the fact, more with the symbolic than with the actual. And so it was. It could not, after all, have been otherwise, for in the strict, literal sense, I had no idea what the now deceased Huey P. Long had been. What I knew was the "Huey" of the myth, and that was what I had taken with me to Mussolini's Italy, where the bully boys wore black shirts and gave a funny salute.

I had no way of knowing what went on in the privacy of the heart of Senator Long. Now I could only hope, ambitiously, to know something of the heart of the Governor Talos of my play *Proud Flesh*. For Talos was the first avatar of my Willie

Stark, and the fact that I drew that name from the "iron groom" who, in murderous blankness, serves Justice in Spenser's *Faerie Queen* should indicate something of the line of thought and feeling that led up to that version and persisted, with modulations, into the novel.

Talos was to become Stark, and *Proud Flesh* was to become *All the King's Men*. Many things, some merely technical, led to this transformation, but one may have some bearing on the question of the ratio of fact and fiction. In 1942 I left Louisiana for good, and when in 1943 I began the version that is more realistic, discursive, and documentary in method (though not in spirit) than the play, I was doing so after I had definitely left Louisiana and the world in which the story had its roots. By now the literal, factual world was only a memory, and therefore was ready to be absorbed freely into the act of imagination. Even the old man by the roadside—the hitchhiker I had picked up on the way down to take my job—was ready to enter the story: he became, it would seem, the old hitchhiker whom Jack Burden picks up returning from Long Beach, California, the old man with the twitch in the face that gives Jack the idea for the Great Twitch. But my old hitchhiker had had no twitch in his face. Nor had I been Jack Burden.

I had not been Jack Burden except in so far as you have to try to "be" whatever you are trying to create. And in that sense I was also Adam Stanton, and Willie Stark, and Sadie Burke, and Sugar Boy, and all the rest. And this brings me to my last notion. However important for my novel was the protracted dialectic between "Huey" on the one side, and me on the other, it was far less important, in the end, than that deeper and darker dialectic for which the images and actions of a novel are the only language. And however important was my acquaintance with Louisiana, that was far less important than my acquaintance with another country: for any novel, good or bad, must report, willy-nilly, the history, sociology, and politics of a country even more fantastic than was Louisiana under the consulship of Huey.

Richard Wright

HOW "BIGGER" WAS BORN*

. . . The birth of Bigger Thomas goes back to my childhood,
and there was not just one Bigger, but many of them, more
than I could count and more than you suspect. But let me start
with the first Bigger, whom I shall call Bigger No.1.

When I was a bareheaded, barefoot kid in Jackson, Mississippi, there was a boy who terrorized me and all the boys
I played with. If we were playing games, he would saunter up
and snatch from us our balls, bats, spinning tops, and marbles.
We would stand around pouting, sniffling, trying to keep back
our tears, begging for our playthings. But Bigger would refuse.
We never demanded that he give them back; we were afraid,
and Bigger was bad. We had seen him clout boys when he was
angry and we did not want to run that risk. We never recovered our toys unless we flattered him and made him feel that
he was superior to us. Then, perhaps, if he felt like it, he con-
descended, threw them at us and then gave each of us a swift
kick in the bargain, just to make us feel his utter contempt.

That was the way Bigger No.1 lived. His life was a continuous challenge to others. At all times he *took* his way, right

*Abridgement of pp. xv-xviii, xxvi-xxix, xlii-xliv, xlvi-1 "How 'Bigger'
Was Born" by Richard Wright. Copyright 1940 by Richard Wright. Reprinted
by permission of Harper & Row, Publishers.

or wrong, and those who contradicted him had him to fight.
And never was he happier than when he had someone cor-
nered and at his mercy; it seemed that the deepest meaning
of his squalid life was in him at such times.

I don't know what the fate of Bigger No.1 was. His swagger-
ing personality is swallowed up somewhere in the amnesia
of my childhood. But I suspect that his end was violent. Anyway, he left a marked impression upon me; maybe it was because I longed secretly to be like him and was afraid. I don't
know.

If I had known only one Bigger I would not have written
Native Son. Let me call the next one Bigger No.2; he was about
seventeen and tougher than the first Bigger. Since I, too, had
grown older, I was a little less afraid of him. And the hardness
of this Bigger No.2 was not directed toward me or the other
Negroes, but toward the whites who ruled the South. He bought
clothes and food on credit and would not pay for them. He
lived in the dingy shacks of the white landlords and refused
to pay rent. Of course, he had no money, but neither did we.
We did without the necessities of life and starved ourselves,
but he never would. When we asked him why he acted as he
did, he would tell us (as though we were little children in a
kindergarten) that the white folks had everything and he had
nothing. Further, he would tell us that we were fools not to
get what we wanted while we were alive in this world. We would
listen and silently agree. We longed to believe and act as he
did, but we were afraid. We were Southern Negroes and we
were hungry and we wanted to live, but we were more willing
to tighten our belts than risk conflict. Bigger No.2 wanted
to live and he did; he was in prison the last time I heard from
him.

There was Bigger No.3, whom the white folks called a
"bad nigger." He carried his life in his hands in a literal fashion.
I once worked as a ticket-taker in a Negro movie house (all
movie houses in Dixie are Jim Crow; there are movies for whites
and movies for blacks), and many times Bigger No.3 came
to the door and gave my arm a hard pinch and walked into
the theater. Resentfully and silently, I'd nurse my bruised arm.

Presently, the proprietor would come over and ask how things were going, I'd point into the darkened theater and say: "Bigger's in there." "Did he pay?" the proprietor would ask. "No, sir," I'd answer. The proprietor would pull down the corners of his lips and speak through his teeth: "We'll kill that goddamn nigger one of these days." And the episode would end right there. But later on Bigger No.3 was killed during the days of Prohibition: while delivering liquor to a customer he was shot through the back by a white cop.

And then there was Bigger No.4, whose only law was death. The Jim Crow laws of the South were not for him. But as he laughed and cursed and broke them, he knew that some day he'd have to pay for his freedom. His rebellious spirit made him violate all the taboos and consequently he always oscillated between moods of intense elation and depression. He was never happier than when he had outwitted some foolish custom, and he was never more melancholy than when brooding over the impossibility of his ever being free. He had no job, for he regarded digging ditches for fifty cents a day as slavery. "I can't live on that," he would say. Ofttimes I'd find him reading a book; he would stop and in a joking, wistful, and cynical manner ape the antics of the white folks. Generally, he'd end his mimicry in a depressed state and say: "The white folks won't let us do nothing." Bigger No.4 was sent to the asylum for the insane.

Then there was Bigger No.5, who always rode the Jim Crow streetcars without paying and sat wherever he pleased. I remember one morning his getting into a streetcar (all streetcars in Dixie are divided into two sections: one section is for whites and is labeled—FOR WHITES; the other section is for Negroes and is labeled—FOR COLORED) and sitting in the white section. The conductor went to him and said: "Come on, nigger. Move over where you belong. Can't you read?" Bigger answered: "Naw, I can't read." The conductor flared up: "Get out of that seat!" Bigger took out his knife, opened it, held it nonchalantly in his hand, and replied: "Make me." The conductor turned red, blinked, clenched his fists, and walked away, stammering: "The goddam scum of the earth!"

A small angry conference of white men took place in the front of the car and the Negroes sitting in the Jim Crow section overheard: "That's that Bigger Thomas nigger and you'd better leave 'im alone." The Negroes experienced an intense flash of pride and the streetcar moved on its journey without incident. I don't know what happened to Bigger No.5. But I can guess.

The Bigger Thomases were the only Negroes I know of who consistently violated the Jim Crow laws of the South and got away with it, at least for a sweet brief spell. Eventually, the whites who restricted their lives made them pay a terrible price. They were shot, hanged, maimed, lynched, and generally hounded until they were either dead or their spirits broken. . . .

Let me give examples of how I began to develop the dim negative of Bigger. I met white writers who talked of their responses, who told me how whites reacted to this lurid American scene. And, as they talked, I'd translate what they said in terms of Bigger's life. But what was more important still, I read their novels. Here for the first time, I found ways and techniques of gauging meaningfully the effects of American civilization upon the personalities of people. I took these techniques, these ways of seeing and feeling, and twisted them, bent them, adapted them, until they became *my* ways of apprehending the locked-in life of the Black Belt areas. This association with white writers was the life preserver of my hope to depict Negro life in fiction, for my race possessed no fictional works dealing with such problems, had no background in such sharp and critical testing of experience, no novels that went with a deep and fearless will down to the dark roots of life.

Here are examples of how I culled information relating to Bigger from my reading:

There is in me a memory of reading an interesting pamphlet telling of the friendship of Gorky and Lenin in exile. The booklet told of how Lenin and Gorky were walking down a London street. Lenin turned to Gorky and, pointing, said:

"Here is *their* Big Ben." "There is *their* Westminster Abbey."
"There is *their* library." And at once, while reading that passage, my mind stopped, teased, challenged with the effort to
remember, to associate widely disparate but meaningful experiences in my life. For a moment nothing would come, but
I remained convinced that I had heard the meaning of those
words sometime, somewhere before. Then, with a sudden glow
of satisfaction of having gained a little more knowledge about
the world in which I lived, I'd end up by saying: "That's Bigger.
That's the Bigger Thomas reaction."

In both instances the deep sense of exclusion was identical. The feeling of looking at things with a painful and unwarrantable nakedness was an experience, I learned, that transcended national and racial boundaries. It was this intolerable
sense of feeling and understanding so much, and yet living
on a plane of social reality where the look of a world which
one did not make or own struck one with a blinding objectivity and tangibility, that made me grasp the revolutionary impulse in my life and the lives of those about me and far away.

I remember reading a passage in a book dealing with old
Russia which said: "We must be ready to make endless sacrifices if we are to be able to overthrow the Czar." And again I'd
say to myself: "I've heard that somewhere, sometime before."
And again I'd hear Bigger Thomas, far away and long ago, telling some white man who was trying to impose upon him: "I'll
kill you and go to hell and pay for it." While living in America I
heard from far away Russia the bitter accents of tragic calcu-
lation of how much human life and suffering it would cost a
man to live as a man in a world that denied him the right to live
with dignity. Actions and feelings of men ten thousand miles
from home helped me to understand the moods and impulses
of those walking the streets of Chicago and Dixie.

I am not saying that I heard any talk of revolution in the
South when I was a kid there. But I did hear the lispings, the
whispers, the mutters which some day, under one stimulus
or another, will surely grow into open revolt unless the conditions which produce Bigger Thomases are changed.

In 1932 another source of information was dramatically opened up to me and I saw data of a surprising nature that helped to clarify the personality of Bigger. From the moment that Hitler took power in Germany and began to oppress the Jews, I tried to keep track of what was happening. And on innumerable occasions I was startled to detect, either from the side of the Fascists or from the side of the oppressed, reactions, moods, phrases, attitudes that reminded me strongly of Bigger, that helped to bring out more clearly the shadowy outlines of the negative that lay in the back of my mind.

I read every account of the Fascist movement in Germany I could lay my hands on, and from page to page I encountered and recognized familiar emotional patterns. What struck me with particular force was the Nazi preoccupation with the construction of a society in which there would exist among all people (*German* people, of course!) *one* solidarity of ideals, *one* continuous circulation of fundamental beliefs, notions, and assumptions. I am not now speaking of the popular idea of regimenting people's thought; I'm speaking of the implicit, almost unconscious, or pre-conscious, assumptions and ideals upon which whole nations and races act and live. And while reading these Nazi pages I'd be reminded of the Negro preacher in the South telling of a life beyond this world, a life in which the color of men's skins would not matter, a life in which each man would know what was deep down in the hearts of his fellow man. And I could hear Bigger Thomas standing on a street corner in America expressing his agonizing doubts and chronic suspicions, thus: "I ain't going to trust nobody. Everything is a racket and everybody is out to get what he can for himself. Maybe if we had a true leader, we could do something." And I'd know that I was still on the track of learning about Bigger, still in the midst of the modern struggle for solidarity among men. . . .

Now, until this moment I did not stop to think very much about the plot of *Native Son*. The reason I did not is because I was not for one moment ever worried about it. I had spent years learning about Bigger, what had made him, what he meant; so, when the time came for writing, *what had made him and what he meant* constituted my plot. But the farflung items of his life had to be couched in imaginative terms, terms known and acceptable to a common body of readers, terms which would, in the course of the story, manipulate the deepest held notions and convictions of their lives. That came easy. The moment I began to write, the plot fell out, so to speak. I'm not trying to oversimplify or make the process seem oversubtle. At bottom, what happened is very easy to explain.

Any Negro who has lived in the North or the South knows that times without number he has heard of some Negro boy being picked up on the streets and carted off to jail and charged with "rape." This thing happens so often that to my mind it had become a representative symbol of the Negro's uncertain position in America. Never for a second was I in doubt as to what kind of social reality or dramatic situation I'd put Bigger in, what kind of test-tube I'd set up to evoke his deepest reactions. Life had made the plot over and over again, to the extent that I knew it by heart. So frequently do these acts recur that when I was halfway through the first draft of *Native Son* a case paralleling Bigger's flared forth in the newspapers of Chicago. (Many of the newspaper items and some of the incidents in *Native Son* are but fictionalized versions of the Robert Nixon case and rewrites of news stories from the *Chicago Tribune.)* Indeed, scarcely was *Native Son* off the press before Supreme Court Justice Hugo L. Black gave the nation a long and vivid account of the American police methods of handling Negro boys.

Let me describe this stereotyped situation: A crime wave is sweeping a city and citizens are clamoring for police action. Squad cars cruise the Black Belt and grab the first Negro boy who seems to be unattached and homeless. He is held for perhaps a week without charge or bail, without the privilege of communicating with anyone, including his own relatives. After a few days this boy "confesses" anything that he is asked to confess, any crime that handily happens to be unsolved and on the calendar. Why does he confess? After the boy has been grilled night and day, hanged up by his thumbs, dangled by his feet out of twenty-story windows, and beaten (in places that leave no scars—cops have found a way to do that), he signs the papers before him, papers which are usually accompanied by a verbal promise to the boy that he will not go to the electric chair. Of course, he ends up by being executed or sentenced for life. If you think I'm telling tall tales, get chummy with some white cop who works in a Black Belt district and ask him for the lowdown.

When a black boy is carted off to jail in such a fashion, it is almost impossible to do anything for him. Even well-disposed Negro lawyers find it difficult to defend him, for the boy will plead guilty one day and then not guilty the next, according to the degree of pressure and persuasion that is brought to bear upon his frightened personality from one side or the other. Even the boy's own family is scared to death; sometimes fear of police intimidation makes them hesitate to acknowledge that the boy is blood relation of theirs.

Such has been America's attitude toward these boys that if one is picked up and confronted in a police cell with ten white cops, he is intimidated almost to the point of confessing anything. So far removed are these practices from what the average American citizen encounters in his daily life that it takes a huge act of his imagination to believe that it is true; yet, this same average citizen, with his kindness, his American sportsmanship and good will, would probably act with the mob if a self-respecting Negro family moved into his apartment building to escape the Black Belt and its terrors and limitations. . . .

The first draft of the novel was written in four months, straight through, and ran to some 576 pages. Just as a man rises in the morning to dig ditches for his bread, so I'd work daily. I'd think of some abstract principle of Bigger's conduct and at once my mind would turn it into some act I'd seen Bigger perform, some act which I hoped would be familiar enough to the American reader to gain his credence. But in the writing of scene after scene I was guided by but one criterion: to tell the truth as I saw it and felt it. That is, to objectify in words some insight derived from my living in the form of action, scene, and dialogue. If a scene seemed improbable to me, I'd not tear it up, but ask myself: "Does it reveal enough of what I feel to stand in spite of its unreality?" If I felt it did, it stood. If I felt that it did not, I ripped it out. The degree of morality in my writing depended upon the degree of felt life and truth I could put down upon the printed page. For example, there is a scene in *Native Son* where Bigger stands in a cell with a Negro preacher, Jan, Max, the State's Attorney, Mr. Dalton, Mrs. Dalton, Bigger's mother, his brother, his sister, Al, Gus, and Jack. While writing the scene, I knew that it was unlikely that so many people would ever be allowed to come into a murderer's cell. But I wanted those people in that cell to elicit a certain important emotional response from Bigger. And so the scene stood. I felt that what I wanted that scene to say to the reader was *more important than its surface reality or plausibility.*

Always, as I wrote, I was both reader and writer, both the conceiver of the action and the appreciator of it. I tried to write so that, in the same instant of time, the objective and subjective aspects of Bigger's life would be caught in a focus of prose. And always I tried to *render, depict,* not merely to tell the story. If a thing was cold, I tried to make the reader *feel cold,* and not just tell about it. In writing in this fashion, sometime I'd find it necessary to use a stream of consciousness technique, then rise to an interior monologue, descend to a direct rendering of a dream state, then to a matter-of-fact depiction of what Bigger was saying, doing, and feeling. Then I'd find it impossible to say what I wanted to say without stepping in and speaking outright on my own; but when doing this I always made an effort to retain the mood of the story, explaining everything only in terms of Bigger's life and, if possible, in the rhythms of Bigger's thought (even though the words would be mine). Again, at other times, in the guise of the lawyer's speech and the newspaper items, or in terms of what Bigger would overhear or see from afar, I'd give what others were saying and thinking of him. But always, from the start to finish, it was Bigger's story, Bigger's fears, Bigger's flight, and Bigger's fate that I tried to depict. I wrote with the conviction in mind (I don't know if this is right or wrong; I only know that I'm temperamentally inclined to feel this way) that the main burden of all serious fiction consists almost wholly of character-destiny and the items, social, political, and personal, of that character-destiny.

As I wrote I followed, almost unconsciously, many principles of the novel which my reading of the novels of other writers had made me feel were necessary for the building of a well-constructed book. For the most part the novel is rendered in the present; I wanted the reader to feel that Bigger's story was happening *now,* like a play upon the stage or a movie unfolding upon the screen. Action follows action, as in a prize fight. Wherever possible, I told of Bigger's life in close-up, slow-motion, giving the feel of the grain in the passing of time. I had long had the feeling that this was the best way to "enclose" the reader's mind in a new world, to blot out all reality except that which I was giving him.

Then again, as much as I could, I restricted the novel to what Bigger saw and felt, to the limits of his feeling and thoughts, even when I was conveying *more* than that to the reader. I had the notion that such a manner of rendering made for a sharper effect, a more pointed sense of the character, his peculiar type of being and consciousness. Throughout there is but one point of view: Bigger's. This too, I felt, made for a richer illusion of reality.

I kept out of the story as much as possible, for I wanted the reader to feel that there was nothing between him and Bigger; that the story was a special *première* given in his own private theater.

I kept the scenes long, made as much happen within a short space of time as possible; all of which, I felt, made for greater density and richness of effect.

In a like manner I tried to keep a unified sense of background throughout the story; the background would change, of course, but I tried to keep before the eyes of the reader at all times the forces and elements against which Bigger was striving.

And because I had limited myself to rendering only

what Bigger saw and felt, I gave no more reality to the other characters than that which Bigger himself saw.

This, honestly, is all I can account for in the book. If I attempted to account for scenes and characters, to tell why certain scenes were written in certain ways, I'd be stretching facts in order to be pleasantly intelligible. All else in the book came from my feelings reacting upon the material, and any honest reader knows as much about the rest of what is in the book as I do; that is, if, as he reads, he is willing to let his emotions and imagination become as influenced by the materials as I did. As I wrote, for some reason or other, one image, symbol, character, scene, mood, feeling evoked its opposite, its parallel, its complimentary, and its ironic counterpart. Why? I don't know. My emotions and imagination just like to work that way. One can account for just so much of life, and then no more. At least, not yet.

With the first draft down, I found that I could not end the book satisfactorily. In the first draft I had Bigger going smack to the electric chair; but I felt that two murders were enough for one novel. I cut the final scene and went back to worry about the beginning. I had no luck. The book was one-half finished, with the opening and closing scenes unwritten. Then, one night, in desperation—I hope that I'm not disclosing the hidden secrets of my craft!—I sneaked out and got a bottle. With the help of it, I began to remember many things which I could not remember before. One of them was that Chicago was overrun with rats. I recalled that I'd seen many rats on the streets, that I'd heard and read of Negro children being bitten by rats in their beds. At first I rejected the idea of Bigger battling a rat in his room; I was afraid that the rat would "hog" the scene. But the rat would not leave me; he presented himself in many attractive guises. So, cautioning myself to allow the rat scene to disclose *only* Bigger, his family, their little room, and their relationships, I let the rat walk in, and he did his stuff.

Many of the scenes were torn out as I reworked the book. The mere rereading of what I'd written made me think of the possibility of developing themes which had been only hinted at in the first draft. For example, the entire guilt theme that runs through *Native Son* was woven in *after* the first draft was written.

At last I found out how to end the book; I ended it just as I had begun it, showing Bigger living dangerously, taking his life into his hands, accepting what life had made him. The lawyer, Max, was placed in Bigger's cell at the end of the novel to register the moral—or what *I* felt was the moral—horror of Negro life in the United States. . . .

Norman Mailer

LAST ADVERTISEMENT FOR
MYSELF BEFORE THE WAY OUT*

If America is rich in talent, which it is, this wealth seems more than equaled by the speed with which we use up our talent. Years ago, in college, I devoured a book of criticism by Joseph Warren Beach, called *American Fiction, 1920-1940;* today, the book would not have to be brought up to date—no one from that generation of major American writers who came before my own has put out work of the first importance since the war, not unless one wishes to assign high seriousness to *The Old Man and The Sea, East of Eden, Fable, The Face of Time,* and the half-dozen monotonously even novels of J. P. Marquand.

Yet what a generation they were—how much more impressive than my own. If their works did not prepare us for the slack, the stupor, and the rootless wit of our years, they were still men who wrote strong, original novels, personal in style—so many of us were ready to become writers because of the world they opened.

To call the role today is depressing. Wolfe is dead and

Fitzgerald is dead; both dead too early; one, a burned-out rocket, the other a gentleman blade who concealed his wounds too long and died lingering over them. Hemingway lost his will to work, or so it seems; Faulkner passed his zenith. Each of them has greatness, and yet neither has written the one novel which would be a monument to his work, and they had gifts on a grand scale.[1] Dos Passos wrote his big work, and none of us has done a novel to come close to it, but the time betrayed him, and he was beached on the dry sands of his political integrity and had to live with the salt water of insufficient recognition. Farrell plowed his broad groove and remained true to himself—he, too, was cheated of a recognition which could match his size, and so he did not have the opportunity to learn about new worlds, and grow; instead he wore down with dignity, and fashion has passed him by. Steinbeck seemed to lose conviction, as well he might—the world became too complex and too ugly for a man who needed situations of Biblical simplicity for his art. And J. P. Marquand, whom Beach saw fit to include, did not do anything new—he just did a lot of very little, and made a gloomy fortune doing it. One must go back to an earlier time, to Dreiser, to Lewis, and to Sherwood Anderson, in order to come across men who wrote across the larger length of their lives and had a career which came close to the limit of what they could do.

America is a cruel soil for talent. It stunts it, blights it, uproots it, or overheats it with cheap fertilizer. And our literary gardeners, our publishers, editors, reviewers and general flunkeys, are drunks, cowards, respectables, prose couturiers, fashion-mongers, old maids, time servers and part-time pimps on the Avenue of President Madison. The audiences are not much better—they seem to consist in nine parts of the tense tasteless victims of a mass-media culture, incapable of

[1] Hemingway's new novel, all these years in the writing since the Second World War, may turn out to be excellent in its way (although I doubt it) but the question to ask will still be whether the Old Man says anything which can bother an eight-year-old or one's grandmother. Hemingway seems to have abused his sensitivity and bravery in such a way as to keep his physical courage by indulging his moral sloth. Now at his worst, he adds to the nausea he once cleared away.

confronting a book unless it is successful. The other part, that developed reader in ten with education, literary desire, a library, and a set of acquired prejudices is worse, for he lacks the power to read with a naked eye. His opinion depends on the sluggish and culturally vested taste of the quarterlies, and since these magazines are all too often managed by men of large knowledge and small daring, the writers they admire are invariably minor, overcultivated, and too literary. Small highly polished jewels reflect upon even smaller gems. The light is private, and they would not have it otherwise. Their real delight is in the abysmal taste of the majority, for a broad vein of good taste in American life would wash away the meaning of their lives.

So the strong talents of my generation, those few of us who have wide minds in a narrow overdeveloped time, are left to wander through a landscape of occult herbs and voracious weeds, ambushed by the fallen wires of electric but meaningless situations. Our promotions are often undeserved, our real efforts are understood too late; the first of us to die will have a fine funeral and his literary stock will boom before the wake is wet. If it were not for some new generation coming to life—a generation which might be more interesting than my own, or so I must hope, it would be best to give up, because all desire is lost for talking to readers older than oneself. Defeated by war, prosperity, and conformity, the best of our elders are deadened into thinking machines, and the worst are broken scolds who parrot a plain housewife's practical sense of the mediocre—worn-out middle-class bores of the psychoanalytical persuasion who worship the cheats of moderation, compromise, committee and indecision, or even worse, turn to respect the past.

There was a frontier for my generation of novelists. Coming out of the orgy of the war, our sense of sex and family was torn in two. The past did not exist for us. We had to write our way out into the unspoken territories of sex—there was so much there, it was new, and the life of our talent depended upon going into the borderland. Instead—and it is the old story—we all learned, one from the trap of another, that what was not trimmed from our pages by an editor's nudge was given away in the hagglings of publisher and author, and that which was left, and some of us insisted upon keeping all or almost all of what we had written, was then distorted, shit on, or ignored by the best and worst of the daily reviewers. And in the quarterlies—God's blessing if the works of four or five of us were compared and dismissed by a bright young academic with a small sense of life.

Now it is getting a little better. Some of us will probably be launched on a second wave of recognition (our contemporaries are getting old enough to have a bit of power themselves), but what a waste there has been. John Horne Burns is dead, a nice talent, sexual, not too dishonest, oversweet but tender—the poisonous stupidities of the reviewers toward his last two novels hurried his going, and who knows what could have happened to his talent, for it had the promise of size. The rest of us are older than we ought to be, ten years used up in two or three of war, and another twenty spent in the fourteen years since. When I come to assess myself, and try to measure what chance I have of writing that big book I have again in me, I do not know in all simple bitterness if I can make it. For you have to care about other people to share your perception with them, especially if it is a perception which can give them life, and now there are too many times when I no longer give a good goddamn for most of the human race. I had the freak of luck to start high on the mountain, and go down sharp while others were passing me. So I saw their faces as they learned to climb, and what faces they were! fear first, with avidity up the ass; their steps—snobbery; the peak, power; and their terror—consequence.

Still! There is the fault of others, and the fault of oneself, and I have my debts to pay. Fitzgerald was an indifferent caretaker of his talent, and I have been a cheap gambler with mine. As I add up the accounts, I cannot like myself too much, for I was cowardly when I should have been good, and too brave on many a bad chance, and I spent my first thirty years abusing my body, and the last six in forced marches on my brain, and so I am more stupid today than I ought to be, my mem-

ory is half-gone, and my mind is slow; from fear and vanity
I paid out too much for what I managed to learn. When I sit
down, soon after this book is done, to pick up again on my
novel, I do not know if I can do it, for if the first sixty pages
are not at all bad, I may still have wasted too much of myself,
and if I have—what a loss. How poor to go to death with no
more than the notes of good intention. *It is the actions of men
and not their sentiments which make history*—the best sentence I've ever written—but I would hate to face eternity with
that for my flag, since I am still at this formal middle of my
life a creator of sentiments larger than my work.

Let me finish with a word about the new book, for the
Prologue to it ends my collection. By present standards of publishing practice, it will be, if I can do it, an unpublishable work.
Since it is likely to take ten years—what with a side-effort or
two to pick up some money—I do not have the confidence
that you will see it in its completed form, except as an outlaw
of the underground like *Tropic of Cancer, Ulysses,* or *Les Cent-
Vingt Journées de Sodome.* If it is to have any effect, and I
can hardly look forward to exhausting the next ten years without hope of a deep explosion of effect, the book will be fired
to its fuse by the rumor that once I pointed to the farthest fence
and said that within ten years I would try to hit the longest
ball ever to go up into the accelerated hurricane air of our
American letters. For if I have one ambition above all others,
it is to write a novel which Dostoyevsky and Marx; Joyce and
Freud; Stendhal, Tolstoy, Proust and Spengler; Faulkner, and
even old moldering Hemingway might come to read, for it
would carry what they had to tell another part of the way.

Saul Bellow

WHERE DO WE GO FROM HERE: THE FUTURE OF FICTION*

We know that science has a future, we hope that government will have one. But it is not altogether agreed that the novel has anything but a past. There are some who say that the great novelists of the twentieth century—Proust, Joyce, Mann, and Kafka—have created sterile masterpieces, and that with them we have come to the end of the line. No further progress is possible.

It does sometimes seem that the narrative art itself has dissolved. The person, the character as we knew him in the plays of Sophocles or Shakespeare, in Cervantes, Fielding, and Balzac, has gone from us. Instead of a unitary character with his unitary personality, his ambitions, his passions, his soul, his fate, we find in modern literature an oddly dispersed, ragged, mingled, broken, amorphous creature whose outlines are everywhere, whose being is bathed in mind as the tissues are bathed in blood, and who is impossible to circumscribe in any scheme of time. A cubistic, Bergsonian, uncertain, eternal, mortal someone who shuts and opens like a concertina and makes a strange music. And what has struck artists

*Reprinted by permission of The University of Michigan Press from *To The Young Writer,* A. L. Bader, editor. Copyright © by the University of Michigan, 1965. All rights reserved.

in this century as the most amusing part of all, is that the descriptions of self that still have hold of us are made up of the old unitary foursquare traits noted according to the ancient conventions. What we insist on seeing is not a quaintly organized chaos of instinct and spirit, but what we choose to call "the personality"—a presentably combed and dressed someone who is decent, courageous, handsome, or not so handsome, but strong or not so strong, but certainly generous, or not so generous, but anyway reliable. So it goes.

Of all modern writers, it is D. H. Lawrence who is most implacably hostile toward this convention of unitary character. For him this character of a civilized man does not really exist. What the modern civilized person calls his personality is to Lawrence figmentary: a product of civilized education, dress, manners, style, and "culture." The head of this modern personality is, he says, a wastepaper basket filled with ready-made notions. Sometimes he compares the civilized conception of character to a millstone—a painted millstone about our necks is the metaphor he makes of it. The real self, unknown, is hidden, a sunken power in us; the true identity lies deep—very deep. But we do not deal much in true identity, goes his argument. The modern character on the street, or in a conventional story or film, is what a sociologist has recently described as the "presentation" self. The attack on this presentation self or persona by modern art is a part of the war that literature, in its concern with the individual, has fought with civilization. The civilized individual is proud of his painted millstone, the burden which he believes gives him distinction. In an artist's eyes his persona is only a rude, impoverished, mass-produced figure brought into being by a civilization in need of a working force, a reservoir of personnel, a docile public that will accept suggestion and control.

The old unitary personality which still appears in popular magazine stories, in conventional best-sellers, in newspaper cartoons, and in the movies, is a figure descended from well-worn patterns, and popular art forms (like the mystery novel or the western) continue to exploit endlessly the badly faded ideas of motives and drama or love and hate. The old

figures move ritualistically through the paces, finding, now
and then, variations in setting and costume, but they are increasingly remote from real reality. The functions performed
by these venerable literary types should be fascinating to the
clinical psychologist who may be able to recognize in these
stories an obsessional neurosis here, a paranoid fantasy there,
or to the sociologist who sees resemblances to the organization of government bureaus or hears echoes of the modern
industrial corporations. But the writer brought up in a great
literary tradition not only sees these conventional stories as
narcotic or brain-washing entertainments, at worst breeding
strange vices, at best performing a therapeutic function. He
also fears that the narrative art, which we call the novel, may
have come to an end, its conception of the self exhausted and
with this conception our interest in the fate of that self so conceived. . . .

Character, action, and language then have been put in
doubt and the Spanish philosopher Ortega y Gasset, summing
up views widely held, says the novel requires a local setting
with limited horizons and familiar features, traditions, occupations, classes. But as everyone knows, these old-fashioned
local worlds no longer exist. Or perhaps that is inaccurate.
They do exist but fail to interest the novelist. They are no longer
local societies as we see them in Jane Austen or George Eliot.
Our contemporary local societies have been overtaken by the
world. The great cities have devoured them and now the universe itself imposes itself upon us, space with its stars comes
upon us in our cities. So now we have the universe itself to face,
without the comforts of community, without metaphysical certainty, without the power to distinguish the virtuous from the
wicked man, surrounded by dubious realities and discovering
dubious selves.

Things have collapsed about us, says D. H. Lawrence on
the first page of *Lady Chatterley's Lover,* and we must each
of us try to put together some sort of life. He offers us a sort
of nature mysticism, love but without false romanticism, an
acceptance of true desire as the first principle of recovery.
Other writers have come forward with aesthetic or political

or religious first principles. All the modern novelists worth
mentioning aim at a point beyond customary notions, customary dramas, and customary conceptions of character. The
old notion of a customary self, of the fate of an all-important
Me displeases the best of them. We have lived now through
innumerable successes and failures of these old selves. In American literature we have watched their progress and decline
in scores of books since the Civil War, from buoyancy to depression. The Lambert Strethers, the Hurstwoods and Cow-
perwoods, the Gatsbys may still impress or please us as readers, but as writers, no. Their mental range is no longer adequate to these new circumstances. Those characters suit us
better who stand outside society and, unlike Gatsby, have no
wish to be sentimentally reconciled to it, unlike Dreiser's mil-
lionaires have no more desire for its wealth, unlike Strether
are not attracted by the power of an old and knowing civilization.

This is why so many of us prefer the American novels
of the nineteenth century, whose characters are very nearly
removed from the civil state—*Moby Dick* and *Huckleberry
Finn*. We feel in our own time that what is called the civilized
condition often swings close to what Hobbes calls the state
of nature, a condition of warfare, in which the life of the individual is nasty, brutish, dull and short. But we must be careful not to be swept away by the analogy. We have seen to our
grief in recent European and especially German history the
results of trying to bolt from all civilized and legal tradition.
It is in our minds that the natural and the civil, that autarchy
and discipline are most explosively mixed.

But for us here in America discipline is represented largely
by the enforced repressions. We do not know much of the delights of discipline. Almost nothing of a spiritual, ennobling
character is brought into the internal life of a modern American by his social institutions. He must discover it in his own
experience, by his own luck as an explorer, or not at all. Society feeds him, clothes him, to an extent protects him, and
he is its infant. If he accepts the state of infancy, contentment
can be his. But if the idea of higher functions comes to him,

he is profoundly unsettled. The hungry world is rushing on
all continents toward such a contentment, and with passions and
desires, frustrated since primitive times, and with the demand
for justice never so loudly expressed. The danger is great
that it will be satisfied with the bottles and toys of infancy.
But the artist, the philosopher, the priest, the statesman are
concerned with the full development of humanity—its manhood, occasionally glimpsed in our history, occasionally felt
by individuals.

With all this in mind, people here and there still continue
to write the sort of book we call a novel. When I am feeling
blue, I can almost persuade myself that the novel, like Indian
basketry, or harness-making, is a vestigial art and has no future.
But we must be careful about prophecy. Even prophecy based
on good historical study is a risky business, and pessimism,
no less than optimism, can be made into a racket. All industrial societies have a thing about obsolescence. Classes, nations, races and cultures have in our time been declared ob-
solete, with results that have made ours one of the most horrible of all centuries. We must, therefore, be careful about
deciding that any art is dead. . . .

American literature in the nineteenth century was highly didactic. Emerson, Thoreau, Whitman, and even Melville
were didactic writers. They wished to instruct a young and
raw nation. American literature in the twentieth century has
remained didactic, but it has also been unintellectual. This
is not to say that thought is lacking in the twentieth-century
American novel, but it exists under strange handicaps and
is much disguised. In *A Farewell to Arms* Hemingway makes
a list of subjects we must no longer speak about—a catalogue
of polluted words, words which have been ruined by the rhet-
oric of criminal politicians and misleaders. Then Hemingway,
and we must respect him for it, attempts to represent these
betrayed qualities without using the words themselves. Thus
we have courage without the word, honor without the word,
and in *The Old Man and the Sea* we are offered a sort of Christian endurance, also without specific terms. Carried to this
length, the attempt to represent ideas while sternly forbidding

thought begins to look like a curious and highly sophisticated game. It shows a great skepticism of the strength of art. It makes it appear as though ideas openly expressed would be too much for art to bear.

We have developed in American fiction a strange combination of extreme naïveté in the characters and of profundity implicit in the writing, in the techniques themselves and in the language, but the language of thought itself is banned, it is considered dangerous and destructive. American writers appear to have a strong loyalty to the people, to the common man; perhaps in some cases the word for this is not loyalty, perhaps it might better be described as *fear*. But a writer should aim to reach all levels of society and as many levels of thought as possible, avoiding democratic prejudice as much as intellectual snobbery. Why should he be ashamed of thinking? I do not claim that all writers can think, or should think. Some are peculiarly inept at ideas and we would harm them by insisting that they philosophize. But the records show that most artists are intellectually active, and it is only now in a world increasingly intellectualized, more and more dominated by the productions of scientific thought, that they seem strangely reluctant to use their brains or to give any sign that they have brains to use.

All through the nineteenth century the conviction increases in novelists as different as Goncharov in Russia and Thomas Hardy in England that thought is linked with passivity and is devitalizing. And in the masterpieces of the twentieth century the thinker usually has a weak grip on life. But by now an alternative, passionate activity without ideas, has also been well explored in novels of adventure, hunting, combat, and eroticism. Meanwhile, miracles, born of thought, have been largely ignored by modern literature. If narration is neglected by novelists like Proust and Joyce, the reasons are that for a time the drama has passed from external action to internal movement. In Proust and Joyce we are enclosed by and held within a single consciousness. In this inner realm the writer's art dominates everything. The drama has left external action because the old ways of describing interests, of describing the fate of the individual, have lost their power. Is the sheriff a good fellow? Is our neighbor to be pitied? Are the baker's daughters virtuous? We see such questions now as belonging to a dead system, mere formulas. It is possible that our hearts would open again to the baker's daughters if we understood them differently.

A clue may be offered by Pascal, who said there are no dull people, only dull points of view. Maybe that is going a little far. (A religious philosophy is bound to maintain that every soul is infinitely precious and, therefore, infinitely interesting.) But it begins perhaps to be evident what my position is. Imagination, binding itself to dull viewpoints, puts an end to stories. The imagination is looking for new ways to express virtue. American society just now is in the grip of certain common falsehoods about virtue—not that anyone really believes them. And these cheerful falsehoods beget their opposites in fiction, a dark literature, a literature of victimization, of old people sitting in ash cans waiting for the breath of life to depart. This is the way things stand; only this remains to be added, that we have barely begun to comprehend what a human being is, and that the baker's daughters may have revelations and miracles to offer to keep fascinated novelists busy until the end of time.

I would like to add this also, in conclusion, about good thought and bad thought in the novel. In a way it doesn't matter what sort of line the novelist is pushing, what he is affirming. If he has nothing to offer but his didactic purpose he is a bad writer. His ideas have ruined him. He could not afford the expense of maintaining them. It is not the didactic purpose itself which is a bad thing, and the modern novelist drawing back from the dangers of didacticism has often become strangely unreal, and the purity of his belief in art for art in some cases has been peculiarly unattractive. Among modern novelists the bravest have taken the risk of teaching and have not been afraid of using the terms of religion, science, philosophy, and politics. Only they have been prepared to admit the strongest possible arguments against their own positions.

Here we see the difference between a didactic novelist

like D. H. Lawrence and one like Dostoevski. When he was writing *The Brothers Karamazov* and had just ended the famous conversation between Ivan and Alyosha, in which Ivan, despairing of justice, offers to return his ticket to God, Dostoevski wrote to one of his correspondents that he must now attempt, through Father Zossima, to answer Ivan's arguments. But he has in advance all but devastated his own position. This, I think, is the greatest achievement possible in a novel of ideas. It becomes art when the views most opposite to the author's own are allowed to exist in full strength. Without this a novel of ideas is mere self-indulgence, and didacticism is simply axe-grinding. The opposites must be free to range themselves against each other, and they must be passionately expressed on both sides. It is for this reason that I say it doesn't matter much what the writer's personal position is, what he wishes to affirm. He may affirm principles we all approve of and write very bad novels.

The novel, to recover and to flourish, requires new ideas about humankind. These ideas in turn cannot live in themselves. Merely asserted, they show nothing but the good will of the author. They must therefore be discovered and not invented. We must see them in flesh and blood. There would be no point in continuing at all if many writers did not feel the existence of these unrecognized qualities. They are present and they demand release and expression.

Vladimir Nabokov

VLADIMIR SIRIN*

. . . But the author that interested me most was naturally Sirin.
He belonged to my generation. Among the young writers produced in exile he was the loneliest and most arrogant one. Beginning with the appearance of his first novel in 1925 and
throughout the next fifteen years, until he vanished as strangely
as he had come, his work kept provoking an acute and rather
morbid interest on the part of critics. Just as Marxist publicists
of the eighties in old Russia would have denounced his lack
of concern with the economic structure of society, so the mys-
tagogues of émigré letters deplored his lack of religious insight
and of moral preoccupation. Everything about him was bound
to offend Russian conventions and especially that Russian
sense of decorum which, for example, an American offends
so dangerously today, when in the presence of Soviet military
men of distinction he happens to lounge with both hands in
his trouser pockets. Conversely, Sirin's admirers made much,
perhaps too much, of his unusual style, brilliant precision,
functional imagery and that sort of thing. Russian readers who

*From Vladimir Nabokov, *Speak, Memory.* J. P. Putnam's, 1966, revised
edition. By permission of the author. Title supplied by the editor. Vladimir
Sirin was the pseudonym used regularly by Nabokov for his works in Russian
prior to his emigration to the United States in 1940.

had been raised on the sturdy straightforwardness of Russian realism and had called the bluff of decadent cheats, were impressed by the mirror-like angles of his clear but weirdly misleading sentences and by the fact that the real life of his books flowed in his figures of speech, which one critic has compared to "windows giving upon a contiguous world . . . a rolling corollary, the shadow of a train of thought." Across the dark sky of exile, Sirin passed, to use a simile of a more conservative nature, like a meteor, and disappeared, leaving nothing much else behind him than a vague sense of uneasiness.

AN INTERVIEW WITH VLADIMIR NABOKOV*
Conducted by Alfred Appel, Jr.

Q: For years bibliographers and literary journalists didn't know whether to group you under "Russian" or "American." Now that you're living in Switzerland there seems to be complete agreement that you're American. Do you find this kind of distinction at all important regarding your identity as a writer?[1]

*From "An Interview with Vladimir Nabokov," conducted by Alfred Appel, Jr., in *Nabokov: The Man and His Work,* L. S. Dembo, Editor (Madison: The University of Wisconsin Press; © 1967 by the Regents of the University of Wisconsin) pp. 19-44.

[1]This interview was conducted on September 25, 27, 28, 29, 1966, at Montreux, Switzerland. Mr. Nabokov and his wife have for the last six years lived in an opulent hotel built in 1835, which still retains its nineteenth-century atmosphere. Their suite of rooms is on the sixth floor, overlooking Lake Geneva, and the sounds of the lake are audible through the open doors of their small balcony. Since Mr. Nabokov does not like to talk off the cuff (or "Off the Nabocuff," as he said) no tape recorder was used. Mr. Nabokov either wrote out his answers to the questions or dictated them to the interviewer; in some instances, notes from the conversation were later recast as formal questions-and-answers. The interviewer was Nabokov's student at Cornell University in 1954, and the references are to Literature 311-312 [MWF, 12], a course on the Masterpieces of European Fiction (Jane Austen, Gogol, Dickens, Flaubert, Tolstoy, Stevenson, Kafka, Joyce, and Proust). Its enrollment had reached four hundred by the time of Nabokov's resignation in 1959. The footnotes to the interview, except where indicated, are provided by the interviewer.—A.A.

A: I have always maintained, even as a schoolboy in Russia, that the nationality of a worthwhile writer is of secondary importance. The more distinctive an insect's aspect, the less apt is the taxonomist to glance first of all at the locality label under the pinned specimen in order to decide which of several vaguely described races it should be assigned to. The writer's art is his real passport. His identity should be immediately recognized by a special pattern or unique coloration. His habitat may confirm the correctness of the determination but should not lead to it. Locality labels are known to have been faked by unscrupulous insect dealers. Apart from these considerations I think of myself today as an American writer who has once been a Russian one.

Q: The Russian writers you have translated and written about all precede the so-called "age of realism," which is more celebrated by English and American readers than is the earlier period. Would you say something about your temperamental or artistic affinities with the great writers of the 1830-40 era of masterpieces. Do you see your own work falling under such general rubrics as a tradition of Russian humor?

A: The question of the affinities I may think I have or not have with nineteenth-century Russian writers is a classificational, not a confessional matter. There is hardly a single Russian major writer of the past whom pigeonholers have not mentioned in connection with me. Pushkin's blood runs through the veins of modern Russian literature as inevitably as Shakespeare's through those of English literature.

Q: Many of the major Russian writers, such as Pushkin, Lermontov, and Bely, have distinguished themselves in both poetry and prose, an uncommon accomplishment in English and American literature. Does this signal fact have anything to do with the special nature of Russian literary culture, or are there technical or linguistic resources which make this kind of versatility more possible in Russian? And as a writer of both prose and poetry, what distinctions do you make between them?

A: On the other hand, neither Gogol nor Tolstoy nor Chehov[2] were distinguished versificators. Moreover, the dividing line between prose and poetry in some of the greatest English or American novels is not easy to draw. I suppose you should have used the term "rhymed poetry" in your question and then one might answer that Russian rhymes are incomparably more attractive and more abundant than English ones. No wonder a Russian prose writer frequents those beauties, especially in his youth.

Q: Who are the great American writers you most admire?

A: When I was young I liked Poe, and I still love Melville, whom I did not read as a boy. My feelings towards James are rather complicated. I really dislike him intensely but now and then the figure in the phrase, the turn of the epithet, the screw of an absurd adverb, cause me a kind of electric tingle, as if some current of his was also passing through my own blood. Hawthorne is a splendid writer. Emerson's poetry is delightful. . . .

Q: Speaking of ideology, you have often expressed your hostility to Freud, most noticeably in the forewords to your translated novels. Some readers have wondered which of Freud's works or theories you were most offended by and why. The parodies of Freud in *Lolita* and *Pale Fire* suggest a wider familiarity with the good doctor than you have ever publicly granted. Would you comment on this?

A: Oh, I am not up to discussing again that figure of fun. He is not worthy of more attention than I have granted him in my novels and in *Speak, Memory.* Let the credulous and the vulgar continue to believe that all mental woes can be cured by a daily application of old Greek myths to their private parts. I really do not care.

Q: Your contempt for Freud's "standardized symbols" extends to the assumptions of a good many other theorizers. Do

[2]Nabokov's spelling.

you think literary criticism is at all purposeful, and if so, what kind of criticism would you point to? *Pale Fire* makes it clear what sort you find gratuitous (at best).

A: My advice to a budding literary critic would be as follows. Learn to distinguish banality. Remember that mediocrity thrives on "ideas." Beware of the modish message. Ask yourself if the symbol you have detected is not your own footprint. Ignore allegories. By all means place the "how" above the "what" but do not let it be confused with the "so what." Rely on the sudden erection of your small dorsal hairs. Do not drag in Freud at this point. All the rest depends on personal talent.

Q: As a writer, have you ever found criticism instructive—not so much the reviews of your own books, but any general criticism? From your own experiences do you think that an academic and literary career nourish one another? Since many writers today know no other alternative than a life on campus I'd be very interested in your feelings about this. Do you think that your own work in America was at all shaped by your being part of an academic community?

A: I find criticism most instructive when an expert proves to me that my facts or my grammar are wrong. An academic career is especially helpful to writers in two ways: 1) easy access to magnificent libraries and 2) long vacations. There is of course the business of teaching but old professors have young instructors to correct examination papers for them, and young instructors, authors in their own right, are followed by admiring glances along the corridors of Vanity Hall. Otherwise, our greatest rewards, such as the reverberations of our minds in such minds as vibrate responsively in later years, force novelist-teachers to nurse lucidity and honesty of style in their lectures. . . .

Q: Could you tell us something about your work habits as a writer, and the way you compose your novels. Do you use an outline? Do you have a full sense of where a fiction is heading even while you are in the early stages of composition?

A: In my twenties and early thirties, I used to write, dipping pen in ink and using a new nib every other day, in exercise books, crossing out, inserting, striking out again, crumpling the page, rewriting every page three or four times, then copying out the novel in a different ink and a neater hand, then revising the whole thing once more, re-copying it with new corrections, and finally dictating it to my wife who has typed out all my stuff. Generally speaking, I am a slow writer, a snail carrying its house at the rate of two hundred pages of final copy per year (one spectacular exception was the Russian original of *Invitation to a Beheading,* the first draft of which I wrote in one fortnight of wonderful excitement and sustained inspiration). In those days and nights I generally followed the order of chapters when writing a novel but even so, from the very first, I relied heavily on mental composition, constructing whole paragraphs in my mind as I walked in the streets or sat in my bath, or lay in bed, although often deleting or re-writing them later. In the late 'thirties, beginning with *The Gift,* and perhaps under the influence of the many notes needed, I switched to another, physically more practical, method — that of writing with an eraser-capped pencil on index cards. Since I always have at the very start a curiously clear preview of the entire novel before me or above me, I find cards expecially convenient when not following the logical sequence of chapters but preparing instead this or that passage at any point of the novel and filling in the gaps in no special order. I am afraid to get mixed up with Plato whom I do not care for, but I do think that in my case it is true that the entire book, before it is written, seems to be ready ideally in some other, now transparent, now dimming, dimension, and my job is to take down as much of it as I can make out and as precisely as I am humanly able to. The greatest happiness I experience in composing is when I feel I cannot understand, or rather catch myself not understanding (without the presupposition of an already existing creation) how or why that image or structural move has just come to me. It is sometimes rather amusing to find my readers trying to elucidate in a matter-of-fact way these wild workings of my not very efficient mind.

Q: One often hears from writers talk of how a character takes hold of them and in a sense dictates the course of the action. Has this ever been your experience?

A: I have never experienced this. What a preposterous experience! Writers who have had it must be very minor or insane. No, the design of my novel is fixed in my imagination and every character follows the course I imagine for him. I am the perfect dictator in that private world insofar as I alone am responsible for its stability and truth. Whether I reproduce it as fully and faithfully as I would wish, is another question. Some of my old works reveal dismal blurrings and blanks. . . .

Q: Do you make a clear distinction between satire and parody? I ask this because you have so often said you do not wish to be taken as a "moral satirist," and yet parody is so central to your vision.

A: Satire is a lesson, parody is a game.

Q: Chapter ten in *The Real Life of Sebastian Knight* contains a wonderful description of how parody functions in your own novels. But your sense of what *parody* means seems to stretch the usual definition, as when Cincinnatus in *Invitation to a Beheading* tells his mother, "You're still only a parody . . . Just like this spider, just like those bars, just like the striking of that clock." All art, then, or at least all attempts at a "realistic" art, would seem to produce a distortion, a "parody." Would you expand on what you mean by *parody* and why, as Fyodor says in *The Gift,* "The spirit of parody always goes along with genuine poetry"?

A: When the poet Cincinnatus C., in my dreamiest and most poetical novel, accuses (not quite fairly) his mother of being a parody, he uses the word in its familiar sense of "grotesque imitation." When Fyodor, in *The Gift,* alludes to that "spirit of parody" which plays around the spray of genuine "serious" poetry, he is referring to parody in the sense of an essentially lighthearted, delicate, mocking-bird game, such as Pushkin's parody of Derzhavin in *Exegi Monumentum.*

Q: What is your opinion of Joyce's parodies? Do you see any difference in the artistic effect of scenes such as the maternity hospital and the beach interlude with Gerty Macdowell? Are you familiar with the work of younger American writers who have been influenced by both you and Joyce, such as Thomas Pynchon (a Cornellian, Class of '59, who surely was in Literature 312), and do you have any opinion on the current ascendancy of the so-called parody-novel (John Barth, for instance)?

A: The literary parodies in the Maternal Hospital chapter are on the whole jejunish. Joyce seems to have been hampered by the general sterilized tone he chose for that chapter, and this somehow dulled and monotonized the inlaid skits. On the other hand, the frilly novelette parodies in the Masturbation scene are highly successful; and the sudden bursting of its cliches into the fireworks and tender sky of real poetry is a feat of genius. I am not familiar with the works of the two other writers you mention.[3] . . .

Q: Although self-parody seems to be a vital part of your work, you are a writer who believes passionately in the primacy of the imagination. Yet your novels are filled with little details that seem to have been purposely pulled from your own life, as a reading of *Speak, Memory* makes clear, not to mention the overriding patterns, such as the lepidopteral motif, which extend through so many books. They seem to partake of something other than the involuted voice, to suggest some clearly held idea about the interrelationship between self-knowledge and artistic creation, self-parody and identity. Would you comment on this, and the significance of autobiographical hints in works of art that are literally *not* autobiographical?

A: I would say that imagination is a form of memory. Down, Plato, down, good dog. An image depends on the power of association, and association is supplied and prompted by mem-

---

[3] Mrs. Nabokov, who graded her husband's examination papers, did remember Pynchon, but only for his "unusual" handwriting: half printing, half script.—A.A.

ory. When we speak of a vivid individual recollection we are paying a compliment not to our capacity of retention but to Mnemosyne's mysterious foresight in having stored up this or that element which creative imagination may use when combining it with later recollections and inventions. In this sense, both memory and imagination are a negation of time.

Q: C. P. Snow has complained about the gulf between the "two cultures," the literary and scientific communities. As someone who has bridged this gulf, do you see the sciences and humanities as necessarily opposed? Have your experiences as a scientist influenced your performance as an artist? Is it fanciful to use the vocabulary of physics in describing the structures of some of your novels?

A: I would have compared myself to a Colossus of Rhodes bestriding the gulf between the thermodynamics of Snow and Laurentomania of Leavis, had that gulf not been a mere dimple of a ditch that a small frog could straddle. The terms "physics" and "egghead" as used nowadays evoke in me the dreary image of applied science, the knack of an electrician tinkering with bombs and other gadgets. One of those "Two Cultures" is really nothing but utilitarian technology; the other is B-grade novels, ideological fiction, popular art. Who cares if there exists a gap between *such* "physics" and *such* "humanities." Those Eggheads are terrible philistines. A real good head is not oval but round.

My passion for lepidopterological research, in the field, in the laboratory, in the library, is even more pleasurable than the study and practice of literature, which is saying a good deal. Lepidopterists are obscure scientists. Not one is mentioned in Webster. But never mind. I have re-worked the classification of various groups of butterflies, have described and figured several species and sub-species. My names for the microscopic organs that I have been the first to see and portray have safely found their way into the biological dictionaries (which is poorly matched by the wretched entry under "nymphet" in Webster's latest edition). The tactile delights of precise delineation, the silent paradise of the camera lucida, and the precision of poetry in taxonomic description represent the artistic side of the thrill that accumulation of new knowledge, absolutely useless to the layman, gives its first begetter. Science means to me above all natural science. Not the ability to repair a radio set; quite stubby fingers can do that. Apart from this basic consideration, I certainly welcome the free interchange of terminology between any branch of science and any raceme of art. There is no science without fancy, and no art without facts. Aphoristicism is a sympton of arteriosclerosis. . . .

Q: I understand that *The Real Life of Sebastian Knight* was written in English in 1938. It is very dramatic to think of you bidding farewell to one language and embarking on a new life in another in this way. Why did you decide to write in English at this time, since you obviously could not have known for certain you would emigrate two years later? How much more writing in Russian did you do between *Sebastian Knight* and your emigration to America in 1940, and once there, did you ever compose in Russian again?

A: Oh, I did know I would eventually land in America. I switched to English after convincing myself on the strength of my translation of *Despair* that I could use English as a wistful standby for Russian.[4] I still feel the pangs of that substitution, they have not been allayed by the Russian poems (my best) that I wrote in New York, or the 1954 Russian version of *Speak, Memory,* or even my recent two-years long work on the Russian translation of *Lolita* which will be published some time in 1967. I wrote *Sebastian Knight* in Paris, 1938. We had that year a charming flat on rue Saigon, between the Etoile and the Bois. It consisted of a huge handsome room (which served as parlor, bedroom and nursery) with a small kitchen

---

[4]In 1936, while living in Berlin, Nabokov translated *Despair* for the English firm, John Long, who published it in 1937. The most recent and final edition of *Despair* (New York, 1966) is, as Nabokov explains in its Foreword, a revision of both the early translation and of *Otchayanie* itself.—A.A.

on one side and a large sunny bathroom on the other. This apartment had been some bachelor's delight but was not meant to accommodate a family of three. Evening guests had to be entertained in the kitchen so as not to interfere with my future translator's sleep. And the bathroom doubled as my study. Here is the *Doppelgänger* theme for you.

Q: Many people are surprised to learn that you have written seven plays, which is strange, since your novels are filled with "theatrical" effects that are patently unnovelistic. Is it just to say that your frequent allusions to Shakespeare are more than a matter of playful or respectful homage? What do you think of the drama as a form? What are the characteristics of Shakespeare's plays which you find most congenial to your own esthetic?

A: The verbal poetical texture of Shakespeare is the greatest the world has known, and is immensely superior to the structure of his plays as plays. With Shakespeare it is the metaphor that is the thing, not the play. My most ambitious venture in the domain of drama is a huge screenplay based on *Lolita.* I wrote it for Kubrick who used only bits and shadows of it for his otherwise excellent film.

Q: When I was your student, you never mentioned the Homeric parallels in discussing Joyce's *Ulysses.* But you did supply "special information" in introducing many of the masterpieces: a map of Dublin for *Ulysses,* the arrangement of streets and lodgings in *Dr. Jekyll and Mr. Hyde,* a diagram of the interior of a railway coach on the Moscow-St. Petersburg express in *Anna Karenina,* and a floor plan of the Samsa's apartment in *The Metamorphosis* and an entomological drawing of Gregor. Would you be able to suggest some equivalent for your own readers?

A: Joyce himself very soon realized with dismay that the harping on those essentially easy and vulgar "Homeric parallelisms" would only distract one's attention from the real beauty of his book. He soon dropped these pretentious chapter titles which already were "explaining" the book to non-readers. In my lectures I tried to give factual data only. A map of three country estates with a winding river and a figure of the butterfly *Parnassius mnemosyne* for a cartographic cherub will be the endpaper in my revised edition of *Speak, Memory*. . . .

INDEX